Structural Adjustment and African Women Farmers

Structural Adjustment and African Women Farmers

Edited by
Christina H. Gladwin

University of Florida Press
Center for African Studies, University of Florida
Gainesville

Copyright © 1991 by the Board of Regents of the State of Florida

Printed in the United States of America on acid-free paper ∞

The University of Florida Press is a member of University Presses of Florida, the scholarly publishing agency of the State University System of Florida. Books are selected for publication by faculty editorial committees at each of Florida's nine public universities: Florida A&M University (Tallahassee), Florida Atlantic University (Boca Raton), Florida International University (Miami), Florida State University (Tallahassee), University of Central Florida (Orlando), University of Florida (Gainesville), University of North Florida (Jacksonville), University of South Florida (Tampa), University of West Florida (Pensacola).

Orders for books published by all member presses should be addressed to University Presses of Florida, 15 Northwest 15th Street, Gainesville, FL 32603.

Library of Congress Cataloging in Publication Data

Structural adjustment and African woman farmers / edited by Christina
    H. Gladwin.
      p.   cm.
    Includes index.
    ISBN 0-8130-1063-2
    1. Women farmers--Africa, Sub-Saharan--Congresses.   2. Women
agricultural laborers--Africa, Sub-Saharan--Congresses.
3. Agriculture and state--Africa, SubSaharan--Congresses.
4. Agricultural subsidies--Africa, Sub-Saharan--Congresses.
I. Gladwin, Christina H.   II. University of Florida. Center for
African Studies.
HD6073.F3A3757   1991   90-19534
331.4'83'0967--do20   CIP

The women are, of course, the biggest single group of oppressed people in the world and, if we are to believe the Book of Genesis, the very oldest. But they are not the only ones. There are others— rural peasants in every land, the urban poor in industrialized countries, Black people everywhere including their own continent, ethnic and religious minorities and castes in all countries. The most obvious practical difficulty is the magnitude and heterogeneity of the problem. There is no universal conglomerate of the oppressed. Free people may be alike everywhere in their freedom but the oppressed inhabit each their own peculiar hell. The present orthodoxies of deliverance are futile to the extent that they fail to recognize this. . . .

The sweeping, majestic visions of people rising victorious like a tidal wave against their oppressors and transforming their world with theories and slogans into a new heaven and a new earth of brotherhood, justice and freedom are at best grand illusions. The rising, conquering tide, yes; but the millennium afterwards, no! New oppressors will have been readying themselves secretly in the undertow long before the tidal wave got really going.

Experience and intelligence warn us that man's progress in freedom will be piecemeal, slow and undramatic. Revolution may be necessary for taking a society out of an intractable stretch of quagmire but it does not confer freedom, and may indeed hinder it.

Chinua Achebe, *Anthills of the Savannah*

Contents

Introduction

Christina H. Gladwin

In the 1980s, development experts and donor agencies agreed on the importance of macroeconomic policies to the development of sub-Saharan Africa. Following the 1981 Berg report, policy reforms aimed at "getting prices right" were made preconditions for new structural adjustment loans and grants in many sub-Saharan African countries (World Bank 1981). Recently, however, debates about the pros and cons of structural adjustment programs (SAPs) have ensued. This volume presents evidence from noted African and Africanist social scientists (anthropologists, economists, political scientists, and sociologists) who take positions on both sides of this debate.

On one side of the debate are those who argue for structural adjustments as a way to invigorate stagnating agricultural and industrial sectors (Bates, 1981; Timmer, Falcon, and Pearson 1983; Due, 1986). They argue that distorted "macro prices" (overvalued exchange rates, artificially low food prices, high wage rates, low interest rates, subsidized input prices) may improve income distribution and the adequacy of food intake in the short run, especially by the poor, whose food consumption can least stand to be reduced. But distorted prices also send critical signals that may negatively affect the efficient allocation of resources and cause *stagnation* of the food supply system and economy in the long run.

> Because most governments wish to affect income distribution in their societies, they are greatly tempted to use government policy in

Christina H. Gladwin is Associate Professor in the Food and Resource Economics Department, Affiliate of the Anthropology Department, and member of the Center for African Studies. She has a Ph.D. from Food Research Institute, Stanford University, and has done extensive fieldwork in Ghana, Mexico, and Guatemala, as well as short periods of fieldwork in Malawi and Cameroon. She is the author of *Ethnographic Decision Tree Modeling* and *Food and Farm: Current Debates and Policies*. She is grateful to Gwen McCann and other members of the Word Processing Unit, Food and Resource Economics, for help in editing this manuscript.

1

an effort to set macro prices, rather than allow them to be determined by market forces. If wage rates can be set high, labor is no longer cheap, and poverty is eliminated. If interest rates can be set low, capital is not scarce, and a country can quickly have a modern industrial sector. If food prices are kept low, food is abundant, and no one will be hungry.... It is no wonder that many countries have tried this approach. When it fails—as it must until the productivity base has been built that will support higher levels of living in the long run—the economy is riddled with serious price distortions. Resource allocations skew income distribution while much of the labor power of the work force is left untapped, and the government faces stagnant growth in both agricultural and industrial output. It is not easy to put such an economy back on track (Timmer, Falcon, and Pearson 1983: 229).

These distorted macro prices were some of the *internal* factors which led to sub-Saharan Africa's economic crisis in the decade of the 1980s. Clearly, there were other internal factors causing the crisis mentioned by both the United Nations' Economic Commission for Africa (1989: 2–8) report and the papers in this volume; they include a narrow production base with ill-adapted technology, an over-dependence on subsistence agriculture, the urban bias of public policies, weak linkages between the modern formal sector and growing informal sector, and poor institutional management. The internal factors were, of course, compounded by *external* factors in the late 1970s and early 1980s. The latter included the oil price hikes of 1973 and 1979, the collapse in world prices of primary (agricultural) commodities which account for 88 percent of Africa's exports, and resulting sharp declines in Africa's terms of trade since 1981. All these factors led to a doubling of Africa's total debt which, although a small percentage (10 percent) of global debt, resulted in the total evaporation of commercial lending flows into Africa and the additional curtailment of loans—or switch to grants—by donor agencies. Africa's economic performance was therefore "particularly dismal" with an average annual growth rate of GDP of only 0.4 percent during the period 1980–1987; and per-capita incomes, already low in comparison to those in Asia or Latin America at the end of the 1970s, steadily declined by 2.6 percent per annum during the 1980s (Economic Commission for Africa [ECA] 1989: i). In addition to the increasing poverty, Africa's productive and infrastructural facilities, as well as social services (education, public health and sanitation, housing and potable water) have "rapidly deteriorated" (*ibid.*).

It is in this context—the context of a decade-long depression—that

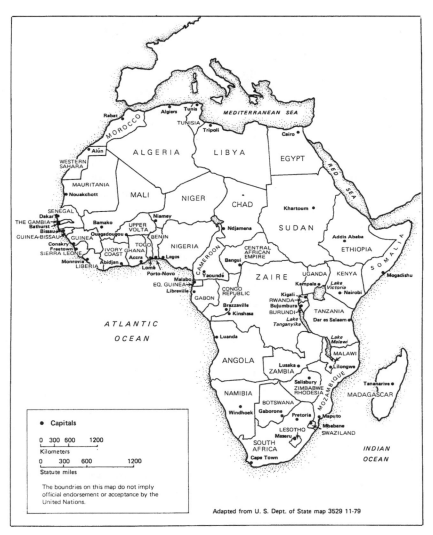

Adapted from U. S. Dept. of State map 3529 11-79

structural adjustment programs and policies (SAPs), supported by the International Monetary Fund (IMF) and the World Bank and adopted by over 30 African countries since 1982 have to be examined. What are the structural adjustment reforms which reportedly can put a distorted economy back on track? Many adjustment packages include: devaluation of overvalued currencies, increases in artificially low food prices and interest rates, a closer alignment of domestic prices with world prices, an emphasis on tradeables/exportables and the gradual withdrawal of restrictions on competition from abroad (trade liberalization), privatization policies (of "parastatals" or large-scale government monopolies), a decrease in government spending, wage and hiring freezes, reductions in employment in the public sector or the minimum wage, the removal of food and input subsidies, and across-the-board reductions in budget deficits as ways to invigorate stagnating economies (ECA 1989: 18–20).

The paper by O'Brien in this volume sets out quite clearly the rationale for structural adjustment reforms in sub-Saharan Africa. Underlying the prescriptions is the neoclassical economics assumption that markets work; markets are generally competitive; and market signals are good guides to resource allocation. Structural adjustment thus means the introduction of more market-oriented policies—liberalization of markets, more efficient use of prices, greater openness to trade, and a bigger role for the private sector. Structural adjustment demands the reduction of budget and balance of payments deficits through fiscal and monetary measures. It demands a public service that is efficient and reliable, with transparent accounting for public monies. It relies on more intensive use of the private sector through divestiture of nonstrategic public enterprises—parastatals—and requires the removal of exchange rate and other biases against exports. Why? Removing distortions and providing proper incentives to the private sector would (1) increase production from underutilized productive capacity in agriculture and manufacturing, (2) achieve a more efficient use of resources, and (3) promote a higher rate of investment which would expand production capacity.

But as Elson (1989: 60–64) points out, adjustment means change, and change means costs as well as benefits, losers as well as winners. The structural adjustment process affects households via: (1) changes in income, through changes in money wages or product prices, (2) changes in prices of purchases, especially food, (3) changes in public expenditure, particularly those in the social sector, and (4) changes in working conditions. Structural adjustment changes will not affect all households in the same way; some will lose and some will win.

A case in point is devaluation of an overvalued currency, whereby a home country's currency becomes *less* valuable in terms of foreign currency. Members of the urban middle- and upper-classes in the home country usually object strenuously to devaluation, because with an overvalued exchange rate, they can import goods cheaply, although it's harder to export. Devaluation realigns domestic currencies with international currencies, thereby making imports more costly; but exports become more competitive. "In theory, devaluation will primarily affect the prices only of internationally traded goods and not domestic goods except for the traded inputs in their manufacture" (Due, this volume).

Who will be the winners and losers? The people who use imported goods—the urban middle- and upper-classes—will feel harder hit by devaluation, because if wages are stable, their purchasing power is reduced. And if devaluation is coupled with an increase in agricultural producer prices, those who benefit will be the farmers and those who lose will be the urban elites. This should stimulate agricultural production in the long run, and encourage import substitution of domestic goods in production, because imports are more expensive. It should also encourage diversified exports, because they become cheaper to foreign buyers with devaluation. Thus exporters should benefit and importers should lose. Do other economic actors lose? As imports get more expensive, domestic prices of substitute products also rise, and this generates more inflation. As Due in this volume points out, price increases often do not wait for inputs to work themselves through the production cycle, but occur immediately after the announcement of devaluation, and affect all consumer goods. Another problem for the losers is the *compounding* of effects of SAP policies with the effects of the sharp declines in world prices of primary commodities and Africa's terms of trade. For those losing out due to declining primary commodity prices, losing out due to SAPs and their emphasis on exportables can be a double whammy.

A related question is: are structural adjustment programs and policies *gender-neutral* (i.e., affecting men and women equally), or merely *gender-blind* (i.e., ignoring the impacts on women and assuming them to be the same as on men)? Authors in this volume agree that there is a difference between the two, and that SAP programs are *not* gender-neutral in operation or effect. In theory, SAP programs should benefit women producers, because much of the emphasis of SAPs is placed on renewing agricultural production, eliminating an urban development bias, and aligning farm-gate prices with world prices. Authors in this volume claim, however, that this will depend on: first, how the policy is implemented in practice; second, what types of agriculture (large- vs. small-scale, export vs. food crops) are in fact supported and encouraged by SAP programs; third, whether or not agricultural price increases cover changes in input costs when subsidies are discontinued; and fourth, whether rural women are in fact *selling* food crops in a market or *buying* food crops to feed their families.

Arguments Against Structural Adjustment

On the other side of the debate are those who argue that structural adjustment programs (SAPs) have failed to stimulate economic growth or recovery in sub-Saharan Africa. Some claim that SAP reforms, despite a heavy focus on agriculture and efforts to increase producer incentives for

There is no question that African women provide most of the labor required to produce the food consumed in sub-Saharan Africa.

farmers, have not only failed to eliminate urban bias and redistribute incomes from the urban to rural sectors but have in fact *worsened* agricultural production and incomes. They have erred by being too macroeconomic in scope (i.e., looking at the economy only from the national or international level) and have ignored the reality of life at the microeconomic or village level in sub-Saharan Africa, where the rural producers—who would supposedly gain from an urban-to-rural redistribution of income under SAP reforms—are *women*. As a result, structural adjustment programs are *not* gender neutral in operation or effect.

There is no question that African women provide most of the labor required to produce the food consumed in Africa, although estimates of women's labor force participation rates in agriculture vary from high estimates of 58 percent (Botswana) to estimates of 46 percent on average (Dixon 1982), with much regional variation (Boserup 1970). In addition, there is no debate that the proportion of African smallholders who are female-headed households is very high by international standards (Due 1989, this volume). Indeed, the only debate surrounds the questions of *how* gender affects rural development and *why* the supposedly gender-neutral SAP recommendations would be undermined by the gender of the food producers to whom they are supposed to provide incentives.

The answer, according to many authors in this volume, lies in the reality of social stratification and differentiation at the village and household level, and imbalances in power relations which affect who gets access to the means of production and who controls the surplus or profit that results from added incentives to produce. Due to social stratification at the village level and inequality in gender relations at the household level, women rural producers are not in a position to benefit from the supposedly gender-neutral effects of structural adjustment policies. The WID literature, by now too vast to cite adequately, testifies to the fact that sub-Saharan African women farmers suffer from unequal access to the modern yield-increasing inputs that an intensification or turnaround of African agriculture will demand (Gladwin and McMillan 1989: 356). Given the SAPs' greater producer incentives, they will not be allowed to respond with an economically appropriate supply response (Lele, this volume), because they lack access to basic inputs of production that men (particularly large farmers) have received: land (Goheen, Peters), credit and fertilizer (Gladwin), labor (Guyer), and in many societies the right to grow cash or export crops at all (Lele, Meena, Elabor-Idemudia). Given the SAPs' greater emphasis on exportables, men who grow export crops may appropriate more of these basic inputs from the women who grow food crops, making their job to feed the family more difficult and their opportunities to generate a marketable surplus even rarer (Lele, Schoepf and Walu, Spring and Wilde).

The result will *not* be that men will take over more of the food production, as is often suggested (Cohen 1989), at least not in the short run (Gladwin and McMillan 1989); because men usually refuse to do work which according to prevailing custom should be done by women (Boserup 1970: 34–35). *The result may be more African food crises in the 1990s,* because women contribute more to the production of food crops than to export crops, which are favored under SAPs. If food production is largely in the nonmonetized sector, as many authors in this volume demonstrate, price signals designed to elicit improved supply responses in agriculture will have virtually no effect. They thus argue that SAPs must be redesigned to stimulate food production that is necessary to enable women to produce the food necessary in both rural and urban areas. Higher food production is also critical to increasing the backward and forward linkages to the manufacturing sector—and thus achieving structural transformation in the foreseeable future (Johnston, O'Brien).

Another result of African women's unequal access to the means of production in both rural and urban areas is that the adverse effects of cutbacks in government spending in social services (health, education) and wages fall hardest on them (Due, Elabor-Idemudia, Meena, Schoepf and Walu). Because women-headed households tend to be the smallest of the smallholders, they are often also *consumers* and not just producers of food products, and as such suffer when food prices rise (Due, Elabor-Idemudia, Gladwin, Lele, Peters). Because women lack the legal rights to acquire larger land holdings, the training to use high-yielding varieties and irrigation, the time to do more work, and the capital to purchase fertilizer and tractors, they cannot raise their incomes. Because women are in charge of reproduction in the household as well as production, they also suffer from SAP-recommended increases in school fees, lack of medicines in the village dispensary, and increases in malnutrition rates (Due, Meena). Because they often depend on remittances from husbands or sons working in urban areas, they also suffer from urban wage freezes or firings. Because women traders depend on an urban clientele to maintain an adequate level of sales, their businesses also suffer from SAP policies which cut back urban consumption (Clark and Manuh).

There is thus agreement among all authors in this volume that SAP policies which increase food prices and reduce job opportunities may increase malnutrition and jeopardize the creation of human capital and the reproduction of the household. Case studies in chapters 4 to 10 show that there are adverse effects of structural adjustment programs which impact on African women, be they farmers, traders, or consumers, rural or urban. Indeed, one might ask if there are *any positive* impacts of SAP programs on African women. Fortunately, chapters 11 and 12 provide some counterevidence to the pessimistic scenario painted in earlier chapters. Guyer's case study of Yoruba women shows that Nigerian SAP policies, the ban on all imported food, and the resulting price hikes have encouraged some entrepreneurial women to start their own farms and cash in on higher producer prices. Ensminger's case study of Orma sedentarized pastoralists shows that the rise in Kenyan meat prices during the 1980s, coupled with government decentralization, has meant greater incomes, education, nutrition, health, and political power for Orma women. In these two studies, both based on two periods of field research (admittedly in less economically distressed nations than those of previous chapters), the welfare of women is not seen to be adversely affected by structural adjustment policies. Are these strikingly different results due to differences in national context, SAP policies, or merely method of analysis? (In chapters 4 to 10, there are almost no local baseline data for measuring *changes* in women's work hours, returns on labor, purchased food, nutrition, or access to cash crops; in chapter 12, there are comparable data collected longitudinally.) The reader should note this area of disagreement between authors in the volume.

But is it important to be looking at the impacts of SAP programs on women entrepreneurs *for equity reasons alone?* No, claim all the authors in this volume. In contrast to the Economic Commission on Africa (1989) report, we are not viewing women primarily as "a vulnerable group" or poor consumers or victims, which carries the danger of deteriorating into paternalism (Elson 1989: 71). Instead, we look at the impacts of SAPs on women producers because that impact will also affect aggregate food production in sub-Saharan Africa. Because women are now at the core of the production system, providing labor to export and domestic crops and in many African societies being solely responsible for food crop production and marketing, for *efficiency* as well as equity reasons it is essential that we understand the impact of structural adjustment and transformation programs on women. If price incentives are to be the solution to Africa's food crises, and women farmers produce most of the food but cannot provide a supply response to increased price incentives, then more African food crises are in store for the 1990s. If credit is a constraint limiting fertilizer use and food production, then it is essential to identify constraints limiting women farmers' use of credit and fertilizer (Gladwin). If "soft government" (Hyden 1983, Cohen 1989) is to be strengthened by SAP policies, then what will be the impact on women, for whom state intervention has often meant more male control of land, labor, and other resources (Staudt 1987)? As Elson (1989: 64) states,

> If greater reliance is to be placed on private enterprise, we need to ask: whose enterprise? The enterprise of the woman farming or trading on her own account, or the enterprise of agribusiness and merchants with monopoly power? The enterprise of a women's cooperative or the enterprise of a multinational corporation?

Confounding these issues is the fact that structural adjustment does *not* guarantee that "structural transformation" of the economy, i.e., substantial shifts in the structure of demand and production, will occur. Most development economists concur that structural transformation of the whole economy is essential to "true" development in the long run. It entails the development of manufacturing and service sectors such that the relative importance of the agricultural sector *declines*, i.e., the percent of the labor force in agriculture and the percent of the GNP from the agricultural sector *declines* as labor specialization proceeds. Although it is not a transformation that has already taken place in Africa, it is the long-term goal of any development policy. As economists O'Brien, Lele, and Johnston point out in this volume, "getting prices right" via structural adjustment policies merely sets the stage *in the short term* for real development to occur; but structural transformation is a long-term process which demands structural changes in the composition of production, consumption, and trade—and not merely changes in monetarist policies. Seen in this light, structural adjustment is a necessary but not sufficient condition for development to occur.

Despite substantial agreement among the authors—on the need for long-term structural transformation, on women's lack of access to basic inputs of production, and on the absence of gender-neutral SAP programs in operation and impact—there are also significant differences among the authors. One, that of method of analysis, has already been noted. Another is national context. The problem is in tracing the poverty of particular groups in particular countries to specific structural adjustment policies. The countries with the poorest economies (Zaire, Tanzania, and Ghana) have long recent histories of severe political/economic dislocation, whereas others (Kenya, Malawi, Cameroon, Nigeria) are better off politically and economically. Compounding the problem of assessing impact is the incredible variation in SAP packages in African countries and the simultaneous presence of macro-level policies that are completely separate from World Bank/IMF-supported SAP policies. Government decentralization policies in Kenya and Zaire (Ensminger, Schoepf and Walu) and the Nigerian policy of cutting off food imports (Elabor-Idemudia, Guyer) are good examples of these policies which one might view as either good or bad structural transformation policies. Their impact is also described in the case studies to be presented because, from a villager's point of view, it matters little what the policy is called if one is poorer and hungrier. At the same time, authors try to separate the effects of different policies while using the *in-context* approach of the case study and preserving the richness of the ethnographic description.

The Carter Lecture Series

The 1990 Carter Lecture Series addressed these issues in a conference January 25–27, 1990, in Gainesville, Florida, by bringing together top scholars in the fields of structural adjustment, structural transformation, and women in development. The Carter Lectures on Africa have been established to honor our colleague Gwendolyn M. Carter, whose distinguished service to African Studies (at Smith College, Northwestern, Indiana, and Florida universities) and to the cause of Africa's welfare and progress has spanned over four decades. To continue this tradition, the lecture series focuses on important frontier problems concerned with African affairs and human development on the continent. The Carter Lectures hope to stimulate further research and act as a catalyst, as Gwen Carter has done, to bring important policy issues and points of view from both African and American scholars to the attention of the educated public. Previous Carter Lectures have focused on the African food crisis and the rise of commercial agriculture in Africa (1986), apartheid in South Africa (1987), and human rights in Africa (1988). The 1990 Carter Lectures with funding from the Ford Foundation both drew on this expertise and set out in new directions, producing this volume.

A Preview

The organization of the papers from the 1990 Carter Lecture Series is the following. O'Brien's paper provides a macro-economic defense of structural adjustment programs (SAPs) mandated by the World Bank and IMF; that perspective has never included considerations of gender distinctions. The paper sets the stage for the rest of the papers which do focus on the gendered effects of SAPs by introducing and distinguishing the concepts of structural transformation and structural adjustment.

O'Brien describes the relevance of structural transformation in the development process as "substantive changes in the structure of production and demand which are signaled by a decline in the importance of the agricultural sector and a rise in the importance of manufacturing." After a brief history of development policies in sub-Saharan Africa, he discusses structural adjustment programs (SAPs) and their causes, and counters the criticisms of the Economic Commission for Africa 1989 report. He concludes that "the verdict is still out" on structural adjustment policies and programs: as Chief Economist for the African Region, World Bank, he follows Elliott Berg in thinking that adjustment policies are "good economic policies." Yet he recognizes that SAPs alone do not ensure economic development in sub-Saharan Africa. Structural adjustment, while necessary, is not a sufficient condition for development to occur; it merely sets the stage for structural transformation to occur.

Uma Lele, agricultural economist at the World Bank, then demonstrates the linkages between women's roles in agricultural production in sub-Saharan Africa, structural adjustment programs, and structural transformation policies needed for real development to occur in Africa. She recognizes the need for structural adjustment policies, claiming they were made necessary by the neglect of agriculture and expansion of the public sector which weakened the industrialization effort. She sees SAP reforms as efforts to correct past discrimination against the agricultural sector, enhance the structure of overall incentives, and introduce fiscal discipline. Yet although the reforms are still needed, she realizes that not all the effects of adjustment are positive in the short run; and adverse impacts of SAPs are bound to be greater on women-headed households. But she claims that the current unsatisfactory scenario must be compared with "the even worse consequences of not adjusting." Without improvements in fiscal discipline and the overall incentive structure, Africa faces a continued decline in per capita income and more massive poverty. The issue for Lele is "thus not whether to adjust, but the speed of adjustment and the mix of measures to ensure that growth is resumed."

Johnston's paper claims that "getting priorities right" during the process of structural transformation should be the goal of sub-Saharan African governments, rather than a narrow adherence to "getting prices right." For countries other than Tanzania and Ghana, price and related distortions may be only *a minor impediment*; and macroeconomic reforms can never be a substitute for the policies and programs needed to foster longer-term agricultural development and structural transformation. Johnston, an agricultural economist from Stanford University, draws on his well-known distinction between a *unimodal* strategy of development which focuses on increasing the productivity of a broad base of small farmers—most of whom are women farmers in sub-Saharan Africa—and a *bimodal* strategy of development which concentrates scarce resources of capital, land, and energy on a small subsector of large farms—owned by (local or multinational) male elites. He claims that the choice of development strategy by government depends critically on the "strategic notions" of government planners who influence decision making, and explores these. He argues that, with a unimodal pattern of agricultural development, sub-Saharan African governments can "get priorities right" by providing an alternative, sustainable model of development to the capital-intensive, nonsustainable, large-scale model that works against women farmers' interests.

Impacts of Structural Adjustment on Women Farmers

Papers in this section present ethnographically rich case studies which look at particular SAPs in particular countries and their impact from the micro or village level, where up to 80 percent of the food is produced by women. For these agricultural producers, a decrease in government spending may mean much higher school fees and no available medicines; wage freezes may mean no remittances from sons/husbands; the removal of subsidies may mean expensive fertilizers are now priced beyond their reach; an emphasis on exportables may mean a decrease in the resources of land, labor, and capital/credit available to their food crops. The result of structural adjustment in the 1980s may be more African food crises in the 1990s; and women, especially female-headed households, will suffer from higher food costs and lower nutrition, more farm work, less control of land and cash crops, and more limited access to health and educational services.

Focusing on East and Central Africa, Due, an agricultural economist at the University of Illinois, looks at the effects of structural adjustment programs on female-headed and low-resource households. She argues that the 25 percent of smallholder farm households which are female-headed and which consume most of their production will *not* be assisted by SAP programs. In addition, expenditures for education and health (including family planning) have been cut by the structural adjustment programs; and inflation has increased markedly. By contrasting the socio-economic position of male-headed (or joint-headed) and female-headed households in Tanzania, Zambia, and Malawi, she shows some of the effects of both production-oriented and consumption-oriented structural adjustment programs. She then suggests some complementary policies to mitigate the impacts of structural adjustment on female-headed households.

Elabor-Idemudia, a sociologist at the Ontario Institute for Studies in Education, claims that the structural adjustment program adopted by

Nigeria after a long internal debate, as a way of putting its economy on the right path to recovery, has so far imparted undue hardships on the lives of its people. She argues that SAP measures of devaluation, privatization, increased market orientation, and cutting of food imports are not necessarily benefiting Nigeria's rural women. Rather, given women's lack of economic power and control over their agricultural products, SAP policies are further subjecting women to increased poverty, powerlessness, and marginalization in terms of access to productive resources and decision-making. She uses 1989 data from two agricultural projects in Bendel and Ogun states, Nigeria, to document these claims. Her results support Elson's (1989: 65) claim that "neither joint decision-making nor equal sharing of resources within households is at all common, and it is quite possible for the level of living of wives to be lower than that of husbands; and for the level of living of girls to be lower than that of boys." She concludes that, after Nigeria's SAP, the quality of life in almost all rural households has deteriorated, with members resorting to eating only one or two meals a day—and using formulas such as "001, 010, or 100" to denote the number and timing of meals rather than verbalizing more accurately their hunger. The hardships brought on the people of Nigeria and the rural poor by structural adjustment cannot be overstressed, in her opinion; and the hardships are more severe for women.

Schoepf, an anthropologist at the Bunting Institute, Harvard, and Engundu, an anthropologist at the Centre de Recherche en Sciences Humaines, Zaire, criticize the use of structural adjustment and other market-oriented policies to address and solve Zaire's economic crisis. They believe that the roots of the crisis go back to pre-independence times; they use case study materials from Zaire to question the pertinence of purely monetary prescriptions for the current ills Zaire is experiencing. Departing from an analysis of class formation and the role of the state, their paper examines the effects of recent policy shifts (devaluation, government fiscal restraint, decentralization, liberalization and privatization of markets) and its effect upon local production and distribution systems with special attention to gender relations and health among poor rural and urban women, who in Zaire are farmers, traders, and consumers.

Meena, a sociologist at the Women's Research and Documentation Projects, University of Dar es Salaam, Tanzania, then describes Tanzania's economic stagnation from the start of the mid-1970s, its causes, and structural adjustment reforms adopted in response to it. In responding to the crisis, Tanzania and the World Bank/IMF disagreed over the details of the structural adjustment program, with the Tanzanian government trying to protect the achievements it had previously made in the social service sector. The IMF, however, was not interested in the issue of maintaining equality in income distribution and provision of social services, as much as it was in stimulating production. Meena first describes the impact of the negotiated SAP package on women farmers and their food production. She then describes the impact of budget cuts on health care and education at the primary, secondary, and university level. She concludes that African states which are committed to long-term solutions of the crisis should best realize that the IMF packages are mainly serving the interest of capital; and adjustment programs will only benefit the people if they are initiated by the people for the interests of the people.

Gladwin, an agricultural economist-anthropologist at the University of Florida, argues that perhaps the most damaging part of SAP packages, in terms of their impact on African women farmers, has been a removal of fertilizer subsidies, proposed in some African countries. The traditional rationale for government's granting of fertilizer subsidies has been the need to increase the profitability and intensity of agriculture, most directly done by decreasing the cost of yield-increasing inputs such as chemical fertilizers, while keeping food prices artificially low. The current emphasis of reducing government expenditures in structural adjustment programs, however, has questioned the social profitability of these subsidies to farmers, even smallholders who cannot easily afford to buy fertilizer. This paper examines the potential impact of recent "fertilizer subsidy removal" programs on women farmers who produce food crops, mainly maize, in both Malawi and Cameroon, countries with an admirable history for food self-sufficiency. The argument is made that a removal of the fertilizer subsidy will decrease fertilizer use drastically, because lack of cash and imperfect credit markets are the main constraints limiting women farmers' use of chemical fertilizers—and not an indigenous belief in organic fertilizers. Because maize is fertilizer responsive, and there are not enough organic substitutes for chemical fertilizer in the local farming systems at this time, a decrease in fertilizer use will decrease maize production, thus jeopardizing not only women's agricultural production and incomes, but also national food self-sufficiency. A more complete structural adjustment, involving higher producer prices, firing civil servants, and dismantling parastatals, would be better than focusing only on removing fertilizer subsidies; and it might open the way for a greater diversity of productive strategies and employment opportunities rather than enforcing a large-scale, capital-intensive agriculture that works against women's interests.

Clark, an anthropologist at the University of Michigan, and Manuh, African Studies Center, University of Ghana, describe the current impact of structural adjustment in Ghana on women traders, which takes place within the context of earlier government intervention in trade which included violent price enforcement. In 1979 and again in 1982, as international and urban-rural terms of trade plummeted, successive governments targeted market women for ideological attack and hostile policies such as price control. Traders' political actions and economic responses conversely grouped them with local consumers. Since the Economic Recovery Program/Structural Adjustment Program began in 1984, trade liberalization and the rehabilitation of transport have removed some significant restrictions on market women's activities. But 1989 survey results by both authors also show that the cumulative effect of years of catastrophic losses from confiscations and interrupted trade left many traders with insufficient capital to operate at 1979 levels. Soaring prices continually raised capital requirements in local currency terms at a rate few traders could match. Those barely hanging on were vulnerable to bankruptcy from minor personal or business crises they could previously have weathered with relative ease. City council traffic and sanitation policies also negatively affect some traders. The broader effects of structural adjustment further limit positive impact.

Impacts of Structural Transformation and Adjustment Policies

Next are papers which explore the additional impact of other macro policies which we term structural transformation policies. They are acting simultaneously and interacting with adjustment policies; and are often misinterpreted as part of SAPs, when viewed from the village level. The impact of these policies is important to analyze because the development process itself may positively or negatively impact on women farmers, depending on whether women's access to productive inputs, capital/credit, markets, technical training, and the political arena is blocked or not (Tinker 1976, Gladwin and McMillan 1989). Policies are analyzed which affect women's production and incomes with new land tenure policies (Goheen), with the entrance of new kinds of farm organizations (Guyer), and with decentralization of government services (Ensminger). In each of these papers, the interactions between the longer-term structural transformation policies and the shorter-term adjustment policies are described, and both of their impacts on women's productive roles and incomes are explored.

Goheen, an anthropologist at Amherst College, looks at women's access to land in Nso in Anglophone Cameroon. She claims that the very categories which have given women status and power in Africa—motherhood—are those which have been undermined and subverted by the marketplace and the differential valuation of male and female work, creating a feminization of poverty which is exacerbated by a growing stratification in rural Cameroon. This has been accomplished primarily by limiting women's access to and control over productive resources—mainly land and education—while at the same time greatly increasing the demands on female labor and income, because women grow the bulk of the food consumed and have the social responsibility for provisioning the household. Thus the long-term weakening of women's access to land, coupled with the current impact of SAPs, threatens the nutritional level not only of the rural household but of a large proportion of the national population.

Guyer, an anthropologist at Boston University, with Idowu, Raw Materials Research Council, Lagos, looks at the diversity of farm organizations and farm sizes in Ibarapa District, Oyo State, Nigeria, and their impact on women's labor force participation in the era of SAP. They claim that there are two interpretations of such diversity. One is populist, represented by the classical work of Chayanov, and the other is class analysis, which focuses on social differentiation and identifies certain kinds of differentiation in class terms. In their view, "class analysis has also highlighted those gender dynamics that have greatly intensified patriarchal control of women's resources and subjected women to more and more complicated and exigent labor routines." Guyer with Idowu claim both forms of analysis are clearly relevant to Africa as production diversifies and differentiates at the same time. The critical questions to answer are: "at what point and in what historical socio-political dynamic should 'diversity' be analyzed as differentiation, an aspect of class relations?" And where class differentiation is present, at what point and in what ways does it constrain the production and welfare of the lower strata including rural women? They then describe the bimodal—or multimodal (Cohen 1989)—nature of Nigerian agriculture as well as Nigerian structural adjustment policies, and analyze their impact on rural women in Ibarapa. They conclude that local farmers, whether small- or mid-scale, male or female, have very different impacts on rural development, class formation, and women's employment, compared to capitalist agribusinesses in Nigeria.

Ensminger, an anthropologist at Washington University at St. Louis, also looks at the differentiation patterns caused by both structural transformation and adjustment policies. In contrast to other papers in this volume, however, her study of the impact of Kenya's macroeconomic policies on women shows that there have been some very positive effects for the women of an East African cattle-herding population, the pastoral

Orma of Northeastern Kenya. Data on terms of trade between 1980 and 1987, household expenditures, anthropometric measures of nutritional status, vaccination, and education by gender show even stronger positive signs for poor households generally and women specifically. These more significant trends are argued to reflect the beginning of genuine structural transformation, a process furthered most recently by Kenyan governmental policy changes favoring administrative decentralization and rescheduling of meat prices. The effect of these policy changes is seen in women's education, nutrition, health, political participation, and economic prospects.

Debate on the Economy of Affection

We also present the transcriptions of a formal debate held during the conference to address the question, "Is the economy of affection a useful model for addressing gender differences in Africa, as well as tracking structural adjustment and its impact on women farmers?" The two-hour debate, trancribed and reproduced here, featured on one side Hyden, a political scientist at the University of Florida, who coined the term "economy of affection" in 1980 to describe networks of relatively autonomous, "uncaptured" peasants living in a peasant mode of production which competes with the capitalist mode and therefore limits development in Africa. In his view, the economy of affection is a way to avoid the top-down approaches of the 1960s and 1970s development literature and analyze the severe problems of underdevelopment that Africa faces.

On the other side of the debate is Peters, an anthropologist at Harvard's Institute of International Development, who argues that African peasants are very involved in exchanges (work groups, wage labor) so that they are neither autonomous nor uncaptured; neither do they withdraw from commercial to subsistence production when the market or state becomes oppressive. She claims that by ignoring peasant interdependence and refusing to disaggregate, Hyden misses the key to social stratification and differentiation, class formation, and agricultural transition that is occurring in Africa today. Because the economy of affection excludes social differences of *all* kinds, including those based on gender, Hyden is forced to ignore women's productive roles and gender relations in production and consumption. She concludes that we are ill advised to continue to ignore gender differences, and should not look to the economy of affection paradigm for help in tracking structural adjustment programs in the short run or understanding the transformation of African rural economies in the long run.

Where Do We Go from Here?

In conclusion, we address more practical questions. Can the most negative effects of structural adjustment policies on women and their families be mitigated, and how? What are the steps being taken by African women themselves to solve the crisis they're facing? What, if anything, can training and extension programs for women do to help African women farmers and traders *as producers* through this crisis? What, if anything, are African universities and the international donor agencies doing? Are there long-term solutions to the basic problem of gender-blindness that development experts are riddled with, and that leads them to design projects which deny equal access to women farmers and so impact negatively on them? The last four papers offer different answers to these practical and fundamental questions.

Trager, an anthropologist at University of Wisconsin-Parkside, and Osinulu, African-American Institute, Nigeria, describe how Nigerian women themselves have responded to the structural adjustment crisis. They claim there has been a recent renaissance of women's nongovernmental organizations (NGOs) in Nigeria in the era of structural adjustment programs and resulting cut-backs in government services in health and family planning programs, income-generating projects, literacy and education activities. Because the Nigerian government does not have the capacity to undertake all development activities, especially in local areas and remote regions, a variety of NGOs, especially women's NGOs, have come to be seen as increasingly important. The authors examine their activities, evaluate their impact in the era of SAPs, and analyze their problems. They conclude that the impact of women's organizations on the development process should be significant, because local women's increased access to information and resources through links with intermediary organizations is a key ingredient to local development. But they warn it is too soon to know if such organizations can counter the negative impacts of structural adjustment; and there is also the danger of too much being expected of them. Just as government before structural adjustment was expected to do everything, women's organizations may erroneously be expected to solve all development problems.

Olayiwole, Principal of the Samaru College of Agriculture, Ahmadu Bello University, Nigeria, then describes how an African university is training both extension agents and rural women how to cope with the new realities of structural adjustment and the economic crisis. She first describes the farming activities of both Muslim and non-Muslim women in northern Nigeria. Then she describes the changes in the education of home economics agents at her agricultural college—changes away from traditional skills of cooking and sewing to the more relevant agricultural skills modern farm women need. In line with Nigeria's Better Life Programme, home economics agents are now taught to work with women to improve the economic welfare of themselves and their families.

Smith and Taylor, University of Florida, then look at the crucial question of how to train an educated African elite to work with lower-strata women farmers. Both home economists, they ask whether a disciplinary home economics program is the best way to prepare students for future work with women farmers; their answer is "no." They suggest that disciplinary programs are not adequate to prepare students to address the many overlapping needs of women farmers in the areas of soil fertility, water use, animal husbandry, forest products use, food storage, nutrition, health, and marketing. They recommend that African faculty themselves decide the future direction of their curricula, and provide an example of a curriculum-planning process that was used successfully at the University Centre at Dschang (UCD), Cameroon; and they take us step by step through this decision process. The result was a set of recommendations for establishing a broad-based multidisciplinary program in Women and Agricultural Households at UCD. The program hopes to bridge both social and technical aspects of agriculture by examining rural women's needs and integrating courses addressing those needs into the nation's primary agricultural institution.

At the donor agency level, the impact of adjustment programs on women is also being discussed and evaluated by the World Bank, the United Nations Economic Commission for Africa, the United Nations Food and Agriculture Organization (FAO), various multinational and bilateral agencies, USAID, and by the affected governments themselves. What should they do? The Commonwealth Secretariat (1989) proposes a six-fold strategy. It first asks that national governments and international agencies broaden their approach to structural adjustment so as to (1) clearly incorporate women's concerns in basic objectives of adjustment and (2) take account of women's special needs in and contribution to economic production, household management, child rearing and caring, and community organization. As part of this strategy, it asks that women's access to credit and key services, including employment, be enhanced in order to increase their opportunities for remunerative and productive work, and that education be given a priority in the 1990s to advance the longer term picture. It focuses on institutionalizing women's concerns though strengthening government and other official machinery in various ways: women's bureaus in strategic areas, women's units in key economic ministries, and "elementary and administrative committees to review legislation and programs." A fourth strategy focuses on external and internal funding mechanisms to target and increase support for women during adjustment programs. A fifth strategy encourages (1) the provision of "accurate, regular and prompt gender disaggregated data on critical social and economic indicators, including access to land and credit, rates of employment and earnings, levels of education, morbidity, mortality and nutrition ..."; (2) the monitoring of the impact of structural adjustment programs; and (3) the carrying out of case studies and surveys. Finally, the Commonwealth Group wishes to initiate an international meeting with appropriate United Nations organizations "to seek consensus on policy goals ... that reflect women's interests" (Commonwealth Secretariat 1989: 10).

Is the Commonwealth Secretariat's list of recommendations a wish list? Are their strategies feasible to follow, or even already in place in some donor agencies? Spring and Wilde of FAO's Women in Agricultural Production and Rural Development Service provide a partial answer by describing FAO programs which link perspectives on structural adjustment with action programs for women farmers. FAO activities include three types: collaboration with multilateral and bilateral agencies including the Social Dimensions of Adjustment (SDA) Project in Africa, advice and assistance to member governments including policy and action projects, and studies that review the adjustment process and disaggregate its impacts. FAO's Plan of Action for the Integration of Women in Development is also discussed, as are FAO staff training programs which are long-term solutions to the problem of gender-blindness in the design of development projects.

REFERENCES

Bates, Robert
    1981   *Markets and States in Tropical Africa.* Berkeley: University of California Press.
Boserup, Ester
    1970   *Women's Role in Economic Development.* New York: St. Martin's Press.
Cohen, Ronald
    1989   The Unimodal Model: Solution or Cul de Sac for Rural Development. *Food and Farm: Current Debates and Policies,* C. Gladwin and K. Truman, eds. Monographs in Economic Anthropology, No. 7. Lantham, MD: University Press of America.
Commonwealth Secretariat
    1989   *Engendering Adjustment for the 1990s.* Report of a Commonwealth Expert Group on Women and Structural Adjustment. London: Commonwealth Secretariat.

Dixon, Ruth
    1982   Women in Agriculture: Counting the Labor Force in Developing Countries. *Population and Development Review* 8(3): 558–559.
Due, Jean M.
    1986   Agricultural Policy in Tropical Africa: Is a Turnaround Possible?" *Agricultural Economics* 1: 19–34.
Elson, Diane
    1989   The Impact of Structural Adjustment on Women: Concepts and Issues. *The IMF, the World Bank, and the African Debt,* Vol. 2, Bade Onimode, ed. London/New Jersey: Zed Books.
Gladwin, Christina, and Della McMillan
    1989   Is a Turnaround in Africa Possible Without Helping African Women to Farm? *Economic Development and Culture Change* 37(2): 345-69.
Hyden, Goran
    1983   *No Shortcuts to Progress.* Berkeley: University of California Press.
Johnston, Bruce, and Roger Kilby
    1975   *Agriculture and Structural Transformation.* Oxford: Oxford University Press.
Staudt, Kathleen
    1987   Uncaptured or Unmotivated? Women and the Food Crisis in Africa. *Rural Sociology* 52(1): 37–55.
Timmer, C. Peter, Walter Falcon, and Scott Pearson
    1983   *Food Policy Analysis.* Washington, D.C.: World Bank.
Tinker, Irene
    1976   The Adverse Impact of Development on Women. *Women and World Development,* I. Tinker and M. Bramsen, eds. Washington, D.C.: Overseas Development Council.
United Nations Economic Commission for Africa (ECA)
    1989   *African Alternative Framework to Structural Adjustment Programs for Socio-Economic Recovery and Transformation,* E/ECA/CM.15/6/Rev.3. New York: United Nations.
World Bank
    1981   *Accelerated Development in sub-Saharan Africa: An Agenda for Action.* Washington, D.C.: World Bank.

I

Structural Adjustment and Transformation

1

Structural Adjustment and Structural Transformation in Sub-Saharan Africa

Stephen O'Brien

> ... it would be extremely helpful if those who deal in the language of economic development could find a way to ease the term "structural adjustment" out of common usage. It is a misleading term because it implies a one-time set of changes with a one-time result. ... In fact, what is at issue is general economic policy. True "adjustment" is in fact an ongoing process of framing good policies, ... more rational decision making procedures and strengthened policy making institutions. In this sense, poor countries, like rich ones, are *never* beyond adjustment (Berg 1989: 28).

Economists define the process of economic development as combining *growth* (rising income or GNP per capita) and *structural transformation* (change in the productive structure of the economy). This development objective, embodying growth with structural transformation of the economy, was the one adopted by almost every African government following independence. In virtually every instance it was pursued through a program of import substitution industrialization led by direct state investment in the productive sectors, particularly in modern manufacturing. The results of this development strategy have been disappointing and, coupled with adverse external circumstances in the 1970s and 1980s, have necessitated structural adjustment reforms.

Why? To understand the causal process and historical circumstances, I

Stephen O'Brien is Chief Economist, Africa Region, the World Bank. He was educated in the Economics Dept., Stanford University, and has taught at Williams College, the University of California at Berkeley, Stanford, and the Institute of Administration of the University of Ife, Nigeria. He has 17 years of experience working in Africa for the Bank: as a Country Economist for Ethiopia and Tanzania, a Senior Economist supervising economic work on Kenya, Uganda, Sudan, Zambia, Zimbabwe, and Malawi, and the Chief Economist of the West Africa Region of the Bank. Currently, he is Chief Economist of the Africa Region.

first describe the relevance of structural transformation in the development process. I then turn to the history of development policies in sub-Saharan Africa. Finally I discuss structural adjustment programs (SAPs) and their causes, as well as counter criticisms of SAPs by the United Nations Economic Commission for Africa (ECA 1989). I conclude that, while the verdict is still out on structural adjustment policies and programs, they alone do not ensure economic development in sub-Saharan Africa. Structural adjustment, while necessary, is not a sufficient condition for development to occur (World Bank 1989a: 62). Rather, structural transformation is essential to development.

Structural Transformation

> The structure of the African economy defines the essential features of Africa's central problem of underdevelopment. The major problems of mass poverty, food shortage, low productivity, weak productive base and backward technology . . . arise from the structures of production, consumption, technology, employment and socio-political organization. . . . Several other problems such as inflationary pressures, instability of export earnings, balance of payments deficits, rising debt burden . . . serve to aggravate the crisis. They are the direct results of the lack of structural transformation. . . . (ECA 1989: 1)

What is normally implied by structural transformation is a decline in the relative importance of the primary (agricultural) sector in both total output and employment, as shown in Table 1-1, and a rise in the share of the secondary (manufacturing) sector. The tertiary or services sector, including government, generally increases slightly in relative importance in the early stages of development, and then more significantly in the later stages; but more relevant is the internal shift from low productivity, largely informal sector activities to modern communications, transportation, finance, insurance, etc. This internal transformation from traditional, low productivity lines of production to more modern, capital-intensive production processes also takes place over time within the primary and secondary sectors, through a change in the product mix and in the technology of production.

Chenery, who coined the term *structural transformation,* states that "economic development can be viewed as a set of interrelated changes in the structure of an economy that are required for its continued growth

Table 1-1. Share of Agricultural Sector in GDP
According to Income Level.

Agricultural Value Added GDP	Average GNP Per Capita
6–10 percent	$3,000
10–20 percent	1,870
20–30 percent	580
30+ percent	290

Source: World Bank 1988: 16.

. . . [and which] . . . involve the composition of demand, production and employment as well as the external structure of trade and capital flows. Taken together, these structural changes define the transformation of a traditional to a modern economic system" (Chenery 1979: xvi). Structural transformation is also accompanied by rising shares of domestic savings and investment in GDP, usually by an increase in the share of production devoted to exports and in the diversity of exported commodities and services.

Historical evidence shows that virtually every country which has experienced sustained growth, and thereby moved from low to middle to high income status, has undergone this type of transformation. "Successful development in virtually all countries has been characterized by an increase in the share of manufacturing in total output. This structural change is both a cause and an effect of rising income" (Chenery 1979: 70).

Why is structural transformation an essential component of long-run development? First, the structure of demand changes with development, due to different income elasticities of demand for different commodities. In essence, food consumption declines as a share of expenditure with rising incomes (Engel's law). The highest rates of growth of consumption relative to income are found in processed food products, manufactured goods, and (modern) services. In order to respond to this changing pattern of demand, an economy should experience a corresponding change in productive capacity. This changing structure of production is also related to productivity change—to differential levels of productivity and rates of productivity growth across sectors. In simple terms, the secondary and (modern) tertiary sectors experience higher rates of productivity growth and factors of production gravitate to sectors where their productivity is highest.

Of course, a developing economy could continue to produce primary products and export them while importing manufactures, but this ignores the opportunities for responding to changing demand patterns in external markets. In fact, changes in the pattern of external trade over time have generally been even more pronounced than changes in domestic demand. "Taken together, the changes in the composition of domestic demand and trade both produce a relative decline in the demand for primary products and a relative rise in the demand for manufactured goods" (Chenery 1979: 79).

Economic Development of Sub-Saharan Africa, The Historical Record

The overall economic performance of sub-Saharan Africa during 1965–1987 is summarized in Table 1-2. These statistics cover the period from the early years of post-independence for most of sub-Saharan Africa up to the most recent year for which aggregated data are available.

If we look first at the 1965–1980 period, prior to the 1980s decade of economic crisis and structural adjustment, we note that overall economic growth was reasonably satisfactory, almost 6 percent per annum, up to the first "oil shock" of 1973. Population growth was already high, greater than 2.5 percent per annum, but there was sufficient margin between economic growth and population growth to provide for a healthy rate of growth of per capita incomes. Personal consumption levels were rising and undoubtedly economic welfare was improving for the majority of Africans. Following the first oil shock there was a marked falling off in the pace of economic growth while, at the same time, the population growth rate was accelerating. The growth rate in per capita production turned negative in the second half of the 1970s, and income and consumption per capita stagnated.

Table 1-2. Growth Rates of GDP, Population, and GNP Per Capita, 1965–1987.

(Average Annual Percentage Growth Rate)			
	1965–73	1973–80	1980–87
GDP	5.9	2.5	0.5
Population	2.6	2.8	3.1
GNP Per Capita	2.9	0.1	-2.8

Source: World Bank 1989: 221, 222, 269.

Table 1-3. Sectoral Shares in GDP at Current Prices.

	Percentages		
	1965	1980	1987
Agriculture	43	30	34
Industry (including mining)	18	33	28
(Manufacturing)	(9)	(9)	(10)
Services	39	37	39

Source: World Bank 1989: 224–225.

Perhaps of equal importance, there was little or no structural transformation of sub-Saharan economies of the sort discussed above. This fact is illustrated by the data presented in Tables 1-3 and 1-4.

At first glance some of the figures in Tables 1-3 and 1-4 would appear to be inconsistent with the conclusion that Africa did not undergo the beginning of structural transformation which is normally associated with long-term development. There was, in fact, a marked decline in the share of agricultural production between 1965 and 1980, and a corresponding rise in the share of the secondary or industrial sector broadly defined. However, closer examination reveals that this shift was almost entirely due to the boom in the oil industry, whose output is included within the mining sector. There was no growth at all in the share of manufacturing in GDP, despite the extensive investments made by most African governments in the establishment of modern manufacturing enterprises. In terms of global comparisons, sub-Saharan Africa's share of world manufacturing value added stagnated, increasing imperceptibly from a minus-

Table 1-4. Structure of Demand and Percentage Shares in Final Expenditure.

	Percentages		
	1965	1980	1987
Consumption	82	79	87
(Government)	(10)	(13)	(16)
(Private Consumption)	(72)	(66)	(71)
Gross Domestic Investment	14	20	16
Gross Domestic Savings	14	22	13
Exports (goods and NFS)	22	26	26

Source: World Bank 1989: 165.

cule 0.7 percent to 0.8 percent between 1960 and 1975 (Meier and Steel 1989: 48). The expansion which took place was heavily concentrated in food processing, textiles, and clothing. There was little backward integration to domestic raw materials or intermediate products. During the second half of the 1970s the steam seemed to run out of the domestic manufacturing sector in most of sub-Saharan Africa; capacity exceeded domestic demand in many sub-sectors and Africa's highly protected infant industries couldn't break into export markets because of their high cost structures.

Other trends were occurring which might appear to have reflected or supported the beginning of structural transformation, specifically the increases in domestic investment and saving during the 1970s. However, a significant proportion of this increase was occurring in the so-called "middle-income oil-exporting" countries, led by Nigeria, which were reaping and spending a tremendous oil-based windfall gain during the 1973–80 period.[1] In low-income Africa the increase in shares of domestic saving and investment was much more modest. More important, the productivity of investment was declining dramatically during the second half of the 1970s, as is clearly borne out by the simple comparison of a 20 percent investment rate with an economic growth rate falling to only 2.5 percent on average (in economist's terms, an incremental capital-output ratio some 4–5 times that prevailing in the 1960s). The low-productivity investment of the 1970s was not laying the ground for sustainable growth into the subsequent decades.

More important trends support the conclusion that, during the first two post-independence decades, sub-Saharan Africa was not undergoing structural transformation. In the external sector, export volumes were stagnating during the 1970s and Africa's share of world trade was declining. Sub-Saharan Africa's share of world exports fell from 3 percent in the early 1950s and 2.7 percent in 1960, to 2.4 percent in 1980 and 1.7 percent in 1985 (Svedberg 1987: 4). Africa's share of developing country exports also declined, from almost 14 percent in 1960 to 7 percent in 1985 (ibid.). In fact, sub-Saharan Africa lost world market shares in almost all of the primary products which were important at the time of independence; even more unfortunate was the fact that these export products in which Africa was losing ground were not replaced by new products. The continued dependence of Africa on primary product exports, and its relatively greater degree of dependence than other low-income developing countries, is shown in Table 1-5.

Within African countries also there was little or no export diversification. In fact, for many countries there was increasing export concentration—the shares of the few leading primary product exports in total export earnings rose, thus making these economies even more vulnerable to the swings in external markets. Sub-Saharan Africa's vulnerability to external markets was also unfortunately increased by the policy of import substitution industrialization since there was little or no development of backward linkages to domestic sources of supply. Additionally, few African countries were able to diversify into the downstream processing of their primary products.

What were the primary causes for this failure of development through structural transformation in the early decades of post-independence? The United Nations Economic Commission for Africa (ECA) lists a number of factors, emphasizing the extreme disadvantages imposed by Africa's initial conditions (the narrow production base with the predominance of subsistence farming, the lack of economic infrastructure, weak human resources and institutional capabilities, political fragmentation, lack of entrepreneurship and capital resources), as well as the adverse effects of an unfavorable external environment—Africa's excessive dependence on the external market in light of the wide swings in prices of primary product producers, growing protectionism in developed countries, the growing burden of external debt at high and fluctuating real interest rates—while giving less emphasis to domestic policy weaknesses (neglect of the agricultural sector or "urban bias," neglect of the informal sector, lack of consistency in domestic policies) (ECA, 1989: chapter 1).

The World Bank, while acknowledging the severe constraints imposed by Africa's initial conditions and the slow pace of improvement despite often heroic efforts, especially in human resource development and institutional strengthening, has given greater stress to domestic policy short-

Table 1-5. Structure of Exports.

Export	Sub-Saharan Africa			All Low-Income Developing Countries		
	1965	1980	1987	1965	1980	1987
Fuels, minerals, metals	34	71	47	22	58	29
Other primary commodities	58	25	39	53	23	22
Total	92	96	86	75	81	51

Source: World Bank 1989: 194–195.

comings. This analysis is contained in a lengthy series of World Bank special studies on sub-Saharan Africa published during the 1980s (World Bank 1981, 1984, 1986). The World Bank is in agreement with the ECA that neglect of the agricultural sector has been a fundamental flaw in the development strategy of sub-Saharan Africa. The combination of overvalued exchange rates, government monopolies of export crop marketing, often through inefficient and high cost crop-marketing parastatals, and price controls on domestic food crops—designed to hold down the cost of living of the urban worker—are negative production incentives for farmers. These more than offset the positive incentive effects of subsidized inputs such as fertilizer and credit. The result was a rate of agricultural growth of less than 2 percent per annum, insufficient to feed the rapidly growing population. Low agricultural production led to growing food imports, stagnation of agricultural export volumes and the loss of export markets referred to above. In addition, the stagnant or slowly growing rural incomes could not provide a dynamic market for the manufacturing sector, nor could primary product exports generate sufficient foreign exchange earnings to finance the import requirements of the modern manufacturing sector. It is today well understood that a healthy agricultural sector is an essential underpinning to dynamic industrial growth, but this critical linkage was absent in Africa during the 1960s and 1970s.

The World Bank also stressed the negative developmental impact of wage and price distortions across all sectors of the economy and focused in particular on the effects of persistently overvalued exchange rates. These overvalued exchange rates make imported capital goods and inputs relatively cheap in comparison with domestically produced substitutes and domestic labor, as well as introducing an "anti-export" bias. Investment in overly capital-intensive manufacturing enterprises was particularly true of public sector firms (Meier and Steel 1989: 90). These biases in pricing and exchange rate policy, as well as heavy reliance on direct allocation by government of imports, domestic inputs, and credit, limited the possibilities for "spread effects" from industrialization—few linkages developed between the largely publicly owned, large-scale manufacturing sector and the small-scale "informal" sector. Thus there grew up in much of Africa a dualistic economy—an embryonic modern, capital-intensive, enclave sector in mining, manufacturing, or plantation agriculture alongside a labor-intensive, low capital-using, low-level technology, traditional sector encompassing both peasant agriculture and urban informal activities. Without the establishment of linkages there was little push or pull to expand or improve the small-scale sector. This dualism has been characterized in the most recent World Bank study as the phenomenon of the "missing middle" (World Bank 1989a: 29).

Experience during the 1980s—The Decade of Structural Adjustment

Much of the developing world has been in crisis since 1979/80. The proximate cause of the crisis was failure to adjust adequately to the two oil "shocks" of 1973/74 and 1979/80, and to the other global economic changes which ensued from these shocks. Most developing countries made certain policy errors of the sort outlined above, undertook investment projects which in retrospect cannot be economically justified, and borrowed heavily abroad to finance both investment and consumption expenditures. Sub-Saharan Africa was particularly vulnerable to the economic crisis of the late 1970s/early 1980s because its still fragile and vulnerable economies had *not* achieved diversification and structural transformation. Other negative factors which particularly impacted Africa, but which were perhaps less clearly perceived in the early 1980s, included the growing competition from other developing countries in Africa's primary export markets, a comparative disadvantage in transportation and communications facilities, a redirection of foreign private investment away from developing countries but away from Africa in particular, and a decline in aid flows to Africa from the Middle East oil-exporting nations.

In sub-Saharan Africa the impact of the economic crisis was broad and deep; hardly any African country was unaffected. For sub-Saharan Africa as a whole, economic output stagnated—between 1980 and 1986 real GDP increased at only 0.2 percent per annum on average. With population growing at 3.2 percent per annum, GDP per capita was falling at 3 percent per year, representing a cumulative decline of over 20 percent during this period. Per capita consumption was falling at a comparable rate. Other economic magnitudes evidenced similar adverse trends: export volumes, after stagnating in the 1970s, fell by 0.5 percent per year; import volumes fell even more sharply, by over 5 percent annually; domestic investment declined as a share of GDP and domestic savings fell even more sharply (Table 1-4). Africa's plight was aggravated by sharply declining terms of trade after 1984, by a net reduction in external resource inflows, and by a mounting external debt burden. Even more threatening to Africa's long-term development prospects was the deterioration in the quantity and quality of social services—health, education, sanitation, water supply—and in social indicators brought on by the economic crisis.

As the economic crisis spread and deepened, more and more developing countries, unable to sustain the economic and financial imbalances they were experiencing, were forced to undertake remedial measures. The term "structural adjustment" has been universally adopted as the label for these programs of policy reform which countries have pursued in their efforts to adjust to changes in the world economy. Many definitions of structural adjustment can be found; here we cite as our authority Elliot Berg, principal author of the World Bank (1981) report on sub-Saharan Africa:

> For most economists [structural adjustment] means changing the structure of production so that the adjusting economy produces more tradeables—import substitutes and exports . . . Restoring equilibrium to the balance of payments is still an important element in the theory and practice of structural adjustment. But nowadays the concept is usually defined more broadly—it means the adoption of measures designed to make an economy more productive, more flexible and more dynamic by using available resources more efficiently and by generating new resources. The importance of domestic policy deficiencies is more explicitly recognized. In terms of specific policy content, structural adjustment in the 1980s has invariably meant the introduction of more market-oriented policies—liberalization of markets, more efficient use of prices, greater openness, and a bigger role for the private sector (Berg 1989: 1–2).

Structural adjustment thus embodies stabilization—the reduction of budget and balance of payments deficits through fiscal and monetary measures—but also relies on more intensive use of the private sector (through, for example, deregulation, contracting out of certain public services, divestiture of nonstrategic public enterprises), removal of exchange rate and other biases against exports, closer alignment of domestic prices with world prices, and rationalization of public sector institutions. The underlying hypothesis is that removing distortions and providing proper incentives to the private sector would: a) lead to a recovery of production from presently underutilized productive capacity (in the economist's terms a move out to the production possibility curve); b) achieve a more efficient use of resources by moving to the point on the production possibility curve where the production mix is consistent with opportunity costs measured in world prices; and c) promote a higher rate of investment which would expand production capacity (shifting out the production possibility curve itself over time).

Common Criticisms of Structural Adjustment Programs

There are now some 30 countries in sub-Saharan Africa which are undertaking, or have attempted at some time during the 1980s, programs of structural adjustment. In virtually all cases these reform efforts have been supported by structural adjustment lending (quick-disbursing loans for balance of payments support) from the World Bank, the International Monetary Fund, and other multilateral and bilateral donors. These Bank/Fund-supported adjustment programs in Africa have become highly visible and have generated debate and controversy. One of the sharpest critics has been the Economic Commission for Africa (ECA 1989: chapter 2). Some of the most common criticisms leveled at structural adjustment programs in Africa have been the following:

1. Structural adjustment programs have been imposed on African governments which are not really committed to their implementation.

2. Structural adjustment programs have ignored or given insufficient attention to the social costs of adjustment, especially to the impact of adjustment measures on the poor and "vulnerable groups."

3. Stabilization and structural adjustment programs together have failed in their immediate objective of restoring economic growth in the short to medium run; stabilization, with its emphasis on controlling excess demand, counter balances structural adjustment, which emphasizes supply expansion.

4. These programs rely excessively on markets and private sector response to market signals; this faith in laissez-faire is misplaced in Africa given the absence of entrepreneurs, small market size which fosters the monopolization of markets, lack of information systems necessary for the efficient functioning of markets, and the noncompetitive nature of many global markets confronting African producers and consumers. Low-supply elasticities in agriculture are cited as the main reason why reliance on price signals to stimulate an agricultural supply response is doomed to failure.

5. Finally, and of greater relevance for this paper, it is argued that existing structural adjustment programs, partly but not entirely because of their reliance on the private sector, cannot generate the long-run development with structural transformation that Africa needs. The criticism is advanced that structural adjustment programs, as currently designed, do not address the economic constraints earlier identified—low levels of technology and human resource skills, small and fragmented markets, weak infrastructure, lack of capital and entrepreneurship, weak institutions, and adverse external environment. Nor do they address rapid population growth or other constraints to long-run development—limited

natural resources, poor soils, harsh and variable climatic conditions, environmental degradation. Furthermore, it is argued that most of these structural obstacles cannot be addressed through market forces; rather they require direct governmental action programs.

Counterarguments

A full discussion of these or other criticisms of structural adjustment is beyond the scope of this paper. These questions have been debated in innumerable seminars over the past few years and have been taken up in a series of World Bank reports (World Bank 1986, 1988; World Bank and UNDP 1989a). However, a brief response will be given to each of the first four points, and a more detailed response to point (5).

1. The first criticism, that adjustment programs have been "imposed" from outside, has validity in a certain sense: African countries have usually not willingly adopted these economic reform programs. Most developing country governments, African as well as others, have attempted to stave off belt tightening as long as possible through continued external borrowing, domestic money creation and, in more than a few cases, through arrears accumulation. Only when all else failed were stabilization and structural adjustment programs introduced. But this took place when the economic and financial crisis was already producing a downward spiral. Food prices were already rising faster than wages as farmers sought to avoid taxation by shifting to other activities or selling in parallel markets. Real wages in the public sector were already falling due to the combined effects of overmanning and reduced fiscal revenues. At the same time recurrent budgets could not meet the nonwage costs of essential public services after paying wages of public servants and interest on the public debt. Overvalued exchange rates led to reduced export volumes, declining availability of foreign exchange, reduced imports through the official market, and a growing premium on ever-scarcer foreign exchange in the parallel market. The emphasis on import-substitution industrialization had led to industrial stagnation, as mentioned earlier; countries were burdened with highly inefficient, protected, import-dependent industrial sectors, usually subsidized and incapable of competing in external markets. The growth of the public sector in the 1960s and 1970s had also led to an impasse. Government budgets were absorbing an unsustainable share of GDP; the growth of state enterprises had led most often not to profitable operations and high public savings and investment rates, but to dependence on subsidies which added to budget deficits. The regulatory

systems, which were supposed to protect the vulnerable, most often bene-fited the rich and powerful more than the poor. They induced corruption, and often stifled enterprise.

While it is true that the IMF and World Bank have played major roles in the design of stabilization and adjustment programs, and bilateral donors are increasingly adopting policy conditionality as the basis for their own structural adjustment loans, most of the measures adopted were dictated by the nature and severity of the crisis and the absence of other means for addressing domestic and external imbalances.[2] What has been true in a number of cases is that programs have been rushed; that is, they have been recommended and adopted in response to the immediate crisis without adequate time for analysis, reflection, or building up the three essential "Cs" within governments—comprehension, consensus, and commitment. This lesson has been well learned over the decade of the 1980s: adjustment programs are doomed to fail if governments are not committed, if they do not accept "ownership" of the program. At present much more effort is being devoted to developing this commitment or ownership. The Policy Framework Paper, which is a statement of the gov-ernment's policy reform program over the coming three years, and which is produced as a joint product of government, IMF, and World Bank, is an important instrument in developing this consensus. To date some 25 countries in sub-Saharan Africa have entered into Policy Framework agreements with the IMF and World Bank, and these agreements have underpinned virtually all of the structural adjustment programs in low-income Africa. Another factor which mitigates the possibility of rushed or imposed adjustment programs is that almost all adjusting countries have by now negotiated from one to several repeat or follow-up adjustment programs with the IMF and World Bank.

2. On the issue of the social dimensions of adjustment, it is now recog-nized that early adjustment programs gave insufficient attention to the social aspects. One reason for this was the general tendency to underesti-mate the time required to restore the momentum of economic growth. In the early 1980s it was widely believed that the period of adjustment to the immediate crisis would be no more than 3–5 years; therefore, the empha-sis should be on correcting economic and financial imbalances. Once the economy was back on a positive per capita income growth track there would be time to turn again to the longer term issue of poverty reduction. It was also generally held that the economic crisis itself was largely respon-sible for any negative social welfare impacts which the population was experiencing, that adjustment per se would have generally positive social

effects, particularly through a reduction in "urban bias" and a stimulus to rural incomes. It was assumed that any social costs which did arise would be short-run or transitional in nature, and that the costs of nonadjustment would far outweigh those of adjustment in any event.

As the adjustment process has extended throughout the 1980s and into the 1990s, it has come to be well understood that social effects cannot be ignored over such an extended period, whether on balance the social impact be positive or negative. Credit for giving the initial emphasis to the social aspects of adjustment should go to UNICEF (1987). The result has been a significant change in the content and focus of structural adjustment programs, in essence to build in the social dimensions in every reform effort. To strengthen the positive impact of adjustment on social programs and on the poor, the World Bank is increasingly focusing on reforms of social policies, on improving data collection to monitor the effects of adjustment on the poor and vulnerable groups, and to improve policy design. It is focusing on designing special interventions to mitigate the short-term burdens of adjustment on the poor, and on social sector adjustment loans and projects to address major social objectives during periods of protracted adjustment. The Social Dimensions of Adjustment Project (SDA), initiated in 1986 by the World Bank, UNDP, and African Development Bank and supported by numerous other donors, is working to improve the volume and quality of data on social effects of adjustment which can then be used to design better adjustment programs which address social problems (World Bank 1990). Some 27 African countries are already participating in the SDA program and active SDA projects will be underway in 15 countries by mid-1990.

Although increasing attention is now being paid to the social dimensions of adjustment, more should be done. A clear task for the future is to further strengthen the link between sustained adjustment and higher consumption and improved social conditions. Higher external aid flows can help achieve this goal. But equally important are improved programs of government spending, which focus a larger share of public resources on well-targeted social programs and provide the right incentives for effective implementation of these programs.

3. With regard to the charge that "orthodox" structural adjustment programs have failed to restore the momentum of economic growth in the short to medium run, it must be acknowledged that this is a difficult question to answer. It involves choice of time periods for comparison (defining before and after adjustment periods, what time lags to allow for); choice of groups of countries to be compared (adjusting vs. nonadjusting); what allowance to make for the strength of adjustment efforts,

how to classify well-managed economies which have avoided crisis; whether to use weighted or unweighted averages for country groupings; how to allow for variations in the external environment, weather, shocks; and, perhaps most important, how to link policy reform measures to economic outcomes (attribution of causality). Numerous efforts have been made to answer many of these questions, including in particular a World Bank/UNDP (1989a) study on the impact of adjustment. The evidence to date is mixed, but there are clear signs that the economic decline is bottoming out and a gradual recovery is beginning for sub-Saharan Africa, and also that adjusting countries are doing better than the rest. For all of sub-Saharan Africa the annual rate of GDP growth has improved from 0.2 percent in 1980-86 to 1.5 percent in 1986-89, reaching 2.8 percent in 1988 and an estimated 3.1 percent in 1989. For low-income African countries, the improvement has been from 1.4 percent in 1980–86 to 3.5 percent in 1986–89. More significantly, the group of 22 low-income countries undertaking structural adjustment programs has achieved an annual growth rate of 4.3 percent during 1988–89.

These figures on overall economic growth performance could be supplemented by additional data on sectoral growth rates and export growth, but a detailed analysis of very recent economic performance is beyond the scope of this paper. In addition, it is still too soon to judge the outcome of structural adjustment programs: *the verdict is still out.* The vast majority of sub-Saharan African countries now undertaking programs of structural adjustment only began their reform efforts in 1985–86 or thereabouts. As we have already seen, the adjustment path has proven to be a long and difficult one; therefore, results based on only two to three years of reforms should be regarded as highly provisional. We do, however, have the case of Ghana, which has been undertaking structural adjustment since 1983 and which has experienced sustained economic growth in the range of 5–6 percent per year for some six to seven years, as evidence of the positive effects of sustained adjustment. In addition, there is considerable variation in the effectiveness with which adjustment programs have been pursued in sub-Saharan Africa. Some countries such as Ghana have implemented reform programs in a sustained manner over several years while others have experienced difficulties in following through on intended reforms or have even been forced to abandon their reform efforts. It must also be emphasized that these aggregate growth rates are still barely equal to, or only slightly in excess of, the rate of population growth. Per capita incomes remain stagnant or are rising imperceptibly. At this pace it would require decades even to return per capita incomes to the level of 1980. Africa's economic recovery is only beginning. It is clear that the scope for improvements in economic management, economic efficiency, and the fuller utilization of both domestic and external resources is still great across much of sub-Saharan Africa.

4. Concerning the charge that structural adjustment programs have relied excessively on the private sector, it must be stated categorically that what is sought in these programs is a better balance between public and private sector roles in African economies, not an abdication of responsibility by the state. It is now generally agreed that governments have become overextended in many African countries; a root cause of weak economic performance in the past has been the failure of public institutions. Nevertheless, governments have a critical role in developing Africa's human resources, in providing a significantly higher level of social services to the entire population, in rehabilitating and expanding essential infrastructure, and in creating the "enabling environment" for private sector activity. At the same time the state cannot do everything and shouldn't try. There is ample evidence of entrepreneurial talent and responsiveness to market signals in the private sector throughout Africa, in the informal sector, in unofficial cross-border trade, in the response of peasant producers to improved prices under liberalization programs, in the oversubscription of share offerings in profitable public sector enterprises in Kenya and Nigeria, and in many other examples which could be cited. Of course, greater reliance on private markets should not lead to the simple replacement of public monopolies by private ones. In this regard, the small size of African economies can present problems. What is required is the removal of restrictions to entry of new domestic competitors and the gradual withdrawal of restrictions on competition from abroad (trade liberalization) which should include efforts to stimulate increased trade and thereby greater internal competition within Africa through regional integration.

In summary, the drive toward greater liberalization of African economies is based on the hypothesis that greater efficiency can be achieved through reliance on competitive market forces and that concentration on strategically important activities will permit the state to function more effectively. What is needed, first and foremost, from the African state is better governance—a public service that is efficient, a reliable legal framework for the enforcement of contracts, an administration that is responsible to the public, transparent accounting for public monies, and scrupulous respect for the law and human rights. These are essential elements of the enabling environment for productive economic activity and enhanced social welfare.

5. We turn now to the issue of structural adjustment in relationship to

structural transformation. At the outset it must be stressed, as is already abundantly clear to all who follow Africa, that the decade of the 1980s has not been a period of sustained growth, broad economic and social development or structural transformation. As has been pointed out above, it has been, until recently, a period of sharply declining incomes and thus of declining economic and social welfare. As might be expected in a period of economic decline, there is evidence of structural retrogression—a declining share of the secondary or industrial sector in production (due primarily to the slump in the world oil market after 1983) with no statistically significant increase in the share of manufacturing (Table 1-3). This was accompanied by a fall in the investment/GDP ratio and an even sharper fall in the ratio of savings to GDP (Table 1-4);[3] a negative rate of growth of export volume resulting in a reduction in the ratio of exports to GDP from 25 percent in 1974–80 to 20 percent in 1987–89; a substantially negative rate of growth of import volume and thus a declining ratio of imports to GDP. In summary, there have been few if any positive trends in the economy of sub-Saharan Africa over the decade of the 1980s, beyond a modest recovery in rates of GDP growth during the past two to three years, and increasing evidence that "structurally adjusting" countries have experienced a more significant recovery than nonadjusting countries.

Does the evidence imply that structural adjustment cannot generate the structural transformation which should undergird successful long-term development in Africa? I would argue that structural adjustment, as it is conventionally defined, is a somewhat different concept from structural transformation, but that it is a necessary precondition for the resumption of sustained economic growth and for broad-based economic development with structural transformation over the longer term. However, as the World Bank's (1989a) report on sub-Saharan Africa acknowledges, structural adjustment while necessary is not a sufficient condition:

> The central objective of future country development strategies is to transform production structures, to reverse the decline in institutions, and to build the foundations for sustainable and equitable growth. The recent structural adjustment programs are important first steps in the right direction—but much more is needed . . . Future country strategies should continue to pursue adjustment programs, which should evolve to take fuller account of the social impact of the reforms, of investment needs to accelerate growth, and of measures to ensure sustainability (World Bank 1989a: 62).

Programs of stabilization and structural adjustment have been primarily concerned with correcting the widespread inefficiencies and distortions which adversely affect the use of *existing* resources—overvalued exchange rates, price controls, subsidization of inefficient production, overmanning in the public service and public enterprises, lack of funding for maintenance which leads to underutilization of existing capacity, and sub-optimal allocation of public sector resources in both recurrent and investment budgets. In the terminology of production possibility frontiers discussed above, these programs have been mainly concerned with step (a)—moving the economy out to the existing production possibility curve. They also concern, but perhaps to a lesser degree, step (b)—the adjustment of the economy to changed relative prices in world markets—initially to the price of oil, today more often to the lower prices of certain primary exports. Finally, they are concerned with establishing the *pre-conditions* for the restoration of higher savings rates, both public and private, and expansion of the level of investment—step (c). But each of these latter two phases requires a longer time frame than was initially envisioned for structural adjustment.

One way of putting the argument is to state that good economic management—the efficient use of all available resources—is always to be preferred over poor management, but by itself good management of existing resources will not produce sustained growth; rather it can only establish a favorable climate for growth. What is needed above and beyond good policies and efficient allocation of public resources is the mobilization of additional savings, both domestic and external, and their investment in high yielding activities—in education for the development of skills and managerial capabilities, in expansion of vital infrastructure, in the expansion of other essential social services, and in the directly productive sectors of agriculture, livestock, forestry, fishing, mining, and manufacturing. Neither growth nor structural transformation can take place without investment, and at the present time investment in Africa is inadequate. In many countries of sub-Saharan Africa the present level of gross investment is too low even to maintain the existing capital stock, both public and private—in other words, gross investment is exceeded by depreciation, with the result that net investment is negative.

Structural adjustment will not lead to self-sustaining growth and structural transformation over the long term unless this savings and investment response can be generated, in both the public and private sectors. What are the causal factors which can induce higher levels of saving and investment? Analysis of the determinants of savings and investment levels in developing countries is extremely complex and beyond the scope of this paper. However, I would like to emphasize again the importance of an "enabling environment" which encourages productive activities in the private sector. One of the elements of this environment is the government's economic policy framework, both overall macroeconomic policy and specific sectoral or microeconomic policies. The initiation of a program of economic policy reform is only the first step; the improved policy framework must be sustained. The critical factors are the stability, predictability, and transparency of the policy regime. Uncertainty increases risk and risk increases the cost of investment. One of the most vital contributions which African governments can make to the long-run development of the continent (perhaps second in priority after the development of Africa's human resources) is the establishment of a well-designed and effectively and consistently applied economic policy framework.

Conclusion

Sub-Saharan Africa has not achieved either sustained economic growth or structural transformation over the first 30 years of independence. Africa's extremely difficult initial conditions and policy weaknesses have delayed the structural transformation that all African countries have sought. External circumstances have been at times supportive but at other times adverse, and adversity has been predominant in the 1980s. Programs of structural adjustment have been efforts at economic reform designed to correct obvious weaknesses in policy and economic management. They aim to enable African economies to cope more effectively with external shocks, whether from weather, terms of trade, or other causes; and to restart the "engine" of economic growth which has been running in neutral or in reverse for too many years. Sustained adherence to programs of economic reform has proven difficult, and the returns are slower in coming than originally hoped, but there is growing evidence that reforms are having a positive impact. Nevertheless, Africa's economic situation is still fragile, just as African economies themselves have remained fragile. What will be required in the future is to sustain and intensify these programs of economic reform, whether they continue to carry the label of "structural adjustment" or not, and to supplement them with a renewed assault on the myriad of constraints which must be alleviated to permit sustained growth, socioeconomic development, and the transformation of Africa's economy over the long term.

NOTES

1. One of the difficulties in discussing statistics for sub-Saharan Africa, especially data for the oil boom years, is the tremendous weight which the Nigerian economy carried in the overall economy of sub-Saharan Africa, as well as the contrary trends in the economies of the oil-exporting vs. the low-income, oil-importing economies. In 1980, for example, Nigeria accounted for over 48 percent of the GDP of sub-Saharan Africa. With the decline in oil prices since 1983, Nigeria's economic decline has been precipitous and dramatic; in 1986 Nigeria's weight in the overall economy of sub-Saharan Africa had shrunk to only 28 percent.
2. "The measures associated with 'orthodox' stabilization programs are thus, for the most part, not imposed by external agencies, but arise out of the imperatives of domestic economic stability" (Berg 1989: 7).
3. For the low-income economies the savings ratio is even lower, having fallen to only 7 percent of GDP in 1987 (World Bank 1989a: 227).

REFERENCES

Berg, Elliot
    1989   Structural Adjustment and Its Critics. Unpublished paper, Elliot Berg Associates, Washington, D.C.
Chenery, Hollis
    1979   *Structural Change and Development Policy.* New York: Oxford University Press.
Johnston, Bruce F., and P. Kilby
    1975   *Agriculture and Structural Transformation: Economic Strategies in Late-Developing Countries.* New York: Oxford University Press.
Meier, Gerald M., and William F. Steel
    1989   *Industrial Adjustment in Sub-Saharan Africa.* New York: Oxford University Press.
Svedberg, Peter
    1987   *The Export Performance of Sub-Saharan Africa.* Institute for International Economic Studies, University of Stockholm, and World Institute for Development Economics Research, United Nations University, Helsinki.
UNICEF
    1987   *Adjustment with a Human Face.* Giovanni Cornia, Richard Jolly and Francis Stewart, eds. Oxford: The Clarendon Press.
United Nations Economic Commission for Africa (ECA)
    1989   *African Alternative Framework to Structural Adjustment Programs for Socio-Economic Recovery and Transformation,* E/ECA/CM.15/6/Rev.3. New York: United Nations.
World Bank
    1981   *Accelerated Development in Sub-Saharan Africa: An Agenda for Action.* Washington, D.C.: World Bank.

1984   *Toward Sustained Development in Sub-Saharan Africa: A Joint Program of Action.* Washington, D.C.: World Bank.

1986   *Financing Adjustment with Growth in Sub-Saharan Africa, 1986-90.* Washington, D.C.: World Bank.

1988   *Report on Adjustment Lending.* Washington, D.C.: World Bank.

1989a   *Sub-Saharan Africa: From Crisis to Sustainable Growth.* Washington, D.C.: World Bank.

1989b   *World Development Report 1989.* New York: Oxford University Press.

1990   *Structural Adjustment and Poverty: A Conceptual, Empirical and Policy Framework.* Washington, D.C.: World Bank.

World Bank and United Nations Development Program

1989a   *Africa's Adjustment and Growth in the 1980s,* Washington, D.C.: World Bank.

1989b   *African Economic and Financial Data.* Washington, D.C.: World Bank.

2

Women, Structural Adjustment, and Transformation: Some Lessons and Questions From the African Experience

Uma Lele

The issues of structural adjustment, transformation, and the impact on women farmers are intricately related to each other. Some specific aspects of their interactions are beginning to be explored rigorously (Collier 1989). However, given the diversity of the problems and the many competing demands on public resources, the numerous macroeconomic, intersectoral, and microeconomic interlinkages which affect women must be explored on a country-specific basis, especially their implications for priority interventions.

Women contribute an estimated three-quarters of the labor required to produce the food consumed in Africa, mostly under conditions of a primitive, hand-hoe technology and low-labor productivity. Data are limited, but suggest that 80 to 90 percent of the poor live in rural areas and that women-headed households comprise well over one-half the rural poor households (FAO 1985). Their children constitute by far the largest majority of the poor. The number of such poor households is growing rapidly in Africa, as evidenced by the accelerated growth in population and simultaneous decline in per capita incomes for nearly a decade. The number living in poverty is projected to double again by 2000 to 265 million, giving Africa the claim to one of the highest concentrations of the poor, along with South Asia (World Bank forthcoming). Although not yet

Uma Lele, Indian, is Manager of the Agriculture Policy Office of the Technical Department in the World Bank's Africa Region. She has a Ph.D. from Cornell University and has held positions in both research and operational complex of the Bank including Senior Economist and Deputy Division Chief of Agriculture in the Agriculture Division in East Africa, Senior Economist in Indonesia Country Programs, and Chief of the Development Strategy Division (then Special Studies Division) of the Economic Research Staff. She is grateful to Beth Porter for research assistance and to Robert Christiansen and Barbara Herz for their comments on the draft. The views expressed in this paper are her own and are not necessarily those of the World Bank or its affiliated organizations.

well-documented (Youssef and Hetler 1983), the share of women-headed households among the poor is also growing rapidly, according to sociological literature and informal sources of information (Buvinic, Lycette, and McGreevey 1983; Buvinic and Yudelman 1989; Rogers 1979; Ahmad and Loutfi 1981). Agriculture is clearly a key sector in the economies of African countries. Furthermore, growth in agricultural productivity is critical to structural transformation, which entails change from predominantly agriculturally based to manufacturing and service sector-based economies. An understanding of the effects of structural adjustment and transformation on women, particularly in facilitating growth in agriculture, is thus essential to the long-term success of any such programs and processes.

Structural Adjustment in Africa

The proximate cause of structural adjustment was the series of adverse terms of trade shocks faced by the primary commodity-producing African countries in the 1970s (World Bank 1988a). Adjustment was also made necessary by the neglect of agriculture and expansion of the public sector, which weakened the industrialization effort. Measures adopted since the early 1980s in well over 30 countries aim to correct past discrimination against the agricultural sector by improving the exchange rate, enhancing the structure of overall incentives, and introducing fiscal discipline. Some countries, e.g., Nigeria and Ghana, have adopted radical reforms to correct the massive distortions. Nevertheless, the initial expectations of donors about the speed of adjustment and the magnitude of the countries' production responses have turned out to be overly optimistic (World Bank 1988a). It is increasingly recognized that reforms will need to be sustained over a considerable period of time if African economies are to resume a sustained growth path.

Continuation of reforms over the long run poses serious sociopolitical problems, however, because not all of the effects of adjustment are positive in the short run. Producer price adjustments have most benefited export crops, which were often heavily taxed. Prices of food crops, on the other hand, have been largely market determined, even when governments have had "monopoly" control of grain marketing, as the share of informal trade in food is often quite large. In addition to the effects of adjustment, several secular factors have also contributed to short-term hardships. For example, food prices have been rising rapidly for nearly two decades due to the failure of food supply to keep pace with the growth in population and notwithstanding the rapid rise in food imports. The number of poor households producing food crops but also relying on the market for wage labor and subsistence food needs has been growing. Urban consumer food subsidies, which in any case benefited only a handful of the poor and especially women, are being withdrawn.

Social indicators—which are an important measure of welfare—made impressive strides until the end of the 1970s, especially in areas such as access to primary and secondary education and improved rural water supply. In the 1980s, however, structural adjustment has not only entailed sharp cuts in public expenditures on essential medical, educational, and other services, but has also led to increased cost recovery in the form of school fees and charges for visits to health clinics. Shortages of foreign exchange have encouraged black markets and privileged access to essential imported supplies such as medicines, production inputs, consumer goods, and transport services. The adverse impact of these developments is bound to be greater than average on poor women-headed households who tend to have less privileged access to such special channels and may not be able to spend the time necessary to obtain scarce goods (World Bank 1989s). The current unsatisfactory scenario must be compared, however, with the even worse consequences of not adjusting. Without improvement in the overall incentive structure, fiscal discipline, and scope for individual initiative, Africa faces the danger of a continued decline in per capita income and an even more massive increase in poverty than reported above. The primary issue in adjustment is thus not whether to adjust, but the speed of adjustment and the mix of measures needed to ensure that growth is resumed, which minimizes the burden placed on the poorest households and which increases the labor productivity of these households so that they can better reap the benefits of national growth.

Structural Transformation

The literature on structural transformation provides insights mainly into the effects of economic growth on households but offers few specific insights into the role of women both within households and in larger societal structures. Kuznets (1957, 1966) has documented a strong inverse relationship between the proportion of the labor force in agriculture and the level of labor productivity and income. Johnston and Mellor (1961) and Johnston and Kilby (1975) have explored the nature of interdependence between agricultural and nonagricultural growth, noting that at an early stage of development when agriculture contains a large share of the labor force and makes a major contribution to GNP, exports, government revenues, savings, and investments, its contribution to the growth of the smaller, but more rapidly growing, manufacturing and the service sectors is critical in the supply of wages, goods, labor, and capital as well as foreign exchange earnings. The manufacturing and service sectors that absorb the growing rural population and provide the goods and services to the farm sector, in turn, constitute the markets for the increased production and productivity in the agricultural sector. Technological change in the agricultural sector is critical for achieving constant, if not falling, real food prices to the nonfarm sector in the course of industrialization by increasing factor productivity and ensuring low wage costs. Several aspects of this structural transformation process have a major impact on women.

First, the decline in the real price of food emphasized by the structuralists must be contrasted with the phenomenon of the secular rise in the real food prices observed in Africa, a symptom of the failure of growth in factor productivity. The implications of rising food prices for poor women, children, and households are discussed later. Second, the literature on transformation stresses that a broad-based increase in factor productivity involving a large number of rural households tends to lead to expenditure patterns and growth linkages that are more conducive to rapid growth in overall employment in the economy than when the benefits of growth in agriculture are skewed in favor of a few households. Third, a broad-based pattern in growth in agriculture tends to create a decentralized pattern in the manufacturing and service sectors, resulting in growth of small towns rather than cities, and enabling households rather than males alone to migrate to urban areas. In contrast, the narrowly based, "bimodal" pattern of growth in agriculture prevalent in most African countries tends to offer fewer employment opportunities generated by the capital-intensive industries, leading to political and social pressures to generate employment in the public sector. The migration of individual males rather than households to mines, plantations, and large-scale industrial complexes augments the size of a few urban concentrations while increasing the number of female-headed households in rural areas.

This paper will first document why African women play an even more important role in the rural economy than their Asian or Latin American counterparts, with a focus on what the special constraints are that restrict their opportunities. It will then explore the implications of this role for the policies which need to be pursued to support women and how development programs actually effect them. Second, based on a recent study completed in the World Bank,[1] the paper will show that African countries which adopted sound economic policies have performed better in agriculture and overall GNP growth and broadened employment opportunities than those which have not. Besides, the breadth of growth has been critical to extending the benefits to women. The origins of the economic crisis leading to the need for adjustment are examined, including the dismal record of external aid to African agriculture. Finally, the effects of adjustment on farming households in general and women farmers in particular are explored. The paper concludes with a discussion of policy implications.

A Case for Focusing on Women Farmers

Women in developing countries work longer hours than men, in housekeeping, child care, fetching fuelwood and water, and in the fields (FAO 1985; Schultz 1989; Collier 1987; Birdsall and McGreevey 1983; World Bank 1989a, 1989f, 1989r). According to FAO, women contribute up to three-fourths of the labor required to produce the food consumed in Africa. Further, aggregate rough data indicate that African women provide about 90 percent of the labor for processing food crops and providing household water and fuelwood; 80 percent of the work in food storage and transport from farm to village; 90 percent of the work in hoeing and weeding; and 60 percent of the work in harvesting and marketing (FAO 1985). Women in Africa typically work up to 16 hours per day, due to their diverse and numerous responsibilities (Kaul 1989). The poorer the household, the larger the share of total output generated from the unrecognized labor of women, and possibly the higher the percentage contribution of women's income to family income (Herz, personal communication). Maternal health and the amount and the quality of the time women have available for child care influence the size and the quality of the population through the effects on fertility and mortality rates and the health and education of children (Schultz 1989).

While cultural diversity makes generalizations difficult, it is evident that African women's greater direct responsibility for the food security and welfare of their households than is typical in Asia and Latin America derives in part from the practice of polygamy. Men have offspring from a number of wives; often several satellite households operate in a common compound. Each wife's interest tends to revolve around the welfare of her own children. Whether men or women command the factors of production (through the right to cultivate land, ability to mobilize labor and technology, and access to information, services, and infrastructure) influences the nature, source, size, and distribution of income within the family, as well as the resultant patterns of consumption, savings, and investment. By focusing on the household as the unit of decision-making and productive activity, as does the structural transformation literature, the implications of these complex intrahousehold effects on overall economic growth are often overlooked (Jones 1983; Schultz 1989; Sen 1987). Consequently, it is important to examine the junctures at which the interests of men and women diverge and converge.

The importance of focusing on female farmers is accentuated by the rising numbers of households which are female headed and may consequently be comprised of only female farmers and their dependents. This trend is of particular concern as female-headed households are among the poorest (Sadik 1989; Youssef and Hetler 1983) and report lower per capita income than those headed by men (Schultz 1989b). In some countries, including Kenya and Malawi, the poorer the household, the more likely it is to be headed by a woman (World Bank 1989i, 1989s). There is a wide variation of the definition of the term "household head," making attempts to identify and enumerate them difficult and reflecting conceptual and methodological biases. Female-headed households include households headed by single mothers, divorced or widowed women, women whose husbands have deserted them (*de jure*) and those headed by women whose husbands are away for an unspecified amount of time, including migrant laborers, or whose husbands make only a marginal contribution to the maintenance of the household due to disability, unemployment, etc. (*de facto*) (Youssef and Hetler 1983). Furthermore, as female-headed households are not homogenous, policies devised to address their needs must take into account the specific social, economic, and political conditions and constraints which they face. Although there has been a significant increase in the availability of census data on households reported by the sex of the head in Africa (from zero of 26 censuses reviewed in 1960 to 13 of 26 censuses reviewed in 1970) (Youssef and Hetler 1983), the availability and completeness of data continue to vary from country to country, and nowhere provide a clear picture of changes over time. The data available indicate, however, that in Africa the percentage of female-headed households is frequently around one-third of the total and in Zambia approaches one-half.[2]

Interactions of Cash Cropping, Income, and Nutrition

The relationship between household income and the source and control of that income is particularly important in Africa where women tend to control income generated from food cropping and men from cash cropping. Even in Kenya, where traditional gender roles are breaking down and women are increasingly playing an important role in export crop production, the income they earn from cash cropping is said to be controlled by men (World Bank 1988b). Control of income within the household is salient as it has been shown that men and women spend household income differently: women are reported to give greater priority in their expenditures to food and children's education than do their husbands (Peters and Herrera 1989, Guyer 1980, and Tinker 1979). The debate about the relationship between cash cropping, control of income, and nutrition is therefore central in the context of both adjustment and transformation.

The shifting emphasis between food crops and export crops is the result of several factors. Food crop prices have been rising for structural reasons, to the benefit of the net sellers of food. As the number of households dependent on the market has been rising and the real wages of these households have been declining, the effect of such food price increases is mixed. Recent adjustment efforts have in general increased the incentives for export crop production, yet during the last two decades international donor community concerns have swung between export orientation and food security, depending on whether growth or equity objectives achieved primacy. Such a lack of consistency discourages farmers from responding to price signals and policy measures. The severe drought in the mid-1970s led to an emphasis by governments and donors on food security. By the end of the 1970s, the loss of world markets in primary commodity exports and the ensuing balance of payments problems contributed to the promotion of export agriculture and led once again to concern about the social dimensions of adjustment: specifically to a focus on issues including food security, health, population, education. These various shifts in emphases have diverted attention from a more fundamental need for broad-based growth in the productivity of both food and export crops, rather than exclusive emphasis on one at the cost of the other.

A number of studies on cash cropping suggest a positive effect of the increased income so generated on education, adoption of new technology and input use in agriculture, food security and nutrition, both at the household as well as at the national level. In the latter case, the effects are through the foreign exchange earnings or savings, government revenues, etc. (Maxwell and Fernando n.d.; Weber *et al.* 1988; Lele, van der Walle, and Gbetibouo 1989; Lele 1989; von Braun and Kennedy 1986; World Bank 1988b). By the same token, gains in household income may not lead to improved health or nutrition if primary health care centers are inaccessible or nutrition information is not available. Kennedy and Cogill observed that in the sugar-growing areas of Kenya, even relatively prosperous rural households lose a considerable number of working days to sickness and spend a significant share of their income on curative medicine due to frequent recurrence of malaria, cholera, and other diseases (Kennedy and Cogill 1988). Expenditures on primary health that are focused on preventive medicine would be more cost effective as well as increasing labor supply and productivity. Even with increased food consumption, however, the effects of cash cropping on nutrition and health may not be positive due to shifts to less nutritious foods or lack of access to preventive health measures. Von Braun and Kennedy conclude that cash cropping activities need to be carefully planned to translate potential nutritional benefits into reality (von Braun and Kennedy 1986).

There is, however, also evidence which questions the positive effect of cash cropping on nutrition. A recent study in Malawi reports that the nutrition of children is better served in households where income is earned in the form of a transfer sent by the male migrant than when income is earned by the resident male growing cash crops, such as tobacco or groundnuts (World Bank 1989j). Nutrition education and other interventions for pregnant women, lactating mothers, and children are important, but they are unlikely to make a macroeconomic impact on the large proportion of people and women living in poverty. To positively affect this population, growth which creates productive employment for the poor and increases their wages is essential. Yet many of the relationships among the various factors in any growth strategy are inadequately understood. For instance, the trade-off between women's increased control of the household income when the husband migrates, and the husband's presence, are subjective and difficult to evaluate. Besides, while women's ability to earn income increases their control of expenditures, women's employment in farming tends to have an adverse effect on the feeding and care of infants, especially among the poorest households where women already have less time for preparation and feeding of children, and who enjoy less support from extended families than their better-off counterparts (Quinn, Chiligo and Gittinger 1988). In Malawi, for instance, the deteriorating status of children's nutrition is attributed to the fact that four or five rather than two preparations of maize meal a day must be fed to children for them to acquire both adequate calories and protein; yet women's growing reliance on wage employment prevents mothers from devoting the time necessary to such tasks. One way women maintain control on household food security in Malawi is by storing physical stocks of food rather than holding cash, as men and other family members tend to "raid" surplus cash more than food stores. Food storage is especially effective if controlled by an elder woman (Peters and Herrera 1989). Female offspring are more often reported to be favored in the allocation of food in Africa in contrast to Asia or Latin America (Sen and Sengupta 1983), perhaps reflecting the greater economic value of women as agricultural laborers. However, these various responses are diverse and must be understood in specific cultural context.

Labor Productivity, Education, Fertility, and the Environment

The low labor intensity of hand-hoe cultivation in a situation of land extensive agriculture in Africa results in long hours of agricultural work and lower levels of labor productivity in Africa than in Asia (Delgado and Ranade 1987) and may also have an impact on human fertility. Frequent failure of labor markets means reliance on family labor for agricultural work (Matlon 1987), and consequently may contribute to the persistence of large families in traditional societies (Caldwell 1978). Recent studies have shown that drops in fertility in response to women's increased access to education have been slower in coming to Africa than in the rest of the developing world, although some drops in fertility rates have been observed recently in a number of African countries, including Botswana, Kenya, and Zimbabwe (World Bank 1989d). The slow response may be attributed to the relatively recent tradition of women's education in Africa, although African women had surpassed their Asian counterparts in primary and secondary school attendance by 1985, albeit starting from a much lower base (Birdsall 1988, Caldwell and Caldwell 1988, World Bank 1989n, Ainsworth 1989) (Table 2-1). The relationship between education and fertility is not clear, however. It has been noted that even a few years of learning at the primary level lowers women's fertility, either directly through increased awareness of contraception or indirectly through reduced demand for children as a result of perceived enhanced income-earning opportunities or by raising the age of marriage and thereby reducing the number of childbearing years (World Bank 1989n). Elsewhere, however, it has been reported that despite expanding education for females, fertility levels have increased (Cochrane 1979, Birdsall 1988). This seeming inconsistency may be explained in part by the observation that fertility may increase with schooling at low educational levels before falling off rapidly at the threshold of secondary education (Cochrane 1983, Timur 1977).

In any case, high growth rates of population have been eroding the gains in per capita income, and few public or private resources have been devoted to investment in the urgently needed social and physical capital. Clearly, living standards cannot be increased unless population growth rates slow down (World Bank 1989n). On the other hand, Boserup, Ruthenberg, and others have argued that increased population is beneficial for intensification of agriculture by facilitating technical change and growth of factor and product markets (Boserup 1965, 1981, Ruthenberg 1971). Boserup's position is consistent with a number of studies that show a positive relationship between the size of the family and household income in situations of surplus land and imperfect labor markets (Sen 1966, 1975). Without active public policy towards the generation of new technology and public expenditures for the provision of the necessary public goods, however, the rate of population growth often outpaces the autonomous rate of technical progress causing deforestation, soil degradation, and inappropriate shifts of land use from livestock to cropping (Lele and Stone 1989; Herz 1974). Here again, as women are the primary providers of fuelwood and fodder in addition to being cultivators, women's education and provision of alternatives to outmoded technologies can play a positive role in consolidating the gains from agricultural intensification through conservation efforts. Furthermore, excluding women through retrograde public policies toward alienation of land for the benefit of a few and restricted rights to new economic opportunities

Table 2-1. Education: Female Percentage of Total Enrollment.

Level/Region	1950	1960	1970	1980	1985
First Level					
Sub-Saharan Africa	28	34	39	44	45
South Asia	28	32	36	37	39
Latin America	48	48	49	49	49
Second Level					
Sub-Saharan Africa	15	25	31	37	40
South Asia	12	22	28	31	33
Latin America	43	47	48	50	50
Third Level					
Sub-Saharan Africa	—	1	3	6	9
South Asia	10	17	21	25	27
Latin America	22	29	35	43	45

Source: Sivard 1985.

can lead to diminishing returns on the land as population densities increase, resulting in a Malthusian trap.

Access to Employment, Extension, Credit, and Technology

Even with a strong commitment to adjustment, improving the overall incentive structure by itself is not sufficient either to resume growth or to ensure that women have equal opportunity to move into jobs of higher labor productivity as the growth process resumes. Women are not able to switch their labor as easily as men because they lack access to information, financial and physical capital, credit, and even markets—contrary to the neoclassical model. Therefore, a variety of "nonprice" factors such as investment in the quality of human resources, and improvement in physical assets, land distribution, institutional development, technology, and services are needed to complement price incentives.

Experience of advanced countries indicates that in order to significantly improve employment practices, distribution of land and other assets, and access to education and institutional finance, women must themselves actively seek changes in legislation, institutions of marriage, divorce, and inheritance. Lacking political power, poor female-headed households are less able to mobilize the capacity of the political, legal, and social institutions to bring about such changes. Not only do women tend to be concentrated in low-earning jobs even in developed countries,[3] but even paternalistic programs directed to alleviate poverty often produce mixed results, as the recent major review of the U.S. experience on poverty programs indicates (Sawhill 1988).

Complex sociocultural factors explain the lack of equal opportunity for women. As Collier notes, women face differential constraints upon their economic activity which include: discrimination outside the household, often in the form of limited access to wage employment; absence of gender-specific role models; asymmetric rights and obligations, e.g., rural women have the dual responsibilities of household maintenance, raising children, and growing subsistence food crops in addition to growing cash crops or working for wages; and the burden of reproduction, with its attendant health deteriorations which limit income-earning opportunities (Collier 1988, 1989). Modifying gender roles takes decades. In traditional African societies there are many additional constraints which hinder the achievement of women's equal rights, despite the well-intentioned constitutional guarantees of such rights.[4] These include, among other things, some retrograde traditional values and customs, unequal access to assets,

Figure 2-1. Women tend to be concentrated in low-paying jobs.

technology and education, and the increasing male bias in the process of modernization (Gladwin and McMillan 1989). Moreover, the rural poor and women rarely participate in the design and implementation of development policies and programs which are intended to benefit them.

Women's income-earning opportunities have been limited by the fact that they have less access to education (Table 2-1), land ownership, institutional credit, fertilizer, and extension services than their male counterparts. A study in Pakistan shows—and its results may have universal validity—that fathers devote greater attention to school-going sons than to daughters. Consequently, even when women attend schools their cognitive skills are sometimes lower than those of men. Although income and family background are similar, the quality of interaction and motivation in the home environment is poorer for girls than boys (Sabot, personal communication). In regard to land ownership, in Kenya only 5 percent of the land titles are in the name of women and women borrowers represent only 10 percent of all loanees (World Bank 1989g). In Malawi, where a matrilineal society prevails, women's control of land seems limited in effect. Besides, women-headed households are a small fraction of those receiving seasonal credit compared to their share of one-third of the total number of households (World Bank 1986a). In Zaire, a woman cannot borrow institutional credit without the written permission of her husband (World Bank 1989p). Clearly, with increased cost of imported fertilizers and pesticides resulting from devaluations and from the removal of subsidies, without access to credit, the poor households that have fewer income transfers from urban employment and are less able to undertake risks are unable to intensify agriculture, as shown in the case of Malawi and Senegal (also see the situation with regard to credit in Senegal in Lele, Christiansen, and Kadiresan 1989). Although women represent up to 80 percent of food producers in some countries, the FAO reports that they are known to receive only 1–2 percent of extension contacts (World Bank 1989l). In Ethiopia, even though women contribute their labor to most phases of food and cash cropping, virtually no effort has been made to target either research programs or extension services to increasing female productivity (World Bank 1989c). Moreover, in Zaire all agricultural extension agents are men, despite the fact that women are primarily responsible for food production, and the services are aimed exclusively towards male household heads on the assumption that they will pass information along to women (World Bank 1989p).

The introduction of technology, even if specifically targeted towards women, does not unambiguously benefit them.[5] Insofar as men gain access to and control of the new technologies, women may be relegated to other time- and labor-intensive activities such that their share of earnings is reduced and they become more dependent on their husbands (von Braun and Webb 1989, Gladwin and McMillan 1989). The introduction of new technologies can also be hindered by the refusal of women to supply labor if they are not adequately compensated (Jones 1983, Dey 1983). Although given appropriate incentives women divert their labor to other cash crops, due to their lesser access to technology and to labor-saving devices and given the demand on women's time for competing household activities, their labor productivity tends to be lower than men's in the same activities. Estimates for Kenyan women's lower productivity per acre compared to men's range from 15 percent (Smock 1981) to 4 percent (Moock 1973), unless they had the same access to education, extension, farm inputs, and credit, in which case women produced 7 percent more (Moock 1973). The productivity per hectare on smallholder farms compared to large farms and estates tends to be lower, in part because small farms dominated by women farmers are less able to mobilize all factors of production including labor (Lele and Agarwal 1989).

Migration and Landlessness

Migration is a device households use to diversify sources and increase the level of income. Whether male members rather than households migrate depends on the extent of land pressure and the nature of urban employment opportunities. Land shortage seems to result in the migration of individual males rather than families, as women remain behind in rural areas to maintain rights to land. By creating labor shortages, male migration to urban areas would appear to reinforce the family's demand for children as a source of agricultural labor. Investment in schooling, on the other hand, withdraws child labor from agriculture.

An impressive spread of universal primary education in Kenya explains in part why real wages have not declined as rapidly as elsewhere in Africa, despite one of the most rapid growth rates of population. A combination of polygamy and women's obligation to meet food security may well reinforce the incentive for a large number of children in circumstances of relatively low apparent cost of rearing children and the high economic return to children's labor in caring for siblings and collecting fuel and firewood (Caldwell and Caldwell 1987; World Bank 1986a). Whereas male migration increases the woman's control of decisions in household activities, whether this control is extended to productive activities is not clear. Once the population density reaches a certain threshold, however, the growing population pressure on the land and the development of labor markets appears to reduce the demand for large families. The recent decline in fertility rates referred to above in countries such as Kenya, Zimbabwe, and Botswana may well be a result of a combination of the growing land pressure, relatively better economic performance, widespread growth of income and education, and availability of family planning programs (van de Walle and Foster 1988).

The determinants of fertility levels or decline are not very well understood in Africa, however. Some demographic literature, for instance, attributes the recent decline in human fertility rates to the opposite factors, namely the decline in income in these countries since the economic crisis began (Cochrane and Farid 1986; World Bank 1989d). That literature suggests, if anything, that the drop in fertility may well be temporary and may be reversed if growth is resumed. Given these conflicting interpretations, it is clear that policy must aim at influencing both the demand for and the supply of children, whereas analysis must continue to improve our understanding of the causal relationships. Investment in labor-saving devices which increase the productivity of women's labor is essential to release their time; steps must be taken, however, to ensure that they benefit from the new technology, rather than the technology being appropriated by men. While some of these investments may assist the poor by enabling them to increase their economic activities through improved infrastructure and easier access to fuels and drinking water, others such as food-processing technologies will reduce the demand for the labor of poor women, as Timmer (1975) has shown in Indonesia.

Much of the discussion above has implicitly focused on households with a surplus output for the market. As pointed out earlier, however, with increasing landlessness or near landlessness of rural households, reliance on the sale of labor for income and on the purchase of food in the market for subsistence has been growing. This higher incidence of landlessness is a result of the increased population pressure on the land, little or no growth in factor productivity in agriculture, and increased control of good quality land by a relatively few politically powerful households, which has led to a substantial movement of populations to marginal areas, as occurred in Malawi, Kenya, and Zimbabwe. The consequent decline in per capita food production has been associated with a rise in the real price of food, with at best stagnant money wages (World Bank 1989f).

In many countries, including Kenya and Ethiopia, women are not permitted to own land. In others, such as Zambia and Tanzania, new land reform laws exclude divorced women from land ownership (Sadik 1989). Many of these landless women-headed households spend nearly 60 percent of their limited income on food. A rapid increase in the price of food substantially reduces their per capita income with the attendant deleterious effects on health, nutrition, and labor productivity. Poverty leads to a vicious circle, namely of the increased need to rely on wage labor, while facing a shortage of labor to intensify production on their own farms. Not only do divorced and widowed women in Malawi indulge in greater "gyanu" work on farms belonging to others than do members of poor households with a male head, but they also face greater incidence of child sickness at home during the rainy season, at a time when demand for agricultural labor outside homes is at its peak (World Bank 1989j). Clearly long-term and predictable employment-earning opportunities generated for women through food for work programs which operate in the off-season can stabilize their income and increase complementarity between cultivation and employment (Mellor and Pandya-Lorch, forthcoming). Evidence from Kenya's Rural Access Road Program indicates, however, that despite considerable success in labor-based road maintenance, less than 10 percent of the wage labor employed consists of females (Kudat 1989), suggesting that design of additional rural roads programs need to devote effort to understanding constraints which inhibit women from being employed.

Interventions

A range of complementary interventions is needed related to food production and distribution, employment, education, and nutrition and health. Particular attention should be paid to the division of responsibilities among men and women and the likely effects of policies and interventions on women's time and families' welfare. The role of local people is key in determining which specific interventions will be appropriate in a given microsociocultural context. While local and international nongovernmental organizations (NGOs) can play an important role in helping to develop and implement such programs, it is difficult for large aid-giving donor organizations such as the World Bank or USAID to make a major economic impact on the lives of women-headed households through their own interventions directly, because they tend to be wholesalers rather than retailers of aid and are too highly centralized in their operations and too distant from the scene of action to develop appropriate rural development programs. Their role must be seen largely as improving the capacity of national, regional, and local governments, voluntary agencies, and private agents to address this mammoth task effectively. This means carefully selecting apex institutions within each country to which financial resources are channelled for further assistance to small-scale local organizations, including those of women. It also means promoting political and administrative decentralization in Africa. In reality, however, women's issues can be captured by elite women who are not democratically elected representatives of the constituencies they insist they serve and whose self-interest may even conflict with that of poor women. Yet the development of indigenous grassroots organizations by women in much of South Asia and in African countries such as Kenya has already demonstrated the impressive organizational ability of women. For such organizations to emerge and make an impact, however, requires a democratic political system. Whereas women in Tanzania, Malawi, and Cameroon have also made significant strides in establishing such community associations, their governments have tended to be less democratically oriented and have hindered the effective participation of these groups in development activities (Lele and Hanak, forthcoming).

Market Interventions

Many previous government interventions such as public sector monopolies of food marketing services and government-imposed barriers to the movement of grain across administrative boundaries actually increased the time, cost, and risks women faced in marketing of food products or encouraged them to sell their surpluses in small lots to avoid breaking restrictions. Similarly, discouragement of private sector hammer mills in rural areas forced women to rely either on hand-pounded sembe and gari or to travel long distances to purchase flour or imported rice. Women who earn a livelihood from the sale of food crops, as do the market women of West Africa, are greatly hindered in their activities by government restrictions, poor physical infrastructure, and the lack of access to credit and transport.

In the past, donors tended to reinforce many of these government interventions by financing parastatals on a scale which would not have been possible for African governments without the level and type of external assistance provided (Lele and Christiansen 1989). Moreover, given the shortage of organizational and human resources and the relative abundance of finances, donors tended to design complex top-down multisectoral interventions which had little or no impact on poor households. To enable import substitution of rice, a labor-saving food particularly demanded by poor women in the cities of West Africa, donors also financed costly large-scale centralized irrigation schemes, which have been a drain on government budgets.

To the extent that adjustment efforts are freeing up markets and improving public sector resource allocation, they will ultimately have a positive effect on women's production and trading activities. Whether such major resource reallocation of government expenditures will take place in Africa is yet to be seen. Donors finance between 30 to 70 percent of public expenditures in many African countries and themselves develop vested interests in past policies and investment. In any case, in the short run the effects of liberalization and privatization on food prices and consequently on the production and consumption in poor food-deficit female-headed households can be unfavorable, as happened in Malawi when the market was privatized in 1987. This poses a strategic problem: liberalization of markets is more easily induced by donors in a period of economic adversity when governments are more willing to undergo reforms, yet reforms need to be preceded by several years of systematic development of alternative marketing channels and accompanied by some stabilization of prices and supplies to protect the consumption of the poor. Markets have often erroneously been assumed to be competitive when donors have pressed for rapid and complete liberalization. Successful market development requires investment in roads, access to credit, improved storage by households and traders, and dissemination of information, conditions which are frequently not met by traditional marketing systems, as numerous recent studies of informal markets show (Christiansen 1989). Given that adjustment is expected to be a phenomenon which will remain for some time, such a long-term approach to the development of markets would seem to be both logical and feasible. While some donor activities reflect an increased time horizon in this manner, most donor assistance continues to be excessively oriented toward the short run, both in its time horizon as well as programming.

Structural Transformation and Adjustment

How have development policies adopted by governments affected the process of structural transformation or intensified the need for structural adjustment? A study on Managing Agricultural Development in Africa (MADIA) in six countries carried out in the World Bank concluded that countries that relied upon their comparative advantage in agriculture performed better both in agricultural and overall growth and diversified their economies more rapidly than those which pursued strategies of diversification at the cost of their traditional agriculture. Moreover, their macroeconomic and sectoral policies have been more important in explaining performance than their luck (Table 2-2). The implications of transformation and adjustment for women can be seen by examining the country experiences. For example, whereas the broad-based growth which occurred in Kenya resulted in a decline in the proportion of population living in poverty, the skewed benefits in favor of a selected few households as in Malawi increased the incidence of poverty, especially among female-headed households (Lele 1988a).

Performances of Selected Countries

Over the 1967 to 1987 period, Cameroon, Kenya, and Malawi experienced relatively fast growth in per capita GDP, while Tanzania, Nigeria, and Senegal experienced no growth or a major decline in incomes. Although both Nigeria and Cameroon enjoyed an oil bonanza, Cameroon performed well, with a large number of small farmers participating in the production of a range of food and export crops, while Nigeria's agricultural sector declined in importance. Exports plummeted and food crop production did not keep pace with the growth of population and rising urban demand promoted by a seven-fold increase in public expenditures. Despite a rise in imports, food prices relative to nonfood prices have risen sharply in Nigeria when compared to the early 1970s.

Even after the adoption of adjustment measures in 1986, which reduced urban demand by encouraging urban-rural migration, food prices have tended to be high in part due to import bans on food. Such high prices should be expected to benefit women producers. However, the prices of most production inputs and consumer goods have risen sharply as well. Thus, when their effect is considered it is not clear that the real income of food crop producers has increased significantly, especially as market margins take up a significant share of prices. Whereas public marketing institutions have been recognized for inefficiency, private markets are often inefficient as well, due to poor infrastructure and lack of information and credit.

Kenya followed Cameroon in achieving rapid growth in food and export crop production. The government gave small farmers access to land, paid them international prices for their major crops, and provided them the necessary public services, thereby facilitating a rapid shift to labor-intensive, high-value crops, while not jeopardizing food production growth. Despite these achievements and the decline in the proportion of the population below poverty, the number of households in poverty increased substantially, especially in the 1980s when overall growth slowed down.

Malawi's overall growth record was similar to that of Kenya. However, unlike Kenya, benefits of growth were highly unequally distributed in Malawi, to the benefit of the estate sector. Smallholder production declined in per capita terms due to the policies of land alienation, restric-

Table 2-2. The Luck Factor, Subsequent Policy Responses, and Comparative Macroeconomic Performance of MADIA Countries, 1960–87.

Country	Luck Factors		Policy Responses		Performance (% growth rates)		
	Initial conditions	Subsequent shocks	Macro-economic policies	Sectoral policies	GDP	GNP per capita	Agricultural sector
Cameroon	F	F	F	F	5.9	2.8	4.4
Kenya	F	F	F	F	5.8	2.1	4.0
Malawi	U	U	F	U	4.4	1.5	2.8
Tanzania	F	U	U	U	3.3	0.2	1.4
Nigeria	F	F	U	U	3.1	−0.2	0.6
Senegal	U	U	U	U	2.2	−0.9	1.2

F = Favorable, U = Unfavorable
Source: Lele 1989. Data on growth rates are from World Bank Data File, 1989.

tions on small farmers regarding rights to grow export crops, and inadequate access to technology, credit, inputs, etc. Women-headed households have experienced the brunt of the decline in real income.

Tanzania and Senegal also performed poorly. Whereas adverse policies played a major part in both countries, Tanzania's more favorable resource endowments, relative to Senegal's, underline the fundamental role that adverse policies played in explaining its stagnation. Genuine strides were made in Tanzania in broadening the access of the rural population, especially women, to social services such as universal primary education and rural water supply. These investments could not be sustained, however, because too little attention was paid to agriculturally led growth, local participation tended to be rhetorical rather than genuine, and individual initiative was squelched. Tanzania's commitment to reforms, initiated in 1986, has been halting at best and parastatals continue to play a major role. Extreme decay in the nation's physical and institutional capital, particularly the road network, poses a major constraint to reaping the benefits of such reforms as have occurred.

During this period, Senegal's agriculture stagnated; any production increases were due to area expansion rather than technological change. Lack of increases in agricultural productivity, deterioration of soil fertility, and vulnerability to variable and harsh fluctuations in climate have contributed to Senegal's low self-sufficiency ratio and high dependence on food imports. Although at independence Senegal boasted impressive social indicators in terms of life expectancy, child mortality, school enrollment, and safe water, there has been little subsequent improvement. Continued stagnation in these areas bodes ill for women and their ability to fulfill their dual roles of production and reproduction.

The above discussion makes it clear that internal economic policies contributed to the macroeconomic crisis by causing stagnation in exports, growing food and capital goods imports, large and uncontrollable budget deficits, the development of parallel markets, and the decay of physical and institutional capital. Nevertheless external factors also caused problems. The two oil price increases in less than a decade and a prolonged recession in the OECD countries in the mid-1970s increased the cost of imports and depressed primary commodity prices. The abundance of official assistance, on the other hand, led to a sense of complacency among governments and donors alike, until balance of payments gaps increased to unsustainable proportions by the beginning of the 1980s.

Much of the foreign aid given in the 1970s had little impact on growth. While project lending expanded rapidly, the integrated rural development projects funded in the agricultural and rural sector were often complex and far beyond the scope of the administrative capacity of the governments to implement. They lacked a technological base and frequently focused on food crops in marginal areas to address well-intentioned concerns about poverty and food security and to meet the government's political objectives, but without achieving growth. On the contrary, many contributed to the growth of low-quality government expenditures and to public interventions which adversely affected women farmers.

Lessons from Adjustment

Structural adjustment has involved the restoration of macroeconomic balance by reducing the current account and fiscal deficits via the reduction of internal demand and increasing supply. It has called for changes in relative prices through adjustment in exchange rate and trade policies, control of money supply and interest rates, and reduction in public expenditures including subsidies. Initial adjustment efforts in the 1980s were focused on relatively short-term issues of restoring external and internal balance, prompted in part by the expectation that the response from the economies to such major adjustments would be relatively quick. As the economic crisis in Africa has been prolonged, however, the scope of adjustment efforts has broadened. There has been a return to the emphasis on the sectoral and household level issues of food security related to technology, as well as physical and social infrastructure. These new efforts can be fruitful if they take into account the development experiences of the 1970s and 1980s. However, the lack of institutional memory in governments and donor agencies frequently prevents incorporation of lessons learned.

Systematic data-based analysis of the adjustment experience has yet to be carried out. Nevertheless, several preliminary observations emerge from the experience to date. First, while price adjustments are necessary to restore macroeconomic balance, *they are by no means sufficient* to achieve a sustained supply response from a large and a growing number of poor households. To achieve such a response requires attention to a variety of nonprice factors of the technological, institutional, and infrastructural nature discussed in this paper. Without these changes, producer price shifts only result in shifts in crop composition rather than an overall increase in output (Lele 1988).

Second, without the access of small farmers to land and new technology (including improved seed and fertilizers which meet their complex subsistence consumption needs), even the shift in composition to more market-oriented crops is constrained by the need of small farmers to meet their domestic subsistence needs. In Malawi, for instance, there are major technological issues related to the promotion of improved flint maizes which women prefer due to their better storage, pounding, and cooking characteristics which did not receive attention until recently, although rural development programs have been underway for nearly twenty years. In Nigeria, the vexing problem of technology for intercropping situations did not receive attention in agricultural research for nearly two decades; meanwhile, extension programs promoted sole cropping technology to small farmers. The result of neglect of these crucial technology issues which small farmers and risk-averse, labor-short, women-headed households face is that the proportion of area required for subsistence cropping has been increasing rapidly at the expense of areas under export crops and livestock. Furthermore, these activities have been leading to substantial deleterious environmental consequences through deforestation and over-cropping.

Third, higher market prices of food crops combined with the uncertainty in the supply of food in the market can increase the risk averseness of farmers at the margin of subsistence and reinforce their emphasis on subsistence production given the high market dependence in a situation of rising market prices. Fourth, while demand for food for home consumption tends to be inelastic, demand for purchased inputs, especially fertilizer, tends to be price elastic.[6] A result of the increase in fertilizer prices is the slackening of its demand growth, especially in the absence of seasonal credit (Gladwin, this volume). Increasing the supply of fertilizer and credit, however, poses complex institutional problems, especially for rural households in remote areas which are poorly connected by transport, and where the indigenous private sector is still weak. In addition, packaging fertilizer in small enough packets to suit the micro needs of small-scale farmers poses logistical difficulties. Failure to address these constraints, which are demanding of human resources and institutions, leads women to work longer hours for subsistence. The ensuing shortage of women's time for timely planting and weeding of their own crops and for attending to the needs of their children increases their vulnerability as well as that of their children. On balance, while structural adjustment concentrated on price adjustments, the next stage is both an adjustment and development process in the effort to increase labor productivity, especially among women.

Conclusion

This chapter has documented the important role of African women in rural social and economic activity. It traced the complex interactions between polygamy and women's responsibilities for food supply and welfare of their households, the relationship of labor supply to agricultural intensification, the distribution of intra-household income and consumption, population growth, and the environment. The chapter explored the impact of food and cash cropping on food security and the effects of increased market dependence of women under conditions of growing population pressure on the land. It then examined the interactions between patterns of industrialization and urbanization, migration of males and households as they relate to agricultural intensification, and women's changing role in the production process and the command of income and household decisions. The chapter demonstrated the need for targeting programs in agriculture, health, education, nutrition, and employment towards women, but highlighted the practical difficulty of achieving this objective, given the limited human and institutional capital in Africa and the low participation of local people in the design of programs. The paper pointed out that while donors can assist women farmers relatively effectively by helping to improve the macroeconomic and sectoral policy and institutional environment, their role in the design and implementation of programs must, by necessity, be indirect.

The experience of adjustment loans in the last decade highlights the need to focus on several important areas. First, it shows that wrong industrialization policies together with terms of trade shocks created the need for macroeconomic adjustment, temporarily diverting attention from the long-term issues of poverty, employment, income, and growth. *The focus on macro adjustment must continue, but it is not sufficient.* Second, this experience demonstrates that a balance must be struck between efficiency-oriented policies and policies involving attention to asset distribution, productive and social services, and income transfers through food price stabilization, food for work programs, etc. These various policies must be considered as complementary rather than competitive as previously assumed. The bulk of adjustment in public expenditures in favor of growth that involves the poor must come from the old costly pursuits, such as large-scale industry and large-scale irrigation. Budget constraints make subsidies on food and fertilizers difficult to accommodate. Moreover, as subsidies tend to benefit the relatively larger market-oriented farmers, there is also reluctance to support their continuation. On the other hand, where poverty and land pressure is intense and the cost of food imports high due to high transportation costs, the budgetary cost of input subsidies can be more efficient and desirable than possible food shortages and food imports. Issues related to the use of input subsidies and their targeting, however, must be considered on a country-by-country basis. In Malawi, for example, while targeted subsidies seem preferable to general subsidies in order to contain the budgetary costs, the statistical information and administrative and monitoring capacity for targeting subsidies effectively simply does not exist. This situation applies in a number of countries. In Nigeria, on the other hand, fertilizer subsidies already amount to nearly 70 percent of the government budget on agriculture and little, if any, of these benefit small farmers, due to the extensive black market in fertilizer.

Third, the issue of export cropping, which has been frequently relegated to the background due to concerns about food security and nutrition, raises important issues of direct and indirect means of reaching poor households. For instance, in Kenya a large majority of farmers are better able to undertake the risk of innovation and to finance it from their own resources due to the higher prices they receive for their export crops, with the result that less than one-third of the households need direct assistance. In Malawi, on the other hand, government discouragement of smallholder cultivation of export crops, in conjunction with the risk aversity of subsistence-oriented households, has resulted in a concentration of subsistence production among smallholders. Despite more rapid population growth in Kenya than Malawi, the real wage has dropped less sharply, in part due to the growth linkages of a broad-based smallholder agricultural growth generated in the Kenyan economy, from which women farmers have benefited.

Finally, if women farmers in particular and poor households in general are to respond more rapidly to improved price signals made possible by adjustment programs, substantial investment is needed in human, physical, social, and institutional resources to address the broader issues of population, agriculture, and the environment, on the one hand, and the intra-household issues of the command of resources and differential access to services between men and women, on the other hand. The task for governments and donors is thus to increase the capacity of local institutions, NGOs, and private agents to identify the potential impact of the structural transformation and adjustment programs on the poor—particularly poor women—and to devise, in conjunction with the affected people themselves, appropriate strategies to bring about more equitable agriculturally based growth.

NOTES

1. The study "Managing Agricultural Development in Africa" (MADIA) was a five-year study (1984–89) undertaken by the World Bank to explain the nature and sources of the agricultural crisis in Africa, particularly the extent to which it originated in resource endowments, historical and contemporary events, external and internal policies, and the economic and political environment. The MADIA study involved detailed analysis of Kenya, Malawi, Tanzania, Cameroon, Nigeria, and Senegal. In addition to the World Bank, seven donors, USAID, UKODA (The British Overseas Development Administration), DANIDA (Danish International Development Agency), SIDA (Swedish International Development Agency), and the French and German governments and the EC (European Community), participated in the study.

2. Available estimates for the percentage of female-headed households in some African countries include: Malawi 34 percent (World Bank 1989i), Kenya 33 percent (World Bank 1989g), Ghana 29 percent (Youssef and Hetler 1983), Mali 15 percent (Youssef and Hetler 1984), Sudan 24 percent (Youssef and Hetler 1984), and Zambia 47 percent (World Bank 1989s). To date, the information from Malawi and Kenya seems to be the more complete and reliable, although Ghana has also improved its capacity to incorporate gender-specific household-headship information into census tables and publications.

3. For instance, in 1980, the shares of female and male employment in manufacturing to total employment were 15 percent and 10 percent, respectively, in Japan and 9 percent and 13 percent, respectively, in Korea. In Japan, whereas the growth rate in nonagricultural employment for women was 45 percent (1960–70) and 20 percent (1970–80), the rate for men was 35 percent and 16 percent. During the same period, however, average female earnings within the same industries were consistently less than half the male earnings in 1965 and by 1980 this differential had increased in several countries. Becker also reports a similar situation for other OECD countries (Lele 1986).

4. In an interesting paper on women's legal capacity and constitutional rights, Marsha Freeman stresses that no constitutional guarantees, such as those provided by most developing countries, are meaningful without the political will of governments and the capacity of the legal systems and institutions at large to enforce them (Freeman 1990).

5. In the Gambia, for instance, women are active in the production and sale of many cash crops. With the introduction of irrigated rice the yields per unit of land increased from 1.3 to 5.9 tons as the share of women's rice fields dropped from 91 percent to 10 percent, reflecting a switch from rice as an individually grown crop under the control of women to a communal crop under the control of men. The benefit of communal cultivation through extended family was greater food security through reduction of

covariate risks (von Braun and Webb 1989). Nevertheless, the introduction of new technology such as that of irrigated rice tends to make women more dependent on their husbands, due to men's greater control of land and greater access to technology.

6. Based on time series data in Malawi, fertilizer demand elasticity is estimated to be between 0.26 and 0.35 with respect to nutrient/maize price ratios; with respect to nonprice factors, this ratio is even higher at between 0.58 and 0.67 (Lele 1988b). For Mali, Gbetibouo estimates price elasticity of demand for fertilizer to be close to −1.2 (Gbetibouo 1990).

REFERENCES

Acharya, Meena, and Lynne Bennett
    1982   *Women and Work in Africa.* Boulder: Westview Press.
Ainsworth, Martha
    1989   Socioeconomic Determinants of Fertility in Cote d'Ivoire. Paper presented at the Population Association of America, Baltimore, MD.
Ahmad, Zubeida M., and Martha F. Loutfi
    1981   Programme on Rural Women. Geneva: International Labor Organization.
Anker, Richard, and Catherine Hein
    1985   Fertility and Employment in the Third World. POPULI 12(2).
Anker, Richard, Mayra Buvinic, and Nadia Youssef
    1982   *Women's Roles and Population Trends in the Third World.* London: Croom Helm.
Becker, Gary
    1981   *A Treatise on the Family.* Cambridge: Harvard University Press.
    1985   Human Capital, Effort and the Sexual Division of Labor. *Journal of Labor Economics* 3: 533–558.
Behrman, Jere R., and Barbara L. Wolfe
    1984   More Evidence on Nutrition Demand: Income Seems Overrated and Women's Schooling Underemphasized. *Journal of Development Economics* 14: 105–128.
    1987   How Does a Mother's Schooling Affect Family Health, Nutrition, Medical Care Usage and Household Sanitation. *Journal of Econometrics* 36: 185–204.
Benavot, A.
    1989   "Education, Gender and Economic Development: A Cross-National Study. *Sociology of Education* 62(1): 14–32.
Benavot, A., and Gita Sen
    1986   Accumulation, Reproduction and Women's Role in Economic Development: Boserup Revisted. *Women's Work: Development and the Division of Labor by Gender,* Elaine Leacock and Helen I. Safa, eds. Boston: Bergin and Gawey.

Beneria, Lourdes
   1982   *Women and Development: The Sexual Division of Labor in Rural Societies.* New York: Praeger.
Birdsall, Nancy
   1988   Economic Approaches to Population Growth. *Handbook of Development Economics,* Hollis Chenery and T.N. Srinivasan, eds. Amsterdam: North Holland.
   1976   Women and Population Studies. *Signs: Journal of Women in Culture and Society* 1 (Spring): 699–712.
Birdsall, Nancy, and William McGreevey
   1983   Women, Poverty and Development. *Women and Poverty in the Third World,* M. Buvinic, M. Lycette, and W. McGrevey, eds. Baltimore: Johns Hopkins University Press.
Boserup, Esher
   1965   *The Conditions of Agricultural Growth: The Economies of Agrarian Change Under Population Pressure.* New York: Aldine Publishing Company.
   1970   *Woman's Role in Economic Development.* New York: St. Martin's Press.
   1981   *Population and Technological Change: A Study of Long-Term Trends.* Chicago: University of Chicago Press.
Buvinic, Mayra, and Sally W. Yudleman
   1989   *Women, Poverty and Progress in the Third World.* Headline Series No. 289. New York: The Foreign Policy Association.
Buvinic, Mayra, Margaret A. Lycette, and William Paul McGreevey
   1983   *Women and Poverty in the Third World.* Baltimore and London: Johns Hopkins University Press.
Caldwell, John C.
   1978   *The Persistence of High Fertility in the Third World.* Canberra: Australian National University.
Caldwell, John C., and Pat Caldwell
   1987   The Cultural Context of High Fertility in Sub-Saharan Africa. *Population and Development Review* 13(3): 409–437.
Christiansen, Robert E.
   1989   Special Issue: Privatization. *World Development* 17(5).
Cleland, J., and G. Rodriguez
   1988   The Effect of Parental Education on Marital Fertiltiy in Developing Countries. *Population Studies* 42(3): 419–42.
Cochrane, Susan H.
   1979   Fertility and Education: What Do We Really Know? World Bank Occasional Paper No. 26. Baltimore: Johns Hopkins University Press.
   1983   Effects of Education and Urbanization on Fertility. R. Bulatao and R. Lees, eds.

Cochrane, Susan H., and Samir M. Farid
　1986　Fertility in Sub-Saharan Africa: Levels and their Explanation. PHN Technical Note 85–13. Washington, D.C.: World Bank.
Collier, Paul
　1988　Women in Development: Defining the Issues. World Bank Working Paper Series No. 129. Washington, D.C.: World Bank.
　1989　Women and Structural Adjustment. Draft. Washington, D.C.: World Bank.
Cornia, Giovanni A., Richard Jolly, and Frances Stewart
　1987　*Adjustment with a Human Face.* Oxford: Clarendon Press.
Dankelman, Irene, and Jean Davidson
　1988　*Women and Environment in the Third World: Alliance for the Future.* London: Earthscan Publications.
Davidson, Jean
　1988　*Agriculture, Women, and Land: The African Experience.* Boulder: Westview Press.
Delgado, Christopher L., and Chandrashekhar G. Ranade
　1987　Technological Change and Agricultural Labor Use. *Accelerating Food Production in Sub-Saharan Africa,* John W. Mellor, Christopher L. Delgado, and Malcolm J. Blackie, eds. Baltimore and London: The Johns Hopkins University Press.
Dey, Jennie
　1983　Women in African Farming Systems. Paper presented at International Rice Research Institute Conference on Women in Rice Farming Systems at Los Banos, The Philippines.
　1984　*Women in Food Production and Food Security in Africa.* Rome: FAO.
Ember, Carol R.
　1983　The Relative Decline in Women's Contribution to Agriculture with Intensification. *American Anthropologist* 85: 285–304.
Fleuret, Patrick, and Anne Fleuret
　1980　Nutrition, Consumption and Agricultural Change. Human Organization 39(3): 250–60.
Food and Agricultural Organization (FAO)
　1985　Women and Developing Agriculture. Women in Agriculture Series No. 4. Rome: FAO.
Freeman, Marsha A.
　1990　Measuring Equality: An International Perspective on Women's Legal Capacity and Constitutional Rights. *Berkeley Women's Law Journal.*
Gbetibouo, Mathurin
　1990　Rapport du Mission. Washington, D.C.: World Bank.
Gladwin, Christina, and Della McMillan
　1989　Is a Turnaround in Africa Possible Without Helping African Women to Farm? *Economic Development and Cultural Change* 37(2): 345–70.

Griggs, Jonathan M.
   1989   Women and Structural Adjustment: A Review of the Literature. Development Economics Research Centre, Department of Economics, University of Warwick.

Guyer, Jane I.
   1980   Household Budgets and Women's Income. African Studies Working Paper 28. Boston: Boston University.

Herz, Barbara
   1974   Demographic Pressure and Economic Change: The Case of Kenyan Land Reforms. Ph.D. dissertation, Columbia University.
   1989   Women in Development: Kenya's Experience. *Finance and Development* 26(2): 43–45.

Herz, Barbara, and Anthony R. Measham
   1987   The Safe Motherhood Initiative: Proposals for Action. World Bank Discussion Paper No. 9. Washington, D.C.: World Bank.

Horenstein, Nadine R.
   1989   Women and Food Security in Kenya. World Bank Working Paper Series No. 232. Washington, D.C.: World Bank.

International Labor Organization and United Nations Research and Training Institute for the Advancement of Women
   1985   Women in Economic Activity: A Global Statistical Survey (1950–2000). Dominican Republic.

Joekes, Susan
   1988   Women and Structural Adjustment: Parts I and II. Paper prepared for the meeting of the WID Expert Group of the OECD/DAC in Paris, France, April 18.

Joekes, Susan, Margaret Lycette, Lisa McGowan, and Karen Searle
   1989   Population Growth, Sustainable Development and the Role of Women. Washington, D.C.: World Bank.

Johnston, Bruce F., and Peter Kilby
   1975   *Agriculture and Structural Transformation: Economic Strategies in Late-Developing Countries.* New York: Oxford University Press.

Johnston, Bruce F., and John Mellor
   1961   The Role of Agriculture in Economic Development. *American Economic Review* 54: 556–93.

Jones, Christine
   1983   The Mobilization of Women's Labor for Cash Crop Production: A Game Theoretic Approach. *American Journal of Agricultural Economics* 65(5): 1049–54.

Kaul, R. N.
   1989   Gender Issues in Farming: A Case for Developing Farm Tools Specially for Women. Paper presented at the Farming Systems Research Symposium, University of Arkansas, Fayettesville.

Kennedy, Eileen T., and Bruce Cogill
   1986   Income and Nutritional Effects of the Commercialization of Agriculture in Southwestern Kenya. Research Report 63, International Food Policy Research Institute.
   1988   The Case of Sugarcane in Kenya: Part I. Effects of Cash Crop Production on Women's Income, Time Allocation, and Child Care Practices. MSU Working Paper #167, Michigan State University.

Kudat, Ayse
   1989   Participation of Women in Rural Road Maintenance in Sub-Saharan Africa. Draft. Washington, D.C.: World Bank.

Kumar, Shubh K.
   1987   Women's Role and Agricultural Technology. *Accelerating Food Production in Sub-Saharan Africa,* John W. Mellor, Christopher L. Delgado, and Malcolm J. Blackie, eds. Baltimore and London: The Johns Hopkins University Press.
   1988   Strategies for Protecting the Nutrition of the Poor During Structural Adjustment. Draft. Paper prepared for regional workshop on Protecting Nutrition During Periods of Adjustment, Bali/Lombok, Indonesia, August 29–September 2.

Kuznets, Simon
   1956   *Towards a Theory of Economic Growth.* Garden City, NY: Double-day.
   1966   *Modern Economic Growth: Rate, Structure, and Spread.* New Haven and London: Yale University Press.

Kydd, Johnathan G., and A. Hewitt
   1986   The Effectiveness of Structural Adjustment Lending: Initial Evidence from Malawi. *World Development* 14(3).

Kydd, Johnathan G., and Robert E. Christiansen
   1982   Structural Change in Malawi since Independence: Consequences of a Development Strategy Based on Large-Scale Agriculture. *World Development* 10(5): 355–76.

Leacock, Elaine, and Helen I. Saba
   1986   *Women's Work: Development and the Division of Labor by Gender.* Massachussets: Bergin and Gawey.

Lele, Uma
   1981   Rural Africa: Modernization, Equity, and Long-Term Development. Science 211: 547–53.
   1986   Women and Structural Transformation. *Economic Development and Cultural Change* 34(2): 195–221.
   1988a Agricultural Growth, Domestic Policies, the External Environment and Assistance to Africa: Lessons of a Quarter Century. *Trade, Aid, and Policy Reform: Proceedings of the Eighth Agriculture Sector Symposium.* Washington, D.C.: World Bank.

1988b   Structural Adjustment, Agricultural Development and the Poor: Some Lessons from the Malawian Experience. MADIA Working Papers. Washington, D.C.: World Bank.

1989   Sources of Growth in East African Agriculture. *The World Bank Economic Review* 3: 119–44.

Lele, Uma, and L. Richard Meyers

1987   Growth and Structural Change in East Africa: Domestic Policies, Agricultural Performance and World Bank Assistance, 1963–1986, Parts I and II. World Bank DRD Discussion Paper, Nos. 273 and 274. Washington, D.C.: World Bank.

Lele, Uma, Robert E. Christiansen, and Kundhavi Kadiresan

1989   Issues in Fertilizer Policy in Africa: Lessons from Development Programs and Adjustment Lending, 1970–87. MADIA Working Papers. Washington, D. C.: World Bank.

Lele, Uma, and Robert E. Christiansen

1989   Markets, Marketing Boards and Cooperatives: Issues in Adjustment Policy. MADIA Working Paper. Washington, D.C.: World Bank.

Lele, Uma, and Ellen Hanak

Forthcoming. *"Soft States," Hard Choices: The Politics of Agricultural Policy in Africa.*

Lele, Uma, and Steven Stone

1989   Population Pressure, the Environment, and Agricultural Intensification in Sub-Saharan Agriculture: Variations on the Boserup Hypothesis. MADIA Working Paper. Washington, D. C.: World Bank.

Lele, Uma, and Manmohan Agarwal

1989   Smallholder and Large-Scale Agriculture in Africa: Are There Trade-Offs Between Growth and Equity? MADIA Working Paper. Washington, D.C.: World Bank.

Lele, Uma, and John W. Mellor

1981   Technological Change, Distributive Bias and Labor Transfer in a Two Sector Economy. *Oxford Economic Papers* 33(3): 426–41.

Lesthaeghe, Ron

1989   *Reproduction and Social Organization in Sub-Saharan Africa.* Berkeley: University of California Press.

Lockwood, Matthew, and Paul Collier

1988   Maternal Education and the Vicious Cycle of High Fertility and Malnutrition: An Analytic Survey. World Bank Working Papers Series No. 130. Washington, D.C.: World Bank.

Matlon, Peter J.

1987   The West African Semi-Arid Tropics. *Accelerating Food Production in Sub-Saharan Africa,* John Mellor, Christopher Delgado, and Malcolm Blackie, eds. Baltimore: Johns Hopkins University Press.

Maxwell, Simon, and Adrian Fernando
n.d.   Cash Crops in Developing Countries: The Issues, the Facts, the Policies. Sussex: Institute of Development Studies.

Mellor, John W., and Rajul Pandya-Lorch
Forthcoming. Food Aid and Development. *Aid to African Agriculture: Lessons from Two Decades of Donor Experience,* Uma Lele, ed. Oxford: Oxford University Press.

Mellor, John W., and Uma Lele
1973   Growth Linkages of the New Foodgrain Technologies. *Indian Journal of Agricultural Economics* 23(1): 38–55.

Mellor, John W., and Bruce Johnston
1984   The World Food Equation: Interrelations among Development, Employment, and Food Consumption. *Journal of Economic Literature* 22(2): 531–74.

Moock, Peter
1973   Managerial Ability in Small-Farm Production: An Analysis of Maize Yields in the Vihiga Division of Kenya. Ph.D. dissertation, Columbia University.

Peters, Pauline E., and M. Guillermo Herrara
1989   Cash Cropping, Food Security, and Nutrition: The Effects of Agricultural Commercialization among Smallholders in Malawi. Cambridge: Harvard Institute for International Development.

Quinn, Victoria, Mabel Chiligo, and J. Price Gittinger
1988   Household Food and Nutritional Security in Malawi. Paper presented at the Symposium on Agricultural Policies for Growth and Development at Mangochi, Malawi, October 31 to November 4.

Rogers, Barbara
1979   *The Domestication of Women: Discrimination in Developing Societies.* New York: St. Martin's Press.

Ruthenberg, Hans
1971   *Farming Systems in the Tropics.* Oxford: Clarendon Press.

Sadik, Nafis
1989   The State of the World Population 1989. New York: United Nations Population Fund.

Sawhill, Isabel V.
1988   Poverty in the U.S.: Why is it so Persistent? *Journal of Economic Literature* 28(3): 1073–1119.

Schultz, T. Paul
1989   Returns to Women's Education. World Bank PHRWD Background Paper Series No. 89/001. Washington, D.C.: World Bank.
1989   Women and Development: Objectives, Frameworks, and Policy Interventions. World Bank Working Paper Series No. 200. Washington, D.C.: World Bank.

Sen, Amartya K.
  1966   Peasants and Dualism With or Without Surplus Labor. *Journal of Political Economy* 74(5): 425–50.
  1975   *Employment, Technology and Development.* London: Oxford University Press.
  1984   Family and Food: Sex Bias in Poverty. *Resources, Values, and Development,* A.K. Sen, ed. Cambridge: Harvard University Press.
  1985   Women, Technology and Sexual Divisions. *Trade and Development.* United Nations Conference on Trade and Development 6: 195–223.
  1987   Notes for the Seminar on Women's Issues in Development Policy. International Center for Research on Women, March 27.
Sen, Amartya K., and S. Sengupta
  1983   Malnutrition of Rural Children and the Sex Bias. *Economic and Political Weekly.* 18 (May): 855–64.
Siandwazi, Catherine, and Shubh K. Kumar
  1989   Effects of Technological Change in Eastern Province on Food Consumption and Nutrition Status of the Population. Prepared for seminar on Growth and Equity in Zambian Agriculture: An Eastern Province Study. (September).
Sivard, Ruth Leger
  1985   *Women . . . A World Survey.* Washington, D.C.: World Priorities.
Smock, Audrey
  1981   Women's Economic Roles. *Papers on the Kenyan Economy: Performance, Problems and Policies,* T. Killick, ed. Nairobi: Heinemann Educational Books, Ltd.
Svedberg, Peter
  1988   Undernutrition in Sub-Saharan Africa: Is There a Sex Bias? Seminar Paper No. 421. Stockholm: Institute for International Economic Studies.
Timmer, Peter
  1975   *The Choice of Technology in Developing Countries.* Cambridge: Harvard University, Center for International Affairs.
Timur, Serim
  1977   Demographic Correlates of Women's Education. Paper presented at the Conference of the International Union for the Scientific Study of Population, Mexico. Vol. III.
Tinker, Irene
  1979   *New Technologies for Food Chain Activities: The Imperative of Equity for Women.* Washington, D.C.: USAID.
Tripp, Robert B.
  1981   Farmers and Traders: Some Economic Determinants of Nutritional Status in Northern Ghana. *Journal of Tropical Pediatrics* 27: 15–22.

van de Walle, Etienne, and Andrew Foster
  1989   Fertility Decline in Africa: Assessments and Prospects. Washington, D.C.: World Bank.
von Braun, Joachim, and Eileen Kennedy
  1986   Commercialization of Subsistence Agriculture: Income and Nutritional Effects in Developing Countries. Washington, D.C.: International Food Policy Research Institute.
von Braun, Joachim, and Patrick J.R. Webb
  1989   The Impact of New Crop Technology on the Agricultural Division of Labor in a West African Setting. *Economic Development and Cultural Change* 37(3).
von Braun, Joachim, Detlev Puetz, and Patrick Webb
  1989   Irrigation Technology and Commercialization of Rice in the Gambia: Effects on Income and Nutrition. Research Report 75. Washington, D.C.: International Food Policy Research Institute.
Weber, Michael, John Staatz, John Holtzman, Eric Crawford, and Richard Bernsten
  1988   Informing Food Security Decisions in Africa: Empirical Analysis and Policy Dialogue. *American Journal of Agricultural Economics* 70(5): 1044–52.
World Bank
  1986a   Population Growth and Policies in Sub-Saharan Africa. World Bank Policy Study. Washington, D.C.: World Bank.
  1986b   Poverty and Hunger: Issues and Options for Food Security in Developing Countries. World Bank Policy Study. Washington, D.C.: World Bank.
  1988a   Adjustment Lending: An Evaluation of Ten Years of Experience. PPR Series 1, Washington, D.C.: World Bank.
  1988b   Report of the Task Force on Food Security in Africa. Washington, D.C.: World Bank.
  1989a   Cameroon: Women in Development Country Assessment Paper. Washington, D.C.: World Bank.
  1989b   *The Challenge of Hunger: A Call to Action.* Washington, D.C.: World Bank.
  1989c   Ethiopia: Women in Development Assessment. Washington, D.C.: World Bank.
  1989d   Fertility Decline in Africa: Assessment, Prospect and Policies: A Research Proposal. Washington, D. C.: World Bank.
  1989e   The Gambia: Women in Development: A Country Assessment. Washington, D.C.: World Bank.
  1989f   Kenya: Food, Nutrition and Development: A World Bank Sector Report. Washington, D.C.: World Bank.
  1989g   Kenya: The Role of Women in Economic Development. A World Bank Country Study. Washington, D.C.: World Bank.

1989h   Madagascar Food Security Study. Washington, D.C.: World Bank.

1989i   Malawi: Country Economic Memorandum: Growth through Poverty Reduction. Washington D.C.: World Bank.

1989j   Malawi Food Security Report. Washington, D.C.: World Bank.

1989k   Mozambique Food Security Study. Washington, D.C.: World Bank.

1989l   Nigeria: Assessment Report on Women in Development. Washington, D.C.: World Bank.

1989m   Role of Women in the Economic and Social Development of the Ivory Coast: Country Assessment Paper. Washington, D.C.: World Bank.

1989n   *Sub-Saharan Africa: From Crisis to Sustainable Development—A Long Term Perspective Study.* Washington, D.C.: World Bank.

1989o   Sudan: Towards an Action Plan for Food Security. Washington, D.C.: World Bank.

1989p   Women in Development: Country Assessment Zaire. Washington, D.C.: World Bank.

1989q   Women in Development in Togo: A Summary Country Assessment Paper. Washington, D.C.: World Bank.

1989r   Women in Development in Malawi: Constraints and Actions. Washington, D.C.: World Bank.

1989s   Women in Development: Issues for Economic and Sector Analysis. World Bank Working Papers Series No. 269. Washington, D.C.: World Bank.

Forthcoming. *World Development Report.* Washington, D.C.: World Bank.

World Bank, World Health Organization, and United Nations Fund for Population Activities.

1987   Preventing the Tragedy of Maternal Deaths: A Report on the International Safe Motherhood Conference. Conference held in Nairobi, Kenya in February. Washington, D.C.: World Bank.

Youssef, Nadia H., and Carol B. Hetler

1983   Establishing the Economic Condition of Woman-headed Households in the Third World: A New Approach. *Women and Poverty in the Third World,* Mayra Buvinic, Margaret A. Lycette, and William Paul McGreevey, eds. Baltimore and London: Johns Hopkins University Press.

1984   Rural Households Headed by Women: A Priority Concern for Development. World Employment Programme Research Working Papers. Geneva: International Labor Organization.

3

Getting Priorities Right: Structural Transformation and Strategic Notions

Bruce F. Johnston

Why focus on priorities? While much attention has been given in the literature on agricultural development to "getting prices right," relatively little attention has been given to the more fundamental question of "getting *priorities* right." In a given situation, policy-induced distortions of "macro prices" (exchange rates, interest rates, wage rates, food prices) may represent a major impediment to agricultural development (Timmer, Falcon, and Pearson 1983: chapter 5). In Tanzania and Ghana, for example, removing such distortions was undoubtedly a precondition for renewed agricultural progress. But elsewhere price and related distortions may be only a minor impediment; and macroeconomic reforms can never be a substitute for the policies and programs needed to foster agricultural development and the transformation of an overwhelmingly agrarian economy into a diversified, increasingly productive economy capable of banishing poverty.

There is in fact considerable justification for the preoccupation with "getting prices right." It is a convenient short hand expression for emphasizing the advantages of moving toward greater reliance on the allocative mechanisms of a market economy, thus subsuming the broader goals of encouraging competition and getting markets to work properly. Roemer and Radelet (1989) state:

Bruce F. Johnston is a Professor, Food Research Institute, Stanford University, and Fellow, American Agricultural Economics Association. This paper draws heavily on a forthcoming book on the political economy of agricultural development and structural transformation by Bruce Johnston, Peter Kilby, and Thomas P. Tomich commissioned by the Economic Development Institute of the World Bank and also supported by the Stanford Food Research Institute and HIID. The author wants to especially acknowledge Thomas Tomich for the concept of "strategic notions," and Peter Kilby for helpful comments; but is solely responsible for this very condensed presentation.

A complete reform package, derived from the neoclassical paradigm, contains five components: (1) freeing markets to determine prices ("letting markets work"); (2) adjusting controlled prices to scarcity values ("getting prices right"); (3) shifting resources from government into private hands (privatization); (4) rationalizing government's remaining role in development (budget rationalization); and (5) reforming institutions to carry out government's new role.

The underlying idea, of course, is that freeing markets so that market-determined prices reflect opportunity costs will encourage a pattern of resource allocation that promotes maximum output and an optimal rate of growth. Hyden (1988: 70) stresses an essential feature of the third and fourth of those five components when he speaks of the need for "reallocation of responsibilities in such a way that a better institutional balance between public, private, and voluntary sectors is achieved...." There is an emerging consensus that the public sector's role should focus on creating an "enabling environment," notably by strengthening the provision of public goods such as education and agricultural research and ensuring that the creation and maintenance of roads and other critical infrastructure are not neglected.

There are so many interventions that appear to be highly desirable that a critical problem is to refrain from committing scarce resources to activities that are *not* of strategic importance. Indeed, a serious problem in sub-Saharan Africa is the tendency for governments to assume responsibilities and to finance public consumption in excess of available resources. The scourge of inflation and a large foreign debt are two of the most serious consequences of this failure to maintain a balance between governmental responsibilities and resources.[1] It is this problem of maintaining a balance between responsibilities and resources that underscores the need to define priorities.

The major theme of this paper is that development planners can adopt *strategic priorities* which will allow sub-Saharan African countries to accelerate the transformation of the structure of their economies and the eradication of poverty. To support this point, I first propose that useful generalizations can be made about strategic priorities. I then describe the common structural/demographic features of late-developing countries that provide a basis for those generalizations. Finally, I explore the concept of strategic notions of policy makers and their ability to reach a consensus on the "right" priorities, and provide a short list of strategic priorities which take account of the great importance of women's farming in sub-Saharan Africa, a role that is examined in detail in other chapters in this volume.

Is It Possible to Generalize about Priorities?

The more orthodox approaches to agricultural policy analysis seem to indicate that it is neither possible nor necessary to generalize about development priorities. Agricultural project analysis provides a basis for ranking alternatives according to quantitative estimates of their benefit-cost ratios. More recently, the Policy Analysis Matrix (PAM) framework has provided what "might be characterized as the application of benefit-cost methods to agricultural policy" (Gotsch 1989: 9). Agricultural project analysis and applications of the PAM framework involve similar calculations and both are specific to the circumstances of a particular time and place.

In a recent manual on the PAM approach, Pearson and Monke (1987) identify three types of policies: agricultural price policy; macroeconomic policies (notably fiscal, monetary, and exchange rate policies); and public investment policies (see also Monke and Pearson 1989). They then use a conceptual framework that focuses on policies, objectives, and constraints to summarize the processes of policy analysis and policy making in these terms:

> Policymakers enact policies (price, macro, or investment) to further government objectives (efficiency, equity, or food security) in the face of economic constraints (supply, demand, and world prices). Policy analysis consists of evaluating price, macro, or investment policy instruments by quantifying the constraints and by estimating the likely impacts of policy on objectives. Analysts can thus identify tradeoffs between objectives and attempt to measure their magnitudes. Policymakers can then better exercise their value judgments about what is desirable policy. (Pearson and Monke 1989: 5).

Note, however, that even though policy analysts attempt to identify and quantify tradeoffs between alternative policies, there remains a need for policy makers to "exercise their value judgments about what is desirable policy."

A major theme of this paper is that useful generalizations can be made about certain *strategic priorities*. The possibility of making useful generalizations which help to identify the *kinds* of policies, programs, and projects that are likely to be appropriate is most significant for *late*-developing countries where 50 to 90 percent of the population still depends on agriculture for income and employment and where the total labor force is increasing at an annual rate of 2 percent or more; in Kenya and a number of other African countries the growth rate of the population of working age is approaching 3.5 to 4.0 percent. That subset of late-developing countries, which includes virtually all of the low-income and many of the lower middle-income developing countries, shares some common features from which important generalizations about development priorities can be derived.

A serious effort to derive useful generalizations concerning strategic priorities is important for several reasons. If possible, decisions should be based on quantitative estimates of the benefits and costs of the relevant alternatives. But a degree of consensus on strategic priorities is essential in order to identify a limited (and manageable) number of options that merit detailed quantitative analysis. Even more important is the fact that many of the critical decisions about strategic priorities *cannot* be based on quantified estimates of benefits and costs. Many key variables are extremely difficult or impossible to quantify but too important to ignore. The fundamental challenge in the design and implementation of an agricultural development strategy is to promote efficient, evolutionary change of a complex and dynamic system. An attempt to apply rigorous optimization or other quantitative techniques to a subset of variables is likely to be worse than decision making that is guided by a more comprehensive attempt to take account of all of the significant variables. That is especially true of the long run in which technology and resources are variables that depend on which historical paths were chosen at successive earlier periods.[2] In a concluding section, I suggest a half-dozen strategic priorities of critical importance to late-developing countries. But first let us consider the common features of late-developing countries that seem to provide a basis for those generalizations with respect to strategic priorities.

Common Features of Late-Developing Countries

Structural/Demographic Characteristics

It is no mere coincidence that no country has achieved the eradication of hunger and other serious manifestations of poverty without *structural transformation* and a *demographic transition.* Because of the interaction between the predominantly agrarian structure of late-developing countries and their high rates of growth of population and labor force, it is inevitable that it will take many years for them to reach the turning point for structural transformation, defined as the time when the absolute size of their farm labor force begins to decline. Moreover, the growth rate of their farm labor force will only be a little less than the rate of growth of the country's total labor force until considerable structural transformation has taken place.

The significance of agriculture's heavy weight in the total labor force combined with rapid growth rates of population and labor force in sub-Saharan Africa needs to be underscored. Seemingly small differences in the initial share of agriculture in a country's labor force and in the rate of growth of its total labor force can have large effects on the time required to reach the turning point. For example, if agriculture's share in the total labor force has declined to 50 percent and the total labor force is growing at an annual rate of 2.5 percent, a 4.0 percent rate of growth of nonfarm employment will suffice to enable the country to reach that turning point in only 16 years. But if agriculture's share in the labor force is still 70 percent in the initial year, 52 years would be required to reach that turning point when the absolute size of the farm labor force begins to decline, assuming again that the total and nonfarm labor force are increasing at annual rates of 2.5 and 4.0 percent. But with the same 70 percent initial share of agriculture in the labor force and nonfarm employment again growing at 4.0 percent, the time required to reach the structural transformation turning point would nearly double to 96 years if a country's total labor force is increasing at 3.0 instead of 2.5 percent.

Demographic Contrasts and Changes in Farm Labor Productivity

The enormous contrast between the demographic/structural characteristics of developed countries and late-developing countries has a number of important implications. For one, that contrast is the proximate cause of the large and growing differences in agricultural labor productivity in the two sets of countries. That is brought out clearly in estimates for 44 countries by Hayami and Ruttan (1985: 120) that partition the changes in labor productivity between 1960 and 1980 into changes in output per hectare and changes in hectares cultivated per worker.

A comparison of the changes in output per agricultural worker in the U.S. and in Bangladesh between 1960 and 1980 provides a dramatic illustration. In 1960 output per farm worker in the U.S. was 47 times as high as in Bangladesh.[3] But between 1960 and 1980 there was a *threefold* increase in farm labor productivity in the U.S. from 94 to 285 "wheat units" whereas in Bangladesh there was a decline from 2.0 to 1.8 "wheat units" per farm worker. As a proximate cause, that change from a 47-fold differential in 1960 to an astounding 158-fold differential in 1980 can be attributed entirely to the demographic contrasts between the two countries.

By coincidence both countries registered increases in output per hectare of approximately 40 percent between 1960 and 1980. But in Bangladesh the increase in output was associated with a 57-percent increase in the farm workforce from 12.1 to 19.1 million, whereas in the U.S. the farm workforce declined from 3.8 to 1.7 million. Consequently, the area cultivated per farm worker in the U.S. increased from 117 to 247 hectares, whereas in Bangladesh the area cultivated per farm worker declined from 0.8 to 0.5 hectares between 1960 and 1980. Because of the much greater degree of specialization in the U.S., where agriculture accounts for less than 4 percent of the total labor force compared to about 75 percent in Bangladesh, it is both necessary and possible for American farmers to augment inputs of human labor with a huge array of purchased inputs. Perhaps even more important is the much greater level of U.S. investments in education, research, and a host of other public and private institutions that directly and indirectly contribute to the productivity of American agriculture.

In the U.S., Japan, Taiwan, and other countries that pursued efficient agricultural strategies, increases in *total factor productivity* (output per unit of total input) have been a major source of increase in farm output. In such countries the growth of output has typically been about twice as rapid as the increase in use of inputs (labor, land, machines, fertilizers), whereas in low-income developing countries the rate of increase in the use of inputs has been nearly as great as the increase in output. In brief, the high levels of productivity achieved in developed and middle-income countries such as the U.S. and Japan are the result of specialization and *balanced* accumulation of capital, including both physical and human capital and also social capital—economically useful knowledge and institutions as well as cultural attributes that sustain the accumulation and efficient use of capital in its various forms.

Finally, this growth of productivity based on specialization and balanced accumulation of capital depends on *structural transformation*, the process whereby an overwhelmingly agrarian economy is transformed into a diversified, predominantly industrial, and highly productive modern economy. Moreover, since increases in output per worker depend on increases in *per capita* stocks of capital in its various forms, completing the second half of the demographic transition is a critical component.

Unimodal Versus Bimodal Patterns of Agricultural Development

Another important implication of the structural and demographic characteristics of late-developing countries is that they confront a choice
between a broad-based *unimodal* strategy aimed at a large subsector of
small-scale units, or a *bimodal* (dualistic) pattern in which increases in
output are concentrated within a small subsector of large-scale units
(Johnston and Kilby 1975, Johnston and Clark 1982). The choice is
often made by default; but there is an unavoidable trade-off between
emphasis on a unimodal vs. a bimodal pattern of agricultural development. This trade-off is gender-related in sub-Saharan Africa, where many
of the small farm units are operated by women (Lele 1986, Gladwin and
McMillan 1989) and most if not all of the large farms are operated by
men (Guyer, this volume).

When agricultural land is scarce, the small size of the average farm unit
will obviously be further reduced if a subsector of large farms accounts for
a large percentage of the available agricultural land. But even if there is
scope for expanding the area under cultivation—as there is in certain
regions of sub-Saharan African countries (Cohen 1989: 9–10)—there is a
trade-off because of the severe cash income/purchasing power constraint
that characterizes the agricultural sector in late-developing countries.
That constraint exists because the urban population dependent on purchased food is very small relative to the number of farm households.
Hence a subsistence orientation is an inevitable characteristic of farm
households. To be sure, a subsector of large farms may be able to escape a
serious purchasing power constraint by accounting for the greater share of
commercial production and farm cash receipts. The resulting bimodal
pattern of agricultural development means, however, that for the great
majority of farm households the purchasing power constraint is exacerbated. To the extent that foreign exchange, licenses for imports, loanable
funds, and other scarce resources are allocated directly by government, as
with state farms, the preferential treatment of the large farm sector and
discrimination against small farms becomes more obvious and extreme.

The initially slow process of structural transformation will only gradually increase cash receipts as domestic commercial sales expand with
growth of the nonfarm population dependent on purchased food. As the
rate of growth of a country's total labor force declines and the weight of
the farm labor force in the total is reduced, the scope for enlarging the
cash receipts of the average farm household is increased. Because that is

inevitably a slow process, expanded production of export crops is likely to
be an attractive option for late-developing countries because it provides a
means of expanding farm cash receipts that is not dependent on the slow
process of structural transformation.[4]

It needs to be stressed that advocacy of a unimodal pattern of agriculture is *not* an endorsement of policies to favor "the poorest of the poor" or
of measures intended to ensure that all smallholders advance in lock-step
so that increases in income differentials are prevented. A unimodal development strategy is *not* an "egalitarian growth path" (Carter 1989: 35) or
an equity argument that "can alleviate income disparities and raise production uniformly across the board" (Cohen 1989: 13). Furthermore,
African experience suggests that a degree of bimodalism may have compensating advantages. Significant involvement of a developing country's
elite in agricultural production seems to protect the agricultural sector
from policies that are too detrimental to farmers (Bates 1981) and also to
encourage government investment in rural infrastructure and agricultural
research and other support services. The contrast between Kenya and
Tanzania is pertinent (Lofchie 1989, Johnston 1989).

There is a substantial risk, however, that African policymakers and foreign advisers will promote the growth of a large-scale farm sector to a
degree that jeopardizes the prospects for success in realizing a unimodal
pattern of agricultural development. In its most recent report on sub-
Saharan Africa, the World Bank (1989: 93) argues that policies should
encourage "medium- and large-scale farming" as well as smallholder agriculture, noting that "educated Africans who might spurn peasant agriculture could be attracted to work in such modern agricultural enterprises."
The argument is seductive but treacherous. There is a strong tendency,
clearly evident in this World Bank report, to ignore the trade-offs that
arise because of the cash income/purchasing power constraint and other
factors that make it *virtually impossible* for a late-developing country to
implement simultaneously successful strategies oriented toward both
smallholders and large-scale farm enterprises.[5] The impacts on African
women farmers left in the stagnating smallholder sector when the lion's
share of national resources of land, capital/credit, and foreign exchange go
to medium- and large-scale male farmers are documented in other papers
in this volume.

Land Reform as a Precondition for a Unimodal Pattern

Because of the attention that has been given to the post-World War II
experience of Japan, Taiwan, and South Korea, there is a tendency to
regard land reform as a precondition for a unimodal pattern of develop-

ment. The redistributive land reform programs carried out in those three countries were indeed successful and contributed to accelerated growth of agricultural output as well as more equal distribution of income among the farm population. There were, however, special circumstances that contributed to the success of those reform programs. In many of today's developing countries the political resistance to effective implementation of redistributive land reform programs is so strong that it is defeatist to assume that such a program is a precondition for achieving a unimodal pattern of agricultural development.

In fact, it is the size distribution of farm *operational* units, not ownership units, that is the critical determinant of the choice of agricultural technology. The patterns of agricultural development in Japan, Taiwan, and Korea were unimodal long before the postwar land reforms; landowners found it more profitable to rent out land in small parcels to be farmed intensively by tenant households. Empirical evidence indicates that small farms have an economic advantage over large farms as long as labor is cheap (owing to its relative abundance and the lack of alternative employment opportunties). But that potential superiority may be offset by various *differentiating factors* that give large farmers a differential advantage over smallholders. Many of those differentiating factors may be a consequence of certain kinds of macroeconomic and sectoral pricing policies. Policies to provide cheap credit and to subsidize inputs are common and invariably bias development in a bimodal direction unless targeted explicitly to smallholders. They create an excess demand situation that gives rise to administrative rationing that in turn gives an advantage to larger, more influential farmers.

Strategic Notions and Development Priorities

One of the major gaps in our understanding of the development process concerns the factors that influence policymakers' decisions about development priorities. Allison (1971) has demonstrated the limitations of relying entirely on a "rational actor model" (Bates 1981) which assumes that governments make choices in a manner analogous to decision making by an individual. In his seminal book, Allison argued that the rational actor model needs to be supplemented by two other models—an "organizational process model" and a "governmental politics model." Those two models direct attention to the role of specific organizations and their organizational routines and interests and to the roles of individuals in a position to influence decisions, because of their positions in the relevant action channels, and who will be influenced by certain individual and group interests.

Collective choice theories such as those set forth by Buchanan and Tullock (1965) claim to be able to explain governmental decision making by extending the self-interest theory of economics to the political domain. In fact, there is no agreed theory of "the political economy of development." Tomich, Kilby, and I have adopted a view of political economy as an approach characterized by explicit concern with political as well as economic constraints and with the importance of seizing political as well as economic opportunities.[6]

The conventional view of the policy process is misleading when applied to the complex, ill-structured problems of development. That conventional view of rational problem solving sees its job as establishing certain objectives and then deciding how those predetermined objectives are to be reached. But one of the central lessons of policy analysis is that ends and means are not distinct entities. Progress in the real world, especially the severely constrained world of late-developing countries, calls for *mutual adjustment of ends and means*. A realistic approach also requires explicit attention to both the desirability and feasibility of alternatives. Leys (1971: 133) puts the matter well when he stresses the need to ask simultaneously "what changes—social and political as well as economic—are within the politicians' 'means,' and what are not; and what patterns or sequences of change, among those that are practicable, will carry the process of economic development farthest and fastest at the least cost in the politicians' resources?"

The importance of viewing social problem solving in late-developing countries as mutual adjustment of ends and means is underscored by the fact that in poor countries certain objectives appear to be so compelling that often there appears to be no humane alternative to stressing what is needed in the hope that an eminently desirable goal will somehow be feasible as well. Thus there is considerable enthusiasm for focusing on hunger as *the* critical problem in Third World countries and calling for direct action to eradicate it. The 1980 report of the Presidential Commission on World Hunger, for example, declared "people who are poor need not be hungry as well" and offered a blanket endorsement for food stamp plans as a direct action that is less costly than general food subsidy programs (Presidential Commission 1980: 40–41). For an affluent country such as the U.S. and for many middle-income countries as well that is a feasible as well as desirable proposition. For low-income, late-developing countries, however, a food stamp plan is an inappropriate, even damaging choice. For those countries no sustainable solution to their pervasive problems of hunger and poverty is possible without structural transformation and substantial increases in farm and nonfarm productivity and output. Their problems of hunger and poverty are more widespread among hard-to-reach rural households than in urban areas, which further underscores the limitations of a food stamp or other direct action program.

In addition to the reasonably balanced investments in physical, human, and social capital required for transforming their predominantly agrarian structure, certain investments in education and health appear to be essential for completing their half-completed demographic transition. The needs for public and private investment and recurrent expenditure for economic and social development are so great that it is exceedingly difficult for late-developing countries to maintain a manageable balance between responsibilities assumed by government and the resources available for carrying out those responsibilities. That common problem of imbalance between responsibilities and resources underscores the critical importance of achieving a workable consensus with respect to development priorities.

Strategic Notions and Reaching a Consensus on Priorities

It is obviously much easier to assert the need for a consensus on development priorities than to offer useful guidance on how it might be achieved. An essential step is to recognize that development is inherently a time-consuming process with a consequent need for patience and persistence. A long-term strategic perspective on the interrelated components of a rural development strategy highlights the importance of *complementary* as well as *competitive* relationships among alternative policies and programs. The focus needs to be on rural development, encompassing but not confined to agricultural development. Success depends on development of the rural nonfarm economy as well as on expansion of farm output. Furthermore, public investments in education, health, and family planning programs that reach a large and growing percentage of a country's rural population are crucial to the progress of structural transformation and the demographic transition.

It is tempting to multiply the list of essential objectives that need to be achieved by a late-developing country. Indeed a defining characteristic of such countries is that *they can't afford to do a great many things that they can't afford not to do*. Study of the historical experience of countries in which well-conceived agricultural strategies have made a major contribution to economic growth suggests that certain strategic notions held by policy analysts and policy makers facilitated a consensus on strategic priorities. In both the U.S. and Japan, for example, widely held strategic notions concerning the importance of education and investing in human resources contributed greatly to their economic progress. Other strategic notions differed in the two countries, but in both the development priorities that were shaped by the strategic notions held by their policy makers were appropriate to their stage of development and the constraints and opportunities that they faced.

In spite of great differences in their resource endowments and historical circumstances, a rich literature on agricultural development in Japan and the U.S. suggests that several strategic notions helped to shape the development of an interacting system of developmental institutions, including primary and secondary schools and institutions of higher education, agricultural research systems, mechanisms for diffusing technical knowledge and innovations, and programs for construction of roads and other rural infrastructure. The increasingly productive agricultural technologies that were developed and diffused in the two countries were very different but well suited to their respective resource endowments.

The concept of strategic notions, as used by Tomich, is less sweeping than ideology but more concrete than "mindset," although akin to both.[7] Even with heroic efforts to quantify costs and benefits of alternative actions, policy makers can only have a notion of the policies and programs that will be effective in furthering the development process. The strategic notions that shape their decisions are based on a combination of conjecture, personal perception of "facts," and vaguely remembered ideas. The beliefs underlying those notions derive from past personal experience and selective interpretations of the experience of others as well as more formal ideas influenced by education and policy research and analysis. Moreover, because those notions are derived from similar backgrounds, they are likely to be shared by many of a country's policy makers. Some widely held strategic notions have been appropriate and highly beneficial. Others have been destructive. There seems reason to believe that African countries have been adversely affected by the sway of imported and changing strategic notions, which has probably been an obstacle to the emergence of strategic notions based more firmly on local experience. It would, however, be defeatist and wrong to assume that African countries cannot draw useful lessons from study and careful interpretation of the experience of countries that have pursued successful strategies of agricultural and rural development.

A Short List of "Right" Priorities

Past experience and the structural and demographic characteristics emphasized earlier provide a basis for identifying certain strategic notions that facilitate consensus on the "right" priorities capable of fostering efficient and equitable development. Equally important, that approach to defining development priorities helps to focus attention on a manageable set of priorities by undermining certain misleading or inappropriate strategic notions.

For example, a strategic notion that has emphasized a dichotomy between efficiency and equity has been widely held. It is almost invariably held by proponents of a dualistic pattern of agricultural development who claim that only large farm units can be efficient. That view ignores the structural-demographic characteristics of a late-developing country that severely constrain sectorwide expansion in the use of "external" purchased inputs, e.g., imported tractors. It is only when structural transformation is well advanced, so that farm labor becomes scarce and expensive and reliance on labor-saving farm machinery becomes socially as well as privately profitable, that economies of farm size become important. In contrast, a strategic notion that is based on a realistic appreciation of the structural-demographic characteristics of a late-developing country and emphasizes policies and programs that foster the progressive modernization of a large and growing percentage of a country's small-scale farm units has important advantages in terms of both efficiency and equity.

It was noted earlier that the interrelated components of a rural development strategy have important complementary as well as competitive relationships. It is essential for development strategies to emphasize concurrent, mutually supporting efforts to accelerate the growth of output and to expand employment opportunities. This inevitably means choosing *not* to undertake many tactically attractive actions. Given the seriousness of the problem of imbalance between resources and responsibilities, food stamp or school lunch programs, for example, which are highly desirable when resource constraints are not too binding, almost certainly do not merit a high priority in a low-income, late-developing country. It is essential to concentrate scarce resources on activities that are complementary and therefore mutually reinforcing and which contribute to widespread and sustained progress in (1) promoting development of the rural economy, farm and nonfarm; (2) accelerating structural transformation; and (3) completing the demographic transition.

Conclusion

My reading of the evidence of past experience suggests that economic and social development will be well served if the strategic notions held by a country's policy makers facilitate consensus on six strategic priorities. Unless perfectly gender-neutral, my recommendations mention how the strategic priority impacts on sub-Saharan African women's roles in farming.

1. *Give priority to government's facilitating and catalytic role while minimizing the role of public agencies in commercial or productive activities.* A major lesson of the experience of the past four decades is that a developing country is not well served by a dogmatic emphasis on either a *laissez faire* or a *dirigiste* approach to defining the role of government. The challenge is rather to strike a balance in allocating functions between the public and private sectors so as to maximize the comparative advantage of each.

2. *Avoid macroeconomic policies that have adverse effects on agricultural development generally and especially on small-scale farm units—which in sub-Saharan Africa are so often operated by women.* This means emphasizing economic stability and predictability, and permitting prices, including interest rates and exchange rates, to reflect the scarcity value of resources, thereby encouraging the allocation of resources toward their most productive use rather than discretionary allocation by administrative rationing that will inevitably be guided by patronage concerns—and in Africa channeled into men's hands. Another major concern must be to avoid allocating capital or foreign exchange to unduly capital- or import-intensive investments in industry. For example, resisting pressures to invest in domestic manufacture of nitrogen fertilizers is especially important because of its enormous opportunity cost.

3. *Face up to the fundamental importance of pursuing an agricultural strategy that leads to a broadly based, unimodal pattern of agricultural development rather than a dual-size structure of farm operational units and a bimodal pattern of development with the two subsectors using drastically different technologies (e.g., African men with tractors, African women with hand-hoes).* The first implication of strategic notions consistent with this lesson derived from past experience and the structural/demographic characteristics of late-developing countries concerns the importance of minimizing *differentiating factors.* It will be recalled that the most common differentiating factors are economic policies such as subsidized distribution of inputs that give large (male) farmers a differential advantage over

(women) smallholders. The second implication relates to the bias of technological change—minimizing reliance on the capital-using, labor-saving technologies favored by large farm units while strengthening research programs which generate *divisible* innovations capable of being used efficiently by smallholders subject to a cash income/purchasing power constraint, e.g., the many excellent Farming Systems programs in Africa that work with women farmers and their food crops. Experience with the Green Revolution in Asia and earlier experience in Japan, Taiwan, and Korea demonstrate that it is considerably easier to generate innovations that are neutral to scale, notably improved seed-fertilizer combinations, under irrigated conditions than with rainfed agriculture. The countries of sub-Saharan Africa face special difficulties in achieving the R&D capacity needed to support broad-based agricultural strategies, not only because they rely mainly on rainfed farming in heterogeneous and often difficult physical environments, but also because the research/extension staff often approach the men in the household to help them improve crops farmed by women. As a result, the women lose their income from the crop that year, and the innovation is not adopted in succeeding years. That underscores the importance of devising cost-effective institutional arrangements capable of facilitating the generation and diffusion of innovations adapted to diverse African conditions. The great potential advantage of Farming Systems Research is that it provides a mechanism for exploiting the potential complementarity between the findings of on-station research by agricultural scientists and the location-specific, empirically based knowledge of a country's farmers, including trial-and-error learning from informal on-farm trials on both men's and women's private fields, with both men's and women's crops.

4. *Expand and improve the rural infrastructure to serve agriculture and rural nonfarm enterprises,* with a particular emphasis on roads and investments in electric power, sewerage, health facilities, schools, and market places in towns of 5,000 to 30,000 inhabitants.

5. *Improve systems of agricultural taxation,* including steps to reduce the disincentive effects associated with the de facto taxation of farmers by an overvalued exchange rate and/or low marketing board prices. In achieving a balance between government responsibilities and resources, it is often as important to augment the resources available through improving local tax systems as it is to cut back on public expenditure. Serious attention also needs to be given to greater use of fees to finance education and certain types of health services.

6. *Undertake certain direct but highly selective measures to enhance rural*

welfare by increasing per capita investments in human capital in the form of education and health. In most of sub-Saharan Africa there has been an enormous expansion of public outlays for education. There is still a formidable challenge, however, to improve the quality of educational institutions at all levels.

Much less has been done toward ensuring that rural areas have access to interlinked health and family planning activities. It is especially important in this instance to be concerned with a proper sequencing of the activities that receive priority. There are cogent reasons for assigning priority initially to activities such as immunization programs, oral rehydration therapy, and nutrition and hygiene education, all concentrated on infants and small children under five and their mothers. Those groups are especially vulnerable and the preventive and promotive technologies available are exceptionally cost-effective. Efforts to integrate different types of activities confront serious administrative problems, but the potential advantages appear to outweigh the drawbacks of linking health and family planning activities. There is a great deal of evidence which suggests that improving the prospects that infants and small children will survive to adulthood, together with parental awareness of those improved prospects, is probably the most important single determinant of the success of efforts to promote family planning. All of the other development priorities will be for naught unless the countries of sub-Saharan Africa begin to make substantial progress in slowing their population growth rates of 3 and even 4 percent.

In conclusion, if policy makers can reach a consensus on these six strategic priorities, then they can achieve structural transformation in an accelerated time period. They can also avoid, as Lele (this volume) has noted, the uncertainties resulting from cyclical shifts in priorities from food security issues to macroeconomic issues of "getting prices right," and back again to food security issues. They can help achieve that balance between governmental resources and responsibilities that is so crucial to growth of output, expansion of employment opportunities, and rural development.

NOTES

1. In a recent essay, W. Arthur Lewis (1988: 22) states that "the principal lesson we have all learned . . . is that inflation is a terrible scourge." In the 1950s, Lewis and most other development economists were much less concerned about the adverse effects of relying on the "inflation tax" to augment other means of financing investments to accelerate economic growth.

2. In principle, the PAM approach can also focus on long-term variables. Pearson and Monke (1987: 9–10) suggest that the PAM approach can "be used to identify the most fruitful directions" for agricultural research. Such exercises can certainly be useful even though the uncertainties in predicting future research results are very great. The emphasis in this paper on deriving generalizations concerning priorities on the basis of historical experience and the implications of the structural/demographic characteristics of late-developing countries is intended to *complement,* not substitute for, efforts to quantify benefits and costs of alternatives once the more appropriate and promising alternatives have been identified.

3. Their estimates of agricultural labor productivity are in terms of output per *male* worker. Given the tremendous importance of female farm labor in developing countries, and especially in Africa, the omission of female labor in the denominator is shocking. There is, in fact, considerable justification for this omission. Owing to deficiencies in the data currently available, international comparisons of agricultural labor productivity would be seriously distorted by using "total agricultural labor" in the denominator because very different definitions are used to determine whether female members of farm households are included in statistical estimates of the farm labor force. Their estimates of agricultural output use the common denominator of "wheat units"; various crops and livestock products are expressed as a ton of wheat on the basis of their price relative to the price of wheat.

4. It seems, however, that the "normal" product cycle whereby countries tend to shift away from substantial exports of primary products, as growth of output and employment in their nonfarm sectors increases the demand for labor and its opportunity cost, is being short-circuited by the current debt crisis. The tendency to shift labor and other resources out of coffee production in Brazil, for example, is being countered by the continuing devaluation of the cruzeiro because of the debt-driven demand for dollars and other convertible currencies to meet extremely heavy debt-servicing obligations.

5. To my knowledge, Malaysia is the only example of successful implementation of what Cohen (1988) refers to as a "multimodal approach." Circumstances that minimize the usual trade-offs are so special in Malaysia—an abundance of agricultural land, comparative advantage in producing two export crops (rubber and oil palm) that face relatively elastic foreign demand, and good access to foreign capital and managerial expertise so that the estate sector does not divert resources from the smallholder sector—that it is "the exception that proves the rule."

6. Our eclectic view is influenced strongly by policy analysis as pioneered by Dahl, Lindblom, and Wildavsky, by the views on bounded rationality and organizational decision making that derive from Simon and March, and a synthesis of those approaches by William C. Clark (Johnston and Clark 1982: chapter 1).

7. The first published discussion of Tomich's concept of "strategic notions" is in Johnston and Tomich (1988). It is discussed in more detail in a forthcoming book by Thomas P. Tomich, Peter Kilby, and Bruce F. Johnston, *Agriculture and Structural Transformation: Rural Development Strategies in Low-Income Countries.*

REFERENCES

Allison, Graham T.
   1971   *Essence of Decision: Explaining the Cuban Missile Crisis.* Boston: Little, Brown & Co.

Bates, Robert
   1981   *Markets and States in Tropical Africa.* Berkeley: University of California Press.

Buchanan, James M., and Gordon Tullock
   1965   *The Calculus of Consent.* Ann Arbor: University of Michigan Press. (Ann Arbor paperback edition, 1983).

Carter, Michael
   1989   Risk as Medium of Peasant Differentiation Under Unimodal Development Strategies in the Semi-Arid Tropics of West Africa. *Food and Farm: Current Debates and Policies*, C. Gladwin and K. Truman, eds. Lantham, MD.: University Press of America.

Cohen, Ronald
   1988   Introduction: Guidance and Misguidance in Africa's Food Production. *Satisfying Africa's Food Needs: Food Production and Commercialization in African Agriculture*, Ronald Cohen, ed. Boulder/London: Lynne Rienner Publishers.
   1989   The Unimodal Model: Solution or Cul de Sac for Rural Development? *Food and Farm: Current Debates and Policies*, C. Gladwin and K. Truman. Lantham, MD.: University Press of America.

Gladwin, Christina, and Della McMillan
   1989   Is a Turnaround in Africa Possible Without Helping African Women to Farm? *Economic Development and Cultural Change* 37(2): 345–69.

Gotsch, Carl H.
   1989   Agricultural Policy Analysis on Electronic Spreadsheets: Commodity and Farming Systems Models. Food Research Institute: Stanford University, Stanford, California.

Hayami, Yujiro, and Vernan W. Ruttan
   1985   *Agricultural Development: An International Perspective.* Baltimore: Johns Hopkins Press.

Hyden, Goran
   1988   Beyond Hunger in Africa—Breaking the Spell of Mono-Culture. *Satisfying Africa's Food Needs: Food Production and Commer-*

cialization in African Agriculture, Ronald Cohen, ed. Boulder/London: Lynne Rienner Publishers.

Johnston, Bruce F.
1989   The Political Economy of Agricultural Development in Kenya and Tanzania. *Food Research Institute Studies* 21(3): 205–64.

Johnston, Bruce F., and Peter Kilby
1975   *Agriculture and Structural Transformation: Economic Strategies in Late-Developing Countries.* New York: Oxford University Press.

Johnston, Bruce F., and William C. Clark
1982   *Redesigning Rural Development: A Strategic Perspective.* Baltimore: Johns Hopkins University Press.

Johnston, Bruce F., and Thomas P. Tomich
1988   The Political Economy of Rural Development: Lessons from Asian Experience. *Conference on Directions and Strategies of Agricultural Development in the Asian-Pacific Region,* Institute of Economics, Academia Sinica, Taipei, Taiwan, Republic of China.

Lele, Uma
1986   Structural Transformation and Women. *Economic Development and Cultural Change* 34(2): 195–221.

Lewis, W. Arthur
1988   Reflection on Development. *The State of Development Economics: Progress and Perspectives,* Gustav Ranis and T. Paul Schultz, eds. Basil Blackwell: New York.

Lofchie, Michael F.
1989   *The Policy Factor: Agricultural Performance in Kenya and Tanzania.* London: Lynne Rienner Publishers, Inc.

Monke, Eric A., and Scott R. Pearson
1989   *The Policy Analysis Matrix for Agricultural Development.* Ithaca: Cornell University Press.

Pearson, Scott R., and Eric A. Monke
1987   *The Policy Analysis Matrix: A Manual for Practitioners.* Falls Church, VA: Pragma Corporation.

Presidential Commission on World Hunger
1980   *Overcoming World Hunger: The Challenge Ahead.* Washington, D.C.: U.S. Government Printing Office.

Roemer, Michael, and Steven C. Radelet
1989   Macroeconomic Reform in Developing Countries. *Economic Reform in Developing Countries,* Dwight H. Perkins and Michael Roemer, eds. Cambridge, MA: Harvard Institute for International Development/ Harvard University Press.

Timmer, C. Peter, Walter Falcon, and Scott Pearson
1983   *Food Policy Analysis.* Washington, D.C.: World Bank.

World Bank
1989   *Sub-Saharan Africa: From Crisis to Sustainable Growth.* Washington, D.C.: World Bank.

II

Impacts of Structural Adjustment on Women Farmers

4

Policies to Overcome the Negative Effects of Structural Adjustment Programs on African Female-Headed Households

Jean M. Due

The structural adjustment programs (SAPs) initiated by the International Monetary Fund and the World Bank and supported by donors are stimulating many tropical African economies through an infusion of foreign exchange, increased agricultural prices, devaluation of overvalued currencies, improved marketing policies, liberalization of important sectors of the economies, and increased competition from the private sector. This paper will argue that the 25 percent of the rural households which are female-headed will not benefit from these policies. In addition the consumption-oriented policies within the structural adjustment programs—reduced expenditures for health (including family planning) and education in particular—have adversely affected female-headed and low-resource households in both urban and rural sectors. Many of these households are forced to bear heavier burdens of food, education, and health costs and are locked into a permanent cycle of poverty. The paper suggests some supplementary policies to assist the most adversely affected families.

Background

There is no doubt that action had to be taken to stop the decline of most economies in tropical Africa in the mid-1980s. With declining foreign

Jean M. Due is Professor of Agricultural Economics, University of Illinois at Urbana-Champaign. She has a Ph.D. from University of Illinois, years of research experience in East and Southern Africa, and is the author of *Costs, Returns, and Repayment Experience of Ujamaa Villages in Tanzania, 1973-1976*, as well as numerous articles about the economics of East Africa and women farmers in international journals such as *Agricultural Economics*. Her current research analyzes funding sources for women's income generation and evaluates income-generating projects in different African countries.

exchange earnings and decreasing domestic revenues due to the decline in primary commodity prices, reduced food production per capita, high rates of population growth, overvalued exchange rates, increasing debt burdens, and high rates of inflation, forceful policies were necessary. Thus, the criticism of the structural adjustment programs must be made with recognition that they are one partial solution to a very widespread malady. The malady had to be treated and few would disagree that economies have improved. The controversy centers around unintentional adverse effects of the structural adjustment programs, which complementary policies can negate to some extent. Examples include the higher food costs of the urban poor, higher education and health costs especially of urban families, and consumer goods whose prices have escalated. These adverse effects have been especially burdensome in urban areas where wages have remained flat; for example, a driver or secretary in Tanzania, even with both husband and wife working, earns 2,000 to 3,000 Tanzanian shillings (Tsh.) per month each; a pair of tennis shoes for a teenage son would cost two-thirds of one month's income. Many of these families are the "working poor." Similarly, female-headed households (FHHs) with only one earner are adversely affected in both urban and rural areas, as will be shown below.

Female-Headed Households

Female-headed households currently comprise 25 to 35 percent of both rural and urban households in most countries of tropical Africa, and may be either *de facto* or *de jure*. A de facto FHH is one in which the husband is away for long periods of time, making it necessary for the wife to do the decision-making and support the family, although there may be income from the husband irregularly. The wife makes decisions about family expenditures and farm operations when the FHHs are rural. A *de jure* FHH is one in which the head is divorced, widowed, or a single parent; in *de jure* FHHs the female head makes all decisions and supports the family; polygamous households are excluded. Many persons will argue that in the extended family system in much of tropical Africa, *de jure* FHHs receive considerable counsel and assistance from the extended family. Yet during personal interviews, women heading these households inform us that they are very much alone under current trying conditions and are almost solely responsible for the welfare of their families.

Contrasts Between FHHs and Male or Joint-Headed Households (JHHs) in Rural Areas

Advocates of structural adjustment policies claim that SAPs are gender neutral and both FHHs and JHHs should benefit from improved agricultural prices and improved, liberalized marketing arrangements. Unfortunately, this is not the case. There are major contrasts between FHHs and JHHs (with both husband and wife present) in rural areas when both types of households are farming. The major factor which differentiates these households is that FHHs, with no able-bodied male (or additional adult female) present, are smaller in size than JHHs and, therefore, have less labor available for agricultural production in a farming system that is very labor intensive. With less labor available, FHHs have smaller crop acreages planted; this results in lower agricultural output, and a higher percentage of production is needed for family consumption, leaving less for sale. Therefore, average and per capita net incomes are lower. Also, FHHs have less access to credit for hiring labor or labor-saving devices and less access to extension services.

Figure 4-1. Female heads of households allocate a greater percentage of their land to food crops.

These results are substantiated from studies in Zambia (Due et al. 1982, Sikapande 1988) and Tanzania (Mollel 1986) shown in Table 4-1, in which data were collected from samples of JHHs and FHHs in the same agro-ecological areas. In Zambia (1982) the mean acreage planted by FHHs was significantly different from that by JHHs (43 percent of JHHs), as were total value of crop production, crop sales, and percent of families visited by an extension agent. In the Tanzanian sample, average crop acreage planted by FHHs was 54 percent of that of JHHs in the same area, and total value of crop production was much lower, as were crop sales and net cash incomes. In both the Zambian and Tanzanian samples, when smallholder farm families were asked about incomes earned from noncereal crop sources—i.e., from brewing beer, selling small quantities of fruits and vegetables, making craft products, and working off the farm, the replies showed that FHHs earned relatively more than JHHs from these types of endeavors. Thus, FHHs were using their labor for opportunities with higher returns than in crop production.

It should be noted also that FHHs plant different crops than JHHs, on average; more of their total crop acreage was allocated to food crops than that by JHHs. The provision of food is a high priority for both types of families but with smaller acreage planted by FHHs it is important to allocate a greater percentage of their land to food crops. As shown in Table 4-1, compared to JHHs the Zambian females planted a higher percentage of their crop acreage to maize, the major food staple, and the Tanzanian FHHs to maize, beans, cassava, and other vegetables.

A study of a larger sample of 123 FHHs was undertaken in Zambia by Hudgens (1988) and data compared with JHHs in the same areas. Hudgens also found that FHHs had less labor available, owned fewer oxen, planted smaller acreages, and had significantly less crop production for sale than JHHs. Sales of JHHs came from maize, beer, cotton, and sunflower; sales of FHHs came from chickens, mushrooms, squash, pumpkins, and beans. Only 2 percent of the FHHs reported income from the sale of maize; with smaller acreage planted, maize is grown primarily for home consumption. Female farmers also reported being busier than their male counterparts during the months of May to July, when labor is needed for bird scaring and maize harvesting and shelling. The fact that fewer FHHs owned oxen than their male counterparts meant they were often forced to hire oxen and labor for land preparation. These costs restricted the total acreage planted as well as purchases of improved seed and fertilizer. Visits by extension agents were also less frequent to FHHs than to JHHs.

The above data from Tanzania and Zambia are further emphasized by

Table 4-1. Comparison of Joint-Headed and Female-Headed Farm Households in Zambia and Tanzania Studies.

	Zambia 1982[1]		Tanzania 1984[2]		Zambia 1986[3]	
	JHH	FHH	JHH	FHH	JHH	FHH
Sample Size	95	17	118	32	97	27
Means of:						
Age	42	44	49	43	41	43
Family size	7.4	4.5 **	NA	NA	NA	NA
Adult equivalents[4]	4.1	2.3*	NA	NA	3.5	1.7***
Acreage in crops	11.5	4.9*	2.7	1.4	6.8	3.0**
Maize	7.6	3.8*	1.7	0.8	5.4	2.4**
Beans	0.3	0.2	0.1	0.1	0.0	0.0
Groundnuts	0.9	0.3**	0.0	0.0	1.0	0.5
Cotton	1.2	0.2*	0.0	0.0	0.0	0.0
Sunflower	0.9	0.3	0.0	0.0	0.2	0.0
Others	0.6	0.1	0.9	0.5	0.2	0.1
Total value crop production	K 1,201	K 368**	Tsh 5,683	Tsh 3,440	K 4,358	K 1,778**
Crop sales[5]	K 763	K 139**	Tsh 1,166	Tsh 329	K 2,904	K 522**
Livestock sales[5]	K 193	K 35*	NA	NA	NA	NA
Farm expenses[5]	K 324	K 85	NA	NA	K 68	K3.0**
Off-farm income[5] & gifts	K 216	K 230	NA	NA	NA	NA
Net cash income[5]	K 848	K 319	Tsh 3,659	Tsh 200*	K 2,836	K 1,775
Percent of families visited by extension agents	57	29	40	28	60	19**
Percent crops consumed	38	64	87	96	35	74

1. Due and White, 1986; crop year, 1982.   2. Mollel (1987); crop year, 1984.
3. Sikapande (1988); crop year 1986.   4. Adults available for farming; adult males and females equals 1.0, children aged 8-11 equals 0.3 and aged 12-17 equals 0.5 adults.   5. K is Kwacha and Tsh Tanzanian shillings.   * Significant differences between means at p < .1; ** significant at p < .05; *** Significant at p < .001.NA - not available.

Sikapande (1988) who, in evaluating the Training and Visit (T & V) extension system introduced into Southern Province, Zambia, in 1983 chose a sample of contact, noncontact, and FHH farm families to ascertain whether or not they benefited equally under the new T & V system.

Sikapande found that few FHHs were chosen as contact farmers. As shown in the right-hand column of Table 4-1, the Sikapande sample confirmed that FHHs had significantly fewer adults available for farming (1.7 compared with 3.5 for JHH), significantly smaller acreage in crops (3.0 acres compared with 6.8), and significantly lower values of total crop production, crop sales, farm operating expenses and net farm income. In the

Sikapande sample, FHHs consumed 74 percent of their agricultural production whereas JHHs consumed only 35 percent. Also, a smaller percentage of FHHs owned or rented oxen than JHHs, had much less access to credit, and were visited much less often by extension agents or contact farmers than JHHs even under the new T & V system. Thus, the T & V systems tried in both Zambia and Tanzania did not assist FHHs.

The Sikapande data also showed significant differences in levels of educations between heads of JHHs and FHHs; FHHs averaged 1.8 years of formal education compared with 4.2 for JHHs. When asked their primary sources of agricultural information, the JHHs stated extension advisors, neighbors, and field days/contact farmers in that order, whereas the FHHs stated neighbors, extension workers, and radio. These important differences in information sources of FHHs relate to the lower number of visits of extension agents or contact farmers; FHHs often lacked knowledge of the name of either the extension agents or contact farmers in their area.

Data from Malawi also emphasized the striking differences between JHHs and FHHs in levels of education, resources, and income. In a 1986 study of 600 farm FHHs, women's groups, and extension agents who had contact with women's groups (Chipande et al. 1986), it was ascertained that 46 percent of the heads of FHHs had *never* attended school, FHHs were at the bottom of the income scale and lacked resources, and had average cash incomes of K166 of which 2 percent came from off-farm employment, 84 percent from the sale of agricultural products (local maize, groundnut, and pulses), and 14 percent from non-agricultural activities (beer brewing, selling processed food, fish, and handicrafts). The authors emphasized that agricultural development strategies in Malawi are directed primarily to crops and not livestock; they recommended small ruminants and poultry for these FHHs as well as fruit canning, and soap and candle making. The authors emphasized that FHHs need activities for income generation in which little cash outlay is required. In spite of the large percentage (69) of FHHs that belonged to women's groups, 45 percent of the income-generating activities were single-person enterprises rather than group enterprises.

Another Malawi study of 100 JHHs and 100 farm FHHs carried out by Phiri (1986) compared sources of household cash income and expenses of the two groups (Table 4-2). FHHs had 58 percent of the cash income of JHHs; FHHs grew relatively more beans, rice, and sugarcane than JHHs and about the same amounts of maize and bananas but acreages of each were smaller. Phiri found that FHHs lacked finance (93 percent of respondents), land (50 percent), skills (18 percent), and inputs

(10 percent) for production. FHHs had fewer extension visits, hired less labor, used less fertilizer, and had less access to credit than JHHs. The Phiri study confirmed the smaller hectarages planted of FHHs (1.4 compared with 1.9 for JHHs), lower cash income and farm expenses, and a net cash income of 58 percent of JHHs (Table 4-2).

Segal (1986), in analyzing data from the Malawi 1983–84 *Annual Sample Survey of Agriculture,* obtained results in comparing FHH and JHH farms that confirm the Tanzanian and Zambian results. FHHs had a smaller household labor force available for farming, employed less hired labor, and had average total cash incomes 68 percent of the JHHs (Table

Table 4-2. Comparison of Joint-Headed and Female-Headed Farm Households in Malawi.

Categories	Malawi 1986[1]		Malawi 1983–84[2]	
	JHH	FHH	JHH	FHH
Means of:				
Household size	NA	NA	4.9	4.0
Adult equivalents	NA	NA	2.3	1.6
Farm size (ha)	1.9	1.4	1.3	0.9
Hired labor-days/year	NA	NA	21	12
Sources of cash income (MK):[3]				
Bananas	263	170		
Cassava	21	16		
Maize	21	16		
Other crops	15	6		
Livestock	4	9		
Subtotal	324	218	217	149
Wage employment	21	7		
Beer brewing	15	1	25	17
Other	7	8		
Total cash income	367	234	243	166
Expenses:				
Farm operation	10	5	NA	NA
Business	56	50	NA	NA
Household	54	35	NA	NA
Total expenses	120	90	NA	NA
Net cash income (MK)	247	144	NA	NA

1. Phiri (1986).   2. Segal (1986); crop year 1983–84.
3. MK - Malawi Kwacha.   NA - not available.

4-2). JHHs provided 75 percent of their caloric needs from home pro-duction whereas FHHs provided only 68 percent. The published study does not include farm operating expenses; this precludes a comparison of net cash incomes, and without these data sets it was not possible to com-pute tests of significant differences between JHH and FHH variables.

Structural Adjustment Prescriptions Are Inadequate for FHHs

Major solutions for the agricultural sector under the structural adjust-ment policies are higher domestic and export farm product prices, lower taxes on export crops, more efficient and competitive marketing arrange-ments, more research on domestic crops, etc. The higher farm product prices have encouraged greater agricultural production. These higher prices, however, will not greatly assist FHHs as little of their production is sold and these households often must reenter the market to purchase food when their own supply is exhausted. Similarly, since FHHs sell only a small percentage of their crop, more efficient and competitive market-ing arrangements are not of much assistance except to the extent that this efficiency decreases the cost of their food purchases. Unfortunately, infla-tion has involved higher food prices and thus higher food costs. Increased research on domestic crops as compared to export crops will assist FHHs if credit is available to enable them to purchase the higher yielding vari-eties, fertilizer, and insecticides, and if the extension services provide the information to FHHs, and if credit is available for labor-saving devices or for hiring labor. When one examines the low average net income of these FHHs (Tables 4-1 and 4-2), can one expect FHHs to repay the credit? Will grants, rather than loans, be necessary for FHHs in the short run?

Effect of SAP on the Agricultural Sector

African agricultural production was especially depressed during the early 1980s and the rate of growth did not keep up with the average 3.5 percent per year population growth. Real export growth, which is primarily agri-cultural, "lagged behind other developing countries and (Africa) had lost half its 1970 world market share by 1983. If Africa's export growth had matched that of other LDCs, its debt service ratio would be about half of what it is today" (World Bank and UNDP 1989: 2). "Under SAP agricul-ture has shown an especially strong improvement with an annual rate of growth in output from 1985–88 triple that of the average over the past 15 years and exceeding population growth for the first extended period since 1970 (ibid: 3). This improvement has also led to an improvement in export earnings."

However, agricultural prices have not increased uniformly; in Tanzania, for example, export crop prices have increased much more than domestic crop prices. Most economists believe that farmers are currently better off than before SAP and that terms of trade and incomes between rural and urban sectors have improved to benefit the rural areas so that the large differential between average rural and urban incomes has narrowed.

How Do JHH Farmers View the Changes since SAP?

I know of few studies which have ascertained farmers' views of the SAP. One survey of 65 farmers in four villages of Morogoro region, Tanzania (Nnyiti 1989), asked farmers their views of changes which had occurred from 1983 to 1989 from the liberalized economic policies. It must be remembered that Tanzania, like Kenya, had very restrictive marketing arrangements before 1983, which made it illegal to move goods privately from one region of the country to another. Sales did occur in local markets (where prices were much higher than official marketing board prices) but only small quantities of farm products could be sold at any one time. In the survey, farmers responded to a number of questions in an area where mixed farming systems prevail; maize, soybeans, sunflower, beans, cowpeas, and other vegetables, bananas, and some cotton are grown. Overall, farmers believed their welfare had improved above the 1983 level but not to the 1976/77 level; new and better houses were being built; 63 percent believed prices and agricultural production had increased; they believed food production per family had increased; farm inputs, consumer goods, and credit were more available; the land area cultivated per family had increased; labor was more scarce as laborers farmed for themselves; and 70 percent of the farmers believed farm investments had increased.

The sampled farmers believed their welfare had improved even though farmers in Tanzania were still receiving (according to Nnyiti) only 28 percent of the world price for coffee, 41 percent for cotton, 38 percent for cashew nuts, 33 percent for sisal, and 7 percent for tea. Farmers commented that food crops can now be sold in the open markets but export crops cannot, and thus there had been a shift to greater food crop production. Farmers commented on the large amount of embezzlement of funds by personnel of marketing authorities and that late payments from the marketing boards have continued. This caused more shifts to open market selling to avoid late payment for crops.

Devaluation

Devaluation, one of the major factors in the structural adjustment programs, was needed to realign domestic currencies with international currencies, thereby making imports more expensive and exports more competitive. In theory devaluation will primarily affect the prices only of internationally traded goods and not domestic goods except for the traded inputs in their manufacture. One would expect food prices to rise with increases in farm gate prices; increased prices of export agricultural products would not affect many domestic consumers as most of those products are consumed abroad. However, using Tanzania as an example, all consumer goods prices, including those of commodities produced domestically, have increased by some 30 percent a year. Larger quantities of commodities are in the shops but prices are very high compared to local incomes. In addition price increases immediately follow any announced changes in currency devaluation as traders anticipate imported goods and import content prices to increase, together with petroleum and transport prices. Even cattle prices increase with devaluation in Tanzania. The price increases do not wait for inputs to work

Figure 4-2. Price increases in shops do not wait for inputs to work themselves through the production cycle; they occur immediately after the announcement of devaluation.

themselves through the production cycle; they occur immediately after the announcement of devaluation. This trend is exacerbated by the high percentage of consumer goods imported (except for food).

With wages flat, real family incomes have fallen dramatically with SAPs and their predecessors. In 1984 the average real wage (salary in manufacturing) in Tanzania was

> 70 percent lower than in 1972 according to official statistics which understate the rate of inflation. At present wages are so low that workers and their families cannot subsist on them. Many workers therefore try to improve their situation through various auxiliary activities, even during work time. This situation results in further deterioration of work motivation and discipline and a further fall in labor productivity (Havenvik et al. 1988: 86–87).

An assistant professor at the University of Dar es Salaam confided to the author that his salary was $55 a month; faculty at the University of Nairobi stated that they could not exist on their salaries unless both husband and wife were working. At present, wage rates in tropical Africa must be among the lowest in the world. This is important background for the consumption-oriented strategies imposed under SAP.

Changes in Consumption-Related Services under Structural Adjustment

Tanzania provides a good example of results of reduction in consumption-related expenditures such as education and health. Since independence the education sector has experienced greater achievements than any other sector (Ministry of Education 1987). In 1960 only 25 percent of the school-aged population was enrolled in primary school and only 10 percent of the adult population was literate. By 1984 universal primary education had virtually been achieved and adult literacy had reached 50 percent by 1981 and 85 percent by 1987 (Ministry of Education 1987). Secondary school enrollment had not achieved similar growth; in 1986 only 11,721 primary school graduates were enrolled out of 380,096 who had completed primary school-leaving examinations. Even though the numbers enrolled in absolute terms had increased, the proportion of the age group enrolled had decreased from 29.2 percent in 1963 to 6.4 percent in 1986 (ibid). Numbers enrolled at higher educational institutions have increased dramatically, as have female enrollments; in 1988, 50 percent of primary school enrollments were female, as were 35 percent of secondary school enrollment and 26 percent of higher education enrollments. These are marked improvements over time.

But the fiscal crisis has forced the government to reduce expenditures on education in nominal terms, and this is reflected in a much more serious decrease in real terms (as shown in Table 4-3); at the same time foreign aid has also declined. The most affected sector has been primary education with a resulting decline in enrollment from 3,727,000 in 1983 to 3,155,000 in 1986 as poor families cannot afford the additional costs thrust upon them, as the government has transferred a major share of responsibility for primary schools to local governments. The quality of education has also declined drastically (Havenvik et al. 1988: 165). At the secondary level, enrollment has increased slightly but expenditure per pupil in constant shillings had declined from 4,400 in 1982 to 3,500 in 1986 (Table 4-3). In addition to the absolute decline in enrollment at the primary level, textbooks and other school supplies are in very short supply at all levels; at the University of Dar es Salaam classes of 200 students typically have access to 2 textbooks in the library! Students and faculty are forced to depend on lecture materials; with teachers at all levels unable to maintain their families on wages paid and undertaking additional income-earning activities, teachers and faculty have less time to prepare lectures and students are affected both by book shortages and teacher preparation. In Zambia the situation is similar to that in Tanzania with crowded classrooms, some half-day classes to accommodate double the number of students (but with teachers receiving the same salary), increases in private schools, and deterioration of quality. A recent copy of the *Daily Nation* (January 20, 1990) highlights the school crisis in Nairobi, Kenya. The article shows parents queuing up for hours to register their children in primary schools and states:

> Over 80,000 children who should be in primary schools are either at home or just roaming the streets; others were working to support their parents instead of learning.... Only 63 percent of primary school-age children in the city were enrolled in 1987.

World Bank staff have argued that teachers' salaries are too high in tropical Africa and that parents should bear a higher proportion of education expenses (Mingat and Psacharopoulos 1985: 35–38), SAPs have forced implementation of the policy with resulting declines in enrollment at the primary level and reductions in expenditures per pupil at both the primary and secondary level; teachers cannot live on their salaries and must undertake other income-generating activities to survive! The real world is much different than the macro view from World Bank offices!

As the government curtailed education expenditures, especially at the secondary level, more private schools have opened with varying levels of

Table 4-3. Expenditures and Enrollment in Primary and Secondary Schools, Tanzania, 1982–1986

Level of Education	1982	1983	1986
Primary:			
Recurrent expenditures (million Tsh)	1,023.7	1,398.2	3,021.2
Recurrent expend. (1980 constant mill. Tsh)	728.1	634.9	646.8
Enrollment (000)	3,276	3,727	3,155
Expend. per pupil (1980 constant Tsh)	222	170	205
Capital expenditure (1980 million Tsh)	31.1	26.1	17.1[a]
Secondary:			
Recurrent expend. (million Tsh)	255.0	349.1	753.4
Recurrent expend. (1980 constant m. Tsh)	181.6	159.8	161.3
Recurrent expend./pupil-current (Tsh)	7,545	8,279	17,410
Recurrent expend./pupil-constant (1980 Tsh)	4,400	3,800	3,500
Enrollment (000)	34	42	43
Capital expend. (current million Tsh)	38.0	49.9	88.2
Capital expend. (1980 constant million Tsh)	22.0	22.7	58.6

a. 1985.   Tsh-Tanzania shillings.
Source: UNESCO 1988 as reported in Havenrik et al. 1988: 164–5.

quality (compared to public education). It is the poor and families with high demand for education who are adversely affected by the SAP in the field of education.

Health

A shortage of foreign exchange has caused a serious shortage of pharmaceuticals in most eastern and southern African countries. This shortage of pharmaceutical and immunization materials has adversely affected the poor particularly, as persons with adequate incomes can purchase some of these materials at pharmacies. Another result of these shortages is that poor people are flooding the emergency wards of regional, mission, and university hospitals hoping to get treatment instead of going to their local dispensaries where they know pharmaceuticals are not available. Emergency ward lines are long and almost unmanageable at these regional hospital facilities. As the situation deteriorates, with less foreign exchange for hospital equipment and supplies as well as drugs, doctors leave in frustration. Often, neither doctors nor nurses have rubber glove protection, to say nothing of availability of condoms for AIDS protection for the general public. Incidence of malaria has increased in areas formerly unaffected. In observing the nominal expenditures for health and education for five countries in Table 4-4, it would appear that expenditures have increased from 1982 to 1985 in most cases (data for 1986, which would more adequately reflect the results of SAPs, were not available for all countries). To conserve space, expenditures in real terms are calculated for health only; with inflation between 10.3 and 28.7 percent per year in East and Central African countries from 1980 to 1987, the expenditure data in real terms show a marked decline. The decline in expenditures per capita is even more striking.

In Tanzania, UNICEF, with Danish funding, provides a supply of immunization and pharmaceutical materials to local rural dispensaries each month; these are not provided to urban dispensaries; at the time the program was initiated, it was the rural dispensaries which were often short of supplies. Currently health supplies are much better in rural than urban areas of Tanzania due to the UNICEF program which is less affected by the SAP except as it affects transport.

It appears clear that children and the poor are most affected by the SAP in the health field. Women suffer due to the shortage of all drugs including family planning supplies. Data are not available on infant mortality but, with less health protection and AIDS, one would expect infant and total mortality figures to show an increase. Clearly eastern and southern Africa's children and poor are at risk as far as health and nutrition are concerned.

Policies to Mitigate Adverse Effects of SAPs

Clearly some of the adverse effects of SAPs especially for FHHs and low-resource families could be mitigated by complementary policies, but these policies would require increased revenues and foreign exchange which the East and Central African countries do not have currently. The foreign exchange is needed especially for pharmaceutical and hospital/health supplies, educational materials and laboratory equipment, and transport—both for roads and for vehicles. Donors could, and are, assisting materially with the foreign exchange shortages; donors could be especially helpful if debts owed foreign governments were forgiven. (Commercial banks should absorb their own losses, as they made bad investment decisions; donor governments should not protect them or collect for them).

It is the human dimension which is most adversely affected by SAPs;

Table 4-4. Expenditures on Health and Education, East and Central African Countries, Selected Years, in National Currencies[1] and U. S. Dollars Per Capita.

	1982	1983	1985	1986	1987[2]
Kenya					
Education nominal (millions)	3516	3802	4410		
Health nominal (millions)	1543	1522	1873		
in 1980 shillings (millions)	1279	1163	1236		
in 1980 $US/capita[3]	9	7	7	6	
percent total expenditures	7.6	7.2	6.9	6.4[2]	6.6
Malawi					
Education nominal (millions)	51.3	55.4	67.1	80.1	
Health nominal (millions)	18.8	28.1	48.8	52.7	
in 1980 shillings (millions)	14.5	20.5	25.8	30.2	
in 1980 $US/capita[3]	3	4	4	4	
percent total expenditures	7.3	9.6	9.9	9.9	7.1
Tanzania					
Education nominal (millions)	2298	2543	1919		
Health nominal (millions)	992	983	1312		
in 1980 shillings (millions)	662	563	584		
in 1980 $US/capita 3	10	9	4		
percent total expenditures	5.4	5.1	5.7	4.9[2]	5.7
Zambia					
Education nominal (millions)	213	195	303	457	
Health nominal (millions)	118	89	144	218	
in 1980 shillings (millions)	75	48	59	80	
in 1980 $US/capita[3]	22	13	12	10	
percent total expenditures	9.6	7.5	7.8	5.5	4.7
Zimbabwe					
Education nominal (millions)	98.6	173.5			
Health nominal (millions)	13.8	17.8	23.4		
in 1980 shillings (millions)	11.5	13.0	14.7		
in 1980 $US/capita[3]	19	17	16	16	
percent total expenditures	3.3	3.1	3.1	6.2[2]	6.1

Sources: 1. International Monetary Fund, Government Finance Statistical Yearbook, 1988 International Monetary Fund, Washington, D.C. 2. World Development Report, 1988 and 1989. 3. Gallager, 1989.

how can East and Central African countries carry out the necessary adjustments to move to structural transformation, growth, and improved balance of payments without adversely affecting human beings in terms of education, health care, potable water, and other basic needs? The liberalization of the economy and other SAP programs have stimulated economies so that there are more employment options. But it is the persons with training and capital who can respond most quickly to these opportunities; the poor are the last to learn of the possibilities and be drawn into higher, or any, income-earning possibilities. This paper will outline only a few possibilities of complementary policies; the author believes that structural transformation of these economies is not going to be accomplished on a five-year horizon but over a much longer period.

Agriculture

Policies which would assist FHHs in their agricultural production are development of higher yielding varieties (which would increase yield without increasing areas planted); ownership of small ruminant animals and poultry; increased credit availability to hire labor, tractors, oxen, purchase oxen and ploughs, etc. as well as credit for other income-generating activities (discussed later) and improved extension services; better trained extension personnel; and radio programs.

Nutrition Supplementation

Present maternal and child-care nutrition supplementation must be continued and expanded to reverse the declining food intake of poor families as food prices have risen. Many of these programs have been supported by donors; expansion especially in poor urban areas is a high priority, with the elderly included. Programs of this type in rural areas would assist FHH and low-resource families.

Debt Forgiveness

Forgiveness of debt owed to international organizations and donors (private bank debtors can negotiate directly, not assisted by governments) would free foreign exchange for use in the education, health, and transport sectors—all of which would directly assist the poor. If pharmaceutical and other medical equipment and supplies, education materials, and transport sector items could be imported with the foreign exchange otherwise allocated to debt payments, the poorest sectors of the population would benefit materially. World Bank loans have contributed materially to the debt burdens of these countries (Lele 1989). Space does not permit a discussion of issues involved but donor governments would benefit also from debt forgiveness.

Reduced Defense Expenditures

Substantial amounts could be transferred to much higher priorities (as in the U.S.) if defense expenditures were reduced from their present levels. A comparison of the percentage of total government expenditures allocated to defense and to health in 1987 (World Development Report, 1989) was:

	Defense	Health
Kenya	9.1 percent	6.6 percent
Malawi	6.6 percent	7.1 percent
Tanzania	15.8 percent	5.7 percent
Zambia	NA	4.7 percent
Zimbabwe	14.2 percent	6.1 percent

Some of these expenditures, especially for Zimbabwe and Zambia, support activities to keep the transport routes open through Mozambique at very high cost.

Credit for Income-Generating Projects

Almost all families in these countries are involved in some kind of secondary income-generating activity to supplement the family income or food supply. These activities should be encouraged; successful activities encourage self-reliance and self-esteem.

Tanzania has just embarked on a bold scheme to provide loans to women for income-generating activities using donor funds; Botswana has used domestic funds for gender-neutral income and employment generation; and Kenya has used donor funds to establish the Kenya Rural Enterprise Program to provide loans to NGOs to on-loan to groups for income generation. Each of these experiments will be summarized briefly.

Botswana's Experience

The Botswana government allocated the equivalent of $19 million for employment generation and enterprise development in 1983. Of this amount $1.6 million or 8 percent was allocated to both men and women for small-scale enterprise development in rural and urban areas. It was hoped that small-scale enterprises would generate employment and income, diversify the economy from mining, cattle, and the public sector, and produce goods for the domestic and export markets. The funds were allocated as a grant rather than a loan; i.e., if funds were utilized to stimulate existing small-scale enterprises or develop new enterprises, they would not have to be repaid.

The availability of funds was widely advertised and rural industrial officers (RIOs) were appointed in rural areas to assist with application completion, evaluate potential projects, train applicants in business management, keep records, input supply, etc., and, when funding was approved, keep financial records of projects funded. These RIOs were located in the agricultural extension offices but the numbers were much smaller than numbers of extension staff.

Of 718 grants approved under the small-scale enterprise program, 46 percent were allocated to women. These women's firms were primarily in knitting, sewing, baking, carpentry, brick making, poultry, and horticulture with smaller numbers in beef drying, jewelry, sorghum milling, and shoe making (Due 1989). The government review team (Smith et al. 1988 and Moradpedie et al. 1987) found that 35 percent of the small-scale enterprises funded were not operating after five years. No data are available on the administrative costs of the Botswana program.

Kenya's Experience

The Kenya Rural Enterprise Programme (KREP) was established in 1984 with funding from a $7 million grant from USAID-Kenya to establish small-scale enterprises through existing NGOs in Kenya. Kenya has a long history of NGO involvement in the country. These NGOs have developed their own groups of participants at the grass roots level. The Kenya Rural Enterprise Programme is an umbrella NGO, registered as a private company, chartered to make loans and grants to other NGOs for small-scale enterprises for both men and women. USAID also recommended that KREP spend the first two years in training NGO staff in social needs assessment, credit supervision, enterprise management, marketing, and input supply. The NGOs could then train their group members in the same areas.

The KREP established the goal of funding viable small-scale enterprise projects in the NGO sector by 1989 to generate employment on the basis of 1:1 for male and female entrepreneurs, recover loans to entrepreneurs at the rate of 80 percent, provide loans at commercial rates (currently 15.5 percent in Kenya) and administrative costs of not more than 20 percent of total loans and, after initial NGO grants, assist NGOs to achieve self-sustaining revolving loan programs in 80 percent of the projects (Kenya Enterprise Programme 1989).

KREP loans were allocated to religious groups (YWCA, Presbyterian Church of East Africa, Catholic Diocese, etc.) and to nonreligious groups such as Tototo Home Industries, home economics women's groups, and community development projects. Two examples of NGO projects were the Isiolo Deanery goat-trading scheme and Tototo Home Industries. The Isiolo Deanery goat-trading scheme involves loans to men in a very poor region of Kenya to purchase and resell goats. This is an individual project under the Catholic Diocese. Tototo Home Industries of Mombasa has been working with community groups on business projects throughout the coastal area for 20 years. Tototo has developed 45 community groups with successful projects in water supply, community health, savings clubs, adult literacy, family planning, and child care. The groups are made up of 25 to 30 persons each of whom 95 percent are women with no formal education. KREP gave Tototo Home Industries a grant of KS (Kenya shillings) 3.8 million in 1987 to improve Tototo's ongoing credit program by extending loans to 15 women's groups currently producing crafts, to expand or start new businesses and hire a training officer to assist with marketing and training.

Data on the repayment experience of the Kenya program are not available; however, the governing board has changed the focus from group lending to individual lending, including some middle-income individuals as well as low-income groups. Women operate 46 percent of the assisted small-scale enterprises and constitute 46 percent of employees.

Tanzania's Experience

The Australian government gave the Government of Tanzania $3 million in 1987 for loans for poor rural women to undertake income generating projects. The Tanzanian government decided to allocate the funds through the already-existing Cooperative and Rural Development Bank (CRDB), established in the early 1970s to provide loans to the rural sector. (CRDB has been reviewed frequently—Due 1978: 1, 2; 1980: 1, 2; 1983.) CRDB has branch offices in each of the 20 regions; funds were allocated equally between regions, with each region receiving 2.5 million Tanzania shillings (Tsh) in 1987. Criteria established were that recipients would be primarily poor rural women who were required to contribute an amount equal to 10 percent of the loan in a building, labor, or cash. No security for the loan was required; the interest rate is 13 percent per annum (when the commercial rate is currently 31 percent). Distribution was suggested as 50 percent agricultural (seasonal inputs for crops and animal husbandry), 30 percent agro-industrial (maize mills, carpetmaking, etc) and 20 percent in other projects. Loans could be made to individuals or groups. Women applied (or their husbands could apply for them) directly to CRDB offices, to District Community Development offices, or other district offices which could assist in application preparation. Officials and women's groups in each region were informed of the loan availability and over 1,800 applications were received in the first 18 months.

I have just returned from spending six weeks reviewing the Tanzanian program with a Tanzanian colleague. (This review was funded by USAID-Tanzania.) Head office CRDB personnel and 4 of the 20 CRDB regional offices were visited to obtain data of total CRDB loans, loans to the women's program, repayment rates, and successes and failures to date. Thirty-two women borrowers in the 4 regions were interviewed to ascertain their experiences with the loans.

When reviewed, the lending program was only 18 months old. What were our findings? Within the first year of the program 471 loans had been approved and 382 dispensed to women for a total of 39.3 million Tanzania shillings (Tsh.) or an average of $714 per loan. The average size of loan granted varied widely by region. Of the four regions visited, the average size varied between $552 and $1,103 per individual or group. It was recommended that more small loans be allocated, as most women are accustomed to managing much smaller amounts of money. Sixty-three percent of the loans were for agriculture and livestock (crops and livestock), 10 percent for agro-industry (maize mills and crafts made from local materials) and 27 percent for other activities (bakery, shoemaking and repair, tailoring, restaurants and hotels). All women visited knew the exact amount of their loans and amounts repaid; all women borrowers had learned to use a bank account. Each loan had generated employment for one additional person, or more fully employed an adult son or daughter. Transport costs are extremely high in Tanzania where roads have been neglected, making vehicle maintenance very expensive. This translates into high administrative costs. The average women client visited had a grade six education, although some had no formal education. The average household size per region visited varied between 6.5 and 9.6. Women with previous entrepreneurial experience were more successful than women without this experience. Most women were not borrowing from sources other than CRDB. Some regions had good experience with group activities; others had bad experiences regarding group repayment.

Repayment rates varied widely by region; after the first year and a half the repayment rate averaged 44 percent; one region had 86 percent repayment and several no repayment. Although the donor made the funds available for poor rural women, only 59 percent of the loans were allocated to rural women and 44 percent to poor women. Urban women, even those on wage employment, are often "working poor"; CRDB branch managers decided to allocate loans to both rural and urban women; urban women hear of the loans earlier and are closer to CRDB offices for assistance in loan applications. Urban loans are also less costly to monitor. Some loans were given to political groups to generate income for the group rather than individuals within the group and to politically prominent women. We see little possibility of additional donor funding if this aspect of the loan program is not corrected promptly.

Given this brief summary of findings, what were the recommendations? Donors and government personnel must be cognizant of the current high transport costs in any lending program (which translate into high administrative costs) and allocate funds and a vehicle to each region to provide better application and borrower monitoring and supervision. CRDB had allocated dedicated, trained personnel to operate the women's loan program in most regions; in others better trained officers are needed. Women interviewed found CRDB personnel very helpful in loan applications and monitoring the program; CRDB Head Office takes six months to complete the legal documentation of the loans; expediting this aspect is urgently needed. Repayment rates must be monitored more adequately especially in regions with low repayment. It would appear that only 44 percent of the borrowers visited were poor women; the majority were middle- and upper-income women. One is aware of the dilemma of providing funds to poor rural women with low levels of education and resources, and with high transport costs of administering the loans. Also, there are many very poor families in urban areas. We recommend that loans be made available to both rural and urban women but that no loans be allocated to upper-income and politically prominent women.

All women visited wanted seminars (of one day's length) to bring together successful borrowers to discuss common problems and solutions and to learn more bookkeeping, livestock management, entrepreneurship, etc. These seminars would need to be located near borrowers' homes and transport provided.

Women interviewed stated that the loans had generated more food and income, especially to pay children's school fees. One woman who borrowed for a dairy project stated, "We now have milk for the children's porridge, tea, and lunches, and money to pay their school fees." Women were also assisting one another in providing the buildings and completing application forms so that their friends could obtain loans.

These have been bold experiments. Women have shown considerable capacity to generate income if credit is made available; they have engaged in beer brewing, crop and livestock production, vegetable and fruit production, candle, soap, footwear, and craft making, stone crushing, tailoring, etc. Credit would have to be more widely available to assist the majority of FH and poor households; administration must be cost-effective and repayment rates kept high.

There are many policy issues in any loan program: the interest rate to be charged, the population targeted, down payment required, size of loan to each recipient, sustainability of the loan funds, group or individual loans, loans or grants, administration of the loan, and whether the credit program should be a minimalist (credit only) or a credit (including education, equity, and/or technical assistance) approach. These policy issues will not be explored further here except to suggest that the credit approach (with education, equity, and technical assistance) appears to be the better approach for African women at this period in Africa's development.

Programs similar to the Botswana, Kenya, and Tanzanian program, if expanded, could greatly assist FHHs and low-resource households in East and Central Africa. These types of programs will not remove other institutional constraints and will change attitudes toward women's entrepreneurship slowly. In the past both developed and developing countries have provided loans at subsidized interest rates and/or given tax holidays to large enterprises to increase employment and production. In contrast little has been done to provide credit for women's enterprises in developing countries until the last two decades. Liedholm and Mead (1987) have shown that small-scale enterprises produce goods which are consumed primarily by low-income persons and utilize less capital and foreign exchange than large-scale enterprises per unit of output. Buvinic (1989), in a major review of donor policies for poor women, concludes that "small-scale and micro enterprise development projects have been among the most successful within the limited range of strategies adopted by donors." Thus in the countries of eastern and southern Africa, small-scale enterprises operated by women would increase consumer goods available, reduce imports, and generate employment and income. The time has come to provide additional assistance to allow women the opportunities previously available only to men and large corporations (where repayment rates have not been spectacular) to stimulate the economies and family incomes and assist in mitigating the adverse effects of SAPs.

Conclusion

The new structural adjustment programs are assisting in stimulating the economies of East and Central Africa. Agricultural production has increased due to improvements in pricing and marketing policies but 25 percent of smallholder farm households which are female-headed and which consume most of their production are not assisted by these policies. In addition the consumption-oriented policies—those affecting expenditures for education and health (including family planning) especially—have been cut in real terms by the SAPs. When total government expenditures must be reduced, it is difficult for governments to maintain funding in these crucial areas. Nutritional supplementation programs, debt forgiveness, reduced defense expenditures, improved financial management, and credit availability for women for various kinds of income-generating activities are therefore suggested as complementary policies to assist in mitigating the adverse effects of SAPs.

REFERENCES

Berger, M.
 1989   Giving Women Credit: The Strengths and Limitations of Credit as a Tool for Alleviating Poverty. *World Development* 17(1): 1017–32.
Bigelow, Ross E., Jim Cotter, Esther M. Nbajah, and Peter G. Ondeng
 1987   *Midterm Valuation of the Rural Enterprise Program of the Rural Private Enterprise Project, Kenya.* USAID Kenya, June 30 (mimeo).
Buvinic, Mayra
 1989   Investing in Poor Women: The Psychology of Donor Support. *World Development* 17(7): 1017–32.
Chipande, G. H. R., M. M. Mowezalamba, L. S. Mwaisanoc, and M. W. Mhango
 1986   *Income Generating Activities for Rural Women in Malawi: A Final Report.* Centre for Social Research, Zomba: University of Malawi.
Commins, Stephen K.
 1988   *Africa's Development Challenges and the World Bank.* Boulder: Lynne Rienner Publishers.
Due, Jean M.
 1980a The Allocation of Credit to Small Farmers in Tanzania and Zambia. *African Studies Review.* 23(3): 33-48.
 1980b *Costs, Returns, and Repayment Experience of Ujamaa Villages in Tanzania, 1973-1976.* Washington, D.C.: University Press of America.
 1983   Update on Financing Smallholders in Zimbabwe, Zambia and Tanzania. *Savings and Development* 3: 261–277.
 1987a Agricultural Credit in Tanzania. *Journal of Southern African Affairs* 3(1): 99–113.
 1987b The Allocation of Credit to Ujamaa Villages and to Small Private Farmers in Tanzania. *Savings and Development* 2: 69–107.
 1990   Experience with Income Generating Activities for Southern African Women (mimeo).

Due, Jean M., and Flavianus Magayane
   1990   Changes Needed in Agricultural Policy for Female-Headed Farm Families in Tropical Africa. *Agricultural Economics*.

Due, Jean M., and Marcia White
   1986   Contrasts Between Joint and Female-Headed Farm Households in Zambia. *Eastern Africa Economic Review* 2(1): 94–98

Gallaher, Mark
   1989   Public Expenditures, Resource Use and Social Services in Sub-Sahara Africa. Draft report prepared for World Bank and UNDP (mimeo).

Havenvik, H. J., F. Kjaerby, Ruth Meena, R. Skarstein, and Ulla Vuorela
   1988   *Tanzania: A Country Study and Norwegian Aid Review*. University of Bergen, Bergen: Centre for Development Studies.

Hudgens, Robert
   1988   A Diagnostic Survey of Female-Headed Households in the Central Province of Zambia. *Gender Issues in Farming Systems Research and Extension*, Susan Poats et al., eds. 373–88. Boulder: Westview Press.

International Monetary Fund
   1988   *Government Finance Statistical Yearbook*. Washington, D.C.: International Monetary Fund.

Kenya Enterprise Programme
   1989   *Programme Report Submitted to USAID/Kenya by Kenya Rural Enterprise Programme*. 1 July 1988 to 30 June 1989, Project Nos. 615-0220-A-00-45005-00 and 615-0238-A-00-7026-00.

Lele, Uma
   1989   *Structural Adjustment, Agricultural Development, and the Poor: Some Lessons from the Malawian Experience*. Washington, D.C.: World Bank.
   1989   Managing Agricultural Development in Africa. *Finance and Development* March: 45–48.

Liedholm, Carl, and Donald Mead
   1987   *Small Scale Industries in Developing Countries: Empirical Evidence and Policy Implications*. Michigan State University International Development Paper No. 9, East Lansing.

Mingat and George Psacharopoulos
   1985   Financing Education in Sub-Saharan Africa. *Finance and Development* March: 35–38.

Ministry of Education
   1987   *Basic Education Statistics in Tanzania*. Dar es Salaam: United Republic of Tanzania.

Mollel, Naftali, M.
   1986   An Evaluation of the Training and Visit (T&V) System of

Agricultural Extension in Muheza District, Tanga Region, Tanzania. MS thesis, Urbana: University of Illinois.

Moradpedi, N. T., and Dr. E. Jones-Dube

1987   *Second Draft Report on the MFDP Consultancy of FAP Evaluation: Background Information on Small Scale Enterprises.* National Institute of Development Research and Documentation, Gaborone: University of Botswana (mimeo).

Muya, Wamahiu

1990   *School Crisis Hits Nairobi.* January 20, p. 18. Nairobi: *Daily Nation.*

Nnyiti, M.

1989   Liberal Economic Policies in Tanzania: Their Effects at the Farm Level. (with a student at Sokoine University of Agriculture). Senior paper, Morogoro: Sokoine University of Agriculture.

Office of Women and Development, USAID

1980   *Income Generating Activities with Women's Participation.* Washington, D.C.: USAID.

Phiri, C.

1986   *Women and Their Economic Activities: A Comparative Analysis of Male-Headed and Female-Headed Households in Thekerani Rural Growth Centre.* Zomba: Department of Rural Development, Bunda College, Malawi (mimeo).

Sikaponde, Enoch

1988   An Evaluation of the Training and Visit (T&V) System of Agricultural Extension in Eastern Province, Zambia. MS thesis, Urbana: University of Illinois.

Smith, Cameron L., Raphael Kaplinsky, John Manz, and Babutsi Beauty Salabe

1988   *Evaluation of Financial Assistance Policy (FAP) and its Role in Botswana Business Development.* Government of Botswana, Ministry of Finance and Development, Gaborone (mimeo).

World Bank

1988   *World Development Report.* Washington, D.C.: World Bank.

1989   *World Development Report.* Washington, D.C.: World Bank.

1989   *Africa's Adjustment and Growth in the 1980's.* Washington D.C.: World Bank and the United Nations Development Program.

5

The Impact of Structural Adjustment Programs on Women and their Households in Bendel and Ogun States, Nigeria

Patience Elabor-Idemudia

In sub-Saharan Africa, women produce over half of the food grown (UNECA 1975a). Yet they continue to experience poverty, hunger, and an immense decline in equity relative to men in their access to the means of agricultural production. Due to unequal access, women have had to resort to selling their labor and have, in the process, been subjected to increased labor exploitation, an increased number of work hours, and increased marginalization with limited economic stability. This has had tremendous impact on the quality of life in their households. Global developments have not helped the situation and have, in some cases, intensified the existing social and economic hardships for women in developing countries by restricting their activities to the uneconomic (informal) sectors of the economy. Ideological notions and practices have maintained the status quo and continue to limit the extent to which women can improve their lot.

Nigerian women are instrumental in many farm activities that contribute to economic and agricultural development but are generally regarded as "unproductive." They are the "invisible" half who are always affected but seldom taken into account. The extent to which women are exploited and denied access to production resources in the agricultural sector is partly due to the duality of the economic system, which may be said to be caught between traditional and modern and which is reflective of the level and stage of capitalism. Women's exploitation is tied to the machinery of the state economy, which promotes capitalism and tends to

Patience Elabor-Idemudia is a Ph.D. candidate at the Ontario Institute for Studies in Education (OISE), Sociology Dept., University of Toronto, Canada. She is a native of Benin City, Nigeria; and has had extensive research/extension/teaching experience working with women farmers and the Rubber Research Institute of Nigeria, Benin City. Her research interests include Third World development with a focus on women and agriculture, and agricultural extension education.

treat women's work as "natural," non-market oriented, and therefore less valued. But a growing literature on women's issues that has appeared during the last two decades has been instrumental in deepening our understanding of the nature and extent of women's participation in economic development.

In Nigeria, as in most African societies, *the disadvantaged groups are the first to suffer when economic, political, and environmental deterioration occurs, and are the last to gain when there are improvements.* Women's inequality at each level of society—generated by the traditional division of labor, the double burden of productive and reproductive responsibilities, and exclusion from education and training—is reinforced by discriminatory ideological and systemic practices inherent in development policies. Since national development plans do not consider women's problems as deserving serious commitment in terms of allocating scarce resources to them, this trend has resulted in women's continuous exploitation in their struggle to cater to their families and themselves. In order to understand the plight of rural Nigerian women and provide an explanation for their exploitation and the undervaluation of their work in agricultural development, there is a need to examine one of several development strategies adopted to revamp the country's ailing economy. This strategy is the Structural Adjustment Policy (SAP) program, which over 30 African countries indebted to the International Monetary Fund (IMF)/World Bank have been coerced to adopt. In focusing on women, reference is made to female-headed households, as recent United Nations estimates indicate that women "serve as head of over one-third of the rural households in the developing world" (Buvinic, Graeff, and Leslie 1978, Leeper 1978: 129, Youssef and Hetler 1983). Because female-headed units are almost invariably poorer than their male-headed counterparts (reflecting both women's lower remuneration and the presence of fewer income producers in the average woman-headed household), problems of family well-being in female-headed households tend to be magnified.

The objective of this paper is to examine and highlight the impact of Nigeria's Structural Adjustment Policy (SAP) on women farmers and their families, as this group constitutes the most vulnerable and usually the lowest-income group in the country. *At a glance, SAP seems to be yielding positive results at the macro level but, on close examination of the micro-level impact, women seem to be worse off now than before SAP.* They are currently being subjected to further subordination and exploitation because of their decreased access to productive resources, and also because of their increased responsibility for maintaining family members who are unemployed or underpaid as a result of SAP. The total impact is analyzed through a case study of two Agricultural Development Projects, located in Bendel and Ogun States, which have been mandated to provide access to production resources to both male and female small-scale farmers; and through a quality of life study of women farmers' households.[1]

The Structural Adjustment Program (SAP) and Nigerian Women

Since the publication of World Bank's Berg Report (1981), most debtor sub-Saharan African countries have had to adopt SAPs as the best way of coping with their stagnating economies.[2] The aim is to boost supply and increase agricultural productivity while at the same time reduce the role of the state and increase the role of the market in resource allocation. SAP policies and programs lay emphasis on:

1. improving the incentives for private sector producers (particularly of export materials) through changes in prices, tariffs and other taxes, subsidies, and interest rates; and

2. releasing resources for private sector use by reducing the resources allocated to the public sector, (thereby preventing the public sector from crowding out the private sector).

Privatization of public sector activities is, therefore, an important objective of the SAP and is advocated by the IMF/World Bank and other donors as a way of reducing public expenditure and increasing efficiency. It is expected to be accompanied by increased competition among private firms and less government intervention in the economy.[3]

The question is whether this thinking meets with the interests and needs of rural dwellers and women farmers who form the majority of the poor in African countries. Women's relationship with the state and the market is a complex one with gender and class implications which have created insurmountable hardship for women (Elson 1987). The fact remains that farm women's work, whether in the household or on the farm, falls into that category which lies "outside the market pricing mechanism" and is often unrecognized or invisible (Beneria 1983).

Theoretically, women's work (both on- and off-farm) does not fit the economist's formulation of economic or productive work because it takes place in the nonmonetized sector or household. It is seen in modern capitalist society as subordinate to and dependent on the market and on market-supplied goods. But it has been well established that, far from being two separate sectors, in a dual economy analysis the subsistence and the capitalist sectors are highly interconnected, because the subsistence sector constitutes a source of cheap labor from which wage labor can be drawn as capital accumulation proceeds. In other words, the latter feeds upon the former (Cook and Kirkpatrick 1988).

To understand the impacts of structural adjustment on women, it is important to know that the Nigerian SAP package adopted in 1985 includes the following changes in the macro economy:

1. The cutting down of government subsidies of social services, food, and productive inputs;
2. The selling of large state-run enterprises or parastatals to private enterprises in order to attract more foreign investment;
3. The devaluation of the Nigerian currency (naira) by over 200 percent and trading in foreign exchange under the Foreign Exchange Market, with huge profits going into the pockets of an exploitative banking industry;
4. The drastic cutting of food imports and other essential commodities without a parallel increase in local food production. This has led to escalating food prices and has in turn resulted in high incidences of hunger and malnutrition;
5. A reduced emphasis on industrialization and increased emphasis on agriculture, particularly cash crop production for export, with focus on large-scale successful farmers at the expense of peasant farmers (Agbroko 1988).

As Elson (1987: 64) points out, these changes translate at the micro and household level into changes in income, prices of purchased goods (e.g., food), changes in public services, and changes in working conditions. The question is: what do all these changes mean for poor rural women and their household members in terms of the quality of life? The answer is partly provided in the case study I undertook in 1989 in Bendel and Ogun States, Nigeria.[4]

The Agricultural Development Projects (ADPs)

Agricultural Development Projects (ADPs) constitute the new strategy which the Federal Government of Nigeria has adopted to implement its agricultural development programs and to integrate women into agricultural development through better extension services and training. The ADPs are jointly financed by the World Bank, the Federal Government, and the respective state governments. They initially began with three projects, first established in Gusau in Sokoto State (1974), Gombe in Bauchi

State (1975), and Funtua in Kaduna State (1976) respectively. As the results started to gain popularity, the number of ADPs were increased, with those established in Ayangba in Benue State (1977), Lafia in Oyo State North (1977), Bida in Niger State (1979), and Ilorin in Kwara State (1980). By 1987, every state—except Akwa, Ibom, and Katsina, which were then nonexistent—had an ADP.

The two major objectives of the ADPs that earned them popularity are: (1) to increase agricultural (food) production, and (2) to increase farm incomes and thereby improve the standard of living of farmers' families in rural areas. These objectives were to be achieved through the provision of a package of farm support services including adaptive research, crop protection measures, and extension services. Due to the need for incentives to motivate farmers, other services such as land development, credit facilities, and tractor-hiring services have become part of the ADP package for farmers. The main targets of the program are small-scale farmers who produce food crops.[5]

Nigeria, as an afterthought, decided to integrate women into agricultural production through a "female farming system approach" that would give them the necessary skills for more efficient production. This female factor was adopted in response to the Lagos Plan for Africa drawn up in 1980, which highlighted actions that governments should take to encourage rural women to increase food production and reduce urban migration (FAO 1984). The Plan of Action stressed: (1) the need for governments to recognize the significance of rural women in food production and therefore improve their skills while making their labor less strenuous; (2) the need to initiate and sustain continuous research and a documentation mechanism for recording the contribution of women to agriculture, especially with regard to food supply; and (3) the need to establish and strengthen the women's division in Ministries of Planning so as to integrate their programs into a national plan of action (FAO 1984). To comply with the Plan, training departments were established in all ADPs and are responsible for identifying the training needs of the project staff and regular farmers in the respective areas serviced by the projects. So far, women have yet to benefit from these objectives as all indications show that they are not the real target clientele of the ADPs. Because there are a limited number of female staff involved with the ADPs, the needs of rural women farmers are not met. Actually, women's needs were never assessed and are not reflected in the projects' plans. This is because past and current practices show that agricultural male staff favor male farmers and completely ignore female farmers. Moreover, efforts of the ADPs have been directed towards male farmers who produce food and cash crops strictly for export to international markets, thereby contributing to and promoting a stronger capitalist economy. In view of this trend, one can speculate that the ADPs and their training components are not aimed at empowering women in any way, nor are they aimed at enabling women to achieve equality with men in gaining access to agricultural production resources.

The Case Study

This study involves field work and data collection in ten Nigerian villages. Five villages are serviced by the Ogun State Agricultural Development Project, and the other five villages are serviced by the Bendel State Agricultural Development Project, both located in Nigeria.[6] The farming system in both locations centers on food crops of maize, cassava, yams, beans, and vegetables (spinach, pepper, tomatoes), plus palm nut in Bendel State and cocoa, cola nut, and soybeans in Ogun State. The study aims to determine the impacts of Nigeria's SAP on women farmers and their households. It involves determining women's access to agricultural inputs, including credit and extension services, from 1985 to 1989 to see if there are any noticeable changes. The study also attempts to determine economic gains (if any) that the women receive from their agricultural labor and how much time they put into everyday work (both productive and reproductive). The study concludes by examining the *quality of life* in the women's households and the strategies adopted by women to survive economic belt tightening.

The parameters adopted in the study include: socioeconomic background; access to credit, farming inputs, and extension services; access to markets; incomes and financial status of household heads; roles in decision making; time budget studies; and quality of life in the households, i.e., nutrition and health care.

Methodology

The data was collected in collaboration with 20 agricultural extension agents working with the ADPs whom I earlier briefed on the objectives of the research. The exercise involved trips to Benin City in Bendel State and Abeokuta in Ogun State, where the two head offices of the ADPs are located, and trips to the ten villages where the women farmers were located. The research was conducted through a combination of methodologies: informal interviews with Ministry of Agriculture officials, ADP administrators, and agents; informal sessions with women at community gatherings; and direct observations of projects and women's activities (for which a daily journal was maintained). Household surveys of farm and nonfarm activities were done through the administration of standardized questionnaires directed at a stratified sample. Criteria for the selection of the households included small-scale farming and location within the area serviced by the ADPs.

Prior to the administration of the questionnaires to the women, a pretest exercise was carried out on five randomly selected women and the findings highlighted some cultural practices and taboos which were infringed upon by some of the questions. The questionnaire was redesigned and expanded to accommodate and respect cultural practices. The research covered a period of six months.

Data and Data Analysis

The sample consisted of a total of 40 respondents: 30 women (15 from each study area) of whom 20 were married, 8 widowed, 2 separated; and 10 men, all of whom were married. The survey showed that 90 percent (36 of 40) of the respondents were in the age category 38–68 years, while the remaining 10 percent (4 of 40) were below 38 years of age. No respondent was younger than 30. None of the respondents had a university education; 10 percent had some level of high school education; 5 percent of the respondents had "modern school" education;[7] 47.5 percent (6 men and 13 women) had some primary education; and 37.5 percent (10 women and 3 men) had no education. About 40 percent of the households (16 of the 40) were headed by women.[8] Only 5 percent (2 of the 30 women) were engaged in wage labor as domestics.

Most (95 percent) of the women were unemployed in the formal sense but 80 percent of them were engaged in income-generating activities such as petty trading, food processing, and food vending in local markets and operating own-accounts farms *in addition to working on family farms.* This is in addition to their domestic roles of childbearing, child care, cooking, fetching firewood, collecting water, and washing clothes. To analyze women's productive and reproductive roles, I separately examine the data on men and women's roles in two sectors—the agricultural sector and the household sector.

The Agricultural Sector

To test if women experienced limited access to production resources, we asked whether there was any difference in women's access to resources within the ADPs. Our data thus include an assessment of women's access to credit, farming inputs, and extension services with the establishment of the ADPs.

When women respondents were asked what sources of credit were available to them to finance their farming activities, 46.6 percent (14 women of 30 women in the sample) said that they depended on their families and kin for financial support, while 20 percent (6 out of 30 women) said that they used their personal savings (Table 5-1). Another 33.3 percent (10 of 30 women) used credit unions, cooperative associations, and moneylenders. Among the men respondents, 40 percent (4 of 10 men in the sample) said that they used their personal savings, while 30 percent said they used loans from the banks. The remaining 30 percent said they used money borrowed from friends.

When the women respondents were asked why they did not get loans from banks, all of them said that they had previously approached various banks for loans but were turned down due to lack of collateral, a condition to qualify for a loan. They were also required to produce written permission from their husbands before they were considered for loans. When the ADP agents were asked why they did not help the women to acquire loans from the banks to support their farming activities, they said that it was not within their mandate to do so. One can only conclude from these findings that women's access to credit facilities has not improved. Rather, it has worsened because women's relatives and kins who were usually in positions to help them with credit have also become victims of economic belt-tightening measures due to SAP and are not too willing to let go of the little that they have.

Farming Inputs

When women's and men's access to farming inputs (fertilizers, tractors, high-yielding seed varieties, and seedlings) were assessed, 56.6 percent of

Table 5-1. Sources of Credit.

Available Sources	Men	Women
Bank	0	0
Family	0	14
Credit union	1	1
Friends	3	0
Moneylenders	0	4
Associations	0	5
Personal savings	4	6
Proceeds from produce sale	2	0
Total	10	30

the women (17 of 30) said that farming inputs were rarely available to them while 26.6 percent (8 of 30) said that inputs were sometimes available to them. Only 16.6 percent of the women (5 of 30) did not provide any answer to the question. When men were asked to assess the availability of farming and production inputs, 90 percent (9 of 10) said that inputs were readily available to them while only 10 percent found inputs to be sometimes available (Table 5-2). This pattern confirms the claim that women's access to farm inputs is limited and at times nonexistent. This may be explained by the fact that almost all the village extension agents are men who do not consider women to be farmers needing farming inputs. They would rather supply the male farmers with inputs that they may share with their wives. Another factor that may be responsible for women's limited access to farming inputs is the latter's high purchasing cost when they are not supplied free by extension agents. Women, by virtue of their poor economic positions, cannot afford these inputs.

Extension Services

When asked the frequency of visits that extension agents made to their farms, 10 percent of the women (3 of the 30) said that their farms were visited every week, 50 percent (15 of 30) said agents visited their farms biweekly, 26.6 percent (8 of 30) said their farms were visited once every month, 6.6 percent (2 of 30) said they received farm visits once a year, and 6.6 percent of the women (2 of 30) gave no answer to the question. When the same question was directed to the men in the sample, 70 percent said that their farms were visited every week, while 30 percent said that their farms were visited biweekly. When access to farm information and training was evaluated, all 10 men said they had received some form of training in agricultural practices from the extension agents, while only

Table 5-2. Availability of Farming Inputs (Fertilizer, Seeds, Pesticides).

Level of Availablility	Men	Women
Very readily available	9	0
Readily available	1	0
Sometimes available	0	8
Rarely/Not available	0	17
No response	0	5
Total	10	30

36.6 percent of the women had received some form of training from the agents.

From these results, it is obvious that women's access to training and extension services is still limited. Although women's access has improved a little since 1985, it is still very limited compared with that of men.

The Household Sector

This section involves a study of time allocation for household members of work activities and leisure, incomes of household heads and other household members, decision-making roles of husbands and wives in households, and evaluation of the quality of life of households through nutritional habits and available health care service.

Time Budget Data

The number of hours in which household members engaged in household activities and leisure was examined. When asked how many hours were spent on various chores during the day, the women were found to spend, on average, 4–6 hours/day on domestic chores (cooking, cleaning, childcare) and 8–10 hours/day on work outside the house engaging in farming activities (ploughing, planting, hoeing, weeding, and harvesting), food processing, food vending, and petty trading in local market. When asked the number of hours of leisure time they had, the women said they had about 3 hours of leisure per day during which they were engaged in mending clothes, giving their children haircuts, knitting, or other activities that they do not consider to be work (Table 5-3). The total work hours of women were found to range from 15 to 19 hours/day in the various households.

When a similar question was directed at the husbands (male respon-

Table 5-3. Time Allocation of Family Members.

| Household members | Activities | | | | |
	Farm work	Cooking, processing	Child care	Total work	Leisure
Men	8	0	2	10	4–6
Women	8–10	6–8	3	15–19	3
Children:					
5–9 yrs	0	2	2–3	4–5	10
10–17 yrs	4	4	4	12	8
18–21 yrs	5	4	5	14	4

dents in the survey), they were found to spend 1–2 hours/day on domestic chores such as mending things around the house and at times child care; 6–8 hours/day on farming activities during the planting and harvest seasons. During off-planting seasons, 4–6 hours/day were spent on leisure activities such as playing games (draft games), attending community meetings, and socializing with men friends. No man in the sample was found to engage in domestic chores, as they were regarded as belonging strictly to the female domain.

All households were found to have dependent children who were in most cases the children of the household heads, others being sisters, brothers, nieces, nephews and other extended kin. The ages of the dependents ranged from about 3 months to 21 years old. The average number of people living in a household was 7.07. A total of about 75 percent of the dependents were primary-school-going children for whom the household heads had to provide school uniforms, stationery, transport money, school fund contributions, and other school needs. About 10 percent of the household members were below the age of attending school, 6 percent were found to be engaged in technical skill training, and 9 percent of children were income earners working in the informal sector and helping to supplement the incomes of the household heads.

In the case of children in the households, the male children within the age group of 1–18 years did virtually nothing within the household and were either away at school, engaged in skill training, playing soccer with friends, or doing their homework. The female children aged 5–9 years were found to be engaged for 1–2 hours/day in domestic chores, helping their mothers with housecleaning, dishwashing, and, at times, child care. Those aged 10–17 years did the same work as those in the previous age group but for a longer period of 5–6 hours/day. Those aged 18 and over, if still living at home, played the role of substitute mothers to their junior siblings when their mothers were away engaging in petty trading or food processing. They also assisted their mothers in food processing, vending, and preparation for household consumption.

Income and Financial Status of Household Heads

Female and male household heads were compared in terms of their income levels, and asked to give details of all members of their households in terms of occupation, income, and contribution to the family budget. In a comparison of women's income to men's, data indicated that the financial position of the majority of women was inferior to that of men: 28 of 30 women had incomes between 1,000 and 2,000 naira, while 8 of 10 men had incomes between 2,000 and 5,000 naira. This meant that households with male heads were financially better off than households with female heads, because 20 of 24 male household heads had wives who, through their engagement in retail trading in the informal sector, supplemented men's incomes. Only 9 percent of children were income earners working in the informal sector and helping to supplement the incomes of the household heads. However, the rising prices of essential commodities and services in the market places considerable drain on the income of the household head, particularly in female-headed households where there is only one source of income.

In an assessment of the financial position of wives, a crucial issue is that relating to the system of allocation and control of income within the home. The assessment indicates that 16 of the 20 married women either had no access to their husbands' income or did not know how much income their husbands earned in a month. Husbands were found to control and manage all household income and to allocate money for grocery shopping; 18 of the 20 women received fixed housekeeping allowances. In these cases the amounts given are fixed by the primary earners, that is, the husbands. Only in 2 households was money management reported to be a joint responsibility of both husband and wife.

Decision Making

Available data show that neither joint decision making nor equal sharing of resources within households happens at all, as Elson (1989) has suggested. When asked who made important decisions regarding household economics and welfare of the children, 75 percent (15) of the 20 married women said that decisions were made by their husbands and handed down for implementation in the households; 12 percent (3 women) said that decisions were jointly made by both husband and wife; the remaining

Table 5-4. Decision-Making Roles of Men and Women.

Decisions Made	Person Making Decisions				
	Husband only	Wife only	Both	Others	Total
Crops to plant	35	2	1	0	40
Crops to sell	20	8	12	0	40
Spending joint income	38	0	2	0	40
Future of children	5	25	2	8	40
Building a house	38	0	2	0	40
Having a baby	30	2	8	0	40

two women said that some decisions were made by their husbands while others were made by wives on an individual basis (Table 5-4). In the case of the 8 widowed women in the study, decisions were made by them in consultation with their older relatives or late husbands' brothers and/or their older children. The two single women made decisions on their own and so did the 10 married men with no input from their wives.

Quality of Life in the Household

The quality of life in the households was determined by examining two essential parameters—nutrition and health care services—that impact on the everyday survival of individuals. The nutritional level in the household was analyzed in terms of consumption of food, the nutrient value of the food, and the pattern of buying essential commodities. The measurement was done through an analysis of the diets of household members and the frequency of meals taken each day. Respondents were also asked how families' food needs were met in a situation where food and commodity prices have continued to rise in the era of structural adjustment. Various responses were given (and shown in Table 5-5) which include: reducing the number of meals per day from 3 to 2 and in most cases to 1 (85 percent of the households), and reducing the quantity of food per meal (all households). Another strategy was to eliminate some essential food items from the diets, particularly protein food items such as beef (85 percent of the households), fish (60 percent of the households), chicken (90 percent of the households), and eggs (95 percent of the households). Many households reported having reduced the quantity of certain staple foods such as yams, plantains, beans, and gari (cassava flour), which they purchase at a particular time, and have resorted to purchasing cheap, non-nutritious food in order to stretch the money. Such foods are more labor-intensive in their preparation. Other foods such as bread, rice, and corn-flakes, which most households had acquired a taste for during the oil-boom days, have now become a matter of the past and can only be found on the dining tables of the rich.

Because people do not like to talk about hunger and reducing the number of meals taken per day, respondents referred to their one-meal schedule by means of "the 0 or 1 formula," where 0 means that no meal is taken and 1 means that a meal is taken. A combination of zeros and ones indicates the frequency and number of meals taken or missed in one day; e.g., 0-1-0 indicates no breakfast, a lunch, and no dinner taken in one day; 0-0-1 indicates no breakfast or lunch but a dinner; and 1-0-0 indicates breakfast taken but with no lunch or dinner. This one-meal schedule is seen as a way of stretching family money, but at times this measure is

Table 5-5. Adopted Survival Strategies.

Measures adopted to survive economic hardship	Number of households	% of N
Reducing number of meals from three to two per day	5	12.5
Reducing the number of meals from three to one a day	30	75
Reducing the quantity of food per meal	40	100
Eliminating food groups from diet:		
Fish	25	60
Beef	30	75
Chicken	35	87.5
Egg	38	95
Milk	38	95
Reducing the quantity of food purchased	40	100
Borrowing money from:		
Relatives	35	75
Friends	10	25
Cooperatives	20	50
Bank	0	0
Sending children out to work for income	10	25

not enough. Some household heads, especially women, have had to resort to borrowing money from relatives and friends as well as from cut-throat moneylenders at high interest rates in order to meet the demands for food of their households. In 25 percent of the households, the children have had to go to work outside their homes in order to bring in some income to help feed the family.

Health Care

The result of all the measures adopted to beat the high cost of living since SAP is an unbalanced diet resulting in both undernutrition and malnutrition, reduced resistance to diseases, and/or poor health. High incidence of kwashiokor, anemia, malaria, diarrhea, and other diseases have been reported since 1985, especially among young children, as have been cases of infant mortality and morbidity (Federal Ministry of Health Records 1988). The situation is due to a number of complex factors, among which are the continuing decline in economic conditions, rapid inflation, decontrolling of prices, and population increases, which have all resulted from structural adjustment programs. Available health care services have deteriorated within the period of structural adjustment and do not meet the needs of the people due to limited funding and understaffing. The "efficient" health care services have shifted from the government to the hands of private doctors whose user fees are beyond the reach of the poor. Most government-owned hospitals have limited supplies of medications whose prices in the private hospitals and pharmacies are not affordable except by the rich. The only available alternative is the purchase of cheap, expired, and sometimes fake medications in so-called patent medicine stores where they can be purchased without a doctor's prescription. Such purchases have at times been fatal.

Summary and Implications of Research Results

Results from this study show that, first, women's access to credit, farm inputs such as fertilizer, and extension services has not improved since the establishment and popularization of the ADPs. In some cases, women's access has gotten worse. This may be due to the fact that very few extension agents are female and the male extension agents do not regard women as fitting their definition of farmers or heads of household, or it may be simply gender bias on their part. The trickle-down theory may also apply here: male agents may erroneously believe that whatever benefits husbands get will eventually trickle down to their wives.

Second, there is a high number of illiterate women, despite the rhetoric of free primary education and adult literacy programs. As a result, the income levels of women are still a lot lower than those of men. This makes it harder for households headed by women to live adequately, resulting in younger members of the household seeking additional wage labor to help sustain the family. Third, available data also show that neither joint decision making nor equal sharing of resources is forthcoming in most households. Yet the majority of household activities and work still fall on the shoulders of the women who spend an average of 15–19 hours of unpaid labor on productive and reproductive activities.

Fourth, the quality of life in almost all rural households was found to have deteriorated with members resorting to eating only one or two meals a day—using formulas 0-0-1, 0-1-0, or 1-0-0 to denote the time of the meal. This practice has resulted in unbalanced diets, undernutrition, and malnutrition and hence declining resistance to diseases. The health of members of most households has therefore deteriorated due to undernourishment and malnutrition; yet the health care delivery system is next to nonexistent. This has resulted in high rates of mortality and morbidity, especially among young children, the middle-aged, and the elderly.

The hardships brought on the people of Nigeria and the rural poor by structural adjustment thus cannot be overstressed. Newspapers, television, and radio reports continue to highlight the discontent in the country and this has, in recent times, been evidenced by a series of demonstrations and riots. The hardship is more severe for women—especially the rural poor—who have been and still are doubly disadvantaged economically, socially, and politically in a patriarchal society like Nigeria, where their plight is not considered serious enough to be included in development plans.

Results show that the majority of women are economically dependent on their husbands, largely due to their lack of education and skills. A good number of rural women have, in addition to farming, set up small retail businesses but unfortunately have not been able to expand because of lack of access to credit. These businesses barely generate enough income for subsistence and for financing children's school expenses. These businesses cannot compete with those of men on equal terms as long as women carry the double burden of unpaid work in the reproduction and maintenance of human resources. In order for women to benefit from gaining access to markets, they need access first of all to public services such as water supply, electricity, health care, education, transportation, and appropriate technology that will reduce the burden of their manual labor. This will, in turn, enable them to acquire the skills they need to enter the market and make use of market access once acquired.

In agricultural production, new intra-household exchange relations are introduced—with unequal distribution of economic power—with SAP emphasis on cash crop and nonfood crop production for export to urban, national, and international markets. Women find themselves being pushed more and more into the private domestic sphere with limited access to production resources. They are restricted more and more to the production of food for family consumption on marginal lands, while men, encouraged by increased access to productive resources in the public domain, are increasingly drawn into cash crop production for export. As Deere (1976: 9) claims, "intrafamilial labour deployment is responsive to the need to attain subsistence in the face of rural poverty."

The above practice, Boserup (1970) claims, marks the beginning of a new division of labor in the social relations of production. Women, who were once self-sufficient, now rely mostly on government handouts and foreign aid while income-generating projects are looked upon as a godsend. Women, with limited skills for alternative jobs in the highly competitive and limited labor market, have become easy targets of subordination and exploitation. Supporting Boserup's claim, Palmer (1985) argues that the separation of domestic and public spheres has meant increased restriction of women to the home, to the production of subsistence food crops, as well as to the production of goods and services required in the household. The impact of this sexual division of labor in the social relations of production is the creation of economic dependency of women on men and lower status for women. Given that in any society money equals power and control, this means that such women have no power and no control over their lives. The resulting production gap and the decline in female status have led many rural women either to abandon cultivation or leave for the urban areas (Boserup 1970: 53–65).[9]

Research findings of this study are similar to ILO studies (1980) which show that women globally put in as many as 16 hours of work a day on farm work, housework, and family care. The nature and type of work have raised the fundamental economic and social issues discussed above. Yet the reality is that women are usually left out when development needs are discussed and new technologies and projects are being designed. Planners fail to recognize women's roles as producers and also fail to recognize their actual roles and potential contribution to development. The image of males as the sole and universal farmers and financial providers juxtaposed with that of women as primarily housewives relegated only to housework—which might or might not include subsistence farming—obscures women's actual productive roles.

Conclusion

It is obvious from the above analysis that women still continue to hold inferior positions in Nigeria and that, despite development strategies and projects like the ADPs, they continue to be worse off than their male counterparts. Structural adjustment programs have worsened, not bettered, their political-economic status. In Nigeria, as in most African societies, the disadvantaged groups are the first to suffer when economic, political, and environmental deterioration occurs, and are the last to gain when there are improvements.

Of several explanations provided in the literature for the continally inferior position of women in developing societies such as Nigeria, two stand out. First, by virtue of their gender, most women and especially the rural poor have been stereotyped into traditional gender roles and have been mostly restricted to the uneconomic private sphere of subsistence agricultural production (Beneria and Sen 1986). This has limited their access to economic power, in comparison to their male counterparts. These gender and class relations have negative implications for resource allocation. Second, women—whether they work outside their homes or not—have increasingly become responsible for catering to the needs of their families in addition to their productive roles. This trend has resulted in increased hardship for them in the era of structural adjustment, in view of government cutbacks in resource allocation to the social services (e.g., health, education, water supply, rural electrification, and transportation). These services, which provide support for meeting women's everyday survival needs, have now fallen further short of doing so.

In view of the findings of this study and their implications of hardship for Nigerian women, the need exists for a reassessment of the objectives of SAP and a reevaluation of the implementation instruments in order to add a human face to SAP programs. If women and their households are to benefit from the expected "gain" of structural adjustment, the need exists to invest substantially in human, physical, social, and institutional resources that address the broader issues of women's subordination, exploitation, and access to farm inputs and social services.

NOTES

1. By "quality of life," I am referring to how everyday human survival needs of food, health care, and recreation and/or leisure activities are met.
2. The Berg Report published in 1981 by the World Bank found the heart of the economic woes of sub-Saharan African countries not to be caused by external forces but by "domestic policy issues" which include overvalued exchange rates, inappropriate pricing policy, excessive state intervention, and costly import substitution policies.
3. In neoclassical analysis, privatization and economic liberalization refer to the removal of various forms of government intervention in the product and factor market which are seen as "distorting" the price signals and "repressing" the market mechanism (Cook and Kirkpatrick 1988: 9).
4. The choice of selected locations was due to my familiarity with the peoples' language, customs, and socioeconomic characteristics by virtue of my schooling and working in the field of agricultural extension in those areas.
5. Small-scale farmers are those farming less than 5 hectares of land; medium-scale farmers are those farming 5–10 hectares of land; large-scale farmers are those farming above 10 hectares of land who receive fewer ADP extension services (Nigerian Ministry of Agriculture).
6. It should be noted that these two projects were set up in response to the Structural Adjustment Program and anticipated rural transformation. Bendel and Ogun States' ADPs were established in 1985 and 1986 respectively to conduct the training of small-scale farmers (both males and females), to provide extension services to the farmers, to provide access to farming inputs (fertilizers, high-yielding varieties of seeds and seedlings and pesticides), and to provide easy access to tractors and other technology

appropriate for small-scale production.

Bendel State is located in the midwestern section of Nigeria, covering a land area of 36,247 sq km, and has a population of 4.31 million (FOS 1984). It is divided into three operational zones for ease of collecting benchmark information. Zone I consists of tropical rain forest in the southeast to derived savannah in the north; farming is the major source of income for 78 percent of the people in this zone. Zone II consists of vegetation varying from high rain forest in the northern and central parts to mangrove swamps in the southern part; farming is the major source of income for 66 percent of the households in this zone. Zone III is characterized by a mixed savannah and rain forest belt in the north and high forest and mangrove swamps in the south; agriculture and fishing are the predominant activities of the people in this zonal area. All zones are characterized by two seasons—rainy and dry (APMEU Baseline Study 1984, Bendel State Statistical Yearbook 1978). The state consists of 20 Local Government Areas.

Ogun State is located in the northwestern section of Nigeria. It is predominantly agrarian, covering a land area of 16,409.26 sq km, with an estimated population of 2.8 million (FOS 1984). The vegetation ranges from tropical forest in the east to mangrove swamp to the south. It is characterized by two seasons—rainy and dry. For ease of administration, the state is divided into four zones comprising of Abeokuta, Ilaro, Ijebu, and Remo. There are a total of 10 Local Government Areas. In a field survey conducted by APMEU (1988) the rural population of the state was found to be 55 percent male and 45 percent female with average rural household size of 5.6, ranging from 4.0 to 7.3.

7. This is a British system of education that falls between primary and secondary levels of academic work. It was established on an experimental basis in Nigeria in 1960 as a new level of education for those who could not proceed immediately to secondary school. It was supposed to provide an avenue for students who performed badly at the primary school level to upgrade themselves in preparation for entrance to secondary school or the job market. It soon failed, as it did not equip its graduates with enough knowledge and skills to acquire jobs; it was phased out in 1966.

8. My definition of *head of household* is based on the economic criteria of who is the main provider of financial needs. Female-headed households include those where men/husbands are members but are not income earners due to job loss or illness, and so do not provide for the financial needs of the family unit.

9. Boserup's (1970) work has been criticized for concentrating on the sphere of production outside the household and for ignoring the role of women in reproduction, and the linkages between women's reproductive and productive activities.

REFERENCES

Adeyokunnu, Titilayo D.
1975   Agricultural Development Education and Rural Women in Nigeria. Department of Agricultural Extension, University of Ibadan (mimeo).

Agbroko, Gabriel
1988   Pains for Gains: Balancing and Aligning a Troubled Economy. *The African Guardian* 3(25), July 4: 14–25.

Agricultural Project Monitoring, Evaluation and Planning Unit (APMEPU)
1982   North-East Report on Baseline Survey.

Ahmed, Zubeida M., and Martha Loìufti
1985   Women Workers in Rural Development: A Programme of the International Labour Organization. Geneva: International Labour Organization.

Akande, Jadesola O.
1980   Participation of Women in Rural Development. *Rural Development and Women in Africa.* Geneva: International Labour Office.

Beneria, Lourdes
1982   *Women and Development: The Sexual Division of Labour in Rural Societies.* New York: Praeger.
1982   Class and Gender Inequalities and Women's Roles in Economic Development: Theoretical and Practical Implications. *Feminist Studies* 8: 157–75.

Beneria, Lourdes, and Gita Sen
1987   Accumulation, Reproduction, and Women's Roles in Economic Development: Boserup Revisited. *Women's Work: Development and the Division of Labour by Gender,* E. Leacock and H. Safa, eds. Boston: Bergin and Garvey Publishers Inc.

Blumberg, Rae Lessing
1981   Females Farming in Food: Rural Development and Women's Participation in the Agricultural Production System. *Women and Crises in Agriculture.* Washington: Office of Women in Development, USAID.
1986   Through the Windows of Opportunity: Enhancing the World Bank's Participation in Agricultural Development Projects in Imo State, Nigeria by Enhancing Extension and Incentives for Women Farmers. Report to Imo State ADP.

Boserup, Ester
1970   *Women's Roles in Economic Development.* New York: St. Martin's Press.

Boulding, Elise
1983   Measures of Women's Work in the Third World: Problems and Suggestions. *Women and Poverty in the Third World,* M. Buvinic,

M. Lycette, and W.P. McGreevy, eds. Baltimore: Johns Hopkins University Press.

Buvinic, Myra, L. Graeff, and P. Leslie
  1978   Women-Headed Households: The Ignored Factor in Development Planning. Washington, D.C.: International Center for Research on Women (ICRW).

Cebotarev, Nera, William Blacklock, and L. Melsaac
  1986   Farm Women's Work Patterns. *Atlantis* 11(2): 1–22.

Cook, Paul, and Kirkpatrick, Colin
  1988   Privatization in Less Developed Countries: An Overview. *Privatization in Less Developed Countries,* P. Cook and C. Kirkpatrick, eds. Sussex: Wheatsheaf Books.

Deere, Carmen Diana
  1976   Rural Women Subsistence Production in the Capitalistic Periphery. *Review of Political Economies* 8(9): 215–26.

Deere, Carmen Diana, and Magdalena De Leal
  1981   Peasant Production, Proletarianization and the Sexual Division of labor in the Andes. *Journal of Women in Culture and Society* 7(2): 338–60.

Dixon, Ruth
  1983   Land, Labour and Sex Composition of the Agricultural Force: An International Comparison. *Development and Change* 14: 347–72.

Dixon-Mueller, Ruth
  1985   Women's Work in Third World Agriculture: Concepts and Indicators. Geneva: International Labour Organization.

Economic Commission for Africa
  1975a   Path to Progress for African Women. Addis Ababa: UNECA/ ATRCW.
  1975b   *Women of Africa, Today and Tomorrow.* Addis Ababa: UNECA Women's Programme.

Elson, Diane
  1987   The Impact of Structural Adjustment on Women: Concepts and Issues. Paper No. 2 for the Institute For African Alternatives (IFAA) Conference on the Impact of IMF/World Bank Policies on the People of Africa. London, September 7–10.
  1989   The Impact of Structural Adjustment on Women: Concepts and Issues. *The IMF, the World Bank, and the African Debt,* Vol. 2, Bode Onimode, ed. London/New Jersey: Zed Books.

Favi, Funmilayo
  1977   Women's Role in Economic Development: A Case Study of Villages in Oyo State. Department of Agricultural Extension, University of Ibadan (mimeo).

Federal Agricultural Coordinating Unit (FACU)
  1986   Directory of Agricultural Development Projects. Issue No. 4, June, FACU/M15/5/12.

International Labour Office (ILO)
    1976   *Employment, Growth and Basic Needs: A One-World Problem.* New York: Praeger.
    1980   *Women in Rural Development: Critical Issues.* Geneva: International Labour Office.
    1984   *Rural Development and Women in Africa.* Proceedings of the ILO Tripartite African Regional Seminar on Rural Development and Women. Geneva: International Labour Office.
    1985   *Resources, Power and Women.* Proceedings of the African and Asian Inter-Regional Workshop on Strategies for Improving the Employment Conditions of Rural Women, Arusha, United Republic of Tanzania, August 20–25. Geneva: International Labour Organization.

Janelid, Ingrid
    1975   *The Role of Women in Nigerian Agriculture.* Rome: FAO.

Lele, Uma
    1976   *The Design of Rural Development.* Baltimore: Johns Hopkins University Press.

Muntemba, Dorothy C.
    1987   The Impact of the IMF/World Bank on the People of Africa with Special Reference to Zambia. Paper No.7 presented at the IFAA Conference on the Impact of the IMF/World Bank Policies on the People of Africa, London, September 7-10.

Okojie, Christiana E.E.
    1987   Accelerated Human Resource Development for the Rural Sector: The Roles of ADPs and the Local Government in Human Resource Development with Special Reference to Women. Paper presented at the ARMTI Seminar on Human Resource Development in Nigeria's Agricultural and Rural Sectors, ARMTI, Ilorin, April 28–30.

Organization of African Unity (OAU)
    1980   *Lagos Plan of Action for the Economic Development of Africa, 1980–2000.* Addis Ababa: Organization of African Unity.

Palmer, Ingrid
    1979   New Official Ideas on Women and Development. Sussex: *Institute for Development Studies Journal* 10(3): 51.

Rogers, Barbara
    1980   *The Domestication of Women: Discrimination in Developing Societies.* New York: Tavistock Publication.

Sen, Gita
    1982   Women Workers and the Green Revolution. *Women and Development: The Sexual Division of Labour in Rural Societies,* L. Beneria, ed. New York: Praeger Publishing.
    1985   Women Agricultural Labourers: Regional Variations in Incidence and Employment. N. Benerjee and D. Jain, eds.

Sen, Gita, and Caren Crown
    1985   *Development Crises and Alternative Vision: Third World Women's Perpectives.* New York: Monthly Review Press.
Spencer, Dunstan
    1976   African Women in Agricultural Development: A Case Study in Sierra Leone. OLC Paper, No. 9. Washington, D.C.: American Council on Education.
Staudt, Kathleen
    1982   Women Farmers and Inequalities in Agricultural Services. *Women and Work in Africa*, E. Bay, ed. Boulder: Westview Press.
Whitehead, Ann
    1982   A Conceptual Framework for Analyzing the Effects of Technological Change on Women. *Development Research Digest* 7: 58–65.
Wilson, Susannah J.
    1986   *Women, the Family, and the Economy.* Toronto: McGraw-Hill Ryerson Ltd.
Women in Nigeria (WIN)
    1985   *Women in Nigeria Today.* Proceedings of the first seminar on Women in Nigeria, Ahmadu Bello University, Zaria, 1982.
World Bank
    1979   *Recognizing the "Invisible" Woman in Development: The World Bank Experience.* Washington, D.C.: World Bank.
    1981   *Accelerated Development in Sub-Saharan Africa: An Agenda for Action.* Washington D.C.: World Bank.
    1983   *World Development Report 1983.* New York: Oxford University Press.
    1986   *Financing Adjustment with Growth in Sub-Saharan Africa, 1986–1990.* Washington, D.C.: World Bank.
Youssef, Nadia, and Carol Hetler
    1983   "Establishing the Economic Conditions of Women-Headed Households in the Third World: A New Approach." *Women and Poverty in the Third World*, M. Buvinic, M. Lycette, and W. McGreevey, eds. Baltimore: Johns Hopkins University Press.

6

Women and Structural Adjustment in Zaire

Brooke Schoepf and Walu Engundu
with Diane Russell and Claude Schoepf

The decade of the 1980s opened with widespread recognition that Africa's agrarian crisis is a general one, not limited to areas struck by drought or insect pests (Schoepf 1981). Numerous studies identified constraints to agricultural development and proposed solutions. One set of policy prescriptions, contained in the Berg Report (World Bank 1981), has been implemented by major multilateral and bilateral agencies under the leadership of the International Monetary Fund (IMF). The Berg Report identifies misguided policies of government interference through price-setting, currency controls, and taxation. These policies privileged urban consumers over rural producers and created a crisis of production. Export crops were neglected (or marketed fraudulently), starving public treasuries of foreign exchange. Bureaucracies grew exponentially, creating still more bottlenecks to production and trade. Loans for unproductive industrial and prestige project investments resulted in slowed, even negative, growth. The results include unfavorable trade balances and overvalued national currencies, which discouraged private investment.

The specific measures recommended for economic stabilization were fashioned into a series of structural adjustments to be adapted to the con-

Brooke Schoepf, an economic and medical anthropologist, is currently a fellow at the Bunting Institute of Radcliffe College, Harvard. She has led research teams in Zaire since 1974. From 1986–90 she directed CONNAISSIDA, investigating ways to prevent AIDS.

Walu Engundu, an economic anthropologist, is a research associate at the Centre de Recherches en Sciences Humaines, Kinshasa, Zaire. Her research focuses on women, health, and development.

Diane Russell's doctoral thesis in anthropology at Boston University focuses on the rice trade in northeastern Zaire. She will be a post-doctoral Rockefeller Foundation fellow.

Claude Schoepf, an agricultural economist, conducted research on farming systems in Shaba and Kivu regions of Zaire.

ditions of each country (World Bank 1986). Adhering to a Structural Adjustment Program (SAP) is a condition for a country's obtaining new IMF credits. In Zaire, policy prescriptions include price liberalization, ending controls on foreign exchange and repatriation of profits, as well as reducing government parastatal holdings through privatization and increasing production of crops and manufactured goods for export in order to generate foreign exchange for debt service. In addition, fiscal policy includes budget restraint, especially in the provision of services, improved customs controls, new taxes on trade, local-level self-sufficiency (decentralization), and devaluation. Basic to the assumptions of structural adjustment is the faith that development can take place in Africa by means of "free" market capitalism, "reliance on market forces," and "getting prices right."

For several years, between mid-1982 and late 1986, Zaire, with its economy in deep crisis, was considered a stellar example of efforts to comply with structural adjustment recommendations. The ills for which structural adjustment was prescribed were real, both in general and in their application to Zaire. But by ignoring the broader political economic causes of crisis, both internally and in the world market, the SAP prescriptions bear little relation to the experience of the preceding century. Thus a review of Zaire's situation may be instructive in identifying the causes of crisis at the macro level. Then we examine some of the effects the implementation of structural adjustment measures have had at the micro level. We describe the effects of structural adjustment policy and programs upon primary producers of food crops, most of whom are women.

Roots of Economic Crisis

Zaire was one of the most industrialized nations of sub-Saharan Africa at Independence in 1960. Much of its political economy was controlled by transnational firms in collaboration with the colonial state. Colonial rule guaranteed the political and economic conditions for profitable operations, including land concessions, infrastructure construction, mobilization of a large supply of cheap labor, low corporate taxes, and unlimited repatriation of profits. The revenues to finance investments and services were accumulated primarily from products and taxes supplied by African peasants, miners, plantation workers, artisans, and petty traders. Following independence the stability of the operating climate was upset as national rulers promoted their own ascension. Peasants strove to obtain larger returns on their labor and, seeking a "second independence," rebelled in many areas. The regime which came to power quelled the rebellions and attracted foreign loans.

Growth between 1968 and 1973 averaged nearly 7 percent annually. It brought increased dependence on copper and other mineral exports that had dominated the colonial economy from the 1920s. Prestige projects and capital-intensive investments made from foreign loans created relatively few new jobs and yielded low rates of economic return. At the same time, dearth of investment in peasant production and transport infrastructure fueled the exodus to cities already crowded with unemployed people.

In 1973 international oil prices rose steeply. Tactics employed by the new class accumulating capital on its own behalf created chaos in the infrastructure. Some internal economic resources were redistributed from foreign owners to the state and to Zairian nationals linked to the inner circle of political power. The management of these windfalls has been much criticized. In 1974 declining international copper prices sent government revenues plummeting while debt service payments came due. Controls were placed on repatriation of profits in apparent violation of the liberal 1969 investment code. Foreign exchange became difficult to obtain at artificially pegged official rates. Spare parts, replacement machinery, and raw materials imports became expensive. As members of the poorly paid bureaucracy used their offices to obtain additional incomes, bribes paid to cut through official red tape and shortages became an increasing drain on profits. Profitability of transnational operations declined, and managers of many firms reported operating far below capacity; industrial output declined. A cumulative negative growth rate of 18 percent occurred between 1974 and 1985, while real prices rose 6,580 percent.

In response to these problems and to recession in the world economy, major investors halted or scaled down proposed new ventures. Plans to develop a free trade zone of export manufacturing and processing dragged. Without new investment commitments, the government could not float loans to begin construction of a new deep water port. Much of the hydroelectric generating potential of the $1.1 billion Inga Complex (dam) remained untapped, an embarrassment to diplomats whose countries had promoted its construction. All this occurred at the same time that terms of trade for Zaire's principal exports continued to decline. Policies to accumulate a national surplus failed as a result of these unproductive strategies which, combined with deepening structural distortions, prolonged world market crisis, and continuing capital drain, resulted in 15 years of crisis.

Recapturing a favorable operating climate has been the subject of continuing policy negotiations between African leaders and the multinational agencies and Western governments during the 1980s. In Zaire mounting debt coupled with the regime's demonstrated political and military weakness gave the institutions of international finance enormous policy-making leverage. This has been deployed to improve both debt reimbursement performance and the operating environment for transnational firms. Policy shifts, as noted above, included devaluation, an end to foreign exchange controls, free repatriation of profits, an end to parastatal monopolies, and decontrol of most food prices.

Women's Labor and Capital Accumulation

In Zaire, as elsewhere in the region, economic crisis and the structures of capital accumulation inherited from the colonial period have contributed to the feminization of poverty (Schoepf 1986b, Walu 1987, Newbury and Schoepf 1989). A brief review of gender differences shows why the effects of structural adjustment policies also are experienced most severely by poor women and children throughout the rural and urban areas.

As elsewhere in sub-Saharan Africa, Zairian women's work in both rural and urban areas is essential to social reproduction (Pruitt, Schoepf et al. 1985). It provides the family food and many other household necessities. In addition, rural women's work provides low-priced labor inputs for cash crops and marketing. Married women are obliged by custom and contemporary social relations to use their incomes in cash and kind primarily to meet the basic food requirements of their families. Peasant men's incomes seldom augment the family diet and, even in the city, women provide significant contributions to household budgets (Schoepf 1978, Pruitt and Reid 1984, Walu 1987, Henn, Russell et al. 1988).

Throughout the post-colonial period, village agriculture has been starved of new investment, especially of investment in technologies that would reduce the labor burden of poor rural women (Schoepf 1980). Production increases have mainly resulted from longer work by peasants on larger fields. Women fled the rural areas in increasing numbers. Currently, Zaire's cities contain as many women as men, yet few wage labor opportunities for women have been created. Women make up only

4 percent of the formal sector labor force. An estimated 40–60 percent of urban men also are without waged employment. They and the majority of women who are without special job qualifications resort to informal sector occupations. The activities of women without substantial capital and connections include petty trade, food preparation, market gardening, sewing, smuggling, illegal home brewing of beer and alcohol, and prostitution (Schoepf 1988; Schoepf and Walu 1990).

Walu's (1987) study of household budgets in Kinshasa documents the substantial contributions of women to family survival. Longitudinal data collected by Walu between 1985 and 1989 show that many poor women's enterprises have failed as a result of the pressures of inflation, often mediated by the women's subordination to husbands and lovers (Schoepf and Walu 1990). Mutually beneficial exchanges between urban and rural kin also are declining and mistrust is growing on all sides. For this reason, as well as others to follow, poor urban women do not perceive return to the village as a solution to their problem of survival. Although hard data are not available, our impression is that for both urban and rural poor people, the social fabric is unraveling under the pressures generated by economic crisis. Case studies lend texture and immediacy to these microeconomic

Figure 6-1. The work of women without substantial capital and connections includes petty trade, food preparation, market gardening, sewing, smuggling, illegal home brewing of beer and alcohol, and prostitution.

generalizations; they suggest how economic crisis leads to crisis in families and society.

Two cases are presented to illustrate the grinding poverty of those with few resources in the city. Mama Mongongo is a widow and a mother of eight, with four children still in school. They live in two rooms without electricity. A water tap and a privy in the yard are shared with six other families. From 1985 to 1987, Mama Mongongo sold cooked food to low-paid workers in the city's central district. At daybreak she walked 4 to 5 kilometers to purchase produce which she then headloaded home to cook on her charcoal burner. Then she carried it to an empty lot, where she lit a fire to keep the food hot for the unskilled workers who were her noon-time customers. Before payday the men expected her to serve them on credit—which many failed to repay. With this trade and some gifts from kin Mama Mongongo was able to meet her rent and daily expenses and pay school fees.

However, in March 1988, Walu noticed that Mama Mongongo was no longer at her accustomed place at noon and visited her home. She reported that her sister's child had died and the obligatory funeral contribution had consumed about half her capital, leaving her without money to purchase raw food supplies. Walu reports, "I found a changed person, very aggressive and at the same time despondent. She no longer wished to reply to my questions." The researcher became part of her support network.

Then one of her older sons gave up looking for work and enlisted in the army. Although the pay is very low, the young man helps his mother somewhat when he is able to collect unofficial fines from travelers whom he threatens on some pretext. Moreover, he obtained a small plot adjacent to the military camp where his mother and his sister grow vegetables. They sell some and consume the rest. However, Mama Mongongo has been unable to meet her landlord's demand that she pay a 22-month advance on her rent. Threatened with eviction, she does not know where she can go. Since she is not able to pay the children's school fees, they can no longer attend school.

In the second case, retreat to the village proved to be an unworkable strategy for an unemployed unskilled worker, his wife, and six children. In 1985 Mama Yoka, the wife, sold food in small quantities from her court-yard on a busy street near a college. She tried several items, including manioc flour, chikwanga (fermented manioc bread), and grilled fish. Although trade was brisk, none of these efforts garnered enough to provide food and school fees. Neighbors helped by feeding the younger children. The eldest daughter completed primary school with high marks and her name appeared on the list of those accepted to the Beaux Arts, one of the best-reputed high schools in the city. However, her parents had no money for fees, uniforms, or books. So, although the girl was willing to walk eight kilometers to school and back each day to save carfare, she was obliged to remain at home.

In 1987 the husband lost his job, so there was no money for rent, either. Admitting defeat, the family moved back to his village. One child died en route and another died after they had settled in the village. People said that "the uncles" had killed the children by sorcery. The husband accused his wife's uncles who, he had been advised, were unhappy with the names given to the children. Mama Yoka, in turn, replied that *his* uncles had done it. However, she told Walu that her children had died as a consequence of malnutrition. Fertile land has become scarce in the community. The husband was allocated fields on barren, eroded land, and their garden had yielded harvests too meager to support the family. In December 1987, having lost the two youngest of her five children, Mama Yoka returned to Kinshasa where her husband has a plot of land in an outlying district. This land is also poor and sandy; only gardens made along rivulets at the bottom of ravines do well. When Mama Yoka came back to visit in her old neighborhood, she brought a symbolic gift of scrawny manioc tubers from her garden. Walu interprets the meager gift as an indication of the family's current desperate straits.

The case studies reveal intersections of class and gender over time. First, while poor women's labor day is lengthened by hours of domestic tasks, middle-class and wealthy women are replaced in much of this work by poorly paid domestics, both male and female. Second, most of the poor women in Walu's network sample are without hope of betterment for themselves and their children. Third, middle-class households are able to maintain their modest consumption levels only in cases where wives' informal sector production and trade brings in two to three times the amount of their husbands' salaries. Some families are elite and wives trade long-distance in luxury goods and food which maintains the family lifestyle and permits husbands to accumulate capital, which they then invest mainly in rental properties and trading. Yet even in these households, gender inequality creates insecurity for women, few of whom are able to own property in their own right (Schoepf and Walu 1990). Thus while gender inequality combines with class inequality to diminish poor women's life changes, as inflation soars, it renders wealthier women unable to take full advantage of their class position. Table 6-1 summarizes the trajectories of twenty households.

Although the sample is skewed toward middle-class families, none were

Table 6-1. Comparison of Women's Enterprises in Kinshasa 1987–89.

Enterprises	1987	1989
Doing very well	2	2
Doing well	4	2
Providing modest comfort/hope	9	5
Eking out subsistence	5	0
Failing or failed	0	11
Total	**20**	**20**

observed to improve their condition. Among low-income households the precariousness of women's small enterprises which hitherto sustained these families is revealed.

Women, Work, and Health

Everywhere that data have been collected, women are found to work longer hours than men in production; their additional domestic labor further lengthens the working day. When women cut corners on food preparation in periods of peak labor demand, as often they must to ensure the next season's food supply, family nutrition suffers. Arduous labor and frequent childbearing combine with poor nutrition to render women's health status especially precarious (Schoepf and Schoepf 1987). Due to their gender-typed responsibilities and subordinate status within the households, however, women have less respite from toil when sick. Pruitt and Reid (1984), for example, found that one in six persons interviewed in rural Bandundu in 1984 reported being ill in the two weeks preceding the survey. Of those, however, women lost 5.5 workdays while men lost 6.5 days.

Structural adjustment requires all health care to be delivered on a fee-for-service basis; consequently, more women report that they are delivering at home. In rural areas too, as health care costs increase, care is becoming less and less affordable to poor women and children who make up 90 percent of health center clientele. Other health consequences of structural adjustment on women's health will be felt in the decade 2000–2010, as women malnourished in childhood tend to be smaller and thus suffer from prolonged labor and even die during childbirth. Since education is also supported by user fees, inflation is likely to mean fewer girls in school in an already unequal situation.

In order to maximize food security in the face of transport problems and rising prices, rural women must grow most of their own provisions or barter locally. However, they cannot withdraw from the market for they must find cash for taxes, clothing, salt, soap, fish, health care, doors and windows, locks, school fees, and other social necessities (Schoepf and Schoepf 1981, 1984, 1987, Newbury 1984, 1986, Russell 1989). In areas with market access women are active in trading their crops. Several studies show that income from crops controlled by women is more likely than men's income to contribute to purchase of food and other necessities for the household (Schoepf 1987, Henn et al. 1988). Local initiatives organized by women on their own, and by women and men together, have made advances in both production and marketing (Newbury 1984, Schoepf 1985a,b). Yet efforts by the poor, even when organized in small groups, are unlikely to be able to avoid the structural constraints described in the cited studies. Why?

Improved Market Incentives Do Not Help Women Producers

What of the market incentives urged by the Berg Report? What has been the impact on women farmers of opening up the market and "getting prices right"? Decontrol of food prices in Zaire led to food production increases in the 1982–83 growing season. Since the 1983 devaluation, however, most of these efforts have been undermined by rising prices of seeds, fertilizer, and consumer goods; peasants must produce more just to survive. In 1985, the government, which had been reluctant to free food prices from controls due to fear of urban unrest, reinstituted maximum prices paid to traders' selling in the cities. This effectively lowered still further the real prices paid to producers. Since traders generally divide up the territory they cover and agree on prices they will pay, peasants are in a poor bargaining position. Yet, because they must have cash, the disadvantages of monopsony are preferred by peasants to no buyers at all, a situation common in the many areas with extremely poor roads and unbridged streams (Newbury 1984, 1986, Schoepf 1986, Russell 1988).

Development Projects Have Not Helped Women Farmers

In areas where large-scale agricultural development projects have brought new resources, entitlements have generally been differentiated by gender as well as by class. Wealthy men have obtained access to trucks, tractors, and credit. Peasant men have gained access to new seeds, fertilizer, and credit, as well as to more labor from wives. Few women have benefited; several projects have added to women's already heavy labor burdens without increasing their incomes (Schoepf 1980, 1985a,b,c, 1987; Henn et al. 1988; Newbury and Schoepf 1989). Yet, knowledge of gender-differentiated resource use has been available since the mid-1970s, at least (Mitchnick 1973).

Sometimes this knowledge has been used to exclude women from projects. Zaire's National Maize Program extended its high yielding technical package to men because planners were aware that women had less access than men to the increased labor that successful composite maize variety production requires. However, their assumption that men could call upon wives for extra labor proved incorrect in southeastern Shaba. In this area matrilineal land inheritance and matrilocal residence supported Lemba women's autonomous decision making (Schoepf 1985a). Women continued to cultivate manioc (in obligatory monocropped fields) on their intercropped gardens, so indispensable to the family food supply. Frustrated by women's resistance to project objectives—to turn the area into a monocrop cornbowl—developers blamed the "lazy peasants."

In north and central Shaba, women were not sufficiently autonomous to be able to refuse their husband's demands on their labor. Russell observed that when Luba Shankadi men began to increase maize cashcropping in 1981, the women dropped the second peanut crop and their family food gardens. In Bas-Zaire where insects and disease attacked the manioc plants in the early 1980s, women sold most of their peanut crop to obtain cash. Since peanut butter was an essential nutrient for toddlers and young children who could not obtain sufficient energy or proteins needed for growth from the manioc-based adult diet, child nutrition suffered (Schoepf 1985).

Women's Lack of Access Has Negative Impacts

When children's diets are deficient, women tend to be blamed for "ignorance" and the remedy is held to reside in nutrition education. Malnutrition, however, should be attributed to land scarcity, poverty, and women's lack of access to and control over food and cash resources. Claude Schoepf (1982), for example, found that women in Kabare Zone, South Kivu, could readily name the five food groups as taught by project-inspired nutrition education. Nevertheless, the zone had one of the highest rates of malnutrition, including kwashiorkor among women and children, because large plantations growing export crops occupied much of the cultivable land, thus reducing the area available for peasant cultivation. Male dominance within the household, men's social obligations, and pressures to pay taxes and tribute then resulted in men's appropriating women's land, leaving them insufficient land for food crop production. On the coffee and tea plantations, women's wages were so low that they were unable to purchase sufficient food to meet their own and children's nutrition needs. In general, where plantations' or peasants' cash crops compete with food crops, land and labor devoted to cultivation of the family food supply is reduced (Schoepf and Schoepf 1987).

While in most areas, norms governing relations between spouses require women to work on husbands' fields, husbands seldom work on, or contribute equally to, women's fields. In areas where men control or own the land, they are able to exercise pressure on women to cede a portion of the proceeds from cash sales. In former times, each spouse controlled the product of her or his labor. Ideological supports for a new pseudotradition were provided by missionary Christianity, by "customary courts" imposed by the colonial administration with the collaboration of male chiefs, elders, and "traditional" healers, and by Western notions of the nuclear family with a single head (Schoepf 1976, Schoepf and Schoepf 1987, Wilson 1982, Yates 1982). The result in many areas was a "double patriarchy" (Dickerman 1984).

Currently, privatization of land ownership combines with postmarital residence and gender ideology to place women at increasing disadvantage with respect to control of productive resources and of their labor (Schoepf and Schoepf 1988). The process of disadvantaging women is occurring even in areas where strong matrilineal ideology until recently protected women's rights to land and labor (Schoepf 1987). Planners have excused the failure to confer entitlements on women by referring to "customary social relations" which they assert will not be altered by project impacts. The fact is that projects have changed social relations by virtue of their assumed gender blindness.

Our interviews reveal a sharp battle of the sexes occurring at the household level. Gender conflicts are framed in normative terms. Moral discourses, elaborated in the process of forging the "double patriarchy" referred to above, serve to mediate the process. As a symbolic practice, gender conflict appears to be overdetermined: present in all classes, it is helped along by economics, politics, and ideology. Gender discourses, superabundant in the mass media as in daily life, serve to obscure and hence to mute other discourses. Fueling intrahousehold struggles, they deflect attention from other arenas in which conflict might be more transformative. One consequence of these combined changes has been the decline in the ability of many peasant households to reproduce themselves (Schoepf 1985c). The crisis of peasant reproduction has led to significant rural exodus, with even more women than men leaving the rural areas. As a result, the food self-sufficiency of the colonial period—achieved through administrative coercion—has given way to increasing food imports with concomitant outlays of foreign exchange. In addition, substitution of manioc for grain along with reduced consumption of fish, meat, and legumes has impoverished the diets of the poor in both rural and urban areas.

The Berg Report's gender blindness did not render government policies gender neutral. The effects of Zaire's structural adjustment program have thus been mediated by women's subordination within the household and by the constraints on peasant productivity and prices. They are also mediated by the state in a manner perhaps unforeseen by planners.

Impacts on Women of Reducing the Budget Deficit

Fiscal reforms contained in the IMF guidelines have been directed at reducing both budget deficits and the taxes levied on large firms. This is accomplished by redistributing the burden to local levels through so-called decentralization. Regional and *collectivité* officials have been directed to raise funds for their own operations as well as for the central government, while services are now supported by user fees. One means of generating these revenues is to levy new taxes on traders. The latter either pass them on to peasants by holding down producer prices or they leave the area, especially where poor roads make rural markets difficult to reach.

Fines are another source of local revenues. They are collected for violation of the myriad regulations governing village life: work on obligatory crops, building latrines and dish-drying racks, owning radios and dogs, keeping livestock, hunting, cutting wood, carrying party cards and baptismal certificates, etc. (Schoepf and Schoepf 1984).

Recently a new program of supervised cultivation, the *Programme d'Autosuffisance Alimentaire* (PRAAL), was instituted by Zaire's Department of Agriculture. Peasants and some urban workers have been summoned to provide labor to clear and cultivate fields under the supervision of agricultural agents who can fine those who fail to report. According to Russell, fines in 1989 are reported to be substantial for poor people—equivalent to a chicken or two.

Since "women are easier to round up and control, while men run away," as one official told Russell, women constitute the vast majority of workers on the PRAAL fields, as in *salongo* (village clean-up) and *anima-*

tion (dancing and chanting slogans). A new juridical basis for mobilizing female labor has been devised. As in the past, work obligations are assigned to household heads, formerly considered to be men. In 1989, Russell found that only women whose marriages are actually registered by the *collectivité* are considered to be married. Under this restricted definition, women living as the spouses of men who have paid bridewealth to their families—and thus are socially recognized in the community as married women—are designated by officials as unmarried household heads. As "free women" they are subject to higher rates of taxation than spouses and are responsible for *corvée* labor. Since most do not have the cash for fines and taxes, they constitute a vast unremunerated labor force.

Russell reports that PRAAL fields are extremely low yielding. Poorly sited and worked reluctantly, the crop of one 14-hectare PRAAL field was estimated equivalent to a well-managed two-hectare manioc plot. She discovered that the model for the PRAAL scheme was a successful *collectivité* which was able to use the women's fields to generate substantial revenue. This allowed it to abolish other local taxes and fines, to electrify the *collectivité* seat, and to buy a Land Rover and a truck to convey produce to market. This *collectivité* not only has a dynamic chief; it has large forest reserves with productive soils and is favorably situated near the diamond mining area of Tshikapa where produce fetches high prices unobtainable in the rural markets of Bandundu. In other words it is an area of "high potential."

Since most rural *collectivités* do not enjoy similar favorable conditions, the model's results are not replicable. Even in the favorable, "high potential" site, women's subordination within the family was used by officials to fuel the process of capital accumulation. Since women have the least control over their labor in family or community, most of the resources extracted from the rural areas were generated by women. New resources accruing to the *collectivité* were not used to lighten women's workloads by means of new technology, but to augment the resources and prestige of officials.

Gender, Trade, and AIDs

Disease epidemics often break out in periods of crisis; AIDS is no exception. Gendered differences in access to resources such as those described in this chapter have contributed to the spread of AIDS during this period of deepening crisis, as more women are forced to use sex with multiple partners to make ends meet (Schoepf et al. 1988a,b; Schoepf and Walu 1990). Epidemiologists report that about 30 percent more women than men were infected with the HIV virus in Kinshasa in 1987.

Women traders often are blamed for the ills of African societies, for high food prices, unsanitary markets, for fraud and capital flight. Irregular sector trade is a major vehicle for capital accumulation; while many traders are women, most of the large-scale operators are male. Yet female traders have been singled out in campaigns against smugglers and currency dealers.

Women traders, who are perceived by many men to be "promiscuous," also are blamed (along with "free women" assumed to be "prostitutes") for the spread of AIDS. However, male long-distance traders have many opportunities for sexual adventures. Moreover, they are likely to have wives in several towns along their routes. Wives and children provide the trader with an identity as a responsible adult, and a reason for being in the town. Affinal kin relations create opportunities for useful patron-client networks, while the women's homes shelter traders from surveillance and provide secure storage for goods. Formal sector economic and political activities also furnish wealthy men with access to multiple partners.

Differences in power, wealth, and ideology combine to make women more susceptible to infection[1] and less able to negotiate safer sex practices with their partners (Schoepf 1988, 1989b; Schoepf et al 1990). Relationships which many women have employed to ensure their own and family survival have turned into their opposite; the AIDS crisis has transformed multiple-partner sexual strategies into a death strategy. Yet deepening economic crisis means that few poor women are able to avoid sex with multiple partners. Blaming women is not only unjust; it is counterproductive to AIDS prevention efforts.

Conclusion

Anthropologists often point to the unforeseen consequences of policies when these are actually implemented. Sometimes they are more properly viewed as undeclared goals. Critiques of the Berg Report emerged immediately following its publication; hence, we can assume that its narrow policy prescriptions were intended to accomplish just what their results have shown. The primary effect of structural adjustment programs has been to continue debt reimbursement and facilitate other capital transfers. A secondary effect has been to mobilize more labor from peasant women. These suggest that the principal aims of structural adjustment programs were to provide more food for the politically volatile cities and save foreign exchange as well as to provide export crops which contribute to debt reimbursement. Thus we conclude that hiding behind reliance on the market, international and bilateral agencies have attempted to rationalize the process of extracting resources, first upward from women producers to officials and traders, thence outward from Africa to the West.

Like most other sub-Saharan African nations and much of the Third World, Zaire is in the throes of economic turmoil. Propelled by declining terms of trade and burdensome debt service, the contradictions of distorted peripheral economies combined with rapid class formation have created what appears to be permanent, deepening crisis. Within Zaire, the overall thrust of current policy is to encourage commercialization of agriculture at all levels. Credit, input supply, and resources of development projects are directed mainly to large- and medium-scale landowners, most of whom are men with political connections. It appears that in this arena, too, the market is an ideological cloak. Hiding behind the market is a political process in which new resources can be garnered to enhance economic power (Newbury and Schoepf 1989).

Gender ideology and the roles it imposes are crucial to this accumulation process, for they justify continuing differences in resource access. Women have less access to and control over productive resources including land and labor as well as project inputs such as credit, improved seeds, fertilizer, and extension information. New agricultural resources including donor-assisted projects, in Zaire as elsewhere, are usually directed to men. Formerly, women were considered "too traditional" to change. The current rationale is that women are "too overburdened" to make efficient use of resources. Since women are the main producers of food for mass consumption, it is clear that raising consumption levels of poor families has not been a priority of the 1980s. Instead, poor women and children are being made to pay with their work and health for past and present policies.

Policy makers who continue to rely on macroeconomic prescriptions to "get prices right" without also taking a close look at the microlevel implications of those normative policies will continue to reproduce, justify, and strengthen economic and sociopolitical inequality. Zaire's crisis continues to be a harbinger of things to come elsewhere on the subcontinent. The case of Zaire indicates that what is needed for Africa's development is not structural adjustment, but structural transformation. Linking macroeconomic factors to microlevel studies with a gendered focus suggests the need for a transformation of societal structures in a manner quite different than that involved in improving the economic indicators to which neoclassical macroeconomists attend.

NOTES

1. Although small-scale female operators in the transborder trade "are only the tip of the iceberg" (as one reporter acknowledged), attacking the tip is safer (*Elima* August 25, 1986; March 4–5, 1988).

REFERENCES

Dickerman, Carol
   1984   City Women and the Colonial Regime: Usumbura, 1939–62. *African Urban Studies* 18 (Spring): 33–48.
Henn, Jean, Diane Russell, D. Smith, B. Horwith, N. Nlandu, G. Mbaranga, M. Kanyangambe, and M. Mwema
   1988   Mission-Wide Evaluation of Women in Development, Sept. 26–Nov. 21. Kinshasa: USAID/Zaire.
Mitchnick, David
   1973   Women and Development in Zaire. Kinshasa: OXFAM/United Kingdom.
Newbury, Catharine
   1984   Ebutumwa Bw'Emiogo: The Tyranny of Cassava, A Women's Tax Revolt in Eastern Zaire. *Canadian Journal of African Studies* 18 (1): 35–54.
   1986   Survival Strategies in Rural Zaire: Realities of Coping with Crisis. *The Crisis in Zaire: Myths and Realities*, Nzongola-Ntalaja, ed. Trenton, NJ: Africa World Press.
Newbury, Catharine, and Brooke G. Schoepf
   1988   State, Peasantry and Agrarian Crisis in Zaire: Does Gender Make a Difference? *Women and the State in Africa*, Jane L. Parpart and Kathleen A. Staudt, eds. Boulder, CO: Lynne Reinner.
Pruitt, William, and Elizabeth Reid
   1984   Bandundu Farm Households Survey. Kinshasa: USAID/Zaire.
Pruitt, W., B.G. Schoepf, E. Gerard, and M. Morand
   1985   Priorite des Priorites, Zaire African Food Systems Initiative Assessment Team Report. April 18. Peace Corps, Washington, D.C.
Russell, Diane
   1988   The Outlook for Liberalization in Zaire: Evidence from Kisangani's Rice Trade. Boston: Boston University, Center for African Studies, WP No.139.
   1989   "Liberalization" and the Local Economy in Zaire: The Case of the Rice Trade in Kisangani. Paper presented at US African Studies Association annual meeting, Atlanta, November 2–5, 1989.

Schoepf, Brooke G.

1976   Recherches en Anthropologie Medicale: Theorie et Perspectives Methodologiques, *Bulletin d'Anthropologie Medicale* (Lubumbashi) 1:2 (Aug.): 20–36.

1978   Women in the Informal Economy of Lubumbashi. Paper presented at Fourth International Congress of African Studies, Kinshasa, December.

1980   Women and Development: Overcoming the Colonial Legacy in Africa. *The Exchange Report: Women in the Third World,* Jill Kneerim, ed. New York: International Exchange of Development Resources.

1981   *The Role of U.S. Universities in International Rural and Agricultural Development.* Tuskegee Institute, Center for Rural Development.

1982   Technology Transfer, Values and Social Relations in Health. *Proceedings of the Tuskegee Institute Inaugural Symposium,* Paul Wall, ed. Tuskegee Institute: Carver Research Foundation.

1983   Unintended Consequences and Structural Predictability: Man and Biosphere in Zaire's Lufira Valley. *Human Organization* 42(4) (Winter): 361–67.

1984   Man and Biosphere in Zaire. *The Politics of Agriculture in Tropical Africa,* Jonathan Barker, ed., pp. 269–90. Beverly Hills: Sage Publishers.

1985a   The 'Wild,' the 'Lazy' and the 'Matriarchal': Nutrition and Cultural Survival in the Zairian Copperbelt, East Lansing: Michigan State University, Women in International Development Working Paper No. 96.

1985b   Macroeconomy, Microeconomy, Women's Roles and Introducing Agricultural Change. Pruitt, Schoepf et al.

1985c   Food Crisis and Class Formation: An Example from Shaba. *Review of African Political Economy,* No. 33: 33–43.

1986   Macrosystem and Gender Roles in Farming Systems Research: The Case of Zaire. Paper presented at the Conference on Gender Issues in Farming Systems Research and Extension, University of Florida, Gainesville, March.

1987   Social Structure, Women's Status and Sex Differential Nutrition in the Zairian Copperbelt. *Urban Anthropology* 16 (1): 73–102.

1988   Women, AIDS and Economic Crisis in Central Africa. *Canadian Journal of African Studies* 22(3): 625–644.

1989a   Knowledge of Women, Women's Knowledge: Texts of 'Tradition' and 'Modernity' in Zaire. Paper submitted for Conference on the Transfer of Knowledge From Europe to Africa, Duke University, September.

1989b   At Risk for AIDS: Women's Lives in Zaire. Colloquium, Murray Research Center, Radcliffe College. December 12.

Schoepf, Brooke G., and Claude Schoepf
    1981   Zaire's Rural Development in Perspective. *The Role of U.S. Universities in International Rural and Agricultural Development*, Brooke G. Schoepf, ed. Tuskegee Institute, Center for Rural Development.
    1984   Peasants, Capitalists and the State in the Lufira Valley. *Canadian Journal of African Studies* 18 (1): 89–93.
    1987   Food Crisis and Agrarian Change in the Eastern Highlands of Zaire. *Urban Anthropology* 16 (1): 5–37.
Schoepf, Brooke, Nkera Rukarangira, Claude Schoepf, Walu Engundu, and N. Payanzo
    1988a   AIDS and Society in Central Africa: A View from Zaire. *AIDS in Africa: Social and Policy Impact*, Norman Miller and Richard Rockwell, eds. Lewiston, NY: Mellen Press.
    1988b   AIDS, Women and Society in Central Africa. *AIDS, 1988: AAAS Symposium Papers*, R. Kulstad, ed. Washington, D.C.: American Association for the Advancement of Science.
    1991   Action-Research on AIDS with Women in Kinshasa. Paper presented at 1st SIECS, Ixtapa, Mexico, October. Forthcoming in *Social Science and Medicine*.
Schoepf, Brooke G., and Walu Engundu
    1990   Women's Trade and Contributions to Household Budgets in Kinshasa. *The Second Economy in Zaire*, J. MacGaffey, ed. London: James Currey.
Schoepf, Claude
    1982   Results of Base-Line Survey in Four Localities near INERA Mulungu Station, Kivu Province. Report for USAID/Zaire.
Walu, Engundu
    1987   La Contribution des Femmes aux Budgets Menagers a Kinshasa. Research Report for the World Bank, June.
World Bank
    1981   *Accelerated Development in Sub-Saharan Africa: An Agenda for Action.* Washington, D.C.: World Bank.
    1986   *Financing Adjustment with Growth in Sub-Saharan Africa.* Washington, D.C.: World Bank.
    1989   *Sub-Saharan Africa: From Crisis to Sustainable Growth.* Washington, D.C.: World Bank.

7

The Impact of Structural Adjustment Programs on Rural Women in Tanzania

Ruth Meena

From the mid-1970s, Tanzania started to experience economic decline and stagnation. The Gross Domestic Product (GDP) stagnated at a rate of 1.5 percent per annum while the real per capita income declined at about 2 percent per annum (Havenvik, Kjaerby et al. 1988) In fact, the 1985 GDP was 10 percent below the 1978 level. Taking population increases into consideration, the real GDP declined at a rate of 12 percent from 1979–85. The rate of inflation has also been increasing. Before 1972 the inflation rate was below 5 percent, but by 1974 it had increased to 10 percent, reaching a peak of 26 percent in 1978. Because of the coffee boom in 1976/77 it decreased to 13 percent, only to increase during the 1980s to range between 20–40 percent.

The crisis has been caused by an accumulation of factors. These include: a deterioration of terms of trade, stagnation of agriculture, the war between Tanzania and Uganda, and fiscal policies which perpetuated the crisis. Between 1977–81, the terms of trade index fell from 133 to 85, or 15 percent below the 1972 level. Agriculture also declined during the 1970s because of drought and declining world prices. The situation worsened when the Tanzanian-Ugandan war forced the government to spend about $500 million or 10 percent of annual GDP.

In responding to the crisis, the Tanzanian government was forced into drawing over its gold reserves at the same time as it requested additional credit from the International Monetary Fund (IMF) to temporarily solve its balance of payment problems. The government of Tanzania was allowed to draw on the low conditional oil facility and received compen-

Ruth Meena is Senior Lecturer and Ph.D. candidate, Department of Political Science and Public Administration, University of Dar es Salaam. She is also a member of the Women's Research and Documentation Projects (WRDP). She has been awarded a Fulbright Senior Fellowship in 1984 and has won the IDRC/Ford Foundation Social Science Research Competitions for Eastern Africa in 1984 and 1986.

satory financing from 1975 to 1976 (United Republic of Tanzania 1986). In the negotiations that followed between the IMF and the government of Tanzania, the IMF provided conditions for its continued support of the Tanzanian government's endeavor to solve its balance of payment problem. These conditions included: devaluation of the currency, imposition of a wage freeze, abolition of price controls, increase of (agricultural) producer prices, increase of interest rates, removal of import controls, and restraints on government expenditure (United Republic of Tanzania, 1986). Some of these conditions had the following gender implications.

Devaluation

Devaluation was required by the IMF on the grounds that it would motivate agricultural producers because it would increase the local value of domestic products. The assumption was that the value that was going to be realized would automatically be transferred to the producers. Further, all the producers, including men and women, would have equal opportunity to benefit from the price increases of agricultural products. It was also assumed that agricultural producers were all going to respond positively to market forces.

This has not always been the case. Between 1973 and 1982, for instance, there was a dramatic decline in production of 14 crops whose export value was 82 percent of the total. This was in spite of the fact that the average weighted price of these crops was 55 percent higher in 1982 than in 1973 (Havenvik, Kjaerby et al. 1989). By implication, an increase of producer prices does not automatically lead to increased production. The relationship between increased producer prices and production increases has to take into consideration *gender*. Questions to be answered include: who are the producers, who controls the products of labor, and how is labor distributed or shared in a given context.

Devaluation has been eroding the real wages of both rural population and urban population alike. When devaluation erodes the real income of peasants, there is a tendency for the male population to migrate to urban areas to seek wage employment. But even if wage employment is available to a significant proportion of the population, wages alone do not enable wage earners to subsist. The female adult population that remains in the rural sector often increases its workload, not only in order to fend for the family, but also to subsidize the wage earner in the urban area.

Indeed, women have always been the "shock absorbers" of socioeconomic crises. Women, whether in the urban or rural sector, have had to engage in some form of informal activity to subsidize household income. The conditions under which these informal activities operate have often been pathetic. Start-up capital for these projects has been extremely low and activities continue without sufficient official support (Chungu, Mandara et al. 1989). And yet it is because of these activities that African governments in severe socioeconomic crises have been able to maintain some political stability.

While women constitute the majority of agricultural producers, and while the law provides for equality in ownership of property and productive assets, in practice women do *not* enjoy the right to land ownership because of many traditions which discriminate against them. By allowing market forces to determine the process of production and ownership patterns, as demanded by the IMF, recovery measures have subjected women to the vagaries of market forces. Under market forces, women who do not control domestic resources cannot compete with men in purchasing land, whereas under Ujamaa policy they would have had access and legal rights to own and control the land in their own right.

Abolition of Price Controls and Removal of Subsidies

The IMF accused the government of bad pricing policies and food subsidies, which had the effect of decreasing farmers' incentives to produce and favoring urban dwellers, because they forced prices of agricultural products down. The proposed reform was to increase producer prices paid to farmers and thus increase their incentives to produce. Unfortunately, several of the assumptions underlying this reform strategy were faulty. First, it assumed that government taxation would permit agricultural producers to control the new surplus. This has not always been the case. Given the fact that the crisis also forced the government to cut its budget, the government has been seeking for ways to offset its own budget deficit, and taxation of farm products has constituted one way of managing the budget crisis.

Second, it assumed that price increases would benefit all producers equally, and all agricultural producers had in practice equal rights in controlling the products of their labor. Although women in Tanzania constitute the majority of agricultural producers, they do not automatically benefit from improvements in the agricultural sector—especially improvements of cash crops which are mainly controlled by men. Recent studies show that increased producer prices which are supposed to motivate farmers have not generated improvements in household income. At the household level, women do not control family resources, including income accruing from the sale of cash crops (Nkoma and Meena 1990).

The issue of price control does not take into consideration the existing sexual division of labor which is unfavorable to women because it demands that women do back-breaking work with tools of low productivity. Women's specific tasks on farm include: land clearing, weeding, harvesting, storing and preservation, headloading, and marketing. To do the weeding, women have traditionally used the hand-hoe as the main tool of production. In our research in a cotton-producing region, we could not find a single woman smallholder owning either an ox plow or tractor or wheelbarrow—tools which make farming easier in this region. The use of tractors or plows for cultivation has remained a dream for women. The whole region has only 308 tractors out of which only 100 are in good running condition, and all these are owned by men. Women cannot even hire tractors because of the increased costs of tractor hiring. Thus, even though cultivation by tractor would make work easier and would increase production, women farmers do not seem to have a choice.

Women thus continue to use small hand hoes which force them to

Figure 7-1. SAPs assume that price increases should benefit all producers equally; but they do not take into consideration the existing sexual division of labor which is unfavorable to women.

bend over for long periods of time as they weed. This activity is tedious and time consuming. Bending over for long periods of time, especially if done by pregnant women, causes back problems and other ailments which are yet to be scientifically analyzed. When weeding is not properly done, crop production is negatively affected. There is thus a need to improve tools used for weeding.

Besides weeding, the cotton crop has to be sprayed against insects and other pests, while soils have to be enriched by adding either animal manure or chemical fertilizers. And removal of subsidies has also meant removal of subsidies of fertilizer and other farm inputs and implements (Gladwin, this volume). Consequently, there has been a constant increase of prices of chemical fertilizers and other agro-chemicals needed for production. From 1985/88 for instance, the price of chemical fertilizers has been increasing as seen in Table 7-1. Similarly, prices of insecticides have been increasing, which limits the ability of farmers to utilize insecticides needed for crop production.

Thus, whereas in 1987/87 a farmer could have purchased a ULV pump by selling 48.99 kilograms of cotton, in 1987/88 the farmer had to sell 61.24 kilograms of his cotton to purchase the same item. Similarly, whereas a farmer needed to sell 131 kilograms of his cotton in 1986/87 to purchase a sprayer pump, and a package of basically needed agro-chemicals—including one liter of thiodine, one 50 kilogram bag of fertilizer (CA), one ULV pump and six batteries for the pump; in 1987/88 the farmer had to sell up to 178 kilograms of cotton to buy the same inputs. Therefore, even if we were to assume that women would have benefited from the increased producer price of cotton, the 20 percent increase in the

Table 7-1. Comparative Farmgate Prices for Farm Inputs for Three Consecutive Seasons.

INPUTS	1985/86	1986/87	1987/88
Fertilizer TSP (50 kg bag)	322.00	533.00	865.00
Fertilizer CAN (50 kg bag)	273.35	375.00	620.00
Fertilizer S/A (850 kg bag)	233.75	410.00	670.00
Thodan	71.90	95.40	335.00
ROPCORD	21.90	95.40	335.00
ULV pumps	719.20	953.20	1430.00
ULV Bottles	5.00	10.00	15.00
Cotoran 500 FW (per 1 ton)	115.70	153.30	695.00
Knsack Sprayer	895.30	3300.00	8000.00

Source: Meena and Kristosia 1988: 23–24.

price of cotton was not enough to pay the farmer for the increased price in necessary farm inputs.

An increase in crop prices has not matched the increasing price of farm implements and inputs which have been rising because of inflation and devaluation. Unless there is a mechanism for controlling prices of these necessary inputs and implements needed by the farmers, the increase of crop prices mandated by structural adjustment policies will not lead to an improvement in the economic status of all farmers.

We also observed that crops which are normally controlled by women such as vegetables, fruits, peas, and beans—food crops—do not get the necessary cash inputs. Why? Since women do not receive cash from the sales of cash crops, they do not have money to purchase agro-chemicals— fertilizers and insecticides—for use on food crops.

In fact, increased producer prices for cash (export) crops may *negatively* affect women by forcing them to spend more of their time on the cash crops and less of their time on their own crops, such as vegetables and fruits. In Mwanza region, for example, there has been a tendency to emphasize cotton and de-emphasize the production of other crops, especially those controlled by women. Horticultural activities constitute a very insignificant agricultural activity in Mwanza region; 7,450 hectares are used for this purpose; and farmers get very low prices for fruits and vegetables (Meena and Kristosia 1988).

While men and women have been jointly responsible for harvesting crops, men have been pulling out from ferrying harvested crops to homes and to primary societies for marketing, due to the increased price of the necessary implements. In Mwanza region, both men and women used bicycles or ox carts to ferry cotton from the farms. Today, bicycles are no longer affordable for the majority of the rural population. For women, it is a distant dream to own and use bicycles since they do not control cash income from the cash crops. Whereas in 1983/84 a bicycle cost 1,874 Tshs (Tanzanian shillings) and in 1984/85 it cost 2,500 Tshs, now it costs up to 20,000 Tshs. Similarly, in 1984/88 a wheelbarrow to transport crops from the farms cost 1500 Tshs; in 1986/87 it increased to 3,000 Tshs; and in 1987/88 the price increased to 10,000 Tshs. Ox carts have similarly increased from 5,000 Tshs to 40,000 Tshs during the same period (Meena and Kristosia 1988).

Price increases of these implements have negatively affected women's workload as women have been responsible for transporting cotton and other crops from the farm to their respective homes and to primary societies before marketing; men are gradually withdrawing from this activity.

When there is alternative means of transport such as a bicycle, wheelbarrow or ox cart, the men cooperate in this activity; otherwise it becomes women's business, thus adding to their labor burden.

Price is thus an ineffective instrument to motivate agricultural producers in increasing production, if (1) there is a mismatch between increases in prices of necessary farm inputs and increases in producer prices, or if (2) there is no mechanism to ensure that the surplus which is accrued from the increased producer price benefits all the producers, including women. A price increase of cash crops whose income is not controlled by women cannot motivate women farmers who have nothing to gain from these increases. Further, in pricing policy there often seems to be discrimination against food crops, especially in those regions which are supposed to be producing some form of cash crops such as coffee, cotton, tea, etc. From 1972, the government of Tanzania started to implement a pricing policy which aimed at discouraging cash crop producers from growing other crops or engaging in other activities which might interfere with cotton production. This policy negatively affected the economic status of women who normally control food crops—grains and all horticultural products. In Mwanza region, for example, there seems to be a deliberate policy to discourage farmers from growing vegetables and fruits; these crops do not get extension services (Mwanza Agricultural Officer, personal communication). The economic return for fruits and vegetables is very low and there has been no price incentive offered for these crops, and yet these are crops controlled by women which provide households with the main source of income and food security. Consequently, there is an observable decline of both fruits and vegetable in this region. In 1985/86, for instance, approximately 1095.93 tons of vegetables were harvested while in 1986/87 only 943.3 tons were harvested.

Expenditure Restraints and Wage Freezes

In addition to price controls, the IMF has advised the government to redirect investment priorities away from "nonproductive" sectors to "productive" sectors and to freeze wages. The implementation of these directives has negatively affected the rural poor, particularly women. Why? First, the inability of the Tanzanian state to adjust the income of workers to correspond with inflation rates has been causing suffering to the people and specifically women during the period of the crisis (Campbell 1986, Kiondo 1988, Nkoma and Meena 1990). Women have been forced to supplement family income by engaging in a variety of activities in addition to their already heavy labor burden. Second, expenditure cuts can involve two levels: either through budget cuts in factor incomes or through cuts in the provision of social services. In either case, it inevitably negatively impacts on the lives of the people. The socio-economic crisis has already reduced the government's capacity to invest in the social service sector as illustrated in Table 7-2 below. Yet the IMF is insisting that the government further cut its budget in what is considered to be a "non-productive" sector—social services.

The Tanzanian state has been relying upon instruments of financial restraint to overcome the crisis, because revenue enhancement measures—increased taxes—would conflict with the interests of the state and international capital. Revenue enhancement measures might have entailed changing patterns of foreign exchange allocation, institutional discipline in financial management, as well as a substantial increase of external resources. Because this option was not selected, the government budget for social services declined in real terms in 1986/87, as shown in Table 7-2. It was also considered easier to administer cuts in public expenditure than to initiate revenue enhancement measures. But such measures have not only undermined the achievements made during the early 1970s; they have also caused great suffering in the lives of the people, specifically women.

Table 7-2. Total Government Recurrent and Development Expenditure by Sector.

	1980/81	81/82	82/83	83/84	84/85	85/86	86/87
Social Services							
Education	1473	1613	1738	2440	2524	2890	2009
Health	688	721	789	981	1020	1131	977
Social welfare	37	52	44	51	54	67	59
Housing and community development	108	45	190	187	209	217	119
Other social services	240	277	176	332	374	448	590
Water and electricity	773	639	597	1027	880	1003	564
Subtotal	3319	3447	3534	5018	5061	5756	4318
Defense	3194	1110	1612	2308	1555	2660	2377
Other sectors	6497	9857	9748	11670	12383	14199	17985
Total	13036	14413	14895	18998	18993	22615	24680
Social Services as % Total	25.5%	23.9%	23.7%	26.4%	26.7%	25.5%	17.5%

Source: United Republic of Tanzania 1980–89.

From the early 1970s, the Tanzanian government started expanding social services, in order to benefit the majority of rural population. The government was pursuing what was considered to be a gender-sensitive social policy that had the full support of the international community. Commending the achievements which the government was making, a UNICEF mission in 1983 observed that:

> Tanzania's experience demonstrates that some of the features of poverty can be eradicated at quite low income levels, within a short period of time, by appropriate selective government policies, in a peaceful manner, and in conditions of political stability (Government of Tanzania and UN Children's Fund 1985: 56).

Cuts in Health Services

Tanzania's Economic Recovery Programme (ERP) did not create the crisis in the health sector, but it made the crisis worse. The impact of the crisis was already being felt in the health sector before the launching of the ERP. The total government expenditure had been decreasing from the peak level of 9 percent in 1973/74 to 5.2 percent in 1984/85 (United Republic of Tanzania Ministry of Health 1980–89). This percentage further decreased to 4.9 percent in 1985/86. Why? The IMF recommended that the community should take a greater role in the provision of its own health services. This recommendation was made at a time when the real income of the people had deteriorated and the state had already invested in infrastructure for health services.

The state had already assumed the responsibility of taking care of the health of the people when it established various institutions such as the Primary Health Care Services, Maternal and Child Health Services, Regional and National Hospitals, etc. During the 1970s there was a rapid expansion of the health services. Rural health clinics increased from 22 at independence to 161 in 1976 to 260 in 1987. Similarly the number of dispensaries increased from 1,847 in 1976 to 2,831 in 1986 (Johnsson 1988). In 1982 there was one rural health center per 75,732 people and one dispensary per 6,846; by 1986 the corresponding figures were 84,231 and 7,736 (ibid.). Similarly health personnel increased from 1.81 per thousand to 1.90 per thousand between 1978 and 1984 (ibid.). The government had also established a Mother and Child Health Services program in 1974. The objective of the program was to achieve universal immunization by 1988. By 1985/86 it was estimated that about 80 percent of all children had been immunized against tuberculosis and 67 percent against measles (Johnsson 1988).

The institutional infrastructure which the health service had established required both financial and human resources for its maintenance. Personnel had to be paid and given instruments to render their services effectively. Physical structures had to be maintained and equipment needed replacement. Rural health centers, dispensaries, and hospitals had to be stocked with medicine and equipment. There was also a growing demand from the people for the expansion of such services.

It was against this background that the IMF demanded the redirection of priories from "nonproductive" sectors—like health—to "productive" sectors. Although the government of Tanzania resisted by attempting to keep constant its allocation to the health sector (Table 7-2), the amount allocated has been affected by devaluation and the changing patterns of the donor community. The declining budget for the Ministry of Health is not only undermining the achievements already made but is also affecting the health of the people in general and particularly that of women and children.

In a 1988 interview with the Director of Medical Services in the Ministry of Health, we were informed that most of the regional and district administrative units did not have sufficient funds to purchase necessary medicine for their hospitals. Although the import support scheme, which aims at improving industrial capacity utilization, has supported pharmaceuticals in improving the production of essential drugs, the situation is that medical stores are overflooded with medicines and hospitals are facing an acute shortage of essential drugs.

Women and children have been the most vulnerable groups affected by government budget cuts in the health sector. By 1978, almost 95 percent of all pregnant women were visiting Maternal and Child Health Services; and 53 percent of deliveries took place in health institutions. More than 56 percent of all deliveries were being done under the supervision of trained medical personnel. In spite of these achievements, maternal deaths have been increasing at an alarming rate due to deterioration in the health services—especially the Maternal and Child Health Services. During early 1988 for instance, 71 mothers died in the Muhumbili Medical Center during the first 13 weeks of January, compared to 65–70 deaths recorded annually in the previous years. Maternal deaths are estimated to be approximating 3,000–4,000 per year (Makaranga 1990) due to poor services and increasing malnourishment among pregnant women.

The condition of women is worsened by the fact that women are overburdened with both productive and reproductive roles. The fertility rate for Tanzanian women continues to be about 7 live births per woman. The mean age of a rural woman at first birth is 17 years and on average mothers in rural Tanzania breastfeed their children for 18 months. This means that rural women are spending 17–20 years being pregnant and breast-feeding children. Unfortunately, this time period coincides with their prime productive years (Havenvik, Kjaerby et al. 1988).

Further, the unequal distribution of labor means that women's health is very important. Studies have shown that, while the labor input of women in agricultural production is 71 percent, men's and children's labor input is 19 percent and 9 percent respectively (Havenvik, Kjaerby et al. 1988). Agricultural production thus depends upon the labor input of women and this in turn will be determined by their health. We do not see the possibility of improving their production while leaving the health of producers and that of their offspring unattended. Investment in health should therefore be considered an investment in human capital, for a healthy population is an asset for any nation. It is thus absurd to separate "productive" sectors from "nonproductive" sectors in countries where productivity is so dependent upon muscle power.

Cuts in Education Services

The IMF package has also provided conditions which discourage the Tanzanian government from investing in the educational sector. This is in spite of the fact that history has demonstrated the relationship between productivity and the level of knowledge of the labor force. In the early 1970s, the Tanzanian government embarked on ambitious educational programs for both youths and adults through the Universal Primary Education and Mass Literacy Campaigns, respectively. In these educational campaigns, there were conscious efforts to bring about equality between the sexes. Whereas in 1960 only less than a quarter of school children attended school, by 1984 universal primary education had been achieved; and half of primary students were girls. By 1987 adult literacy had reached 85 percent; and women constituted a very significant percentage of the new literates (United Republic of Tanzania 1980–89).

As with health services, Tanzania's Economic Recovery Programme (ERP) did not create the crisis in education, but it made the crisis worse. Before the launching of the ERP, the education sector was already experiencing an education crisis which resulted from unavailability of resources. The amount of government allocation to this sector had already started to decline in relationship to other sectors. While in 1981/82 the government allocated 18 percent of the total budget to education, this percentage decreased to 8 percent in 1984/85.

One of the demands of the IMF package on the education sector was that education had to pursue policies for adjustment, revitalization, and expansion (IBRD 1987). Cost recovery measures in the education sector included transferring the responsibility for the construction of primary schools from the government to the people, introducing cost sharing measures by instituting school fees at increased levels, encouraging and promoting Self Reliance Activities, and promoting private involvement in the education services (IBRD 1987).

The above conditions have the following gender implications. First, in places where the majority of the male population has migrated to urban areas seeking employment opportunities, women will be called upon to contribute their labor in the construction of these primary schools. This will further increase their labor burden. Second, cost sharing will mean that women will shoulder the burden of school fees either by paying them directly, or by supplementing family income, thus enabling their husbands to pay school fees. Third, permitting market forces to control enrollment at all levels will subject women to competition based on financial power rather than intellectual ability. Such competition might eliminate intelligent persons—especially women—whose labor is crucially needed for the survival of communities.

The IMF educational package has negatively affected both the quality and quantity of education at all levels. The introduction of user charges in a period when there has been actual erosion of real wages and real incomes has negatively influenced the amount and quality of education being offered to the children of the poor. The effect of user charges on the education process is yet to be carefully analyzed.

The freezing of wages of the workers as a measure to control and reduce government expenditure will further erode teachers' salaries, which were already low by any standard. In 1983, primary school teachers were receiving an annual salary which was an equivalent of US$662 against US$1,233 for Kenya and US$2,255 for sub-Saharan Africa (UNESCO 1988). The erosion of teachers' wages will mainly affect a large percentage of women who seem to constitute the majority of primary school teachers living in the rural sector. By implication, this will force such women to engage in extra activities to supplement their salaries at the expense of professional improvement.

The financial dimensions of the adjustment program in the education sector will have a much more long-term effect than anticipated by the architects of the ERP. A UNESCO mission observed that:

Overall, the results have not been satisfactory so far: communities responded rather poorly to the challenge; fees are not collected regularly and there is no accountability or control mechanism; textbooks remain unpurchased in stores and the ESR activities yielded little (for secondary schools and technical colleges around three percent of their recurrent budget) for lack of initiative, shortage of initial capital, overloaded timetables and lack of control and accountability (Government of Tanzania and UNESCO 1988).

In terms of quality and quantity all levels of the education sector are being negatively affected. In the primary education sector, for instance, the UNESCO mission was worried that the quality has deteriorated to such low levels that the "system has started to turn out illiterates" (Government of Tanzania and UNESCO 1988). It was also observed that in tests of English, mathematics, Kiswahili, and numerical skills in a representative sample of primary schools, 75 percent of pupils scored below 15 points out of a total of 50.

The government has been spending less and less on primary schools than on other sectors of education. Less than US$30 is allocated as per capital recurrent expenditure per primary school pupil. The actual amount is low in absolute and relative terms, when compared to other levels, as illustrated in Tables 7-3 to 7-5.

Given the above picture it is obvious that the government cannot purchase necessary teaching materials or pay a sufficient amount to the teachers to motivate them or spend sufficient amounts of funds to maintain the physical structures. It also means that it will be difficult for government to expand primary schools to keep pace with population growth. Indeed both the learning and the working environment is demoralizing.

Table 7-3. Percentage Distribution of Public Expenditure on Education by Level of Education.

	1982			1986		
	Revenue	Capital	Total	Revenue	Capital	Total
Administration	6.0	15.9	7.1	5.0	17.6	7.7
Primary Education	53.2	19.8	49.6	56.6	12.1	47.1
Secondary Education	13.3	14.1	13.3	14.1	20.0	15.4
Teacher Training	5.7	12.4	6.4	6.5	6.5	6.9
Technical Education	1.7	14.9	3.2	1.5	20.9	5.4
Higher Education	12.6	10.7	12.4	12.5	15.5	13.1
Adult Education	7.5	12.2	8.0	3.8	6.3	4.4
	100.0	100.0	100.0	100.0	100.0	100.0

Source: Government of Tanzania and UNESCO 1988.

Table 7-4. Primary Education Unit Recurrent Expenditures (in Tsh constant 1980 prices).

	1981	1982	1983	1986
Recurrent Expenditures (Tsh billions)	803.8	728.1	634.9	646.8
Enrollment (000)	3538	3276	3727	3155
Unit Recurrent Expenditure (Tsh)	226	222	170	205

Source: Government of Tanzania and UNESCO 1988.

It is no wonder that enrollment rates have been declining while the drop-out rates at primary school for both sexes is alarming (United Republic of Tanzania, Ministry of Education 1987). Drop-out rates for primary education, level one, for instance, increased from 2.2 percent in 1980/81 to 9.1 percent in 1985/85. Between 1982 and 1986, on the other hand, enrollment rates for standard one to seven decreased by 68 percent (United Republic of Tanzania, Ministry of Education 1982-86). This trend is undermining the attempt to build up a literate labor force for the rural sector. If this trend continues unchecked, it will finally mean that the investments which have been made in education have been wasted. Given the fact that women play a big role in both production and reproduction, their level of education has a positive impact on the quality of life for communities. Given the fact that the quality of primary education determines the quality of other levels, there is a genuine need to keep and maintain this quality at whatever cost.

Secondary education has similarly been affected by the economic crisis and its condition is being worsened by the implementation of the ERP. Tanzania has an unusually small secondary school sector. When compared

Table 7-5. Trends in Public Capital Expenditure on Total Education and Primary Education (in Tsh 000's).

	1981	1982	1983	1984	1985
1. Total for Education	354,828	270,205	346,329	478,284	591,050
2. Total for Primary Education	54,075	53,650	57,329	56,983	65,290
3. Total for Primary Education in Constant 1980 Prices	40,411	31,127	26,141	—	17,127
4. (2) as % of (1)	15.2	19.9	16.6	11.9	11.0

Source: Government of Tanzania and UNESCO 1988.

Table 7-6. Recurrent Expenditure on Public Secondary Education.

	1982	1983	1984	1985	1986
In Tsh (million)					
in current prices	255.0	394.1	329.0	475.2	753.4
in constant 1980 prices	181.6	159.8	—	131.6	161.3
Unit Revenue Cost					
in Tsh current prices	7545	8279	10355	11175	17410
in constant 1980 prices	4400	3800	—	2900	3500

Source: Government of Tanzania and UNESCO 1988.

to other countries in sub-Saharan Africa, after Rwanda it has the smallest (UNESCO 1988). In 1983 only 3 percent of primary school leavers had places in secondary schools, compared to 19 percent in Kenya and 20 percent for sub-Saharan Africa. This percentage has increased to 5.5 percent in 1986 and has had a slight increase to 6.3 percent in 1987/88 (United Republic of Tanzania, Ministry of Education 1988). The increase in enrollment of secondary schools has resulted from expansion of private secondary schools. Both public and private schools compete for the same resources for textbooks, teachers, and other instructional materials. The private schools in the majority of cases are in a disadvantaged position in terms of resource availability. This is reflected in the performance of these schools in the national examinations. As in the primary schools, there has been an acute shortage of teaching materials at this level. The science laboratories have gone without equipment and science practicals have ceased to be taught. The performance of girls in science seems to be negatively affected as the number of female students qualifying for science subjects has deteriorated over the past years (United Republic of Tanzania, Ministry of Education 1980).

Less expenditure on secondary education has the following implications to the education sector generally and to the economy. If the government is unable to expand this sublevel it will imply that a significant pro-

Table 7-7. Capital Expenditure on Public Secondary Education.

	1982	1983	1984	1985	1986
In Tsh (millions)					
in current prices	38.0	49.9	56.9	80.1	88.2
in constant 1980 prices	22.0	22.7	—	21.0	58.6

Source: Government of Tanzania and UNESCO 1988.

portion of its labor resource will remain with only a primary education. This will have a definite impact on productivity. Poorly prepared secondary school pupils will be ill-prepared to cope with university education, especially when the university is also going through a similar crisis. In the final analysis it will mean producing university graduates who are not well equipped to manage the high-level manpower positions in the economy. Finally, secondary school leavers are mainly employed in the middle-level jobs as technical staff, machine operators, craftsmen, clerical staff, teachers, etc. Without a sound educational background these professionals will neither be able to cope with professional training nor will they manage properly the skill demands placed on them by their respective jobs and professions. In the long run inadequacies at this level will have a tremendous impact on the productivity of the economy.

Similarly, education expenditure for higher education has also been affected by the crisis and ERP.[1] In the academic year 1988/89 the University of Dar es Salaam was allocated less than two-thirds of its required budget. Already the university was going through a crisis of teaching material, lack of textbooks, maintenance funds, etc. The university had already been forced to reduce practical training for students and resort to theoretical learning, a contradiction of the principles spelled out in the Arusha Declaration. The university was also forced to postpone the academic year of 1988/89 because it had run out of funds. This was costly because salaries had to be paid to those who service this institution, even though those services were not rendered. Time was also wasted when students boycotted classes because their allowances did not correspond with the costs of food and other services they required.

The limited learning environment at the university affects female students in a special way. Those who are already mothers find it hard to maintain their families with the allowances they are getting. Some of them resort to cost-saving measures, which include cooking their own food in the hostel where cooking facilities have never been made available. The effect of this on their performance is yet to be studied. The scarcity of reading material seems to have given some students time to waste, and some of them exploit this idleness to harass the female population through a provocative sexist wall literature. The recent case of suicide committed by a female student because of sexual harassment by male students cannot be isolated from the impoverished intellectual atmosphere at the university campus.

The inability of the government to expand female education will doom women to nonskilled jobs including traditional agricultural activities. It will, moreover, limit women's participation as managers, intellectuals, and politicians. The present trends of female employment, and of women's participation in politics and in the general management of the economy confirms this (Meena and Mtengeti 1988).

The impact of the deterioration of the education sector on labor productivity will be of a long-term nature; and the quality and the amount of basic education will determine the long-term recovery of the economy. If Tanzania is to maintain the educational sector, it is necessary to increase the amount of capital allocated to this sector amd not consider it as a nonproductive sector. There is also a need to motivate teachers and students. This can be done by improving conditions of work through matching real wages and conditions of living. An increase of drop-out rates and declining trends in enrollment rates are economic wastes. Such trends cause underutilization of both physical infrastructure and human resources. Policies of adjustment should therefore minimize resource waste and ensure maximum resource utilization. For the education sector, this means full enrollment and optimal teacher-student ratios.

The Issue of Equity in Income Distribution and Social Services

Before the signing of the 1986 agreement between the Tanzanian government and the IMF, the government had attempted to pursue compromise reform measures—a compromise between the conditions which the IMF was imposing and its own egalitarian policies. Thus, a National Economic Survival Program (1981–82) and Survival Adjustment Program (1981–82) were implemented as middle-road reform programs which attempted to implement some of the conditions of IMF without giving in totally to the IMF's conditionality. The Tanzanian government was attempting to protect the achievements which had been made in the social service sector. SAP had, for instance, spelled out the following objectives:

> 1) to reduce the rate of inflation through adjusting the government's budget to the levels consistent with the growth of the national economy; 2) to achieve a balance of payments adjustment so as to alleviate the extreme scarcity of foreign exchange and the consequent under-utilization of domestic production capacity; 3) to achieve an increase in the productivity of parastatal enterprises and an improvement in public sector management; and 4) to maintain equity in income distribution as well as the provision of social services and other basic needs to the majority of the population (United Republic of Tanzania 1986).

The IMF, however, was not interested in the issue of maintaining equality in income distribution and provision of social services and accused the Tanzanian government of over-involvement with equality issues at the expense of production. Even though the expansion of the social service sector had been made possible because of international support—including the World Bank support of the Basic Service Strategy—Tanzania was accused of over-expansion of its social service sector.

Following SAP, the government devalued the currency by 40 percent while producer prices were increased by 50 percent. There was a further move to liberalize agricultural marketing when the government ended the grain monopoly of the National Milling Corporation and when the Crop Authorities were dissolved and replaced by cooperative societies which had been dismantled in 1972. The government also took some measures to reduce the government deficit by freezing hiring, by reducing ministries, and by reducing subsidies which included subsidies on farm inputs and implements. Prices of consumer goods were also raised. Enterprises which had their own foreign funds were permitted to import their own goods. The attempt to make a compromise with the IMF failed as it rejected the reform measures which it considered insufficient to shock the economy and stimulate growth. It finally forced the Tanzanian government to enter into the agreement in 1986 which ended the struggle between attempts to build an egalitarian society vs. attempts to open the economy to market forces (via the IMF package).

The Economic Recovery Programme (ERP 1986–89 or ERP1)

Unfortunately, the IMF package has been totally gender blind; i.e., women seem to be absent from the reform measures. ERP was mainly directed at measures to devalue the currency, improve capacity utilization in industry, redress budget deficits, carry out parastatal reform, and redirect money away from government to productive activities (United Republic of Tanzania 1986). The main thrust was to increase production without caring who was to produce and who was going to benefit from the production. As a result, the implementation of ERP1 resulted in over-burdening women as they engaged in a variety of activities due to inflation and devaluation. The result has been that their health and the health of their children has been badly affected, while their productive and reproductive roles have threatened their very lives.

The government of Tanzania has just finished implementation of ERP1 and has endorsed ERP2, also referred to as the Economic and Social Action Programme (ESAP) (United Republic of Tanzania 1990). Yet indicators to measure the effect of ERP1 on various sectors of population and particularly women are yet to be developed. Like the previous reform programs, ERP2 is clearly gender insensitive. It considered seven priority areas, none of which mentioned women. ERP2, however, seems to have realized the social costs of ERP1; it provides a special program for minimizing social costs. But like ERP1, ERP2 does not consider women as a particularly vulnerable group that has been forced to bear more than an equal share of the social costs of adjustment programs. Traditional areas of priority are still devaluation, trade liberalization, budget restraints, price policies, and sectoral policies (United Republic of Tanzania 1990).

By implication, the implementation of ERP2 will continue to have adverse effects on women. Devaluation will continue to erode the real incomes of both the rural and urban population. The absence of women from ERP2 implies that women will continue to pursue personal adjustment programs for the benefit of their families and their communities, unsupported by concrete material support except for lip-service given in recognition of the innovative strategies that women have developed to cope with the crisis. Given the fact that women constitute the majority of the labor force, adjustment programs which ignore their contribution and their vulnerability cannot effectively promote growth. Neither can they adjust effectively to the crisis.

Conclusion

The Tanzanian government has been forced by the IMF, World Bank, and all the Western States to pursue reform measures which undermine their own gender-sensitive development projects. The government has also been forced by these pressures to reduce the amount of expenditures on the social services on the grounds that the social service sector is a nonproductive sector. On a short-term and long-term basis, however, the productivity of the nation will be negatively affected by decreases in expenditures on education and health. It is illogical to postpone investments in education and health services on whatever pretext. It is even more illogical in the Tanzanian context because agriculture, which plays a central role in the economy, depends upon labor productivity for any increased output, which then depends on the education and health of the labor. It is difficult to separate productive from nonproductive investments within this context.

Because of the above observations the following recommendations can be made. Efforts should be made by African states to balance investments in various sectors of the economy as they pursue SAP programs. Adjustment programs that tend to ignore the welfare of the people are bound to perpetuate the socioeconomic crisis of the 1980s that necessitated SAPs. A well-educated and healthy population is an investment to be treasured. *Adjustment programs will only benefit the people if they are initiated by the people for the interests of the people.* African governments have to learn from African women, who have demonstrated unsurpassed innovativeness in developing survival strategies to cope with the crisis. They have thus enabled the governments to maintain some political stability. African states that are committed to a long-term solution of the ongoing socioeconomic crisis should best realize that the IMF packages are mainly serving the interests of capital.

NOTES

1. A Dean of Faculty of Medicine lamented that in the past three years fewer and fewer students are qualifying for medicine and the few who qualify have to be given expensive, time-consuming remedial courses. The number of girls qualifying for medicine has also declined.

REFERENCES

Brock-Utne, Birgit
    1988   A Critical Analysis of World Bank Report No. 6934, Education Policies for Sub-Sahara Africa: Adjustment, Revitalization, and Expansion. The Bureau of Education and Scholarships for Overseas Studies, NORAD, Oslo, Norway.
Campbell, Horace
    1986   The IMF Debate and the Politics of Demobilization in Tanzania. Paper presented at the Second Triennial Congress of OSSREA in Dldoret, Kenya, July.
Chungu A., Richard Mandara, et al.
    1989   Strengthening Strategies to Improve the Economic Situation of Women in Tanzania: Morogoro Feasibility Study Report. Institute of Production Innovation, University of Dar es Salaam.
Ellis, Frank
    1980   Agricultural Pricing Policy in Tanzania 1970–79. Implications for Agricultural Output, Rural Incomes and Marketing Costs. Economic Research Bureau, University of Dar es Salaam.
    1982   Agricultural Pricing Policy in Tanzania. *World Development* 10(4): 263–83.
    1983   Agricultural Marketing and Peasants. State Transfers in Tanzania. *Journal of Peasant Studies* 10(4): 214–43.

Government of the Republic of Tanzania and United Nations Childrens' Fund
  1985   *Analysis of the Situation of Children and Women.* Dar es Salaam:
          Government of the Republic of Tanzania and United Nations
          Childrens' Fund.
Government of the United Republic of Tanzania and UNESCO
  1988   *Sector Review: The Financing of Education in Tanzania Overview.*
          UNESCO Education Financing Division, EFM/140. Paris:
          UNESCO.
Havenvik, H. J., F. Kjaerby, Ruth Meena, R. Skarstein and Ulla Vuorela
  1988   *Tanzania: A Country Study and Norwegian Aid Review.* University of
          Bergen, Bergen: Centre for Development Studies.
Hyden, Goran
  1986   African Social Structure and Economic Development. *Strategies for
          African Development,* J. Berg and W. Seymour, eds. Berkeley:
          University of California Press.
International Bank for Reconstruction and Development (IBRD)
  1987   *Education in Sub-Sahara Africa: a World Bank Policy Study.*
          Washington, D.C.: The World Bank and IBRD.
Johnsson, Urban
  1988   The Health Sector in Tanzania 1980–87. Paper presented at the 5th
          Economic Policy Workshop, May, Dar es Salaam.
Kiondo, Andrew
  1989   The Nature of Economic Reform in Tanzania. Seminar Paper,
          University of Dar es Salaam.
Makaranga, Revocatus
  1990   Wanawake 4,000 Hufariki Kila Mwaka Kutokana Na Matatizo Ya
          Uzazi! *Mzalendo Jumapili February 4, 1990.* Govt. Printer, Dar es
          Salaam.
Meena Ruth, and Rogathe Kristosia
  1988   Small Scale Farm Input Study. Research Report for NORAD, Dar
          es Salaam.
Meena, Ruth, and Asha Rose Mtengeti
  1988   *Wanawake Katika Siasa Na Uongozi Tanzania.* Dar es Salaam:
          Educational Publishers and Distributors, Ltd.
Nkoma, Alice, and Ruth Meena
  1990a   Coping Up Strategies for Urban Poor Women. Research Report for
          UNICEF, Dar es Salaam.
  1990b   The Impact of Structural Adjustment Program on Rural Women.
          Staff Paper, Women's Research and Documentation Projects
          (WRDP), University of Dar es Salaam.
United Republic of Tanzania
  1983   *A Structural Adjustment Plan.* Gov't. Printer, Dar es Salaam.
  1986   *Economic Recovery Programme.* Gov't. Printer, Dar es Salaam.
  1987   *Basic Education Statistics in Tanzania (BEST) 1982-1986.* Ministry
          of Education, Dar es Salaam.

1980–89   *Budget Speeches.* Ministry of Health, Dar es Salaam.

1980–89   *Budget Speeches.* Ministry of Education, Dar es Salaam.

1980–89   *Budget Speeches.* Ministry of Finance and Planning, Dar es Salaam.

1990   *1990 Economic Recovery Programme II (Economic and Social Action Programme) 1989/90–1991/92.* Govt. Printer, Dar es Salaam.

8

Fertilizer Subsidy Removal Programs and Their Potential Impacts on Women Farmers in Malawi and Cameroon

Christina H. Gladwin

Since the early 1980s, development experts and donor agencies have agreed on the importance of structural adjustment reforms aimed at "getting (macro) prices right." Adoption of these reforms was made a precondition for new grants in many sub-Saharan African countries. In both Malawi and Cameroon, one such required reform was government's gradually decreasing fertilizer subsidies available to the small farm sector. The aim of this paper is to review fertilizer subsidy removal programs in both countries for their potential impact on women farmers who bear most of the responsibility for food crop production. Because women produce, store, and market the food in both countries, these programs will adversely affect aggregate food production and food security if they adversely affect women producers.

It is first necessary to briefly review both sides of the debate about the pros and cons of fertilizer subsidies. On one side of the debate are those who argue for structural adjustments as a way to invigorate stagnating agricultural and industrial sectors (Bates, 1981; Timmer, Falcon, and Pearson 1983; Due, 1986). They argue that distorted "macro" prices (artificially low food prices, high wage rates, low interest rates, overvalued exchange rates) send critical signals which may negatively affect the efficient allocation of resources and cause stagnation in the long run. As a corollary, they have argued against governments' using fertilizer subsidies to increase the profitability of intensive agriculture while keeping food prices artificially low (Timmer, Falcon, and Pearson 1983: 288). Only when total fertilizer use is low and the ratio of incremental grain yield to

Christina Gladwin is Associate Professor in the Food and Resource Economics Department, Affiliate of the Anthropology Department, and member of the Center for African Studies. She has a Ph.D. from Food Research Institute, Stanford University, and has done extensive fieldwork in Ghana, Mexico, and Guatemala, as well as short periods of fieldwork in Malawi and Cameroon. She is the author of *Ethnographic Decision Tree Modeling* and co-editor of *Food and Farm: Current Debates and Policies*.

fertilizer application is high can such subsidies be cost-effective, relative to higher output prices or greater food imports. As fertilizer use becomes more widespread, the costs of the program rise dramatically and the production impact per unit of fertilizer subsidy drops, as few nonusers of fertilizer remain to be converted to users. Thus, fertilizer subsidies can keep farm profitability high and consumer prices low only for a short time. After that, the short-run distortions will impede an efficient long-run growth strategy.

On the other side of the debate is a clearcut argument that is repeated over and over by farmers, extension agents, and people in ministries of agriculture in countries which have initiated a fertilizer subsidy removal program, such as Malawi and Cameroon. It is as follows: If there is no fertilizer subsidy, there will be little or no fertilizer bought by smallholders, especially by women farmers who are the smallest of the smallholders, because lack of cash (and credit) is the main constraint limiting smallholders' use of chemical fertilizers. Without chemical fertilizer, there will be less fertilizer-responsive foods (e.g., maize) produced to feed the cities and countryside, and there are no viable, practical organic substitutes for chemical fertilizer in local farming systems at this time. Thus a decrease in fertilizer use will decrease maize production, jeopardizing not only women's agricultural production and incomes, but also the high level of food self-sufficiency currently enjoyed by both Malawi and Cameroon. If not enough maize is produced, governments will have to import maize, the main subsistence crop, or suffer greater levels of malnutrition. Implied in this argument is the assumption that the cost of importing maize will be greater than the cost of subsidizing fertilizer.

But, counter the subsidy removal advocates—usually found in the World Bank, USAID, and the Ministry of Finance—one way to offset the rising price of fertilizer is to increase producer prices of food and cash crops, which are kept artificially low. It is true that producer prices are kept artificially low: in Malawi in 1986/87, maize prices had been low relative to other cash crops, e.g., tobacco, cotton, groundnuts. In Cameroon in 1989, farmgate prices of coffee, used by smallholders to buy fertilizer for maize and coffee, were one third to one half of world coffee prices.

Unfortunately, governments are more likely to decrease fertilizer subsidies than to increase artificially low producer prices, because since colonial times, paying farmers less than the world price has been the way African governments *tax* farmers (Bates 1980). In 1989, for example, the Cameroonian government was in the second year of a Fertilizer Subsector Subsidy Removal Program (FSSRP), but it also cut farmgate coffee prices in half in December, to keep them at one-third the world price. Thus farmers were faced with a double whammy: a 100 percent decrease in producer prices and a 50 percent increase in the price of fertilizer.

Even when government does increase producer prices, it is unclear whether increasing the price of maize can by itself substitute for keeping the price of fertilizer low, as most smallholders do *not* sell maize and are in fact maize-deficit households themselves (Lele, Peters, this volume). Because 55 percent of Malawi's smallholders cultivate less than 1 hectare of land, with 0.6 hectares of that planted to subsistence crops (the local maize variety and groundnuts) that are not usually sold, they are not maize-surplus households. Lele (1989: 16) terms the structure of Malawi's agriculture a "dualism-within-dualism" structure, whereby smallholders are split into two groups: a minority who have a farm size large enough "to produce a marketable surplus and capable of taking risks and a preponderant majority experiencing stagnation or near economic paralysis." Increasing the producer price of maize will thus be detrimental not only to the urban poor but also to the majority of Malawi's smallholders who are maize-deficit households. According to Harrigon (1987), the only hope of increasing their incomes is to encourage their use of fertilizer on local maize varieties, so that more of their land can be taken out of subsistence and planted to cash crops.

Her results are supported by the 1984 FAO land resources report, which assesses the potential for food production within each country in the Third World from its own lands and based on estimates of present and projected populations in the year 2000 (FAO 1984). It concludes that potentials of land to produce food are limited but vary considerably between and within countries. Malawi, in contrast to Cameroon, is one of the densely populated, land-scarce countries that must intensify production, i.e., raise input levels from "low" to "medium" levels, in order to avoid massive food imports or famines by the year 2000. A *low* level of inputs roughly corresponds to use of no fertilizer or biocide on traditional crop varieties with no long-term conservation measures; a *medium* level corresponds to use of a basic package of fertilizers and biocides on some improved crop varieties, with simple long-term conservation practices. For countries like Malawi, the report concludes, intensification and an increased use of fertilizer is essential.

As Falcon (1987) points out, not all subsidies are bad. One food policy should not be mandated for all sub-Saharan African countries, but mandated reforms should depend on the particular conditions faced by the country in question. In a previous paper (Gladwin with Tower 1988), I argue that conditions in Malawi support a 55 percent fertilizer subsidy because smallholders tend to apply a *suboptimum* amount of fertilizer due to their lack of cash or credit for fertilizer. In this case, there is a net gain in efficiency from a fertilizer subsidy because the value of the increased net output of the agricultural sector from the fertilizer subsidy exceeds the cost of the subsidy disbursed.

In this paper, 1989 data from men and women farmers in Cameroon are joined with 1987 data from Malawi to see the impact of fertilizer subsidy removal programs and the resulting increased price of fertilizer on women farmers who bear most of the responsibility for food crop production in both countries. In Malawi, women produce the local variety of maize, which is 90 percent of maize production and the staple food crop, while men produce cash crops of tobacco or hybrid maize; in Cameroon, women produce the food crops (maize, yams, beans) while men produce coffee, the cash crop. Because the main factor now limiting fertilizer use by women is lack of cash or credit, an increased price of fertilizer will lead many women farmers to drop it or not start to use it. The result could be a decrease in aggregate maize production in both countryside and city. Note that this argument is *not an equity argument* but an efficiency argument; fertilizer subsidy removal programs could adversely impact women farmers and through them, aggregate food production. Thus, in the first section, I show that even with present levels of fertilizer subsidies, fertilizer use is now very low, suboptimal in both countries. In the second section, it is argued that a removal of the fertilizer subsidy and increase in fertilizer prices could decrease fertilizer use to even lower levels, because lack of cash and imperfect credit markets are the main constraints limiting women farmers' use of chemical fertilizers. The third section explores the imperfect credit markets in both countries. I conclude that, because maize is fertilizer responsive—in contrast to cassava or millet—and there are no viable organic substitutes for chemical fertilizer in the local farming systems at this time, a decrease in fertilizer use will decrease maize production, thus jeopardizing not only women's agricultural production and incomes, but also the high level of food self-sufficiency currently enjoyed by both countries.

Fertilizer Use Is Suboptimal

Economic theory says that farmers will increase fertilizer use until the value of the product (e.g., maize) produced by the last additional bag of fertilizer (called the value of the marginal product of fertilizer VMP) just equals its marginal cost or price. At that "optimal" quantity of fertilizer, the ratio VMP/P equals one. Previous empirical studies of Third World farmers, however, suggest that farmers increase fertilizer use until the ratio of the marginal product of fertilizer to its real price (p_f/p_m) is not one but greater than or equal to *two* (Timmer 1974: 200, Gladwin 1976). The ratio is usually two or more because farmers cannot base their decisions to use or increase fertilizer on the criterion of profit maximization alone. They also face constraints such as lack of cash, lack of credit, lack of knowledge of how to apply the fertilizer, and presence of risk and/or uncertainty about the weather, markets, etc. They usually do not know just how much fertilizer they are applying, because they manually apply it with bottle caps or handfuls. In Africa, an additional problem is that farmers usually do not know the exact size of their fields: in Malawi (and Cameroon), a plot is called an acre (hectare) but may not be an acre (hectare). Because farmers discount profit for these other factors, they usually end up applying a "suboptimal" quantity of fertilizer and the ratio VMP/P is greater than one.

Another reason farmers apply low levels of fertilizer stems from the nature of the sexual division of agricultural labor in the African household (Gladwin and McMillan 1989). Although allocation of labor rules vary across regions, even within the same country, in Malawi and N.W. Cameroon women produce the subsistence crop maize and men produce a cash crop: tobacco and hybrid maize in Malawi and coffee and cocoa in Cameroon. The very nature of this division of labor leaves women without any cash with which to buy the fertilizer for maize. Either they are dependent on their husbands to buy fertilizer for them, or they must take some food away from the family to sell to buy fertilizer for the next season. This is very hard for women to do; it is impossible in a maize-deficit household, i.e., one which regularly produces less maize than it consumes. The result is that men buy fertilizer for women's maize if they have the money after buying fertilizer for their cash crop, and women apply a suboptimal quantity of fertilizer on subsistence maize.

To see if farmers in the Malawi sample also applied a suboptimal quantity of fertilizer, a small personal survey of Malawian smallholders was conducted in May 1987. The sample consisted of 40 smallholders in three agricultural districts: Lilongwe, Kasungu, and Salima. Although farmers in this sample were on average bigger, more experienced farmers than is the norm (with average landholdings of 3.02 hectatres), their experience with fertilizer allowed us to elicit the history of their fertilizer use.[1] To elicit an estimate of the VMP of fertilizer, farmers were asked about their cropping patterns in 1985/86 and 1986/87: crops, acreage, fertilizer use, manure use, and yields received. Then they were asked about past changes in fertilizer use: the year, quantity applied with or without credit, on what crop, yields received, and reasons for the change.

Results are summarized in Table 8-1, from 38 observations of initial adoption and increases in fertilizer use and corresponding increases in maize yields, and show that the average ratio of VMP/P is 3.2 for the local maize variety (the women's crop) and 4.5 for hybrid maize variety (the men's crop). Because the ratio is greater than one, fertilizer use is suboptimal in Malawi, leaving open the possibility that fertilizer subsidies could be cost-effective, relative to higher output prices (Timmer, Falcon, and Pearson 1983: 288).

Although the same calculations were not done with the Cameroon data, fertilizer use on maize is very low in the areas sampled: Kom region of the North West province of Cameroon, the major maize-producing area, and Dschang in the West province.[2] In Kom, women who grow the maize on hillside plots 1–3 hours from their compounds either don't use

Table 8-1. Farmers' Ratios of the Value of More Fertilizer on Maize.

| Year | Pf/Pm | Ratio = Pm * MPf/Pf: | |
		Local	Hybrid
1960–70	4.4	3.3	
1970/71	4.4	1.8	
1971/72	4.4	3.2	
1972/73	5.5	1.2	
1973/74	5.5	1.7	
1974/75	4.7	1.4	0.8
1975/76	3.6	1.3	
1976/77	3.4	1.9	2.8
1977/78	3.4	4.0	
1978/79	3.4	9.3	3.8
1979/80	2.6	−1.0	
1980/81	2.6		
1981/82	1.5	5.4	5.4
1982/83	2.3	2.4	8.3
1983/84	2.5	3.2	2.4
1984/85	2.9	0.8	1.9
1985/86	3.4	3.9	
1986/87	3.4	4.3	
AVG	3.2	4.5	
(n)		(26)	(12)

Source: Personal Survey 1987.

any fertilizer or have just started fertilizing maize in the mid-1980s and on average use one 50-kilo bag per hectare. In villages around Dschang, maize plots are sometimes mixed with coffee, but again, women are responsible for fertilizing the maize and apply roughly 1 bag per hectare. For this reason, fertilizer use is very low and expected to be suboptimal.

Smallholders' Decisions Between Chemical and Organic Fertilizers

In this section, it is argued that a removal of the fertilizer subsidy will decrease fertilizer use to even lower levels, because lack of cash and imperfect credit markets are the main constraints limiting women farmers' use of chemical fertilizers. To show this, a model of farmers' decisions whether or not to use chemical and/or organic fertilizers is tested on data from Malawi and Cameroon. The decision model in figures 8-1a, b, c, and d explains why some farmers use *both* chemical and organic fertilizer, while others use *only chemical,* while some use *only organic* (defined as animal manure, compost, or certain kinds of green manure). It also shows which constraints to chemical fertilizer use are most important: farmers' lack of capital or credit, or their indigenous beliefs in organic fertilizers (manure/compost) as the right way to fertilize their crops, or their fear of dependency on chemicals.

This decision is a crucial one in countries like Malawi and Cameroon that import all chemical fertilizer or its feedstocks. It is especially critical in Malawi, which is land-locked and faces high transport costs to the sea (due to the cutting of the Beira railroad line in Mozambique). It is a key decision for those policy makers interested in the potential of *sustainable agriculture* or low-input agriculture (Brush 1989).

Because the outcome chosen by the farmer is different for different crops, this model is specific to the main food crop: maize in Cameroon and the local (not hybrid) variety of maize in Malawi, which constitutes 90 percent of maize production and is the staple food crop. Also for simplicity of modeling, it is here assumed that every farmer incorporates some green manure or crop residues on maize during the "banking up" of soil around the secondary roots after the second weeding and fertilizing (in Malawi) or during the initial turning under of the soil, after the land is taken out of fallow (in Kom, Cameroon). This use of crop residues is no doubt beneficial to soil structure, but is not the same slow-release nitrogen fertilizer as animal manure or compost. Hence organic fertilizer here means manure and/or compost but not crop residues.

The model posits that farmers must first pass a set of simple "elimination-by-aspects" constraints (Tversky 1972) in Figure 8-1a. The decision tree is read from top to bottom, with the alternatives the farmer must choose between listed in the parentheses at the top of the tree (e.g., Apply organic; chemical; both; neither). Note that the tree model doesn't predict quantities of fertilizer applied; to predict quantities, a researcher must use a linear programming model. All farmers are individually asked the questions in the *decision criteria*, denoted by < >, all of which have to be passed on a path to a particular *outcome*, denoted by [ ]. The decision criteria may be simple constraints (e.g., "Have the cash to buy the fertilizer you need?"). Alternatively, the alternatives may be ordered on some factor or aspect (e.g., "Is the cost of buying fertilizer less than the cost of getting it on credit?") A further complication is that the criteria may be "semiorders," by which the alternatives are ordered if there is more than a noticeable difference between them (e.g., a difference in cost of 5 Kwacha per bag of fertilizer).

The methodology of decision-tree analysis requires decision criteria to be elicited from one subset of farmers in the region and tested against actual choice data collected from another set of farmers (Gladwin, 1979). A test of the model is provided by comparing the outcome chosen by the farmer in real life with the outcome that the model sends him/her to (i.e., his/her data to), via his/her responses to the questions on the questionnaire. If the model successfully predicts 90 percent or more of farmers' choices, it can be assumed to be an adequate description of farmers' decision processes. If not, further elicitation of more accurate decision criteria from the farmers themselves is necessary, since they and only they are the experts on how they make their decisions. The decision criteria in this model were elicited from Guatemalan farmers who made similar choices in 1977–79, and tested on farmers in Malawi and Cameroon. The credit decision criteria were elicited during the first nine interviews in Lilongwe and Kasungu, and further tested in interviews with 30 farmers in Malawi and 35 in Cameroon. After passing Figure 8-1a, farmers then must have a need or motivation to use either or both kinds of fertilizer (Figure 8-1b). They then pass to a set of resource constraints specific to each kind of fertilizer, and will use that kind if they satisfy or pass each constraint (Figures 8-1c and 8-1d). Farmers will use both kinds of fertilizer if they think the crop needs both, and they pass both sets of resource constraints.

Elimination Criteria

Farmers must first pass a simple set of constraints in Figure 8-1a which eliminate use of both organic and chemical fertilizers if: their type of soil

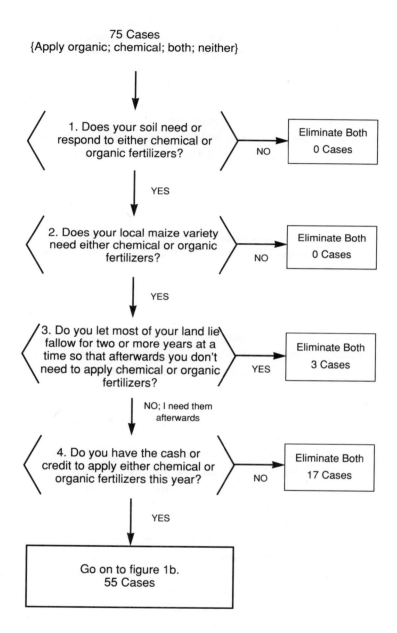

Figure 8-1a. The Decision Between Organic and Chemical Fertilizers on Maize: Stage 1 Constraints.

doesn't need or respond to either kind of fertilizer (criterion 1), *or* their type of local maize seed doesn't need either kind of fertilizer (criterion 2), *or* they let most of their land lie fallow for two or more years (as women do in Kom, Cameroon, by rotating three maize fields) so that after the fallow period it doesn't need either chemical or organic fertilizers (criterion 3), *or* they lack the cash or credit for either chemical or organic this year (criterion 4). If a farmer is eliminated at this first stage of the decision process, he or she doesn't have to decide between organic and chemical fertilizers because both are eliminated and the decision is simple.

Stage-Two Criteria

Farmers who pass "stage-one" criteria do have a complicated decision, however, and continue on to stage-two criteria in Figure 8-1b. If they think that their maize variety *needs* both kinds of fertilizer to produce good yields (criterion 5), they are sent on to both sets of resource constraints in Figures 8-1c and 8-1d. If they think maize needs only organic fertilizer (criterion 6), they are sent only to Figure 8-1c. Similarly, if they think maize needs only chemical fertilizer (criterion 6), they are sent only to Figure 8-1d.

Farmers will apply organic fertilizer to maize, in Figure 8-1c, if: they have enough animals to make enough manure or compost to use on their maize (or a crop such as tobacco rotated with local maize)[3] every two or three years (criterion 8), *or* they can buy the manure/compost they need (criterion 9) *and* they have or can get transport (e.g., an oxcart and oxen in Malawi) to carry the manure/compost to their fields (criterion 10), *and* they have the time or (full- or part-time) labor to carry it to their fields (criterion 12), which are not too far away to carry manure to (criterion 11). If all these constraints are passed, the model predicts that the farmer applies manure and/or compost to maize (or a crop rotated with local maize). If a farmer fails *one* constraint, the model predicts no manure/compost is applied.

In Figure 8-1d, farmers will apply chemical fertilizer to maize if: there was chemical fertilizer available at the time needed, either to buy or get on credit (criterion 13), *and* the farmer had either the cash or credit at the time needed to get the fertilizer (criterion 14), *and* the farmer could take the risks associated with chemical fertilizers (criteria 15–17).

The Risk Subroutine

The main risk of chemical fertilizer is what I call the "dependency" of the land on chemical fertilizer. Farmers in both countries claim that their land

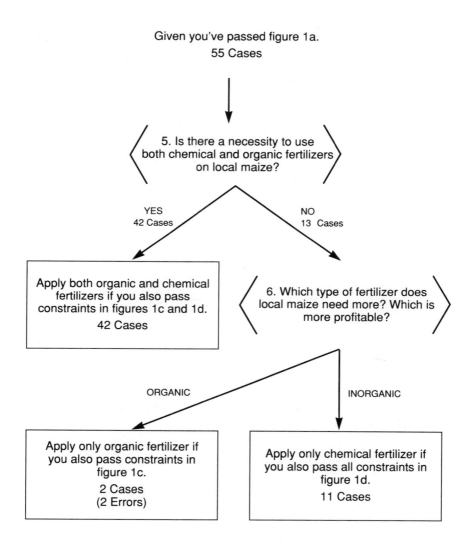

Figure 8-1b. Motivations to Use Chemical, Organic, or Both Fertilizers.

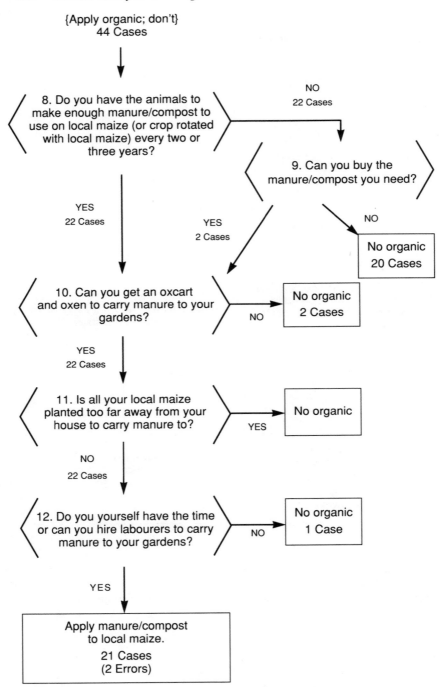

Figure 8-1c. Resource Constraints to the Use of Organic Fertilizer.

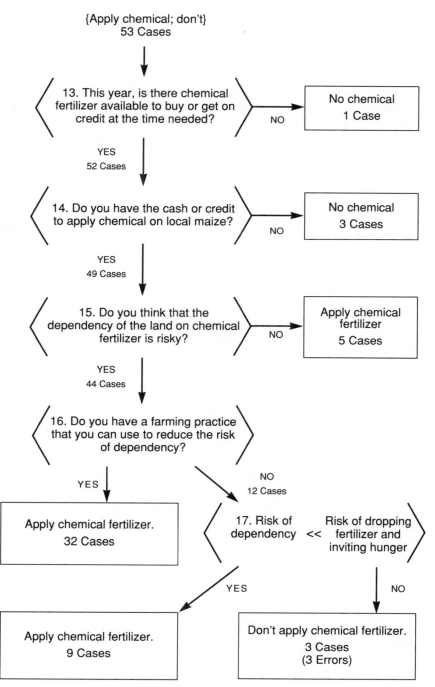

Figure 1d. Resource Constraints to the Use of Chemical Fertilizer.

(and in some cases their traditional seeds or germplasm) gets dependent on chemical fertilizer such that, if they stop applying it for one year, their yields decrease *drastically*. Whether or not this is due to a change in the land (or seed) itself, as ecologists have argued, or merely in farmers' expectations of the yields they should get from the land, as chemical advocates claim, is irrelevant for our purposes of assessing whether farmers will take the risk of chemical fertilizer. What is relevant here is whether the farmers themselves believe that their land becomes dependent on chemical fertilizer, and whether they consider this dependency to be dangerous or risky (criterion 15), and whether they will take the risk (criteria 16–17). If farmers are worried about the dependency of the land on chemicals, the model predicts that they will take the risk only if: *either* they have a farming practice or way to reduce the risk substantially (e.g., also apply manure) (criterion 16) *or* they feel they must take the risk anyway because they cannot now return to using only manure/compost without a drastic reduction in their yields (criterion 17). With the latter line of reasoning, they are weighing the future danger of being overly dependent on fertilizer with the present risk of dropping it now, suffering a reduction in maize yields now, and "inviting hunger" now. As was the case with manure/compost, the model predicts that chemical fertilizer will be applied if all the constraints on chemical fertilizer are passed, and not otherwise.

The reader should note that in all stages of this decision model there is a capital or credit constraint. Results of testing this model should thus allow us to compare the limiting effect of the cash/credit constraints with the limiting effect of farmers' beliefs that their maize variety doesn't need chemical (or organic) fertilizer, or that leaving the land in fallow for two years is a good substitute for chemical fertilizer. If farmers do have such beliefs, they will drop out of the decision process in the model at criteria 2 or 3 and not even reach the cash/credit constraints in criteria 4, 9, and 14. This allows us to determine just how important lack of cash/credit is, as a factor limiting farmers' use of chemical fertilizer.

Results

The model was tested via personal interviews with 40 smallholders in Malawi in 1987 and with 35 farmers in Cameroon in 1989. Results of the test of this model show that lack of cash or credit (criterion 4) was the main factor limiting fertilizer use. No farmer had a type of soil or variety of maize that did not need either chemical or organic fertilizer. Most (23) Cameroonian farmers (in Kom) had a two-year fallow, however; but they said they still needed chemical or organic fertilizer after the fallow, so that only three believed maize did not need chemical or organic fertilizers. But eight of 40 farmers in Malawi and 9 of 35 farmers in Cameroon did not use either chemical fertilizer or manure due to lack of cash/credit.

Thirty-two farmers in Malawi and 23 farmers in Cameroon went on to the tough decision between organic and chemical fertilizers. Of these 55, 42 farmers believed that both kinds of fertilizer were necessary, while 11 farmers believed only chemical was necessary on local maize, and two farmers felt only organic was necessary. (However, the model erred in these cases, because they in fact use both chemical and organic.) Thus the model predicts that 53 farmers will use chemical fertilizer if they can also pass all the constraints on chemical (availability at the right time, cash/credit, and the farmer's willingness to take the risks of fertilizer). Forty-three farmers will use organic if they can also pass the constraints on organic (enough animals to make it or the cash to buy it, an oxcart available, enough time to apply it, and maize gardens close enough to their home so they can deliver it).

Results of putting the cases down the set of chemical fertilizer constraints show that 46 of the 53 farmers pass them and should apply chemical fertilizer. Three of the 7 cases sent to the outcome "Do not apply chemicals" are errors, however, and do apply chemical fertilizer. Only one farmer does not have fertilizer available to buy, and three do not have the cash/credit. Forty-four farmers believed that chemical fertilizer use was risky and the land became *dependent* on chemical fertilizer after initial use, so that once you started it, you had to keep applying more and more of it. However, 5 of 49 farmers did not think this was risky; 32 more farmers had a farming practice to reduce the risk (complementary manure application, planting of a leguminous tree during fallow; appropriate crop rotations, etc.). Twelve more farmers had no farming practice to reduce the risk; 9 felt they *had* to take it because otherwise, their yields would decrease drastically if they dropped chemical fertilizer. Three farmers believed that the land's future dependency on fertilizer is riskier than "inviting hunger" now by dropping fertilizer, but they are errors because they use chemical fertilizer anyway.

Results of putting the 44 cases down the set of organic constraints show that *only 19 cases end up applying manure/compost to local maize*, two cases are errors and the remaining 23 farmers could not pass one constraint or another. The biggest constraint here is lack of enough animals to make the manure/compost: 20 farmers had neither enough animals nor could buy manure. Of the 24 who had manure available, 2 farmers could not get hold of transport, and one farmer (a big commercial farmer) did not have the time to transport manure. Two farmers are errors of the model because they did pass the organic constraints and should have applied organic but "didn't want to waste time with manure when chemical fertilizer was available nearby."

Thus results show that only 19 farmers apply manure/compost while 46 of 75 farmers apply chemical fertilizer. *Although the majority of farmers claim that both kinds of fertilizer, organic and chemical, are necessary, more farmers can pass the chemical constraints than can pass the organic constraints.* For both kinds of fertilizer, *lack of cash/credit* is the biggest limiting factor: 17 farmers fail to pass the capital constraint in Figure 8-1a; 20 farmers cannot buy animals or manure in Figure 8-1c; and 3 more cannot pass the cash constraint for chemical fertilizer in Figure 8-1d.

Supporting these results showing that lack of cash is the main constraint limiting fertilizer use are data from asking farmers directly, "If the price of fertilizer increases from 3,000 to 4,500 CFA (in Cameroon), what will you do? Increase fertilizer, decrease, or stay the same?" Data from Cameroon show that 25 of 33 farmers will decrease fertilizer use or stay at 0 bags, 2 more will stay at present levels of use, and only 6 of 33 farmers will increase fertilizer use. Data from Malawi show that 23 of 29 farmers asked would decrease fertilizer use, 3 would stay at present levels, and 3 would increase fertilizer use. Thus in both countries, 48 of 62 farmers would decrease fertilizer use if the price increased by 50 percent.

Inadequate Credit Facilities

The final part of the argument is to show how and why credit markets are imperfect in Malawi and Cameroon, and why expansion of credit is not a good substitute for a fertilizer subsidy in a country where government wants to increase fertilizer use and safeguard food security. In Malawi, seasonal credit in kind for crop production now reaches *16* percent out of the 1.3 million farmers, or 206,000 farmers. Only about *6* percent of the smallholder production area is currently financed by credit, mainly through "farmers' clubs" which enable them to get credit for fertilizer, on average a 0.4 hectare package, via the Smallholder Fertilizer Revolving Fund. There are also women's clubs through Malawi's Women's Programme that give credit to women for groundnut seed and/or fertilizer; their default rate is even lower than that of the farmers' clubs. In 1985/86 the seasonal credit volume was 19.96 million kwacha at interest rates of 10 percent; recovery rates have been a high 97 percent, but the expansion of these clubs has been slow.

Women's use of credit is not proportional to their importance in

Malawi's agriculture. In 1980/81, 28.4 percent of households were headed by women. Dixon (1982) estimates that 50 percent of agricultural labor is performed by women and Kydd and Christiansen (1982) show that 69 percent of Malawi's full-time, year-round farmers are women; yet women household heads account for only 25 percent of credit club members in 1986/87. It is not clear whether women are systematically excluded because they are women or because most (72 percent) of them are the smallest of the smallholders with less than one hectare of land.

To answer these questions, smallholders' decisions to join a credit club and the clubs' decisions to admit members were modeled in Malawi. (I present this model and then discuss its applicability to the case of the Cameroon.) The farmer's decision to join a credit club is shown in Figures 8-2a and 8-2b, which combine in a logical order the reasons why some farmers get credit for fertilizer, while others decide to buy it with cash. The first seven criteria in the tree are "elimination-by-aspects" criteria that rapidly eliminate a farmer from a farmers' or women's club. They include conditions such as: the farmer is rejected for admission to a farmers' club by other club members (criterion 1); the farmer is so hopelessly poor that he/she expects to be denied entrance to the credit club so won't even try to join (criterion 2); the (woman) farmer is married to a member of a farmers' club and he by law must get the fertilizer on credit *for* her (criterion 3), unless he (or his whole club) has defaulted on a previous loan and now cannot receive credit (criterion 4); there is no women's club in the area which gives credit for fertilizer directly to the women (criterion 5); women lack confidence in or familiarity with credit clubs so that they won't take the risk of not repaying the loan (criterion 6); the farmer or his/her whole club cannot now receive credit due to a previous default on their part (criterion 7). If any of these conditions holds, credit as an option is eliminated for the farmer.

If the farmer "passes" these constraints successfully, he or she passes to the ordering aspect in criterion 8, on which he or she minimizes the cost of acquiring fertilizer. If the cost of buying fertilizer is much less than the cost of getting it on credit, the farmer "goes down" the lefthand path of the tree. The farmer then *buys* fertilizer if: he/she has enough cash to buy all the fertilizer needed (criterion 9) *and* he/she hasn't other more pressing needs for the cash such as school fees, clothing, etc. (criterion 10); *or* he/she has other uses for the cash so needs the credit, *but* thinks there's a risk of not being able to repay the loan (criterion 11), *and* this risk of non-repayment is *greater* than the risk of "inviting hunger" if you grow maize varieties (local or hybrid) without fertilizer (criterion 12). Why is not repaying a credit loan so risky? Farmers in default report that club mem-

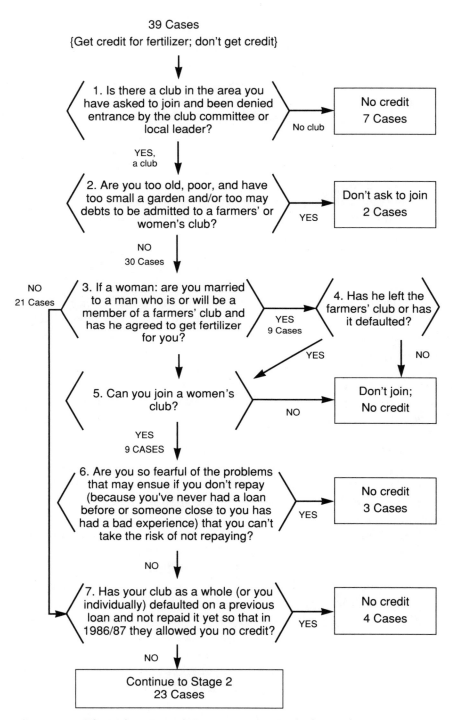

Figure 8-2a. The Malawi Farmer's Decision to Get Credit for Fertilizer.

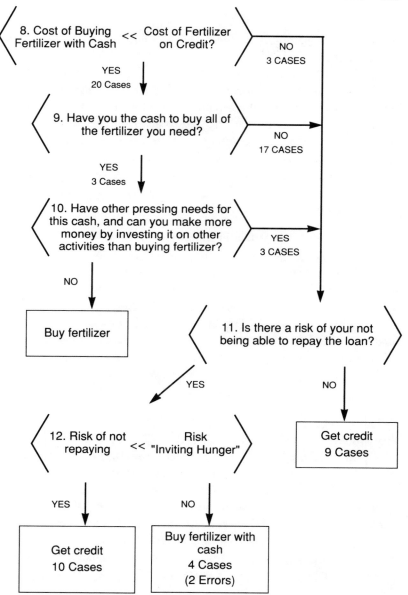

Figure 8-2b. Stage 2 of the Malawi Farmer's Decision to Get Credit.

bers and extension agents steal their animals, oxcarts, and even the doors and roofs to their houses to hold until the farmer or a family member repays the loan.

On the other hand, the farmer "goes down" the right hand branch of the tree and *gets the credit* for at least some of the needed fertilizer *if* he/she thinks there is little difference in the costs of acquiring fertilizer *or* he/she doesn't have all the cash needed to buy it *or* has other more pressing needs for this cash *and* can also pass the risk constraints. The farmer will take the risks of credit, i.e., of not being able to repay the loan, if he/she thinks "you invite hunger if you grow local maize without fertilizer," and judges the danger of hunger to be greater than the danger of not being able to repay the loan (criterion 12).

Results of Testing the Model in Malawi

The model was at first tested without criterion 2, which eliminates the hopelessly poor who don't even try to join a credit club, and with a more restricted version of criterion 6, which read, "Have you never had a loan before so that you're afraid of not being able to repay a (large) fertilizer loan?" With data from 39 farmers, the model originally tested failed to predict the choices of six farmers, for a success rate of 85 percent. Since this is a poor success rate for decision tree models, I looked for a pattern in the model's failures. The pattern was clear: the model failed to predict the choices of six women household heads, five of whom had less than two acres.

The failures showed up at the risk minimization criteria. Women said they would not join a credit club because of "the way they get money back"; but that yes, hunger was more dangerous and risky than their not being able to repay credit. The model thus predicts these women should get credit; but they don't. For them, the risk of not repaying credit is such an important constraint that it doesn't belong at the bottom of the tree but should be higher up the tree in the elimination stage, because it eliminates any possibility of their joining a credit club. Therefore, criterion 6 was expanded from a special case of one woman who had never had credit before, to include more cases of women farmers who were afraid to take the risks of credit.

Another way the original model was incorrect was in being too optimistic. It did not allow for the fact that the smallest smallholders might feel hopeless in their poverty, and this would cause them to not even *ask* to join a club to get the credit and thus get the fertilizer and produce the maize to get them out of their impoverished condition. Such was the situation of at least two women household heads: they weren't denied entrance to a club in criterion 1 because they felt their case for admission to the club was so hopeless that they didn't even ask to join. Poor women without a cash crop to pay back a fertilizer loan *do not want credit*, because they can't pay it back with subsistence maize production. To correct for these errors of the model, criterion 2 was added in the elimination stage, where it rapidly eliminates the smallest (women) smallholders from getting credit.

Given these two corrections to the model in Figure 8-2, it now predicts 95 percent of the 39 farmers interviewed, 21 of whom got credit in 1986/87. Of what use is the model? It shows policy planners why 18 farmers did *not* get credit: seven farmers either had no farmers' club in their village or were excluded from that club for reasons given below; four farmers were in clubs that had previously defaulted and so were denied credit in 1986/87; three (women) farmers were too fearful of not repaying to even consider joining a club; two (women) farmers were too hopelessly poor to even try to get into a club. All these farmers eliminate the credit option rapidly, in the first stage of the decision process. Only 23 farmers pass to the "hard core" decision process where they compare the two options, getting credit vs. buying fertilizer, on two aspects, cost and riskiness. In this stage, 19 farmers pass all constraints listed in the model and get at least some credit for fertilizer. Two more farmers, big farmers, felt that buying fertilizer was cheaper than getting credit and there was no risk of hunger because they had enough land to plant enough maize; but they feared not repaying the credit so they bought fertilizer. Two women remain as errors of the model because they get credit when they should buy fertilizer.

Results from Cameroon

Can this model be used to predict farmers' credit decisions in the Cameroon? Only in a trivial way can the model be applied, because there are practically no credit clubs for Cameroonian farmers. Most farmers interviewed in Kom and Dschang say no to criterion 1, "Is there a club in your area that you can join?" Only three farmers in Kom and two in Dschang reported belonging to a credit club; those in Kom were started in 1986–87 and were women's clubs started by MIDENO, a rural development program in the North West province, on the same model as the Malawi Women's Program. In 1989, women farmers received their first credit for fertilizer and, at the time I left Kom, they were meeting to repay the loan for the first time.

What credit is in Cameroon is supplied either through the local coffee cooperative, the local credit union, or the indigenous *njangi* or *tontin* systems of saving. Members of the local coffee cooperative sell their harvested coffee in January and receive their next year's fertilizer at the same time, to be applied in February through April to both coffee and maize. This is called "credit" but strictly speaking, *this is a cash transaction*, and the cooperative does not give more fertilizer than can be paid for with last year's coffee. Members of local credit unions save on a monthly basis for a year and borrow against that collateral during the second year; but they cannot borrow more than they have saved. Thus they do not receive credit per se. Members of an *njangi* can do the same, i.e., build up their collateral to borrow during the second year, or put money into a common pot every month to receive twelve times that amount once a year. Almost every Cameroon belongs to an *njangi*; but again, strictly speaking, this is not credit since the borrowing limit is the amount of prior savings. Thus only MIDENO credit clubs give credit, and these are very few and very new.

Policy Recommendations

What policy recommendations can be formulated from these results? Because the most frequent limiting factor to credit use in both countries is *no available credit club* in one's own village or exclusion from that club, policy planners should continue to push to expand numbers of clubs and eliminate some of the local club restrictions which exclude farmers. Because the next limiting factor, for five of the 18 "no credit" cases in Malawi, is fear of not repaying a loan and losing assets, policy planners should develop new terms of repayment which do not scare off farmers, especially women, from getting credit. One way to do this is to expand the number of women's clubs via MIDENO or the Women's Program. Another way is for government to strengthen each club's "credit fund" which the club uses to loan to individual members when they default. Several women reported that the credit fund of their club up to now has been too small; thus the risk of default has been very high. But with a strengthened credit fund, each club could give amortized disaster loans to farmers in default.

These policies will probably not, however, reach the smallest of the smallholders, including the many women-headed households who are too poor to want credit. Only a grant of supervised fertilizer for a couple of years will be sufficient to shock some of these farmers out of their "hopeless" constraint. Once they are shocked out of this constraint, they might proceed to use the same decision criteria as their more hopeful neighbors who can afford to compare the costs of credit vs. buying fertilizer. Now, however, they cannot.

Conclusion

When farmers' fertilizer use is suboptimal, and the value of the marginal product of fertilizer exceeds its price by the factor two, the optimal fertilizer subsidy can be substantial (55 percent of the world price). Why is smallholders' use of fertilizer suboptimal? Results of testing the model of farmers' decisions between chemical and organic fertilizer show that lack of cash and credit are the main constraints to fertilizer use in both Malawi and Cameroon. Organic substitutes for fertilizer (manure/compost or a fallow cycle with leguminous trees planted at the start of the fallow) are not substitutes for chemical fertilizer in the eyes of women farmers; they are complements, and expensive ones. Animals and animal manure are too expensive, too inconvenient, and maize fields are too far away to transport it, while the fallow cycle is too short in the region sampled to be a viable substitute for chemical fertilizer in maize production. In turn, one of the main factors limiting farmers'—especially women farmers'—use of credit is their aversion to the risks of not being able to repay loans in bad years. Poor women farmers *do not want* credit because they don't have a cash crop to sell to repay the loan with.

Clearly, an expansion of credit clubs will not be fast or easy; nor is credit a substitute for making fertilizer cheap enough for poor farmers, usually women farmers, to get with cash provided by husbands, sons, or njangi savings. Given these conditions, an expansion of the credit market is not a substitute for keeping the fertilizer subsidy at present levels, 55 to 65 percent of the world price.

Why have governments in Malawi and Cameroon initiated fertilizer subsidy removal programs? The answer to this question lies in the political arena. Unfortunately, fertilizer subsidy removal may be the *least bitter pill* that African governments have to swallow in a structural adjustment "lending" program. Because of the economic crisis facing many African governments, it is hard for them to raise artificially low producer prices to world prices; since colonial times, their budgets have depended on taxing farmers in this way. Similarly, it is harder to fire excess civil servants, who are their voting constituencies, than to make fertilizer more expensive for poor (women) farmers who live hours away from the capital. Likewise, it is politically unwise to dismantle a parastatal marketing board employing an elite group of educated voters, in order to substitute a more economically efficient system of periodic markets employing, again, rural women.[4]

Is there a solution to this dilemma? Clearly, a more complete structural adjustment, involving higher producer prices, a reduced number of civil servants, and the dismantling of parastatals, would be better than focusing only on removing fertilizer subsidies. It might open the way for a greater diversity of productive strategies and employment opportunities rather than enforcing a large-scale, capital-intensive agriculture that works against women's interests. But given the political realities of structural adjustment, on the one hand, and the economic rationality of women farmers who are responsible for food production in both Malawi and Cameroon, on the other hand, one solution is to *target fertilizer subsidies at smallholders, especially women farmers, for food production.* If fertilizer subsidies are removed completely, the African food crisis of the 1970s will pale in comparison to that of the 1990s. Leaving fertilizer subsidies at present levels—and even increasing them—is obviously the optimal food-security strategy in countries where lack of capital is the main limiting factor to fertilizer use; yet governments may lose needed structural adjustment grants with this strategy. A compromise would be to target fertilizer subsidies at smallholders' food production, as Malawi has done. Because women produce the food in most African cultures, one way to do this is via women's credit clubs like the MIDENO clubs in Cameroon and those of the Women's Program in Malawi. Will there be too much leakage of this subsidy to men's cash crops? The answer comes from one husband in Kom who allows his wife to fertilize her maize while he neglects to fertilize his coffee: "I don't like to be hungry."

NOTES

1. In other respects, the sample is fairly representative of Malawi smallholders: 26 farmers were credit club members, and 14 were not; 22 farmers got credit for fertilizer in 1986/87, while 18 did not. Seventeen farmers were women household heads, three were couples interviewed together, and 20 were male household heads. (Dixon [1982] estimates that 50 percent of agricultural labor is performed by women in Malawi.) Of the 40 farmers interviewed, 33 were household heads. Questions about the sexual division of labor and income within the family revealed that groundnuts is a women's cash crop while tobacco, cotton, and hybrid maize are men's cash crops, and local maize and beans are grown for the whole family's consumption.

2. The Cameroonian sample was chosen to be representative of smallholders

in the North West (Anglophone) province and (Francophone) West province. In Wombong Down, Kom, 25 smallholders were interviewed: 14 women, 10 men, 1 couple. Of these, 21 were maize-deficit households—they had to buy maize—and only 5 of 25 got credit for fertilizer. Around Dschang in West province, only 11 farmers were interviewed: 7 women, 4 men. Of these, only 2 were maize-deficit households, 5 sold maize, and only 2 got credit.

3. Farmers in Kasungu, Malawi, normally rotate tobacco (the man's cash crop) with local maize every other year. Farmers that I interviewed apply quite a bit of manure on tobacco: 20 to 50 oxcarts per acre. Given that the effects of manure and/or compost last for two or more years because they are slow-release fertilizers, this manure is also considered to be applied to local maize for the purpose of testing this model.

4. Why has USAID singled out fertilizer subsidy removal programs instead of tying them to other structural adjustment programs? In the words of one USAID officer, "The political climate was right to push it through. But now that the government has decreased the price of coffee, we're afraid we're stuck."

REFERENCES

Bates, Robert
  1981   *Markets and States in Tropical Africa.* Berkeley: University of California Press.
Dixon, Ruth
  1982   Women in Agriculture: Counting the Labor Force in Developing Countries. *Population and Development Review* 8(3): 558–59.
Due, Jean
  1986   Agricultural Policy in Tropical Africa: is a Turnaround Possible? *Agricultural Economics* 1: 19–34.
Falcon, Walter
  1987   Aid, Food-Policy Reform, and U.S. Agricultural Interests in the Third World. *American Journal of Agricultural Economics* 69(5): 929–35.
Food and Agriculture Organization
  1984   *Land, Food, and People.* Rome: United Nations Food and Agriculture Organization.
Gladwin, Christina
  1976   A View of the Plan Puebla: An Application of Hierarchical Decision Models. *American Journal of Agricultural Economics* 58(5): 881–87.
  1979   Cognitive Strategies and Adoption Decisions: A Case Study of Non-Adoption of an Agronomic Recommendation. *Economic Development and Cultural Change* 28(1): 155–73.
  1989   *Ethnographic Decision Tree Modeling.* Newbury Park, CA: Sage Press.

Gladwin, Christina, Kathleen Staudt, and Della McMillan
   1986   Providing Africa's Women Farmers Access: One Solution to the
           Food Crisis. *Journal of African Studies* 13 (Winter 1986-87):
           131–41.
Gladwin, Christina, and Della McMillan
   1989   Is a Turnaround in Africa Possible without Helping African
           Women to Farm? *Economic Development and Cultural Change*
           37(2): 345–69.
Harrigon, Jane
   1987   Price Policy in Malawi. Mimeo, Ministry of Agriculture, Lilongwe,
           Malawi.
Kydd, Jonathan, and Robert Christiansen
   1982   Structural Change in Malawi since Independence: Consequences of
           a Development Strategy Based on Large-Scale Agriculture. *World
           Development* 10 (5): 355–75.
Lele, Uma
   1989   Structural Adjustment, Agricultural Development and the Poor:
           Some Lessons from the Malawian Experience. Washington, D.C.:
           World Bank.
Nyondo, F.
   1987   Price Responsiveness of Producers of Basic Food Crops in Malawi.
           M.S. Dissertation, Food and Resource Economics Department,
           University of Florida.
Stuart, C.
   1984   Welfare Costs of Additional Tax Revenue in the United States.
           American Economic Review (June): 352–62.
Timmer, C. Peter
   1974   The Demand for Fertilizer in Developing Countries. *Food Research
           Institute Studies* 13(3): 197–224.
Timmer, C. Peter, Walter Falcon, and Scott Pearson
   1983   *Food Policy Analysis.* Washington, D.C.: World Bank.
Tower, Edward, and Robert Christiansen
   1987   A Model of the Effect of a Fertilizer Subsidy on Income
           Distribution and Efficiency in Malawi. Working Paper No. 27,
           Duke University, Durham, NC.

9 Women Traders in Ghana and the Structural Adjustment Program

Gracia Clark and Takyiwaa Manuh

Since 1984, Ghana has figured prominently as an example of whole-hearted adherence to World Bank-endorsed policies aimed at changing the balance between economic sectors. Its Structural Adjustment Program (SAP) has included massive devaluation of the Ghanaian cedi, which has made it possible to increase the domestic price of export commodities, leading to expansion in production of cocoa and mineral production, restraints on wages and government expenditures, transfer of resources to sectors producing tradeables that generate or save foreign exchange, and creation of a more favorable climate for foreign investment and local private enterprises.

Women traders in the marketplace system offer a key window on this adjustment process. SAP programs rely on traders to transmit price information to small farmers and manufacturers who sell almost entirely through markets and who allocate their resources based on price signals. Effective stimulation of production also depends on the availability of producer inputs and consumer goods supplied mainly by traders. Several studies have documented the vital link traders provide between producers and consumers as well as their demographic importance (Robertson 1984, Clark 1988 and forthcoming). Sales accounted for 14.6 percent of economic activity in the 1984 Ghana Census; women traders were 89

Dr. Gracia Clark is an assistant professor at the University of Michigan with a joint appointment in the Center for Afro-American and African Studies and the Department of Anthropology. She received her doctorate from the University of Cambridge. She has worked on contract for ILO, ODA (UK), and UNIFEM on food systems, commercial policy, and appropriate technology.

Ms. Manuh, Ghanaian, is a graduate of Wesley Girls School, Cape Coast, and has a L.L.B. degree from the University of Ghana, Legon, and a L.L.M. degree from Dar-es-Salaam, Tanzania. She has been a Barrister and Solicitor, Supreme Court of Ghana. Currently she is a research fellow, Institute of African Studies, Legon. Her publications include *Law and the Status of Women in Ghana,* and she has carried out numerous international consultancies.

percent of sales workers. Market conditions thus closely reflect changes in production and consumption levels for most of the Ghanaian population.

This paper considers SAP in the historical context of a long-standing process of negotiation and adjustment of the terms of trade, the balance of power between national and international socioeconomic groups, and opportunities for expansion in commerce and production. This perspective allows us to distinguish the effects of recent structural adjustment policies from the continuing effects of the economic crisis and to compare these effects with the avowed aims of SAP.

The modification of the structure of opportunity available to individuals and households as a result of the crisis and specific policy responses provides the unifying framework for analysis. This emphasis was developed by Ghai and Alacantara for their analysis of the economic crisis in Africa, Latin America, and the Caribbean (UNRISD 1989). They suggest that, in the crisis, profitable opportunities arise only for individuals and groups with strong international connections and a few daring entrepreneurs. Artisans and small farmers producing for the internal market are especially impoverished, along with most bureaucrats, technicians, and professionals. Current trends in market trading traceable to SAP clearly confirm this interpretation of its overall impact.

Economic Decline and Responses in Ghana: The ERP/SAP

From a combination of internal and external factors, the Ghanaian economy gradually ground to a halt between the mid-1970s and the mid-1980s. This coincided with a generalized crisis for most sub-Saharan African countries, which saw real GDP per capita declining about 20 percent and average income per capita falling almost 30 percent between 1980 and 1985/6, and led to massive deterioration in the quality of life. Worsening terms of trade raised oil prices while prices of cocoa (Ghana's major export), gold, diamonds, and timber fell. Output fell steadily and Ghana's share of the world market for cocoa fell from 33 percent in the 1970s to 12 percent in 1982/3 (Statistical Service 1988). Food self-sufficiency also declined from 83 percent in 1961–66 and 71 percent in 1973–80 to 23 percent in 1982, resulting in a fourfold increase in food imports from 1972–82 (Tabatabai 1986, cited in ILO/JASPA 1989).

These economic developments led the Ghanaian government to major policy shifts away from its commitment to self-reliance and popular mobilization proclaimed on its assumption of power on 31st December

1981 (Green 1988; Loxley 1988). The Economic Recovery Programme (ERP) drawn up in 1983 comprised two phases. A traditional stabilization program from 1983–86 aimed to reduce fiscal deficits, balance of payments deficits, and external debt arrears. A medium-term plan from 1986–88 proposed structural reforms to enhance the conditions for growth, improve the structure of incentives through fiscal, monetary, exchange rate, and trade policies, stabilize wage bargaining through income policies, and reduce the role of the state in economic activity.

The means to achieve these goals were the typical IMF/World Bank tools. Demand restraint measures included budget and wage restraints and credit ceilings. Currency devaluation and price reforms switched resources to tradeables (exports and efficient import substitutes). Reforms in the financial sector, state enterprises, and public sector management and import liberalization aimed to improve the medium and long-term efficiency of the economy. These resulted, inter alia, in massive retrench- ments, higher costs for social services, and price rises associated with a hundredfold devaluation of the Cedi during the period 1983–89.

Most accounts present Ghana's adjustment process as a success made possible by government measures, sustained good weather, and substantial capital inflows of US$1,567 million from 1984–88. The budget deficit has been wiped out, with meager surpluses in 1986, 1987, and 1988, while the balance of payments deficit has fallen sharply. GNP increased at about 4.7 percent annually between 1984–88, and the agricultural sector has recorded some growth, although not sustained (Table 9-1).

Shifts in the structure of opportunity show up in further analysis of growth rates within and between sectors. Mining, extractive industry, and services have gained at others' expense. Cocoa production increased by 37 percent between 1983 and 1988/89, much faster than other agricultural activities, and in real terms, higher than total GDP (see Table 9-2). Higher cocoa producer prices exacerbate the differentiation in rural incomes, since 32 percent of cocoa farmers earn 94 percent of cocoa income (ILO/JASPA 1989:16). Since 1984 the terms of trade for food producers have declined by half relative to nonfood consumer items as well as cocoa, in response to government policies of exchange rate adjust- ments and higher returns to cocoa farmers (Table 9-3).

These price levels lower real incomes for both farmers and traders of local foodstuffs. Meanwhile they face increased competition from imports now readily available. Despite these reduced opportunities, agriculture and the informal sector are expected to absorb the bulk of the large num- bers of unemployed workers displaced from public and private employ- ment (ILO/JASPA 1989).

Table 9-1. Selected Economic Indicators, Ghana 1985–89.

	1985	1986	1987	1988
1. Basic Indicators				
Per Capita GDP (1975 prices) Cedis	426	436	446	441
Growth rate of per capita GDP (1975 prices) %	2.4	2.3	2.3	3.4
Growth rate of real GDP (%)	5.1	5.2	4.8	6.2
Annual rate of inflation (%)	10.4	24.6	39.8	31.4
2. Growth of Production (%)				
Real GDP	5.1	5.2	4.8	6.2
Agriculture	0.6	3.3	0.0	3.6
Industry	17.6	7.5	11.3	10.3
Manufacturing	24.3	11.1	10.0	9.2
Mining	6.5	3.1	7.9	35.8
Services	7.5	6.5	9.4	7.6
3. Structure of Production (% of GDP)				
Agriculture	51.6	50.7	48.4	47.2
Industry	13.0	13.3	14.1	14.7
Manufacturing	8.5	9.0	9.4	4.7
Mining	1.2	1.1	1.1	1.4
Services	38.0	38.5	40.2	40.8
4. Structure of Demand (% of GDP)				
Government Consumption	15.4	14.9	18.4	NA
Private Consumption	77.1	75.8	73.9	NA
Gross Fixed Investment	9.0	8.3	9.6	NA
Exports of Goods and Non-Factor Services	8.0	10.8	13.3	NA
Imports of Goods and Non-Factor Services	9.6	9.8	15.3	NA
5. Public Finance				
Health Expenditure/GDP (%)	1.2	1.1	1.3	1.2
Health Expenditure/Total Budget (%)	8.7	8.3	9.3	9.0
Real Per Capita Expenditure (1975 Cedis)	0.08	0.09	0.10	0.11
Education Expenditure/GDP(%)	3.0	3.3	3.6	3.5
Education Expenditure/Total Budget (%)	22.3	23.9	26.5	25.1
Real Per Capita Education Expenditure (1975 Cedis)	0.20	0.27	0.31	0.31
Total Expenditure Deficit/GDP (%)	−1.6	0.6	1.2	0.9
6. Balance of Payments				
Current Balance/GDP (%)	−2.5	−2.0	−2.2	−2.0
7. Employment and Wages				
Recorded Employment	464,483	413,737	NA	NA
Growth Rate (%)	3.0	−10.9	NA	NA
Real Minimum Wage Index (1970 = 100)	34.6	35.9	32.1	30.7
8. External Debt				
Total Debt Stock (Million $)	2176	2656	3124	3063
Total Debt Stock/GNP (%)	49.1	47.5	63.3	60.0
Total Debt Service/Exports of Goods and Services (%)	24.0	27.7	45.9	61.4

Source: *Quarterly Digest of Statistics,* Statistical Service, Accra, various issues; World Bank Debt Tables 1988–89.

Table 9-2. Agricultural GDP Growth Rates 1983–88.

	Growth Rate (Percent)				
	1985	1986	1987	1988	1989
Subsector					
Agriculture and Livestock	−1.9	0.2	−0.3	6.0	1.0
Cocoa Production and Marketing	13.2	18.2	3.3	6.3	6.7
Forestry and Logging	0.1	1.2	1.5	3.4	1.6
Fishing	11.9	14.0	−10.1	2.3	4.1
Total Agriculture					
Memo Item:					
Total GDP Growth	5.1	5.2	4.8	6.2	1.9

Source: *Quarterly Digest of Statistics,* September 1989. Statistical Services Accra.

The Programme of Action to Mitigate the Social Costs of Adjustment (PAMSCAD)

Recognition of the negative effects of SAP on the most vulnerable groups in Ghanaian society and the continuing crisis led to the formulation of PAMSCAD in 1987. It aims to reduce the social costs to those identified by the 1989 Ghana Living Standards Survey as at risk: the rural poor, especially in northern Ghana, and underemployed and unemployed persons in the urban informal sector. While still under modification, it allocates a modest US$85 million to provide basic needs through community initiative projects, employment generation for the unemployed, and women's programs including credit and skills and management training. Mitigation of social costs does not extend to traders despite their importance to the ultimate effectiveness of response to the SAP. None of the PAMSCAD schemes includes traders, and neither does the World Bank-initiated private small and medium enterprise development project. The Bank of Ghana announcements of these credits in the *Daily Graphic* in October 1988 outlined application criteria that specifically excluded trade and primary agriculture. This reflects both the persistent view that

Table 9-3. Ghana: Relative Prices of Food 1977–87 (1977 = 100).

	1977	1980	1981	1982	1983	1984	1985	1986	1987
Terms of Trade Food/Non-Food Consumer Items	108	96	91	112	138	86	60	57	42
Relative Prices of Food/Cocoa Production	100	131	92	125	184	136	64	51	42

Source: Loxley 1988.

traders' work benefits none but themselves and traders' continuing relative weakness vis-à-vis the state political formation, as the next section demonstrates.

The Historical Development of the Structural Configuration

The basic questions asked and answered by both the architects and critics of structural adjustment have not been coined anew. Pricing levels, the level of openness to external trade, and the balance of opportunity and control between different local and international groups have been issues for state intervention for centuries. Rather than getting the politics out of trade policy, SAP continues this tradition of active negotiation over terms and conditions of trade. Current participants in the process seek changes that would create both long and short-term advantages in price formation and the structure of economic opportunity. Their interests and strategies owe much to their historical experience with past and present opponents.

In what is now Ghana, as to some extent throughout West Africa, the relative strength of various economic groups has been largely settled and readjusted through the medium of trade. Sophisticated trading networks with North Africa predated coastal contact with European ships, facilitating incorporation into imperial trading systems, but also preserving considerable local initiative within those systems. In each historical period, state actors considered the procedures and terms of trade legitimate political issues because they directly affected the relative power and opportunity of their constituents and themselves.

Early Trade Issues

Local chiefships grew up around control of trade routes and regulation of trade, with local chiefs defending the interests of leading traders. Coastal chiefs negotiated prices (literally the exchange rate between imports and gold, the local currency) with ship captains (Harrop 1964). They gave the largest traders official status and required outsiders to trade through them (De Marees 1602). In the early years, chiefs could and did refuse to deal with captains not meeting their conditions and paying debts (Hopkins 1973).

The paramount chiefs of Asante, the largest inland chiefship after 1800, established an elaborate system of border markets, customs duties, state-sponsored traders, and state loans for trade (Wilks 1975). This reserved for Asante citizens trading opportunities in luxury and military goods and also in the substantial trade in fish, salt, and other foodstuffs. It also enabled chiefs to divert trade to politically cooperative routes.

Under British colonial rule, British trading firms enjoyed the advantages of state support through physical protection, subsidized facilities, and favorable policies. On the coast after 1850 (extending to Asante after conquest in 1900) the largest firms consolidated control of imports and exports by bankrupting or buying out independent African and European traders. They reorganized trade through employed agents or shopkeepers and passbook customers (mainly uneducated women) who could not transfer their accounts between firms (Howard 1978). Firmer subordination of import trade brought feminization. Ambitious coastal men became educated professionals rather than traders with restricted prospects.

Confrontations over control of export trade led to state takeover of this sector. Asante men, once active in chiefly trade, moved rapidly into cocoa farming as cocoa replaced palm oil and rubber exports after 1900. The large exporting firms bought through male agents and independent brokers, largely outside marketplaces. As price levels fell in the 1930s, they tried to preserve their profits by dividing up the territory to prevent competition. The cocoa boycott of 1937–38 protested both the plummeting terms of trade between cocoa and imports and the restricted opportunities for independent brokers, who included many chiefs and other large farmers. A simultaneous boycott of consumer imports organized by market women enabled the cocoa producers to hold out as long as they did, and attracted as much official hostility (Hopkins 1965). The authorities responded by setting up the Cocoa Marketing Board, which collected through employed agents with local monopolies, as the firms had.

The colonial authorities also tried to control terms of trade and opportunities for accumulation in local foodstuffs production and trade. They wanted to keep wages low for themselves and the mining companies and reduce provisioning costs in the barracks and prisons. Food prices rose during both World Wars, when conscription raised institutional populations and made farm labor scarce. Farmers sought to preserve their real incomes as wages and prices of inputs and consumer goods soared. Price controls to prevent such "profiteering" were only attempted in the mining towns and regional capitals where British employer interests arose.

Nationalist Trade Policies

Nationalists before and after independence tried to redress the worsening terms of trade by supporting price controls for imported consumer goods. During World War II, they pressured the British to add import price controls and defended market women against official charges of responsibility for price inflation. They protested when the British frequently adjusted imports prices upwards to preserve the profit margins of British firms against rising costs and shipping losses. They also protested against the accompanying quota system which explicitly protected the British firms market share against African, Syrian, and United States firms able to undercut them with supplies from other sources (Kay 1972).

Their support of traders weakened after independence because the new government faced some of the same wage and supply pressures as the colonialists. Kwame Nkrumah, the first president (1957–66), adopted colonial rhetoric blaming monopolistic market women for shortages. He did reverse colonial priorities by emphasizing import price controls and allocations. He intervened in local foodstuffs pricing mainly through attempts at state distribution through public corporations and cooperatives.

Opportunities in market trading continued to be limited by its increasing marginalization and subordination. State commerce and regulation expanded the importance of bureaucratic processes from which traders were excluded along with most ordinary Ghanaians. Both Nkrumah and his successor, Dr. Busia (1969–72), consulted civil servants and educated businessmen rather than traders on economic policy, despite their support for both political parties as propagandists and fundraisers. Market women now allied with their customers in populist actions over workers' buying power. For example, they demonstrated against the 1961 austerity budget and aided the associated railway strike (Drake and Lacy 1966).

Trade Regulation under the Military

Under Generals Acheampong and Akuffo (1972–79), an elaborate licensing system for imports and foreign exchange continued to restrict trading opportunities for market women in favor of leading military personnel and their associates. Access now depended on personal connections rather than party loyalty or educational qualifications. The sudden commercial prominence of high officials' family members and romantic partners was resented by established market traders as well as the general public.

Import price controls for consumer goods were retained, but enforced intermittently. This kept both legal and illegal channels operational, under very disparate terms of trade. Public sales of goods at control prices in very small quantities took place at short notice, almost always in urban areas. Large workplaces such as factories and government agencies managed to negotiate allocations for workers occasionally, but not small businesses or the self-employed, such as traders. Urban traders thus had only a slightly better chance of obtaining some cheap goods than rural traders or farmers, and only if they were young and strong enough to stand in often violent lines (Clark 1988).

The current head of state, J. J. Rawlings, made a determined attempt to adjust the terms of trade through strict price controls of both imports and local foodstuffs during 1979 and the years of 1981–84. The terms of trade had eroded by then to the point that the young officers and urban workers he championed could not afford imports. The government also could not afford to import legal supplies, making extension to local foodstuffs rather logical.

Direct attacks on market traders were among the first events in both governments. Ordinary retailers bore the brunt of confiscations, forced sales, and beatings, although official news releases claimed they were aimed primarily at large-scale wholesalers. Policy statements elaborated goals of restricting opportunity in trading: reducing traders' profits and economic influence and making trading less attractive than farming or other productive occupations.

Price controls also restricted food farmers' opportunities, and they proved they could respond promptly, gravely disrupting urban food supplies. In 1979 and again in 1982, erratic and violent price enforcement discouraged farmers from sending food to market, harvesting what matured, and planting crops destined for sale (Clark 1988). They also complained the lack of consumer goods gave them no motive to sell. Farmers' refusal to market through official channels put them tacitly on the side of traders, who consistently offered them higher prices and brought out consumer goods.

Food price enforcement rearranged some power balances in the marketplace system. Rural traders had two advantages over urban traders then: they made less convenient targets for confiscation and could grow some food. Traders selling more valuable, usually more profitable processed foodstuffs (like cooking oil) and imports or manufactures also made more attractive targets. Many tried selling ice water, but soldiers began breaking their jars.

The events of 1979 were dramatic, but the longer period of enforcement in 1982–83 had a deeper impact because the government made a more thorough effort to uproot the market system rather than punishing corrupt individuals. Trading in the market was outlawed for many imports and manufactures and new marketing channels were organized through local Committees for the Defense of the Revolution. While these never functioned well enough to effectively collect farm produce or distribute farm inputs and consumer goods, several aspects of trade did come to a standstill.

While wishing to keep working, traders still identified strongly with consumers on the terms of trade issue. Despite traumatic personal experiences, many supported the idea of price controls as such. The military refused to allow them to collaborate in setting overall price levels, as craft and transport organizations had done.

These long crises *widened gaps between high and low capital traders* within the marketplace. No traders were located in Kumasi who had sufficient control of access to goods to actually *profit* from the instability, but large traders could afford to stay home when conditions were worst. Smaller traders living on daily or weekly earnings had to keep coming to market despite real physical danger and risk further financial losses. Large traders lost capital, but saved some to resume business later. The poorest traders lost weight and lost children. Many medium-scale traders survived personally, but became permanently dependent on the remaining large traders for finance, especially after 1983. Relatives or colleagues who might have provided temporary loans after an individual business catastrophe were suffering themselves. This polarization of the market has continued to intensify with the disproportionate impact of SAP on the poorer traders.

Impact of Recent Structural Adjustment Policies

A survey of market traders in Accra and Kumasi and open-ended interviews of traders in Kumasi Central Market were conducted to provide different kinds of information about the impact of ERP/SAP. They focused on changes in trading patterns perceived by traders, and on distinguishing those linked to specific policy changes from those arising from preexisting economic problems. Manuh surveyed 209 traders in Accra and Kumasi in September and October 1989. The sample included traders in the staple commodities of consumption. In order to compare their positions before and after SAP, only persons who had traded for more than five years were selected.

The questionnaire covered shifts in business volumes and commodities traded over time, credit sources, knowledge of the ERP/SAP and its impact on business, services, consumption, and expenditure patterns. The majority of respondents were Akan, married, and bore full responsibility for all household needs. Their mean age was 31–40, the mean household size was 5–7 persons, and 48.3 percent had primary or middle-school education. The majority retailed local food items they bought from other traders in the market. Their average number of years trading was more than 15 years; 41.1 percent had been trading local foodstuffs then, most of whom still did.

Clark interviewed about thirty traders in Kumasi Central Market in December 1989 and January 1990. Enterprise heads who had been fully documented in 1979 were relocated, almost all of whom had also been contacted in 1983 or 1984. Changes in trading practices could thus be dated in relation to major policy initiatives and infrastructural improvements.

First, open-ended questions solicited traders, perceptions of current conditions and their most pressing constraints. Further questions focused on expansion or contraction of enterprise personnel or activities, changes in credit or other relations with associates, and new travel patterns in response to transport improvements. Each trader was interviewed two or three times to encourage less obvious issues to surface. Shifts in gender and ethnic trading roles reflecting shifting overall opportunity structures were also investigated.

Interview Findings

Traders volunteered three major comments on current conditions they considered directly linked to recent government policy changes. The first refers to falling overall demand with the statement "they don't buy." Traders attributed this to high prices arising from devaluation, directly in the case of imports or manufactures and indirectly for local foodstuffs. They said farmers justified their higher farmgate prices with reference to higher prices for farm inputs and higher wages to farm workers. These prices limited demand because of the low buying power among consumers, described with the statement "there is no money." Since wage and budget constraints under SAP expressly aimed to restrict demand, this can be considered a direct intended result of SAP.

The same phrase "there is no money" also was used to refer to traders' own serious lack of capital. The cumulative effect of years of catastrophic losses from confiscations and interrupted trade left many traders with insufficient capital to operate at 1979 levels. Soaring prices continually raised capital requirements in local currency terms at a rate few traders could match. Those barely hanging on were vulnerable to bankruptcy from minor personal or business crises they could previously have weathered with relative ease.

The capital squeeze forced many middle-level traders to withdraw into less profitable operations, widening the gap between rich and poor and closing off avenues of upward mobility. Those no longer able, for example, to fill a truck with yams lost economies of scale and could no longer go on the road. Retailers who could no longer buy in wholesale quantities had to switch to cheaper commodities or buy from intermediaries. Some had given up their market stalls and become hawkers, selling fried snacks or boiling pineapple skins for medicine. Larger traders surviving now placed their capital with direct agents or employees rather than giving credit to autonomous customers as before.

Traders appreciated that physical harassment by soldiers and police had stopped with the deregulation of market trade. Adverse economic conditions, however, prevented them from taking advantage of their new security to expand. The exceptions were mainly in imported and import-substitution commodities, which rebounded from a virtual halt just before ERP and remain lucrative for those who can meet the capital demands. Secondhand clothing, for example, has expanded dramatically since fewer can now afford new ready-made or custom-sewn clothing. Turnover seemed highest in these commodities, so expanding enterprises may have brought in capital from outside sources.

Paradoxically, more people are seeking a livelihood from trading while opportunities within the marketplace system are shrinking from restricted demand. The pressure on the lower ranks of trading is immense from displaced traders from higher levels and new entrants from other economic sectors. Traders complain that the flood of desperate new competitors simply subdivides a limited income, but recognize a right to work for persons with no realistic alternative.

Redeployed public sector workers join those laid off by the private formal sector and young people not finding jobs in either one. Rising numbers of male traders reflect the restricted opportunities in these predominantly male sectors. Young men swell the ranks of secondhand clothing and other gender-integrated commodities. They have even appeared in the female-dominated local foodstuffs yards, creating novel gender tensions when they expect female deference.

Traders did appreciate the recent improvement in road quality and number of vehicles available, since they are heavy transport users. While not strictly an ERP/SAP policy, Ghana's good World Bank standing attracted the donor funds that rehabilitated major trunk roads. Faster trips and more frequent and reliable schedules reduced the amount of capital and labor tied up in slow trips, long waits and searches for trucks, risk reserves for truck breakdowns, and fatigue-related illness. It also reduced the numbers of traders employable on certain routes, since smaller numbers could handle a given volume.

Some intermediary roles seemed to be gradually disappearing with increased efficiency. Specialist travelers based in urban areas found their familiarity with transport facilities and operators brought less competitive advantage now over traders from district towns and villages. Kumasi buyers could go straight to the farms in more areas, rather than patronize local periodic markets. The effects were most dramatic along the rebuilt trunk roads, but the higher vehicle numbers extended some effects to smaller roads that were still passable.

Survey Findings

Shifts in type of commodity traded and business volume reflect changes in the structure of opportunity between 1978 and 1989. The greatest drops were in imported items, with lesser shifts in local food items (Table 9-4). Reasons for shifts cited included lack of supplies, lack of capital, and government restrictions, in that order.

Business volume also declined considerably up to 1984. The proportion of traders reporting *good business volumes* was 68.9 percent for up to 1978, 60.4 percent for 1979–81, 37.5 percent for 1982–83, 22.5 percent for 1983–84, and 27.8 percent for 1987–89. The dramatic decline between 1981 and 1983 reflects government measures when traders were harassed and markets were virtually closed down. Improvement after 1984 was not significant.

Business volumes had increased since 1984 for about 42 percent of traders and declined for 15 percent. Most of the increase was for traders in imported food and non-food items. Thirty-two percent found trade to be good now, 32 percent found it to be the same, and 34 percent found it to be bad or disastrous. Profit levels had increased for only 12.3 percent of the traders.

Looking specifically at different categories of traders, it was found that traders in local food items fared best between 1978–84, while traders in imported items fared worst. Traders in imported food items reported zero volume of business in 1982–83. Following the fortunes of the 68.6 percent of traders for whom business had been good up to 1978, 31.9 percent said business was bad in 1979–81, 33.3 percent said it was bad in 1982–83, 40.3 percent said it was bad in 1984–86, and 43.8 percent said it was bad in 1987–89.

For the majority of traders (52 percent), the period from 1978 to 1984 had been bad in terms of trade volume and profitability. Lack of capital, supply problems, and government restrictions were the main reasons. For a few (14.8 percent), it has been better.

Table 9-4. Shifts in Commodities Traded, 1978–1989

	Local Food	Local Non-Food*	Percentages Imported Food	Imported Non-Food*	Missing	Total
Up to 1978	62.7	19.6	3.8	4.8	9.1	100
1978–1981	54.5	21.5	11.0	9.1	3.9	100
1982–1983	60.8	28.2	2.9	7.2	0.9	100
1984–1986	52.6	27.8	11.0	8.6	0.0	100
1987–1989	57.4	31.1	3.8	7.7	0.0	100

Total Number of Traders: 209
*There appears to have been confusion between locally produced non-food items and imported ones, and percentages under local non-food may consequently be inflated.

When traders' lack of access to credit is borne in mind, lack of capital becomes a real constraint. About 90 percent of traders have no access to institutional credit. They rely mostly on relations and kin, susu contributions, money lenders, and other traders for credit. The few with access to bank credit expressed dissatisfaction with high interest rates, credit limits, and the high savings required to qualify for overdraft facilities.

Structural Adjustment Program Policies

Most traders were aware of major government policy directions in the area of trade and the economy through other traders and the radio. They knew of trade liberalization and the abolition of price controls, since most had been affected by price controls. Surprisingly, there was no significant difference between traders who regarded price controls as necessary and/or useful and those who did not. The traders' position was that the government would be entitled to expect sales at approved prices if they made goods available to them directly.

Overall, the majority of traders saw government policies as adversely affecting trade from 1984 on, as there was less purchasing due to higher prices. Sources of supply had widened, with more availability of transport and better roads for local items and the liberalized climate for imported items. However, traders also reported greater competition from new entrants. In addition, they have had to pay additional taxes as a result of the government policy of widening the tax net, noting increased market tolls and exactions.

Since ERP/SAP, traders reported more cordial relations with several social groups. They felt consumers no longer regarded them as profiteers and hoarders. Relations with soldiers and police had also improved greatly, and traders believed the government regarded them more favorably. Relations with city officials had gone through more twists and turns.

Traders were dissatisfied with measures aimed at improving sanitation and relieving overcrowded markets because of mistreatment of hawkers, loss of capital, and relocation of traders to remoter, less profitable markets.

Traders noted improvements in roads and transport, in market infrastructure, and in the disposal of waste and sanitation. Those in Accra mentioned the construction of the new 31st December market in Accra, with its bank, post office, health post, and childcare center. Those in Kumasi believed siting a bank within the market precincts would assist them. All wanted further improvements to the working environment and credit programs.

As consumers themselves, traders reported positive and negative effects of ERP/SAP. Almost equal numbers said their quality of life had eroded (31 percent) or improved (29.7 percent). Although goods are more available, with more choice, higher prices bar access to goods and services. Traders reported higher expenditures on household needs, with food taking up to 50 percent of total expenditure. With cost-recovery conditionalities in social services, the higher charges for water, electricity, transportation, and health care now consume a major share.

Analysis

Consideration of survey and interview findings together reinforces the importance originally suggested for a framework embracing the terms of trade, the structure of opportunity, and the relative balance of power between various socioeconomic groups. The most significant impact of SAP has come through devaluation and changes in relative pricing, although the credit squeeze compounds its effects. Falling demand and the influx of new traders both reflect and demonstrate the dropping relative power of traders and other disenfranchised groups.

Devaluation and Pricing

The deregulation of prices and continuing devaluation of the cedi have brought worsening terms of trade and higher prices for both locally produced and imported items. Higher prices for goods and services and charges for social services led to lower consumption levels confirmed by the Ghana Living Standards Survey. The majority of traders perceived negative consequences from high prices for their quality of life.

As intended, higher price increases than wage increases under SAP have decreased overall demand for goods. The volume of trade has not improved significantly from the crisis levels just before SAP, keeping trading incomes low. The widening gap between rich and poor specifically reduces the buying power of the poorer segments of the population who are most likely to purchase most of their needs in the market.

Traders themselves mainly fall into these same lower-income categories. Imports and manufactures are beyond reach; even local food prices force painful nutritional choices. Fees for medical care, schooling, water, and electricity are prohibitive for many. As women, these traders bear a disproportionate burden in compensating with their own labor for services and supplies cut back or forgone and the falling real incomes of other family members. *Belt tightening becomes an empty phrase under these conditions.* These women either never owned belts or have long since sold them to buy medicine.

Credit

Higher prices also increase demands for working capital in a period when the credit squeeze makes expanding capital very difficult. Smaller autonomous traders either become tied agents or employees or are replaced by these. This concentrates power and income in fewer hands, creating more opportunities for abuses. The few large traders surviving face less competition, so they can increase profit margins and find associates willing to accept more direct control.

Traders may not have ever had access to bank credit, but its restriction affects them indirectly. Relatives and associates that might earlier have qualified for bank loans now compete with them for informal loan funds. Meanwhile, higher fees for medical care, schooling, and utilities reduce the amounts available. The high current interest rates for bank loans make them less attractive to those who still qualify.

Increased credit to the informal sector would make a substantial contribution to economic recovery by generating employment. The ILO/JASPA report considers credit a general constraint to the informal sector. Commercial banks have been reluctant to lend to small producers and require collateral and other conditions they can rarely meet. Most traders see capital as their greatest obstacle and request credit assistance, despite the lack of official interest and deliberate exclusion of traders from PAMSCAD and other credit schemes.

Redeployment

The retrenchment of workers in the public and large-scale private sectors without any organized "redeployment" has sent large numbers of would-be traders into the market. Sectors supposedly favored by SAP have apparently not been able to respond sufficiently with increased production or income to compensate appreciably for shrinking sectors. Despite the express intent of SAP, imports have driven out local import substitutes in rice, cooking oil, clothing, and other commodity groups. Employment cutbacks have extended to many smaller private and informal businesses, which depend heavily on orders and consumption financed by the formal and public sector.

Planners seem to take for granted the ability of these displaced workers to find at least minimal subsistence in an informal sector without any additional resources. In fact, its income-generating capacity is severely restricted by some of the same conditions hampering the formal sector. Traders show considerable sympathy for the newcomers, even across the accepted gender and ethnic boundaries of the marketplace. For all their renowned ingenuity, however, they cannot spin gold from straw. Creating additional jobs within a shrinking volume of trade simply slices the cake thinner and thinner for all concerned.

Urban Infrastructure

Market traders have gained from prominent improvements in urban infrastructure under SAP. They gain in comfort and efficiency from the gradual improvement of city streets, trunk roads, and vehicle numbers. Improved garbage collection and proposed public toilet rebuilding give priority to high-use areas such as markets. Major market rebuilding projects have been completed in Accra and proposed in Kumasi.

Extensive street clearance campaigns around official markets, major shopping areas, and intersections have mainly harmed other categories of traders. They target hawkers (with no fixed locations), streetside kiosks, and unofficial locations housing small and medium-scale traders, producers, and service workers. Confusing and contradictory implementation intensifies hardships, for example, by requiring and then confiscating expensive improvements. These measures probably leave traders with market stalls better off by reducing competition. They also eliminate the trading options most accessible to traders with few social or financial resources.

Conclusion

Rather than reversing the effects of the prolonged economic crisis on market traders, the ERP/SAP seems to have continued or intensified them.

The terms of trade and structure of opportunity for traders have been worsening for decades. Continuing polarization between high and low capital traders has deepened hardship at the lower end without allowing significant expansion at the higher end.

Aggressively hostile actions towards traders have largely ceased under SAP, but capital shortage and falling demand seem to be equally effective in limiting their trading. Recovery in trading volume and income has been surprisingly slight, given the extreme political, social, and climatic crisis conditions immediately preceding SAP in 1982–83. Traders benefit from general infrastructural improvements, but suffer more from policies restricting demand and money supply.

PAMSCAD is intended as a palliative to many of the hardships admittedly created by SAP in the short term. Its planned interventions, though modest, aim to provide basic needs for the highly vulnerable groups identified. The ILO/JASPA study also recommends concrete measures to address unmet needs of the redeployed and underemployed youths. None of these programs consider traders as among their constituency, although they expect the marketplace system to contribute substantially to meeting the needs of others.

Official reluctance or refusal to help traders deal with the new demands made upon them may well reflect continuing hostility to them and misunderstanding of their function in the Ghanaian economy. After all, trade liberalization arose as much from external pressure as from internal conviction (of government, traders, or consumers). The local belief that traders contribute nothing to the broader economy—and the longer-term mistrust of market women—undermine SAP policies of trade liberalization and privatization. Increasing the structure of opportunity for traders or their power relative to other social groups looks counterproductive.

Unfortunately such exclusion of market traders from economic planning and resources threatens the whole process of economic growth, inside or outside of SAP. Their own standard of living is inseparable from levels of consumption and production in other sectors, but reverse linkages are equally strong. Impoverishment of the marketplace system makes it less effective as a distributive network and an employment generator for nourishing the productive and human resources of the nation.

REFERENCES

Clark, Gracia
    1988   *Traders Versus the State.* Boulder: Westview Press.
    forthcoming Food Traders and Food Security. *The Political Economy of*

African Famine: The Class and Gender Basis of Hunger, R.E. Downs, D. O. Kerner, and S. P. Reyna, eds. London: Gordon and Breach.

De Marees, Peiter
1602 *Chronicle of the Gold Coast of Guinea.* Translated 1985 by A. Van Dantzig and Adam Smith. Oxford: Oxford University Press.

Drake, St. Clair, and Leslie Lacy
1966 Government Versus the Unions: The Sekondi-Takoradi Strike, 1961. *Politics in Africa: 7 Cases,* Gwendolen Carter, ed. New York: Harcourt, Brace and World.

Economist Intelligence Unit
1989 *Country Profile, Ghana 1989–90.* London: Economist.

Ghai, Dharan, and Cynthia Hewitt de Alcantara
1989 The Crisis of the 1980s in Africa, Latin America and the Caribbean: Economic Impact, Social Change and Political Implications. UNRISD Discussion Paper No. 7, Geneva.

Ghana Government
1987a *National Program for Economic Development.* Accra.
1987b *Programme of Actions to Mitigate the Social Cost of Adjustment.* Accra.

Green, Reginald
1988 Ghana: Progress, Problematics and Limitations of the Success Story. *IDS Bulletin* 19 (1).

Harrop, Sylvia
1964 The Economy of the West African Coast in the 16th Century. *Economic Bulletin of Ghana* 8:15.

Hopkins, A. G.
1965 Economic Aspects of Political Movements in the Gold Coast and Nigeria, 1918–39. *Journal of African History* 7:133.
1973 *An Economic History of West Africa.* New York: Columbia.

Howard, Rhoda
1978 *Colonialism and Underdevelopment in Ghana.* London: Croom Helm.

International Labor Organisation (ILO)
1989 *From Redeployment to Sustained Employment Generation: Challenges for Ghana's Programme of Economic Recovery and Development.* Addis Ababa: ILO.

Kay, G. B.
1972 *The Political Economy of Colonialism in Ghana.* Cambridge: Cambridge University Press.

Loxley, John
1988 *Ghana: Economic Crisis and the Long Road to Recovery.* Ottawa: North-South Institute.

Republic of Ghana Statistical Service
1989 *Ghana Living Standards Survey.* World Bank Social Dimension of Adjustment Project Unit, First Report. Accra.
1988 *Quarterly Digest of Statistics* (various issues). Accra.

Robertson, Claire
    1984   *Sharing the Same Bowl: A Socioeconomic History of Women and Class in Accra, Ghana.* Bloomington, Indiana: Indiana University Press.
Tabatabai, A.
    1986   Adjustment Policies and Access to Food in Ghana. *International Labor Review* 127 (6).
World Bank
    1989   *Debt Tables, 1986–89.* Washington, D.C.: World Bank.

III

Impacts of Structural Transformation and Adjustment Policies

10 The Ideology and Political Economy of Gender: Women and Land in Nso, Cameroon

Miriam Goheen

These are trying times in Cameroon as in much of sub-Saharan Africa. Per capita incomes throughout the subcontinent have fallen continuously during the 1980s while prices have increased dramatically. Economic performance and living standards are now significantly worse than in the 1970s (Commonwealth Secretariat 1989). In rural Cameroon, the current economic crisis and its consequences are evident in the routine of daily life. Posters in the banks portray an industrious ant piling up savings while admonishing bank patrons to do the same as a prophylactic against the more disastrous effects of the "Crise Economique." Women's lapas are worn and faded, their voices tired and urgent as they gather around cooking fires to share gossip about market prices and strategies on how best to sell dear and buy cheap to maximize time and money. Taxi parks are crammed full of young boys jostling each other in search of the occasional odd job or just passing time—boys who in better times would be sitting in the classroom—while in the bars men drink palm wine in place of bottled beer and regale each other with financial hard-luck stories, complaining of the salaries and coffee money owed them for the past six months or eight months or year.

High prices, low incomes, long waits for salaries and wages already earned: the economic crisis has cast a shadow on the fortunes of most people in Nso in western Cameroon. It has settled most heavily on the lives of poorer farmers and women (categories which substantially overlap) and those who depend on them. The importance of women's informal sector earnings and of crops produced for consumption to total household income has increased dramatically as have demands on female time and labor. Higher prices paid for agricultural products have not increased real

Miriam Goheen is an assistant professor of cultural anthropology at Amherst College, Massachusetts. She has a Ph.D. in anthropology from Harvard University and has done extensive fieldwork in the Grassfields, North West Province, Cameroon.

239

rural household income since the markup is accompanied by higher marketing costs, and higher prices for essential manufactured goods and for services such as education and health care. While most men can confine themselves to income-generating pursuits, most women, in addition to being heavily involved in food production and assuming the burden of provisioning the household, take prime responsibility as home managers, child bearers, and caretakers of children and the elderly (Commonwealth Secretariat 1989). Women have borne the brunt of the economic crisis; it is they who have had to find the means for families to survive.

Public Policy and Gender

It is unsettling and ironic that national economic and agricultural policy favors elite farmers at the expense of small rural producers, the majority of whom are women. Women's work in the food sector is a major source of rural family welfare. Furthermore, women's sales of surplus food represent by far the major source of Cameroon's commercial food supply (Guyer 1987). Yet arguably, the policies of Cameroon's current one-party state can best be understood as an attempt to consolidate political hegemony by meeting the interests of the capitalist, professional and upper-level bureaucratic and military classes at the expense of rural smallholders in general and women farmers in particular (Ntangsi 1987, Koopman [Henn] 1989). Agricultural policy, including land allocation and acquisition, is seriously biased in favor of the urban and governmental elite rather than rural smallholders (Koopman [Henn] 1989, Goheen 1988b).

Although they respond more quickly and efficiently and positively to new market opportunities by increasing food production than do men, women food farmers are virtually never included in policy discussions and their interests are rarely if ever given serious consideration (Koopman [Henn] 1989). This paper is an attempt to explain why this is true, in particular with regard to access to land, and why in the long run it is such bad policy for this to be so.

Ideology regarding gender categories has been a primary stumbling block to women's access to resources, particularly to land, in the current political economy. The cultural categories of gender in Nso today, as in the past, link farming-female-food as a gender marker. The designation of women as primary food farmers and providers has sometimes been problematic but it has until recently effectively encouraged a relative equality and complementarity between male and female qualities (Kaberry 1952,

Goheen 1984). With changing material conditions, which are increasingly determined by the political economy of the marketplace and commoditization, the complementary roles played by men and women have become much less equal. Women in Nso are discovering ironically that the very qualities which have assured their status and power are those which have been undermined and subverted by the marketplace and the increasing differential valuation of male and female work. The contradictions in women's role as primary food farmers have deepened, and there is now evident a "feminization of poverty"—a poverty exacerbated by a growing social stratification in rural as well as urban Cameroon.

Changes in the status of women's roles have resulted partly from the changing meaning of the limits set on women's access to and control over productive resources—especially land and education—and from a simultaneous increase in the demands on female labor and income. In Nso, people are not starving, but some are hungry and malnourished, and almost half the population of rural villages has only a minimally adequate diet (Ariza-Nino et al. 1982). The weakening of women's entitlements to land, labor, and credit potentially threatens the nutritional level not only of the rural household but of a large proportion of the national population (Guyer 1987, Hill 1986). In Cameroon women grow the bulk of the food consumed nationally; women in Nso grow virtually all the food consumed locally as well as significant amounts of the national supply of corn, beans, and Irish potatoes.[1]

A decline in national food self-sufficiency over the past decade has intensified the government's interest in developing commercial agriculture in Nso and the surrounding region. The decline in food self-sufficiency has become an area of focus and political concern for the current regime. Until the mid-1980s Cameroon was almost entirely self-sufficient in food production. This was a source of pride and nationalist rhetoric from the central government. By 1984–85 the percentage was under 90 percent; food imports rose in that year by nearly 8 percent for a total of 40 billion FCFA (Ngu 1989).[2] This trend has continued into the present, increasing—in rhetoric at least—a national emphasis on agricultural development and commercialized agriculture in the Grassfields region, including Nso.

The social relations of production in Nso and the struggles over their changing meaning have created a discourse in which female voices, which should be at the center of these conversations, are instead muted and often silent. Changing material conditions have exacerbated contradictions in the division of labor, especially where these involve gender roles. I will argue in this paper that a resolution of these contradictions is important to the production of an adequate food supply and that a necessary step to resolving these contradictions is an understanding of Nso gender ideology, which emphasizes women's obligation to farm food crops while denying them ownership of the fields. The relevance of women's labor to the production of an adequate food supply will be placed in context through an exploration of the relationships among the household economy, the political economy of land, and gender ideology, along with the cultural norms and practices in which these are embedded in the production and reproduction of inequalities.

I will argue four points in this connection. First, women's labor is the most critical factor in the social reproduction of Nso society. Second, while gender is central to an understanding of agricultural production and food sufficiency, it is not always sufficient: it must be understood in the context of increasing rural stratification. Third, rural stratification leads to differential access to resources, the most important of which are land and education, which in turn are related to access to the national bureaucracy. Fourth, in a context of increasing stratification and land privatization, Nso authoritative discourse,[3] which places responsibility to provide food and income on women but gives them no control over productive resources, increases gender inequality, marginalizes and impoverishes women, and endangers local and national food self-sufficiency.

Women's Labor in Social Reproduction[4]

Historically the Nso chiefdom has been the largest and most powerful chiefdom in the Bamenda Grassfields in what is today the Northwest Province (NWP) of Cameroon. This Province is today one of two anglophone provinces in a largely Francophone country. Land area is 1,730,000 hectares—approximately 3.8 percent of the national territory. With a population well over one million, the NWP is one of the most densely settled areas in the country, with an average of over 53 persons/km². Over 85 percent of the population lives in rural areas, compared to 72 percent nationwide. In Bui Division, whose boundaries follow the boundaries of the Nso chiefdom, the population is approximately 200,000, with a density of well over 65/km², most of whom are designated as rural dwellers. Good arable farmland with even marginally adequate transport access is in short supply—a situation which has been exacerbated by both population growth and government programs encouraging agricultural development and land privatization (Scott and Mahaffey 1980, Goheen-Fjellman and Matt 1981, Goheen 1984). We will examine this relationship in more detail in the next section; suffice it here to say that while it is essential that women maintain access to land within the household economy, this is becoming costly in terms of both time and money.

In order to understand the seriousness of women's marginalization in terms of access to land, we must first have a working knowledge of the domestic economy which relies so heavily on women's labor and their contribution to household subsistence. The household is the basic unit of production. Over 90 percent of food consumed is homegrown and 85 percent of all income is produced within the household economy—that is, through sale of agricultural products rather than wages or salary. Women's production is primarily subsistence oriented. They till, plant, weed, and harvest virtually all food crops—activities which require year-round, almost daily attention.

While women's labor is allocated to household subsistence, men's labor is allocated to growing cash crops and to investment in capital-intensive and often status-oriented activities. Men and women most often work in different sectors of the economy and do not necessarily combine or allo-cate their time and resources to maximize the commodity output of the household as a unit (Guyer 1980, 1984, Guyer and Peters 1987, Goheen 1988a). Husbands and wives keep separate budgets and each is expected to meet expenses—personal, production, and specific family expenses such as medical and school fees—from his or her own earnings. Men and women have different networks and obligations within and between households. The growth of the market economy has created new needs and new visions, increasing both expectations and the amount of cash needed to reproduce the rural household. Thus new demands have been levied on both male and female incomes.

An overwhelming percentage of the food supply is produced by women; they cultivate over 90 percent of the food available to the house-hold. The cultural tradition which places the responsibility to feed the family on women leaves most female farmers with relatively little mar-ketable output and little time to increase production. Yet women con-tribute 42 percent of the household income in cash value, including the market value of their subsistence crops; one-quarter of actual cash expenses are paid by women's cash income. Women's expenditures are dominated by supplements to the household food supply such as condi-ments, palm oil, salt, soap, etc. Virtually all of a woman's cash income is spent on household items and children's education, while men divide their expenditures between capital-intensive items within the household such as zinc for roofing, furniture, school and medical fees, and items outside the household, including gifts to relatives and friends, and payments to men's fraternal organizations where they wine and dine—their compatriots.

The household in Nso can be seen as the principal place where commodity and noncommodity relations come together. Women's production is oriented toward the production of subsistence (use value) while men's is oriented toward creating capital—both material and symbolic—a much more individualistic quest. The point is not that men are uninterested in the welfare of their families, but rather that they are not held socially responsible for the family's basic food security. They rarely purchase items routinely used on a daily basis to prepare the family meals; when they do purchase consumables these tend to be "prestige" supplements such as sugar, tea, white bread, or meat.

By assuming the social responsibility for provisioning the household, women's labor underwrites and supports men's activities outside the household. Women produce, provision, reproduce, and underwrite the reproduction of social relations not only within the household but within the larger society as well. While obviously critical on the home front, the importance of women's labor transcends the local scene. A significant amount of work on men's coffee farms is done by women, the proceeds of which accrue to the male household head; thus women's labor supports both export and food crops. And women have, throughout Cameroon's recorded history, managed to feed both the rural and the urban population (Guyer 1987, Koopman [Henn] 1989). Clearly it is crucial that women maintain access to land if they are to continue to underwrite not only the local nutrition and the reproduction of social relations but also the adequacy of the national food supply.

Growing Privatization and Concentration of Land

While nutrition levels are not yet critical, many households are at risk and are increasingly vulnerable in the context of a process of commoditization and the further development of markets among differentiated rural producers. Land issues loom large since guaranteed access to land is essential to the ability of rural subsistence farmers to continue to feed the household at even a marginally acceptable nutritional level. Land is increasingly scarce and expensive—especially arable land within reasonable trekking distance from rural villages—and it is becoming scarce and privatized in ways which potentially marginalize small farmers, especially women (Goheen 1988b).

Throughout Nso there is an uneasiness that the commoditization of land and escalating land prices will lead to the marginalization if not outright disenfranchisement of small rural producers. National policies aimed ostensibly at stemming the tide of dependence on imported foods have instead encouraged land speculation by a growing rural elite who file for large amounts of land for "development projects," which more often than not develop personal fortunes rather than the national food supply. Land for farming even in outlying villages is becoming scarce and often expensive, much to the dismay of most Nso farmers who consider access to land to be a right of citizenship. A critical aspect of this potential disenfranchisement is the fact that the majority of the small rural producers are women. While individual households have to date been able to gain access to enough land to more or less adequately satisfy subsistence needs, some are having difficulty doing so and many women trek long distances to farm. Since women are viewed as competent to manage the crops but not to own the fields, the trend towards privatization has undermined women's secure rights of usufruct under the traditional tenure scheme. This ideology is played out in the allocation of new land through government development projects that not only discriminate against women but often directly exclude them from participation.[5]

If we just look at national statistics these apprehensions appear unfounded, and consequently land tenure issues until very recently have been largely ignored in national and international development schemes, with the exceptions of Davison (1988) and Reyna and Downs (1988). These statistics do not allow us an adequate reading of the meaning of land use patterns, and clearly do not give a clue as to regional patterns. Cameroon is an extremely diverse country, both culturally and ecologically. Land tenure patterns, farm size, and population density vary from one region to another.

National bureaucrats and others in positions of local and regional power use their influence to manipulate the national land ordinances to further their individual positions, both by acquiring substantial amounts of land themselves and by helping others to do so in return for personal favors. It is well known that "they" have differential access to large tracts of land, but names and figures are elusive. Fingers are pointed and rumors abound, but the actual facts do not appear to be a matter of public record (Goheen 1988b, Jua 1989).

While not yet national issues, land scarcity and land distribution have become local issues in the more densely populated rural areas like the Northwest Province, including Nso. These conflicts are reflected in the increasing confrontations between farmers and herders and in the growing number of court cases involving land disputes. The issues are complicated by a local ideology which stresses that farm land for subsistence production should be both free and freely available to all. The current conflicts over land in Nso involve a complex set of issues, which include struggles over the meanings of land, of communal commitment, and of gender.

Land Use, Abuse, and Conflicts

As noted earlier, the Grassfields is viewed as a potential breadbasket by a national government beset by economic problems and sensitive to the political implications of increasingly large food deficits and imports. With a healthy climate and diverse ecological zones, the region has long been a rich agricultural area and center of long-distance trade. But while the government has a keen interest in developing commercial agriculture in and around Nso, this goal is more easily envisioned than accomplished. Although ecologically diverse and agriculturally rich, this is also an area of steep escarpments cut by low-lying valleys. Poor roads, high transport costs, and consequent low farmgate prices have discouraged commercially oriented food production. Farmers receive less than one-third of retail prices; transport costs account for two-thirds of the markup (Scott and Mahaffey 1980). Most of the fertile low-lying farmland has no road access during rainy season and limited access at any time; many villages have seasonally restricted market access, while much of the area with good market access is either planted with coffee or too steep for mechanized commercial farming.

Transport costs have clearly been a critical stumbling block to increased production. But access to other resources—to arable land and credit for capital inputs—is also a critical factor. The government in Yaounde, while slow to respond to improving the roads, attempted to encourage increased production by instituting a number of land ordinances in 1974 ostensibly aimed at land reform and opening up new areas for production (United Republic of Cameroon 1974, Goheen 1984). Although these ordinances were expressly instituted to clarify land use rights and give small farmers a surety of tenure so as to encourage expansion, they have instead, by virtue of their ambiguous content and relationship to customary tenure, created increasing stratification between the uneducated small village farmers who cannot take advantage of them, and the better-educated rich farmers who can and do. Since customary tenure arrangements are an integral part of traditional subsistence agriculture, the state-promoted economic development of agriculture and privatization of land title have created complex changes in tenure relationships and arrangements at every level of society. At the same time, customary tenure has remained the primary mode of access to farmland for most people in Nso—for virtually all women—and the ideology that farmland should be free and available to all Nso citizens remains a salient theme in local politics.

Rights over control and access to land and the meaning of these rights have become a source of growing controversy and debate. Farmer-herder competition for land and population growth, the most visible source of scarcity, are relatively obvious and conversations about these, while often acrimonious, remain within a familiar discourse. Two other conflicts are also changing the social relations of land control. The first stems from competition over land for commercial as opposed to subsistence use. This appears on the surface often to be a gender conflict. The second concerns the ambiguous relationship between customary tenure arrangements and national land policy. This may on first reading be interpreted as a national-local conflict.

The Role of "Modern Big Men"

But to reduce this problem to a two-factor formula is to oversimplify a complicated set of issues. These conflicts are actually the expression of an increasingly obvious rural economic stratification; that is, they are the result of large-scale land acquisition by the new rural elites which both limits the amount of land available to smallholders and commoditizes land and its use, especially in and around the larger villages. I have referred elsewhere to these new elites as "modern big men" to distinguish them from traditional lineage heads; but traditional-modern is a false dichotomy. The modern big men are actively involved in traditional politics: they obtain titles in secret societies and have become familiar faces at the Fon's palace. (*Fon* is the name by which Grassfield chiefs are known). These men have in effect become the new lineage leaders. The participation of the new elites in local cultural and political practices combined with their access to the state facilitates new forms of accumulation which are protected by the old hierarchical order. Land is becoming concentrated in the hands of this new elite—who are almost exclusively male. The position of power of this new elite is both anchored in local tradition and reinforced by its access to the state; new relations of domination become fused with the hierarchy of traditional politics. This collaboration has facilitated the acquisition of land by these new elites through national land allocation grants, which must be approved by both national and traditional authorities.

Women are not precluded in law from access to national land grants. But since in local belief and practice women own only the crops and not the fields, women very rarely file successfully for these land grants. The marginalization of women producers has not been replaced with increased agricultural production by these new capitalist farmers. To date, little of the land acquired by national grant has been brought into production. Instead it is used for speculation and as surety on loans and investments in commercial ventures and urban properties which bring more immediate returns (Jua 1989). Disturbingly, the practices of these new elites reduce the amount of land available to smallholders and limit the amount of capital invested in food production.

The emerging rural stratification in Nso isn't a question of traditional/modern or local/national or simply male/female: it is a question of differential access to resources through knowledge of how to manipulate both national laws and local institutions. The modern big men take advantage of the ambiguous juxtaposition of national land ordinances with customary tenure arrangements, grafting new inequalities onto the already existing relations of domination. We cannot view the national context and the local context as discrete units nor as directly opposed. But the goals of national policy may ultimately be at odds with local needs and with local values stressing self-sufficiency and freely available land. The struggles over land for subsistence as opposed to cash crops are not simply a gender issue. Given that access to land is crucial to the rural standard of living—indeed to the ability of most households to grow sufficient food—it is important to understand the ability to control land in terms of both gender hierarchy and stratification between households.

New Forms of Stratification

Throughout Nso history, titled men have enjoyed status and power, a power reinforced by religious beliefs, ritual obligation, and an elaborate code of etiquette. But the material effects of these inequalities have by and large been mediated by obligations between leaders and their dependents, obligations which have ensured access to land to satisfy subsistence needs. What is new is the ability of the new elite to accumulate significant

amounts of individual wealth with little consideration of the marginalization of others with regard to access to productive resources. The discourse
which emphasizes the ideology that farmland should be free is today not
supported by existing material conditions. The fusion of new relations of
domination and traditional forms of power protects new forms of accumulation and legitimates new forms of stratification. Within these new
forms of stratification gender ideology has contributed to a weakening of
women's inalienable rights to land. The ways in which the discourse
regarding gender has succeeded in materially reproducing and maintaining women in a marginal position must be placed within the context of
this growing rural stratification.

Household income in Nso, ranges from a high of 7 million FCFA (US
$35,000) to a low of 14,500 FCFA (US $72.50). (Average annual household income was 447,270 FCFA [US $2,236] with a standard deviation
of 427,980 FCFA [US $2,136], indicating a high degree of stratification
within the entire sample.) Farm size and nutrition levels too are unequally
distributed (Goheen 1988a). Since credit access often depends on farm
size and cash crop production levels, small farmers—male and female
alike—have little access to credit. Jua (1989) notes that no small farmers
have been given government loans and that the government "displays an
inordinate penchant to give loans mainly to civil servants and wage earners wishing to engage in agriculture." Government loans tend to increase
the wealth of these civil servants and wage earners without substantially
increasing agricultural production nor the actual amount of capital
invested in agriculture.

The marginalization of the small farmer is apt to increase in the next
few years. The food and export crop section of the Sixth Five Year Plan
(1986–91) highlights a program to offer credit, production subsidies, and
other incentives to so-called "medium scale farmers," defined as persons
who own and supervise production on 50–100 hectares. The average food
farm in Nso is 1.2 hectares; even if the amount of land under cultivation
for coffee were added to this, few households have more than five hectares
available for food and cash crop production in combination. The
"medium scale farmer" of the sixth Five Year Plan are typically local
bureaucrats or large-scale entrepreneurs or, even more likely, urban-based
elites who may or may not use their credit advantage to increase agricultural productivity (Koopman [Henn] 1988). And clearly, these "medium
scale farmers" are not female.

The situation of small producers, especially women, is getting worse.
In the context of rather rapid commoditization of land and deepening

market relations, access to scarce capital for labor, transport, and expansion becomes more critical. In poorer households women must trek further to farms. Their land lies fallow for shorter periods of time, decreasing its fertility and yield. They contribute a higher percentage of cash income to the household budget and pay a higher percentage of "male" expenses, such as medical and school fees.

Gender Categories and the Authoritative Discourse

In Nso today, gender ideologies assert the fundamental differences between male and female qualities; these are realized in differences in tools used, crops grown, plots cultivated, and the division of labor. Social categories of women as producers, provisioners, and caretakers (of food and children) and men as hunters, warriors, and big men—as protectors, status seekers, and authority figures—are reproduced in the division between male and female in production and in the reproduction of the domestic economy.

As is the case with all power relations, gender relations are determined by the material conditions of everyday life. It is an everyday life in which women's work is assigned no real value. It is an everyday life where, although women produce most of the crops, they are denied ownership of the fields; an everyday life where women are assigned the longest, hardest, most tedious tasks, tasks whose definition as "women's work" involves a downgrading of status and value. It is an everyday life in which the definition of male and female qualities has remained static while material conditions have changed and one in which the complementarity once denoted by gender categories has been lost with the changing material conditions which are increasingly determined by the political economy of the marketplace and commoditization. A woman's everyday life in Nso today is experienced as one in which male/female cultural categories and qualities guarantee inequality.

Structural Change and Continuity in Women's Position

Women's role as primary farmers has remained essentially the same since Phyllis Kaberry (1952) wrote her classic study *Women of the Grassfields* in which she called women "the backbone of the country." Today, as in the past, women in Nso derive a good deal of their status and sense of pride from their position as primary food producers. A woman without a farm is suspect as lazy, a bad citizen, even immoral—clearly not capable of fulfilling the obligations of an adult Nso woman. Today Nso women are working longer hours, traveling long distances to farm, are more actively involved in marketing, and are cultivating twice as much land as they were thirty years ago, in order to earn the cash to fulfill their obligation to provision the household. Their control over land has weakened, and their access to credit, labor, fertilizer, and education is much less than that of men's access to such resources. State policies regarding land allocation and agricultural credit for development programs widen the gap between male/female access to crucial assets, while local norms and ideology perpetuate static ideals of male-female roles and spheres of influence.

To understand the dynamics of local and national agricultural production we need to understand the ways in which the structural positions occupied by both farm women and "big men" are justified by gender ideology and the ways in which these are reproduced by local practices. Differential access by gender to critical resources—land, labor, credit, and education—is central to this understanding. It can be argued that women as a group have been differentially impoverished by the current economic crisis. But gender itself is not a homogeneous, undifferentiated category. The importance of gender should not blind us from exploring other unequal dimensions of stratification which, while not independent of gender, are not entirely coterminous. These include overall access to education, to wage and salaried jobs, to capital, and, perhaps most important, knowledge of and access to the national bureaucracy (Hart 1982, Kennedy 1988, Lubeck 1987, Nafziger 1987).

Conclusion

I have argued that women in Nso have borne the brunt of the economic crisis. Women have continued to assume the social responsibility for feeding the household and for finding the means for their families to survive. The sale of their surplus production is a significant contribution to the urban food supply while the labor they perform on men's coffee farms contributes to cash crop production and thus to government revenues. Yet national economic and agricultural policies favor elite farmers at the expense of small producers, the majority of whom are women.

Placing elite farmers at the center of the national program to increase food production has troubling implications for the future of the economic welfare of rural smallholders. If the schemes for large-scale capitalist farming succeed, elite farmers will be able to outcompete traditional farmers, and women will lose their only source of income. Even more worrisome is the likelihood that elites will gain control of large tracts of land and fail to develop the food sector, opting instead for export crops or for investments outside the agricultural sector. Women in Cameroon feed both the rural areas and the urban centers. If they lose their ability to do so the overall picture is bleak. Clearly any national policy which fails to incorporate women's concerns is not only discriminatory but also jeopardizes the long-term utility of the policy itself.

Gender is a—if not *the*—critical factor to an understanding of the consequences of changing relations of production and the implication of these for agricultural production and food self-sufficiency in Cameroon in general and Nso in particular. Although women in effect underwrite the food sufficiency and the social reproduction of Nso society, they are essentially excluded from ownership, inheritance, and real control of land both by the current structure of customary tenure and by national land and development policies. As a group, women also have less access to other crucial resources than do men. But gender in and of itself is not sufficient to our understanding; gender must be understood within the context of a rapidly growing rural stratification—a stratification in income and farm size, in education and access to credit, in employment opportunities, and by unequal access to the national bureaucracy. The power position of the new elites and their differential access to resources including land are facilitated by their roots in local cultural and political patterns— patterns which exclude women from land ownership. What Vaughan (1987: 131) notes regarding women's entitlements in Malawi is pertinent here: "... the gender dimension does not always override that of class and employment, but the fact that it sometimes does is nevertheless of interest."

Finally, I have argued that gender in this context cannot be understood without a comprehension of local gender categories and qualities and the ways in which these are maintained in the daily reality of male control of ownership and access to resources. Gender categories assign to "male" the qualities of protectors, status seekers, and authority figures, and to "female" the qualities of producers, reproducers, and provisioners of both food and children. These qualities are reflected in patterns of income, expenditure, and investment, as well as by tools used, crops produced, land farmed, and the division of labor, and are reproduced by daily practices—what Bourdieu (1977) calls "the mundane workings of everyday life." Farming-food-female are linked as gender qualities, although women's role as farmers is limited by the fact that they are precluded from owning the fields. This ideology has been central to women's exclusion from control over critical resources, especially but not exclusively from national land and development projects. If the connection between farming-food-female is to be reproduced in a way that does not ultimately marginalize women's labor and put women (and those who depend on them) at risk, the "farming" in the equation must include ownership of the fields as well as the crops. Otherwise, women in Nso and those who depend on them could find themselves impoverished, marginalized by contradictions in the very roles which once gave women status and power.

NOTES

1. See Guyer (1987) and Meilink (1989). According to a 1981 report of the Ministry of Economic Affairs, Cameroon, food production comes mainly from two sources: 1) the "traditional" smallholder sector and 2) agricultural projects in the modern sector. The former is by far the most important, accounting for 90 percent of total grain production (millet, sorghum, and maize), almost 100 percent of starchy leguminous plants, and 90 percent of fruits and vegetables. The traditional smallholder sector is overwhelmingly female. See Scott and Mahaffey (1980) for agricultural statistics for the Northwest Province. The Northwest Province grows approximately one-third of the national food supply of corn, beans, and Irish potatoes. Kumbo, the capitol of Nso, is a major market in the province, second only to Bamenda, the provincial capital, as an assembling point for foodstuffs shipped out to major urban centers.

2. Ngu argues that the dependence of Cameroon on oil while paying lip service to agricultural development accounts for a good deal of the current economic crisis. He claims that export instability is both undermining the legitimacy of the state and exacerbating the current crisis. Food shortages in major urban centers are predicted by a 1981 USAID-Yaounde study and report, *Plan Alimentaire a Long Terme.* Large deficits are predicted for corn (40–60 million tons), beans (8–15 million tons), and Irish potatoes (5–10 million tons), all of which are major exports from the Grassfields region to major urban centers. Deficits are also predicted in palm oil, banana, plantain, rice, groundnuts, vegetables, wheat, cassava, and sweet potatoes. Meilink (1989) also records declining per capita food production beginning in the early 1980s, while the two major cities in Cameroon, Douala and Yaounde, are experiencing annual growth rates of 6–7 percent. The future of food self-sufficiency in Cameroon does not look bright.

3. By *discourse,* I follow Foucault (1971) in meaning not only the language used to describe gender and other relations of power in Nso but also the social institutions that help constitute and reproduce that language,

including institutions such as the division of labor, the family, and marriage patterns. The term also includes ways of thinking about social institutions as well as the practices which reproduce and sometimes transform these. Following Raymond Williams (1977), *authoritative discourse* is a set of practices and the ideology that reproduces those practices.

4. The quantitative data on which much of the following discussion is based were obtained from a survey of 72 households in eight Nso villages in 1981. The information is supplemented by observations and interviews with Nso farmers and bureaucrats over a two-year period (1979–81) of fieldwork in Nso and from two months of fieldwork in the summer of 1988. The survey included information on land access, nutrition, marketing opportunity, and production choice (Goheen 1984 and 1988a).

5. When in Nso, I questioned the District Officer as to why women had not been granted land within the Young Farmers' Resettlement Program since they are obviously the primary food farmers. The DO replied, "Well, you see, this program is designed to keep young families in the countryside and of course no self-respecting man would want to move to his wife's farm." Whether or not this is true is an empirical question but ideologically it has served to keep women from acquiring land through government development programs in Nso. Another example: A very well educated Cameroonian man from the Grassfields region questioned me as to what I meant when I asserted that women were often discriminated against in national development programs. I pointed out that women had great difficulty getting access to land and therefore were precluded from participation in the Young Farmers' Resettlement Program or effectively from acquiring national land under development projects in general. He said, "Oh, well, *land*—of course you cannot be giving women land: it would destroy our whole social system!"

REFERENCES

Ariza-Nino, Edgar, M. Goheen-Fjellman, and L. Matt
  1982   *Consumption Effects of Agricultural Policies: Cameroon and Senegal,* Center for Research on Economic Development, University of Michigan.
Bourdieu, P.
  1977   *Outline of a Theory of Practice.* Cambridge: Cambridge University Press.
Commonwealth Secretariat
  1989   *Engendering Adjustment for the 1990s.* London: Marlborough House.
Davison, Jean
  1988   *Women, Land, and Agriculture: The African Experience.* Boulder: Westview Press.
Foucault, M.
  1971   *L'Ordre du Discourse.* Paris: Galliuard.

Goheen, Miriam
  1984   Ideology and Political Symbols: The Commoditization of Land,
           Labor and Symbolic Capital in Nso, Cameroon. Ph.D. dissertation,
           Harvard University.
  1988a   Land and the Household Economy. *Women, Land, and Agriculture:*
           The African Experience, Jean Davison, ed., pp. 90–105. Boulder:
           Westview Press.
  1988b   Land Accumulation and Local Control: The Manipulation of
           Symbols and Power in Nso. *Land and Society in Africa,* S. Reyna and
           R. Downs, eds., pp. 140–162. Hanover, N.H.: University of New
           England Press.
  1991   Buying Legitimacy: Secret Societies, Titles and the Modern Big
           Men of Nso. *African Transformations,* Jane Guyer, ed. Madison:
           University of Wisconsin Press.
Goheen-Fjellman, M., and L. Matt
  1981   *Effects of Demand Aspect on Production and Nutrition.* In-country
           report for USAID Contract DSAN-C-02770, Yaounde.
Guyer, Jane
  1980   Female Farming and the Evolution of Food Production Patterns
           Amongst the Beti of South Central Cameroon. *Africa* 50: 341–56.
  1984   *Family and Farm in Southern Cameroon.* Boston: Boston University
           African Research Series 15.
  1987   *Feeding African Cities.* Manchester: International African Institute,
           Manchester University Press.
Guyer, Jane, and Pauline Peters
  1987   Conceptualizing the Household. *Journal of Development and*
           Change, Special Issue, pp. 197–214, June.
Hill, Polly
  1986   *Development Economics on Trial: The Anthropological Case for a*
           Prosecution. Cambridge: Cambridge University Press.
Jua, Nantang
  1989   The Petty Bourgeoisie and the Politics of Social Justice in Cam-
           eroon. *Proceedings/Contributions: Conference on the Political Economy*
           of Cameroon: Historical Perspectives, Peter Geschiere and Piet
           Konings, eds., pp. 737–96. Leiden: African Studies Center.
Kaberry, Phyllis M.
  1952   *Women of the Grassfields.* London: H.M. Royal Stationery Office.
Kennedy, Paulᵢ
  1988   *African Capitalism: The Struggle for Ascendancy.* Cambridge:
           Cambridge University Press.
Koopman (Henn), Jean
  1989   Food Policy, Food Production and the Family Farm in Cameroon.
           Proceedings/Contributions: Conference on the Political Economy of
           Cameroon: Historical Perspectives, Peter Geschiere and Piet Konings,
           eds., pp. 531–556. Leiden: African Studies Center.

Lubeck, P. M.
    1988   *The African Bourgeoisie.* Boulder: Lynne Rienner Press.
Meilink, H .A.
    1989   Food Price Policy and Food Production in Cameroon. *Proceedings/ Contributions: Conference on the Political Economy of Cameroon: Historical Perspectives,* Peter Geschiere and Piet Konings, eds., pp. 587–596. Leiden: African Studies Center.
Nafziger, E. Wayne
    1987   *Inequality in Africa: Political Elites, Proletariat, Peasants and the Poor.* Cambridge: Cambridge University Press.
Ngu, Joseph N.
    1989   The Political Economy of Oil in Cameroon. *Proceedings/ Contributions: Conference on the Political Economy of Cameroon: Historical Perspectives,* Peter Geschiere and Piet Konings, eds., pp. 109–146. Leiden: African Studies Center.
Ntangsi, Joseph
    1987   The Political and Economic Dimensions of Agricultural Policy in Cameroon. Manuscript, World Bank, Washington, D.C.
Reyna, Steven, and R. Downs
    1988   *Land and Society in Africa.* Hanover, N.H.: University of New England Press.
Scott, W. and M. Mahaffey (Goheen)
    1980   *Agricultural Marketing in the Northwest Province, Cameroon.* Yaounde: USAID.
United States Agency for International Development (USAID)
    1981   *Plan Alimentaire a Long Terme.* Mimeo. Yaounde: USAID.
Vaughn, Megan
    1987   *The Story of an African Famine: Gender and Famine in 20th Century Malawi.* Cambridge: Cambridge University Press.
Williams, Raymond
    1977   *Marxism and Literature.* Oxford: Oxford University Press.

11

Women's Agricultural Work in a Multimodal Rural Economy: Ibarapa District, Oyo State, Nigeria

Jane I. Guyer with Olukemi Idowu

My title borrows a term from Ronald Cohen (1989) to refer to the distribution of farm size. As he notes, many African rural economies are already multimodal and have been so in differing ways for a long time. Economic history suggests that the African past has seen various kinds of diversity in farm size depending on the social organization of production and including plantations worked by slave labor (Cooper 1977), vertical integration on the basis of highly polygynous marriage (Guyer 1984a), and the mobilization of large numbers of kin and junior dependents under powerful leadership (Bohannan 1954). The issue I want to address is not whether a multimodality policy is creative in increasing total production or productivity levels, but what the social basis and social dynamics are of the particular kind of multimodality developed under the political and economic conditions of the 1980s, including structural adjustment programs.

There are two interpretative frameworks in tension with one another, although both stress the centrality of diversification. One tends towards

Jane I. Guyer is associate professor of anthropology at Boston University. She has carried out research on the division of labor, gender, and economic history in Nigeria and Cameroon. Her published work includes a monograph entitled *Family and Farm in Southern Cameroon* and an edited volume entitled *Feeding African Cities: Studies in Regional Social History.*

Olukemi Idowu is a researcher with the Raw Materials Research Council, Lagos, Nigeria. Her research on large farms was sponsored by the Women's Research and Documentation Centre, University of Ibadan.

The field research on which this paper is based was undertaken by Guyer in Oyo State in 1968–69, financed by National Institutes of Mental Health; July 1987, financed by the Joint Committee on African Studies of the Social Science Research Council/ACLS; January to March, and July 1988, financed by National Science Foundation. Affiliation with the International Institute of Tropical Agriculture, Ibadan, and the Institute of African Studies, University of Ibadan, is gratefully acknowledged. Field research by Idowu was undertaken under the NSF grant and the sponsorship of the Women's Research and Documentation Centre, University of Ibadan.

populism, represented in classical theory by Chayanov (1986), in Nigeria by the current official rural development policy, and in feminist work by the conclusions of an international conference on women held in Paris in 1984 (ORSTOM 1985). Diversity of productive strategies, market opportunities, economic organizations, and employment is seen as both economically productive and socially creative. The conference conclusions were particularly striking: women's welfare appears to be enhanced, above all to be less vulnerable to permanent marginality and to rapid and devastating fluctuation, in rural economies characterized by diversity (Guyer 1984b). The populist position is not in principle opposed to diversity in the size of enterprises; indeed Lenin's classic criticism was that it did not give enough analytical and theoretical attention to clearly evident differentiation amongst the peasantry. A populist position does not have to be unimodal in any radically egalitarian or uniformitarian sense.

Class analysis, by contrast, focuses precisely on differentiation and identifies certain kinds of size differentiation in class terms. In works sensitive to feminist arguments, class analysis has highlighted those gender dynamics that have greatly intensified patriarchal control of women's resources and subjected women to more and more complicated and exigent labor routines (Harrison 1979, Sabean 1978).

Both forms of analysis are clearly relevant to Africa as production diversifies and differentiates at the same time. The interpretative issue with respect to case material is one of identifying thresholds: at what point and in what historical sociopolitical dynamic should "diversity" be analyzed as differentiation, an aspect of class relations? And where class differentiation is obviously present in a particular rural economy, at what point and in what ways does it constrain the possibilities for diversification in production and market relations, and hence the current welfare level and future prospects, of the lower strata including rural women? The particularity of African twentieth-century history is that efforts at developing large-scale wage labor have a very checkered record outside of the settler economies characterized by extensive land alienation and repressive legislation. Elsewhere agricultural entrepreneurs of all kinds, from the state to religious leaders, struggle with workable means of mobilizing, motivating, and managing a labor force. Large enterprises have gone bankrupt, relocated, destroyed their ecological base, and demanded heavy subsidies, as well as, in places, becoming rooted in local relations of production (Dinham and Hines 1983, Williams 1988). As a result, the relations between the "modes" in multimodal agricultural systems are shifting and unstable, complicating any simple interpretation of long-term historical trajectories as either diversification or differentiation.

Figure 11-1. Class analysis has highlighted those gender dynamics that have greatly intensified patriarchal control of women's resources and subjected women to more and more complicated and exigent labor routines.

The Nigerian situation demands particular care because the economy has always demonstrated an enormous and rapid responsiveness to short-run shifts in conditions,[1] such that long-term structural changes are difficult to identify. There is absolutely no doubt that Nigerian society is stratified, but the presence and influence of established holders of capital in the agriculture sector is a shifting one because their economic portfolios are highly diversified.

Current political-economic commentary from Africa simplifies the problem by making a theoretical and heuristic distinction between the indigenous sector financed from local resources on the one hand, and large-scale enterprises in plantation or contract peasant farming that are largely financed from national or international capital on the other (Mkandawire and Bourenane 1987). Hence the designation "bimodal," even where regional economies are actually much more varied if judged empirically by farm size. This seems to me a very useful distinction since resource access depends on analytically separable dynamics in the two cases and involves different institutions. Analysis of other categories of farm size—other modes—that appear in the empirical material can be undertaken subsequently and in context.

With respect to a particular region, the relevant questions about the 1980s are: First, how have the bimodal—local and national/international capital—sectors developed, separately and in relation to one another? Second, how have the varied kinds of diversity (or multimodality) in the local sector—which may or may not be interpretable as class differentiation—responded to the changing scenario, including the activities of large-scale enterprise? Finally, does this shifting configuration have particular structural characteristics and cumulative implications for women, their welfare, economic activities, and organizations?

Nigeria in the 1980s

Responses to structural adjustment depend heavily on the preexisting dynamics of national economies and the specific nature of the policies. Although the Nigerian agricultural sector taken as a whole seems to have stagnated during the period of the oil boom, there were certainly some areas of growth and reorganization. Watts's book on agriculture during the oil boom period "demonstrates clearly that in Nigeria, the agricultural sector expanded and varied new forms of accumulation took place which transformed the social relations of the countryside" (Watts 1987a: 7). The cities grew so rapidly that it is unrealistic to imagine that the increased mouths were entirely fed from imported wheat, rice, and Brazilian beef. Transport was greatly extended through infrastructural development and the purchase of cheap vehicles with overvalued naira. Food production was certainly stimulated: Tiv yams and Northern tomatoes developed their own markets in Ibadan, beef from the North and Niger was transported to the south in fleets of trucks, rice from West Cameroon and the Abakaliki area of Eastern Nigeria filtered into the rest of the country, poultry farms became numerous around the major cities, and cassava farming seems to have been extended almost everywhere.

The traditional export crops and raw materials for Nigerian industrial production suffered more than the food sector because of very high costs and intense competition with a relatively booming food sector. As one erstwhile tobacco producer in Ibarapa said to me tersely, during those years "kò pé," it didn't pay. The Nigerian Tobacco Company (NTC) employee at the local office told me that farmers took the inputs and grew food crops instead; the NTC annual report for 1977 notes "we are experiencing increasing competition from food crops which, while not giving such a high cash return as tobacco are not nearly as work intensive" (NTC 1977: 8). As Andrae and Beckman (1987) have argued for cotton and Ugwu and Okereke (1985) have argued for cassava for the Nigerian Root Crops Production Company at Enugu, it was the supply link between indigenous agriculture and the capitalized industrial sector at home that was fraught and fragile under oil boom conditions.

The food sector was heavily promoted in places by the World Bank Agricultural Development Projects (ADPs) that were started in the North in 1976 and have since expanded their influence into the rest of the country, taking over the infrastructure and activities of the River Basin Development Authorities in 1987. Cheap tractors and other farm machinery also made it possible for a multimodal pattern to develop—for a segment of the professional and business class to go into arable farming as one activity in their economic portfolio, for small farmers to expand acreage, for local entrepreneurial spirits to increasingly specialize and commercialize their output, and for a few corporate businesses to develop an agricultural arm, for a variety of reasons including heavy government pressure to invest in Nigeria.

The Nigerian Structural Adjustment Program (SAP)

The Nigerian structural adjustment policies were initially locally developed rather than imposed by the international financial organizations.

Three of the provisions, and one unintended implication, are particularly relevant. First, devaluation of the naira from parity with the dollar to a present level of about 10 to the dollar between 1986 and 1989 rearranges the entire profitability accounting process, with particular and dramatic impact on the expense of imported inputs such as tractors and other machinery. Where machinery used to be relatively cheap and labor expensive, the inverse is now the case, such that the place of capitalization in production is being drastically reassessed over the few years of grace during which old machines are still usable. Given the well-known and constantly reiterated conclusion that labor is the bottleneck in Nigerian agriculture (Adegeye 1977, Titilola 1987: 364), the changing relationship between capital and labor is the dominant emerging issue.

Second, a total embargo was placed on the import of grains in order to stimulate local production. In spite of smuggling, bread is now far too expensive to figure in local diets, and the breweries and animal feed industries have had to convert both the production process and their supply networks to local sources.[2] In the grain-based industries, the industrial-agricultural links have had to be forged, quickly and apparently fairly successfully in at least some cases.[3] It is worth noting briefly here that this provision of the Nigerian structural adjustment policy is potentially fragile, since it is under diplomatic pressure from the U.S. as a restrictive measure preventing American grain imports (*New York Times*, Dec. 29, 1989).

Third, government institutional measures have been taken to try to vitalize the small-scale sector: provision of services through the Directorate of Food, Roads, and Rural Infrastructure, credit facilities through the People's Bank, and stimuli to agricultural research and seed multiplication. The Raw Materials Research Council was launched to give marketing advice to farmers and small-scale industrial processors, as one of many private and public attempts to firm up the agriculture-industry linkage that remains problematic.

Finally, one unintended consequence of all this taking place at once— including occupational restructuring as formal sector workers are laid off or forced into retirement and political activism picks up for the phased return to civilian rule—is a general instability and unpredictability in market conditions for everything. Liberalization of the marketing boards subjects prices to various winds of change. For example, the cocoa price has fluctuated wildly as it was exposed for the first time in decades to an unstable world market, while a momentary boom was caused by big businessmen using exports of almost anything as a means of access to hard currencies. Food prices rose very rapidly in early 1988, in part because of drought.[4] Adjustment processes that amount to earthquakes in economic conditions for particular crops, sectors, and regions may swamp the effects of other cumulative changes and crack the institutional bases of established economic activities. At the same time, some policies continue from pre-SAP days, notably the World Bank ADPs.

This then is the context for interpreting the implications of structural adjustment programs for rural women in a particular region: the agricultural sector was already developing multimodal characteristics; the various modes found different aspects of the SAP configuration beneficial or threatening; and the entire response that we are trying to assess, between 1986 and 1989, builds on the achievements made and the problems set up under other conditions. Their roots in those other conditions are highlighted by discussing each of the farming modes in the historical order in which it made its appearance and ways in which it has grown since then. Particular attention is given to the two most important general questions raised by SAP: how is the dramatically changed capital/labor cost ratio being managed by different categories of farmer? And what is happening to the institutional links between farmers and processors, from the artisanal to the industrial?

Ibarapa District, Oyo State

Ibarapa has been within the supply hinterland of Ibadan and Lagos for over a hundred years. Just outside the cocoa belt in derived guinea savanna, its products have selectively become incorporated into the regional distribution system, starting with savanna grass for thatching and egusi-melon seeds, adding yam products and cowpeas in the 1940s, cassava and maize from the 1950s, and fresh produce (tomatoes, peppers, okra) in the 1960s and 1970s as the transport system greatly improved. During the Civil War when transport was extremely limited the entire gamut of products was processed locally into a dried form (yam flour, dried peppers, dried okra).

When I carried out field research there in 1968–69, the backbone of agricultural production was a male smallholder peasantry, supported since their settlement in the region in the middle of last century by peak period female labor in harvesting, processing, and porterage, and since about 1960 by a supply of migrant wage labor from the Benoue region (Idomas) in clearing and heaping of new farms. The only tractors were owned by the Nigerian Tobacco Company for whom a small number of men were contract farmers (Daly, Filani, and Richards 1981). With the current agricultural practice of four years cultivation to eight years fallow, and a mean farm size of just under three acres, Ibarapa almost certainly offered more cultivable land than the current population could use. In any period of growth it would seem a prime candidate for innovation.

When I returned in 1987 innovations had indeed taken place. Male farm size had increased by about 40 percent to 4.1 acres, beginning with the increased influx of laborers from Benoue and the Republic of Benin in the mid to late 1970s and picking up more momentum with the development of commercial tractor hire from the late 1970s onwards. On the same sort of timetable and for the same reasons a small group of local farmers with entrepreneurial ambitions, tough physical constitutions, and good social networks had greatly expanded farm areas to 10 and as much as 60 acres. Beyond them in farm size is the prominent professional group who use savings, salaries, local status, and regional/national networks to support their farms of over 100 acres.

These people must be distinguished from corporate agribusinesses which first moved into Ibarapa in the mid-1970s and further developed following the promulgation of the Land Use Act in 1978. The act vested ownership of land in the state and allows acquisition of rights of occupancy from the customary occupants for areas up to 500 hectares. Two of the farms developed have been over 1,000 acres (Texagri and Temperance Farms, later Obasanjo Farms), while the third is about 700 acres plus livestock sheds and other substantial grounds (United Africa Company/Marquis). Another large stretch of land said to be five square miles has been allocated to an urban-based group but not yet developed.

The final major new category of farmers consists of local women. They have gone into farming in their own account, starting from a stable low of about 10 percent before the mid-1970s and picking up in spurts until 1988 when 69 percent claimed to have farms of their own, with a mean size of just under two acres.

Any discussion of Ibarapa on the eve of SAP thus has to start from at least four categories of farmers, working in diverse and differentiated ways: local male small-scale producers, local women, a socially heterogeneous category of locally based mid-scale farmers, and corporate agribusiness. The expansion of much of their activity has been made possible by low car and tractor prices during the civilian regime of 1979–83 when imports were rendered very inexpensive by the high international value of the naira. I am not claiming anything about the technical or social desirability of this particular pattern of diversification, but simply emphasizing that class differentiation and productive diversity were already laid down and women were deeply implicated.

Four Farming Modes in the Context of SAP

Male Small-Scale Farming

The Yoruba population of Ibarapa originates primarily from Old Oyo in the savanna to the north, settling in Ibarapa initially in the 1840s and at the present sites at the end of the 1890s. Compound histories indicate that the incoming refugees brought classic Oyo culture with them: urban settlement and administration, specialist occupations, savanna farming techniques, and religious cults. Farmer (*agbè*) is an occupational designation applying primarily, although not categorically, to men. Although almost all able-bodied men do have a farm, in 1968 there was some considerable diversity of farm size, depending on whether farming was considered a primary activity or simply a subsistence support to the considerable number of hunters, weavers, embroiderers, blacksmiths, religious functionaries, teachers, and others. Subsistence farms were about one-quarter to one-third the size of "farmers'" farms. I argued in my dissertation on the town of Idere (population of 10,000) that the other major differentiating factor in farm size and income was seniority within sibling groups, in a society where all senior men carry heavy ceremonial obligations that have to be financed (Guyer 1972).[5]

The male peasantry has become, I would argue, considerably less diversified since 1968. With the intensification of urban food demand, the rising cost of living, and extended consumer ambitions, many of the non-farming specialists have greatly extended their farms. Now everyone from the motor-bike mechanic and the primary school teacher through the eighty-plus-year-old chief has an extensive farm. Seniority has become a more complex process in both its perquisites and its obligations. New variations have emerged but their contours are difficult to interpret for the moment. Hence, I will discuss this entire category of male small holders, working farms of 6 acres or under, together.

Before discussing these farmers, their demographic profile is worth pausing over. Whether there has been a net loss of men from agriculture over the oil boom period is a difficult question to address. Suffice it here to say that I was surprised to find that of the 66 farmers in the old sample, only eight had left farming and moved away, while a whole new cohort of younger farmers has become established. The occupations of the children of those still farming suggest that the male farm population is at the very least maintaining itself, replacing the dead, chronically ill, and the emigrants.

There have been two notable changes in these farms: an increase in mean size of about 40 percent from 2.9 acres to 4.1 acres, and a shift towards the sale of perishable crops. The growth period began in the mid-1970s with vastly improved transport, Beninois workers, and the beginnings of tractors for hire. In 1988, 59 percent of the small-scale male farmers studied had used tractors to clear 54 percent of total cultivated land. Tractor use was therefore widespread by this time.

The results of these longer-term changes for women were various. First and foremost, the unpaid porterage duties (head-carrying) they owed to husbands and male kin have decreased very significantly. Their harvest duties have correspondingly increased, but most of this work is remunerated. The increased production stimulates some primary processing on their own account, particularly of cassava, but the long-term trend seems to me towards fresh sales of all crops to specialist processors closer to the centers of consumption. Such a development would drop many very small female operators out of the processing occupations that they had as independent income sources since about the 1940s and 1950s, unless the increased cost of transport revives the importance of processing at the production end rather than at the consumption end.

I would sum up these developments as *an overall decline in women's routine obligations* and opportunities in their older occupations, and *a rise in their peak period activities*, on which men are increasingly and critically dependent. In the small-scale sector the male farmers have been absolutely unable to chisel down the harvest wage, or effect any change in its in-kind composition (a set quantity from the harvest per day of work, plus food). In real terms it may even have risen for the still-major commercial crop of egusi-melon, to which have been added tobacco and tomatoes as potentially calling for wage workers. The configuration represented here must be kept in mind as part of the dynamic through which women have gone into own account farming in unprecedented numbers.

The SAP conditions both stimulate and stifle the direction of change. They stimulate it because some young men have in fact returned to the rural areas, prices for food crops have generally been advantageous, demand has been increased by the grain import restrictions, and market roads have been kept in good condition. They stifle it because tractors are becoming expensive and perhaps unavailable in the longer run, the Beninois laborers are more difficult to recruit because Nigerian wages are disastrously low when converted into francs CFA, the cost of some consumer needs (medicine, school needs, cloth) has risen, and the stock of transport vehicles is becoming rickety and expensive to maintain. For a full contextual analysis, one should include the decline in certain infrastructures affecting health, such as clean water and medical facilities. In a guinea-worm endemic area, it is not unusual to see 20 percent of the population incapacitated for work during the dry season. Hence, of course, the critical importance of effective government expenditure.

The net effect of SAP on male smallholder farm size and total production I would gauge to have been very positive in the immediate first year or two when the capital stock was still working, and then problematic. The policy expectation is that the response of an ingenious and experienced entrepreneurial sector will turn it positive again, although the future of machinery in agriculture under present price conditions is far from clear. Without tractors, I would expect mean farm size to fall, and farmers to concentrate on the highest-value crops which also use the most hand labor. If market transport costs rise and scarcity sets in as it did during the Civil War, local processing might go through another revival.

In summary, one can envisage the logical scenario aimed at by policymakers: higher local employment in agriculture and processing, and the substitution of cheaper for more expensive inputs; but with lower levels of mechanical support it looks more like retrenchment and recapitulation than growth.

Female Small-Scale Farming

In 1968 most women did not farm in their own right, and I thought of women's farming as a minority pattern. Piecing together evidence from two fairly congruent sources,[6] I would hazard an estimate of 10 percent as the proportion of women who had farms of their own of some sort in the 1960s. A sizable group of them probably farmed truck vegetables in the river basin in the dry season and did not have the standard rain-fed crops at all. In my 1968 sample of 66 farmers, two were women with arable crop farms, i.e., farms with standard crop rotations.

In 1988 a brief survey of 222 women suggested that 69 percent currently claim to have their own farms. Judging by the year at which they started farming, there were two intensive growth phases: 1976 and plateauing at the same rate until 1984, and then a very rapid and continuing growth after 1984. Almost half (44 percent) of the women now farming claim to have started since 1984, that is, since the economic crisis and structural adjustment programs set in. The first conclusion to draw is that women's farming does not bear a simple responsive relationship to economic conditions.

By analyzing in detail the farm practices and occupational histories of 40 women, it seems to me that farming first became attractive to women when transport increased the marketing possibilities at the same time as introducing new competition into trade and processing. The women who took up farming at that time did not substitute it for their other occupations so much as use it to balance out crises in their trades and provide their own raw materials for processing. Although it may have been a defensive move at the time, this category has subsequently taken farming fairly seriously, somewhat expanding their farms (mean of 1.7 acres by comparison with 1.3 acres for the later cohort) and diversifying their crop repertoires (only 61 percent of farm area in cassava by comparison with 79 percent for the later cohort). They have not, however, caught up yet with the farm size and cropping pattern of the very long-term women farmers (mean farm size 3.4 acres and 54 percent in cassava). The women who took up farming after the economic crisis and under SAP conditions have a different profile; their farms are smaller, more uniformly cassava farms, and their other occupations seem more marginal.

Women see farming as a viable occupation for a cumulatively expanding set of reasons. Before the oil boom growth there was always a small category of women who liked farming and/or had limited access to a man's food farm to support their children. Probably nothing dramatic has happened in the domain of marriage stability or longevity to reduce this core since then. As markets opened up, the ensuing volatilities in trade and processing became more dangerous and had to be balanced by another income source. At the same time women became relatively freed of routine porterage obligations, giving them some increased flexibility in their daily schedule. Experts are also fairly convinced that the population growth rate soared, and certainly the women themselves mentioned the need to feed more mouths as a reason for farming. Finally the steadily intensifying demand for fresh produce and competition in trade in the SAP era, accompanied by steep rises in certain consumer costs, make it imperative and potentially viable that women make an income from the farm.

Even more than the male farmers, however, women are dependent on the price and availability of commercial inputs. Forty-two percent of women's farm land was cleared by tractor, and 57 percent by hired labor. By contrast, men did clear some of their own land (19 percent). Women also hire more labor for weeding than men. Some operate more like farm managers than farmers. For the moment, *in the first years of SAP implementation when the demand for cassava from the poor urban population is enormous and tractors are still on the scene, there is a veritable boom in women's farming.* Inevitably, however, such enterprises are much more vulnerable to the rapid rise in the price of inputs and the unpredictable fluctuations in produce prices. It is conceivable that women's farming could be reduced if tractors become unavailable and the ensuing competition for labor drives wages up.

Local Large Farmers

There were no farmers at all in this category in 1968. They grew up in the mid to late 1970s and early 1980s, and are very idiosyncratically varied. In 1988 there were about nine farmers in the town of Idere with total areas over 10 acres, with the largest "homegrown" one at about 50 acres. Their main characteristic in common is that they have, or developed, diverse income sources with which to finance the greatly increased need for mechanization and hired labor. Unlike the small farmer's case, it is completely unfeasible for large farmers to substitute their own labor to increase efficiency; one is in business or not, and in fact two farmers came to my notice who cultivated a large acreage one season and nothing the next.

For obvious reasons this is probably the most vulnerable category of all to price instabilities. By 1988 these farmers were already stretching the imagination and the purse to acquire tractors and hold onto a dependable labor force.

While they constitute a very small numerical group, the mid-scale farmers are quite important in that they are locally based innovators with deep roots and connections who are quick to see possibilities and dangers vis-à-vis the wider regional system. For example, it was larger farmers who were most vigilant over very extensive land alienation to outsiders under the Land Use Act. They attract resources in the shape of transport, tractors, and some political attention, and they tend to be brazen enough to deal with the authorities. They also "provide" harvest employment to quite a large number of women. "Provide" is in quotes because it is precisely the conditions of work in a deepening agricultural wage labor market that need to be examined.

Women work for the larger farmers in several capacities: fertilizer spreading is a minor task, harvesting is still the critical one. Five larger local farmers' *egusi* harvest records were kept for 1988. They needed a total of 512 woman days of work (102 per farmer) by contrast with 14 per farmer for 16 male small-scale farmers. One large farmer generates about the same harvest work as seven smaller farmers, but are the conditions the same? A comparison of the bags of egusi distributed in wages and the cost per woman/day of food suggests that women do slightly better in the small-scale sector: larger farmers devote 13.4 percent of the harvest to wages whereas small farmers devote 16.1 percent; larger farmers pay 61 kobo per woman day for food whereas small farmers give 97 kobo. This is all entirely logical, since the small farmer hires his closest female kin and affines, and hence stands to gain indirectly from their good will and the income they make, whereas the larger farmer is trying to put pressure on

Table 11-1. Female Harvest Wages by Mode of Farm, August 1988.

Mode	A Value/food	B Percent total harvest in kind	C Naira (in cash or value of B)	D Total (A+C)
Agribusiness (N = 3)	None	NA	4–5.25	4–5.25
Local Male Large (N = 5)	.61	13.4	8	8.61
Local Male Small (N = 16)	.97	16.1	8	8.97
Local Female (N = 3)	1.19	17.6	8	9.19

The apparently increasing proportion of the harvest given in wages in kind from the largest to the smallest local farms must reflect the degree to which the measure is full. The difference is slight, and not enough to be terminologically distinguished through the standard words applying to the fullness of market measures.

I have valued all measures at the current market price for a standard measure. Since the market measure is almost certainly filled to a lower level and rises in price over the year, this 8 Naira (column C) represents the lowest possible naira value of the harvest wage in kind.

the wage. It is worth noting that the difference in "efficiency" between these two groups is small by comparison with the more striking decline in the wage when women work for cash for corporate business. Table 11-1 summarizes wages for comparable harvesting tasks performed by women in the four farming modes.

A last word might be added to the effect that women do depend on working the egusi harvest as they have always done, and so far there is no shortage of workers and no complaint as long as the larger farmers keep close to the old standards and working conditions. Were they to collapse, the loss would be felt, even if very locally, to the villages directly supplying the labor.

Corporate Agribusiness

Ibarapa has seen three major corporate farm ventures, and land acquisition on a vast scale rumored at five square miles by another. The legal basis for large-scale land acquisition in the south was laid down by the Land Use Decree, now Land Use Act (Francis 1984, Omotola 1982). Occupancy rights can be acquired from those holding them under customary tenure at the discretion of a Land Allocation Advisory Committee based initially at the local government level and later at the state level. An agreement has to be reached, generally mediated by a major local figure or by lawyers, and in principle the land acquired cannot exceed 500 hectares. It is quite clear from a number of cases that occupancy of land has been achieved through a large variety of agreements and can easily exceed the upper limit. For example, a high-ranking merchant bank officer told me of credit extended to an agricultural entrepreneur in Eastern Nigeria for rice development on six miles of river, and a Nigerian Breweries' advertisement boasts the acquisition of 8,000 hectares in Niger State to "create a local source of raw materials."

It would be too hasty, however, to conclude that land is being irrevocably amassed in huge chunks by corporate business. The deals are increasingly made and they are very large, but the ability of the businesses to survive and to maintain their claims in the long run is another matter. When the Texaco farm of 3,886 hectares closed in 1987 (*The President,* July 3, 1988), the customary occupants are said to have mounted a vigorous campaign for not only the land to revert to them but the improvements as well: a *gari* factory and farm buildings. It was said to be quite unclear for the moment whether the farm could be sold or not. A lawyer who mediated a different vast land deal thought that customary occupants might have a good case if they wanted to get rid of the new occupants, and in any case everyone concerned was convinced that life could be made utterly miserable for newcomers if the former owners wanted to harass them. Whether all this is a pipe dream, or whether it applies only to those enterprises with the least clout, will largely determine the place of fully capitalist agriculture. A staunch supporter of private freehold and leasehold land ownership attacks the futility of the 1978 Land Use Decree:

> The Land Use Decree is one of the worst pieces of legislation thrust upon the helpless citizens of this country.... All businessmen in enterprise of any sort need security and continuity of land tenure which are not supplied by a mere right of occupancy. (Adedapo Adeniran, *Daily Times,* March 22, 1988).

The coming ten years will be critical to the future of rural landholding in the district. While from the strictly ecological point of view there may be room for a few plantations, their very concentration dispossesses some local farmers or moves them onto other land, and their sheer size may mortgage the future for a rapidly increasing population that has intensified and extended its own agricultural activities. The "homegrown" large farmers are already trying to think up ways of controlling land alienation because they, of course, hold their own farms in customary occupancy. Policy measures to promote corporate agribusiness would have to firm up the provisions of the Land Use Act because evidence seems to suggest that it is applied in quite indeterminate ways with quite indeterminate results.

The companies acquiring land in Ibarapa have so far been too well-connected to feel deeply vulnerable to land disputes. The Texaco farms in a village just over the Ogun State line and at Igbo-Ora in Ibarapa saw their first season in 1976. General Obasanjo, who initiated the Land Use Act while head of state, has two farms founded in the early 1980s. The Lanlate farm has two sites of 450 hectares and 560 hectares respectively, and 1,500 hectares have been newly acquired. The Igbo-Ora farm is much smaller, heavily capitalized, and entirely devoted to poultry. The United Africa Company (UAC)/Marquis farm was founded in 1984. All, then, had been on the drawing board at the very least before economic crisis became evident about 1983 and were capitalized before the SAP programs so dramatically altered input prices.

The purposes were varied. The Texaco farm seems to have been a political response to pressures from the Nigerian government for foreign oil companies to invest locally under the Feed the Nation policy of the mid-1970s. The other two farms appear to be efforts to develop vertical integration in farming and processing. Obasanjo's farms all relate to one another, the arable farms providing grain for feed for the poultry and livestock sections. The UAC/Marquis farm is primarily a technologically sophisticated pig-raising enterprise, with crops on about 700 acres to provide grain for the feed mill, a planned slaughterhouse, and a sausage-making plant. Much of the output is destined for another branch of UAC, the Kingsway Rendezvous snack chain in the major cities.

Beyond land acquisition the major economic impact of these vertically integrated enterprises within the region is in the labor market, and women figure very prominently in the labor force for all except the poultry farm. The Texaco farm employed over 140 women per day as cassava peelers for the *gari* factory. The UAC/Marquis farm and Obasanjo farms may each employ 300 to 400 casual laborers a day for the harvest season, picking maize, cowpeas, and egusi. The daily wage was between 4 and 5.25 naira in 1988, while the UAC manager suggested that piecework rates could enable a fast worker to earn as much as 11 naira. The farms provided transport to work but did not give meals.

At these rates it is not necessarily easy to recruit enough labor and both the UAC and Texagri managers expressed difficulties in the past. The value equivalent of the small-scale in-kind payment is higher than the agribusiness daily wage,[7] and it includes food, is less rigid about the time worked, and is close to home. *Hence the agribusiness workers tend to be poorer, foreign, or in urgent need of cash.* The forces that generate the basic core supply of middle-aged women to large-scale farming and agribusiness are probably still familial and conjunctural in their lives: widows with children, unsuccessful traders, wives of men in poor health, and so on. None of the farm workers interviewed by Ms. Idowu had a farm of her own, so one must be open to the possibility that pockets of land shortage may be developing for people who cannot work too far from home, such as mothers bringing up their children with little other support. The location, not just the size, of large plantations is relevant to their interface with local communities. The farm owners, of course, want to be near settlements for the labor supply and transport, whereas the local farmers are clearly affected.

Other short-term workers may be generated through the recruitment organizations that have grown up over the past few years. Both UAC and Texagri managers expressed concern, however, that there were moments when the major sources hardly sufficed and they suffered from competition with other employment possibilities.

The total labor supply has been increased beyond this minimal level under SAP conditions, in part by the increased recruitment of teenage labor. Older workers were emphatic that having such young co-workers was a new development. The costs of education and clothes have risen along with other items, leaving many school-age young people with the necessity of providing some support for themselves. One young girl was working until she had enough money to buy a pair of shoes to go back to school in. Taking days off school to work in the fields can be their only way of staying in school in the long run. The same rise in unavoidable consumer costs such as medicine increases women's demand for wage work to meet sudden expenditures; one very large-scale and eminent local farmer said that women come to his house in greater numbers than before to ask for work.

The future for corporate agribusiness is probably more secure than for the local mid-scale farmers. The biggest farms are branches of vast international enterprises with the capacity to subsidize over the shorter run if their boards see it as worthwhile. They can maintain water supplies, generators, transport, pedigree breeding stock, tractors, combines, improved seed, fertilizer, and so on, and allow time for the development of solid industrial linkages to poultry concerns, feed mills, breweries, and retail outlets. Like any business they are likely to put downward pressure on the wage if they can. If they are able to do so, it will be an indicator of pockets of fairly deep economic distress among subcategories of the female population at particular moments in their lives.

Towards Some Interpretations

On Diversity and Differentiation

If some sort of larger-scale farming is to be promoted, the vast difference between the companies and local mid-scale farmers needs to be looked at carefully. They link differently to industry and to the labor force, and they are very differently accountable within the local political and legal arena. As long as the mid-scale farmers hold their land in customary occupancy they cannot become a rooted, hereditary squirarchy, and however successful they become in their lifetimes their prominence in agriculture cannot be passed on. In an area like Ibarapa that is not yet at the limits of its land supply, there is room for these people to be very productive and enterprising while they have the strength. While they are "middle class" by current income and life-style—making the Pilgrimage to Mecca, building houses, educating children, some with salaries and pensions, building up strong regional and national networks, developing access to state resources—the processes of resource reallocation are deeply embedded in the home communities to which they belong and will set in sooner or later unless actively controlled by their immediate heirs.

In this area of Nigeria, then, one has to make a conceptual distinction between, on the one hand, a markedly differentiated category in agricultural practices and life-style that cannot yet transform itself into class, and on the other hand capitalist agribusinesses. The former, while for some purposes one might want to analyze it in class terms, shows more of the institutional characteristics of the small-scale sector and offers employment to women on somewhat similar terms. The important question about them is how an expansion of their activities would affect the small-scale sector. The labor question would simply be struggled over, and I think the outcome is both indeterminate and on-going from year to year as other conditions change. Unless land shortage sets in, the critical dynamic seems to be the market for produce. For the most part, mid-scale farmers search for mid-scale buyers, rather than simply selling in the rural wholesale markets, mainly, I think, because of their lack of transport and storage infrastructure for the quantities in which they are now dealing. It is possible that contract farming for industry and marketing to large-scale buyers would be more attractive to these than to the small-scale farmers who want to take advantage of all positive price fluctuations and therefore find it difficult to honor contracts made when other conditions prevailed. If so, the market will tend to segregate institutionally into a) vertically integrated agribusiness, b) contract farming and marketing, and c) the rural wholesale sector. All patterns of growth in this area, however, depend on the capital/labor price ratio and availability, because every category of farmer has had, and would prefer to continue to have, access to tractors.

Conclusion

In summary, it seems to me that critical assessment of the SAP policies requires several steps. First of all, the direction of change in the economy *before SAP* needs to be established because in the immediate time frame these conditions will be at least as important an influence on developments as the specific SAP policies. At the macro-level the decline in commodity prices is a decisive influence that began before structural adjustment and is not clearly ameliorated by its provisions. At the local level the bases for both diversification and differentiation in Ibarapa agriculture were laid long before the SAP era, including the relatively increased competition for women in trade and processing and the movement of women into farming.

Second, the specific provisions of SAP need to be noted. It is the idiosyncracy of Nigeria's SAP, the grain embargo, rather than its typical features that most closely affects the farmers in Ibarapa in the short run. The long run will equally depend on specific, and perhaps idiosyncratic, political developments around the various emerging problems and bottlenecks. The issue to watch here is the cost of mechanization versus labor for various different categories of the farming population. SAP is not a single generic package with respect to agriculture, but a set of policies subject like any other to revision, competition, confusion, nonimplementation, and regional differentiation in effects.

Finally, with respect to the more generic effects on women, the reduction in cash available for consumer purchases has made all women aware of the general reductions in the standard of living. The awareness of crisis seems to have encouraged a much higher level of activism than the relatively greater availability of cash fostered in the 1970s. The direction of change for rural women so far leads towards greater differentiation with some diversification as well. Limiting their markets through massive imports or extensive support for agribusiness would promote differentiation at the expense of diversification. If the activism focuses on this whole set of issues over the coming period of political debate and return to civilian rule, it could contribute in a major way to the very long-term struggles over agricultural policy that everyone now seems to accept to constitute the true reality of "structural adjustment."

Women's situation in the current dynamic is the most difficult to summarize. A major factor worth noting is their experimentation with activities such as farming on their own account that they have done in much smaller numbers before, and their maintenance, even at a lower level, of their old occupations. They now have to engage with land tenure rubrics, bargain with laborers, develop crop repertoires, assess new crops, and so on, as well as keep abreast of the market conditions for trade and processing. Yoruba women's reputation as hard and bold bargainers is largely based on urban marketwomen; many rural women are new to dealing with the issues they face as farmers. This in itself may provoke the greater activism that rural development policy is claiming to promote, and certainly a lot of press is given to women's organizations in Oyo State more broadly.

Unless the economy goes into absolute decline, the demand for female wage labor in local men's farming will increase. If the terms are commensurate with traditions, women will welcome this development as yet another way to earn a living. They have always been in the labor market as well as self-employment, and the more possibilities the better. They also, of course, employ wage labor themselves, including other women. Full-time wage work on terms set down by corporate business is a different situation altogether, offering somewhat poorer working conditions but more regular employment than the local sector.

If transport is maintained, women's trade is likely to become polarized as fresh produce takes over the markets and the incursions of large outside traders expand. Full-time produce buyers will still operate; all women will do processing from time to time as a minor economic activity, but broad-based participation in primary processing for sale will probably decline in favor of farming. Perhaps cooked food provision will increase as expanded farm work by some women offers others an economic niche in substituting for domestic work.

The future of women's farming is therefore quite central to the maintenance of diverse occupational opportunities for women. Without farming, the village-based woman's income-earning possibilities will come under pressure. There is no predicting the long-term future here because the rights to land and labor will be struggled over as all categories compete for their resources and markets. But Yoruba women have earned independent incomes for a very long time, they need them more than ever, and if at all plausible to do so they are likely to organize rather than allow marginalization. I think no one would have predicted the present expansion of women's farming in the early 1970s. The literature has customarily designated the Yoruba as a "male farming system." But the longest tradition seems to be for all adults to generate resources to meet their own ritual and social obligations. Short of a cultural revolution, women will continue to generate economic niches that allow them to do this, and indeed try to make the greater contributions that the high prices induced by SAP demand.

NOTES

1. See Berry (1987) for the concept of the "disappearing peasantry" applied to the oil boom period. Colonial agricultural history contains cases of unanticipated responsiveness, for example the massive expansion of cassava production for starch during World War II that resulted in destruction of some of the commodity, and administrative plans for regional specialization to prevent the demise of the oil palm economy in favor of cassava. Nigerian produce pours over the borders into the franc zone under some conditions and pours in the other direction under others. During the present period, "camels ... [are] ... used to smuggle grains ... for Maradi and other towns in the Republic of Niger" (*Daily Times,* January 22, 1988. For historical cases, see Watts 1987b).

2. "Foreign Flour Floods Market—Mill Boss" (*Daily Times,* March 17, 1988), but "Brewers and Bakers Grumble but Govt Insists on Ban on Wheat Importation" (*The Nigerian Economist,* April 27–May 10, 1988).

3. For example, "a friend involved in major agribusiness ... needed large local supplies of maize to replace the easy access to large-scale importation before the recent ban. A group of women had been worrying him as to what business they could do with his organization. He thought he had dismissed them when he retorted that if they could supply his organi with six lorry loads of grains every day, he would pay them cash down. They disappeared for a week or two. Indeed, he thought he had got rid of them. Then one day about ten days later the lorries started to roll in and neither side has looked back since then" (Mabogunje 1989)

4. "Food Crisis Looms. Poor Harvest All Over" (*Daily Times,* January 18, 1988). "(A) Bag of Maize That Was Sold for N25 This Time Last Year, Now Sells for Over a Hundred Naira" (*Newswatch,* February 29, 1988).

5. Field work was undertaken in 1968–69, the summer of 1987, January to March 1988, and the summer of 1988. I worked from a basic sample of 66 farmers from the small town of Idere and three of its farming villages. In 1988, I reinterviewed the 35 farmers from the old sample who were still farming around Idere (33 men and 2 women) and 8 who were not, and added three new categories—a cohort of young men (17), women (38) and mid-scale farmers (9)—as well as carrying out interviews with landowners, a lawyer, tractor owners, chiefs, farm laborers, traders, transporters, market mediators (*pàràkòyí*) and others.

6. A sample of 222 women was interviewed briefly, being the total resident female populations of four compounds, during a holiday when the farm village population was maximally represented in town. A new sample of 38 women farmers and 2 from the old sample was interviewed more extensively.

7. According to market interviews the standard measure of egusi paid to women harvesters was worth 8 naira in the rainy season and 8.50 naira later in the year. The measure given to the women is also much fuller: *fowókó*, a term referring to the measurers putting their arm all around the rim before filling it. The market measure is never filled in this way.

REFERENCES

Adegeye, Adeduro J.
  1977   An Evaluation of Food Crop Farming inside Old Cocoa Groves. *Nigerian Agricultural Journal* (14)1: 40–45.

Andrae, Gunilla, and Bjorn Beckman
  1987   *Industry Goes Farming. The Nigerian Raw Material Crisis and the Case of Textiles and Cotton.* Uppsala: Scandinavian Institute of African Studies, Research Report No. 80.

Berry, Sara S.
  1987   Oil and the Disappearing Peasantry: Accumulation, Differentiation and Underdevelopment in Western Nigeria. *State, Oil and Agriculture in Nigeria*, Michael Watts ed., pp. 202–222. Berkeley: Institute of International Studies.

Bohannan, Paul
  1954   *Tiv Farm and Settlement.* London: HMSO.

Chayanov, A.V.
  1986   *The Theory of the Peasant Economy.* D. Thorner, B. Kerblay, and R.E.F. Smith, eds. Madison: University of Wisconsin Press.

Cohen, Ronald
  1989   The Unimodal Model: Solution or Cul de Sac for Rural Development? *Food and Farm: Current Debates and Policies*, Christina Gladwin and Kathleen Truman, eds., pp. 7–34. Lantham, MD: University Press of America.

Cooper, Frederick
  1977   *Plantation Slavery on the East Coast of Africa.* New Haven: Yale University Press.

Daly, M.T., M.O. Filani, and P. Richards
  1981   *The Ibarapa Planning Atlas. Processes and Problems of Rural Development in Ibarapa Division, Oyo State, Nigeria.* Ibadan: Department of Geography, Technical Report No. 1.

Dinham, Barbara, and Colin Hines
  1983   *Agribusiness in Africa.* London: Earth Resources Ltd.

Francis, Paul
1984   "For the Use and Common Benefit of all Nigerians": Consequences of the 1978 land nationalisation. *Africa* 58(3): 5–28.

Guyer, Jane I.
1972   The Organizational Plan of Traditional Farming; Idere, Western Nigeria. Ph.D. dissertation, University Microfilms, Ann Arbor.
1984a   *Family and Farm in Southern Cameroon.* Boston University African Research Studies No. 15.
1984b   Women in African Rural Economies: Contemporary Variations. *African Women South of the Sahara,* Jean Hay and Sharon Stichter, eds., pp. 19–32. London: Longman.

Harrison, Mark
1979   Chayanov and the Marxists. *Journal of Peasant Studies* 6(1): 86–100.

Mabogunje, Akin
1989   Women in Business and Agribusiness in Nigeria. Keynote address given on the occasion of the Workshop on Women in Business and Agribusiness, Ibadan, December 5–8.

Mkandawire, Thandika, and Naceur Bourenane
1987   *The State and Agriculture in Africa.* Dakar: CODESRIA.

Nigerian Tobacco Company
1977   Annual Report.

Omotola, J.A.
1982   *The Land Use Act. Report of a National Workshop.* Lagos: University Press.

ORSTOM (Office pour la Recherche Scientifique et Technique Outre Mer)
1985   *Femmes et Politiques Alimentaires.* Paris: ORSTOM.

Sabean, David
1978   Small Peasant Agriculture in Germany at the Beginning of the Nineteenth Century; Changing Work Patterns. *Peasant Studies* 7(4): 218–24.

Titilola, S.T.
1987   The State and Food Policies in Nigeria. *The State and Agriculture in Africa,* Mkandawire and Bourenane, eds., pp. 354–76. Dakar: CODESRIA.

Ugwu, B.O., and O. Okereke
1985   The Problem of Inadequate Supply of Raw Cassava for Industrial Cassava Processing; A Case Study of the Nigerian Root Crops Production Company, Enugu, Nigeria. *Agricultural Systems* 18: 155–70.

Watts, Michael
1987a   *State, Oil and Agriculture in Nigeria.* Berkeley: Institute of International Studies.
1987b   Brittle Trade; a Political Economy of Food Supply in Kano. *Feeding African Cities. Studies in Regional Social History,* Jane Guyer, ed. Manchester: Manchester University Press/Indiana University Press.

Williams, Gavin
   1988   The Development of Capitalist Agriculture in Africa? Paper pre-
           sented to the Annual Conference of the Canadian Association of
           African Studies.

12 Structural Transformation and Its Consequences for Orma Women Pastoralists

Jean Ensminger

While there is now a growing literature analyzing the effects of structural adjustment upon agricultural societies in Africa, there is to my knowledge little if anything written about the effects of such policies upon pastoral societies, let alone the specific effects upon women in herding societies. In this chapter I consider the impact of these changes on the pastoral Orma of northeastern Kenya. In particular, I shall analyze the effects of two major policy shifts by the government of Kenya, which fall under a broad definition of structural adjustment, or macroeconomic and political changes designed to utilize government resources more efficiently (Jaycox 1988). The first of these is the rescheduling of agricultural and meat prices which took place between 1980 and 1987. The Orma are major marketers of meat, while they purchase substantial quantities of maize flour and sugar, all price-controlled agricultural commodities. The second policy change to be considered is the decentralization of the government bureaucracy, which officially began on the 1st of July 1983 (Government of Kenya 1987).

The case study material discussed in this paper is based upon two periods of field research among the Orma. The first of these (from July 1978 to February 1981) represents the baseline study, while the second (April to December 1987), is the period during which the effects of these changes were monitored. The data reported here are from two household economic surveys of most residents within the same 15 by 20 mile area around the market town of Wayu. Of the 230 households resident in

Jean Ensminger is assistant professor of anthropology, Washington University at St. Louis, with a Ph.D. from Northwestern University. She wishes to thank the following institutions for generous research support: Fulbright-Hays, the Ford Foundation, the National Science Foundation (BNS-7904273), the Rockefeller Foundation, and the National Institutes of Health (SSP 5 R01 HD21327 DBS). She also wishes to acknowledge the fine institutional support provided by the National Museums of Kenya and the Institute for Development Studies, University of Nairobi.

1979, 174 (76 percent) were surveyed, while of the 214 households resident in 1987, 180 (84 percent) were surveyed.

The Galole Orma and Their Place in Recent Kenyan Economic History

The Orma of northeastern Kenya are riverine cattle pastoralists with lesser numbers of sheep and goats. They reside in Tana River district, which borders the coast of Kenya, the Somali and the Wapokomo to the north and east, the Wakamba to the west, and the Giriama to the south. They are Islamic, Eastern Cushitic-speaking people of the Oromo language group.

This case study was carried out in the geographic center of Orma territory with the population known specifically as the Galole Orma, after the seasonal river which cuts the territory from east to west on a parallel with Hola, the district headquarters of Tana River. In 1979, 39 percent of Galole households were settled in villages with shops and were strongly integrated into the market economy as commercial beef producers. The other 61 percent were less involved in the market economy and to a greater extent nomadic. This group was generally more self-sufficient in meeting their subsistence needs, which consisted primarily of dairy products, supplemented only when necessary with purchased maize flour, sugar, tea, and cooking oil. By 1987, the market town population had increased to 63 percent from the 39 percent figure of 1979 and, although still pastoral, was engaged in much more floodplain agriculture, conditions permitting.

The findings presented in this chapter ought to be interpreted keeping in mind the historical position of the Orma in the 1970s and 1980s, as well as the recent economic history of Kenya. During the great Sahelian drought of the early 1970s, the Orma lost approximately 70 percent of their livestock. This period coincided with a major wave of sedentarization within the Wayu survey area and the permanent incorporation of those households into market relations, at least for their subsistence needs during the dry season (Ensminger 1984). Large numbers of households impoverished during this drought never recovered self-sufficiency as pastoral producers, though almost all maintain small herds to this day. The significant point to note is that major economic stratification occurred among the Orma in the early 1970s, thus predating the period under study here. In the 1970s the poor fended as best they could with help from wealthy relatives, government famine relief, and limited employment prospects in the area. It was not until the 1980s that significant new employment prospects for the poor appeared, reflecting an increasing economic diversification of the economy, or what may be interpreted as the beginning of true structural transformation.

As Lele (this volume) and Bates (1989) have noted, Kenya has fared better economically than most other African nations. Because economic management has historically been better, Kenya needed less-drastic structural adjustment corrections. Thus, the Orma case described below may appear to be at odds with the other case studies from different African nations presented in this volume, which indeed it probably is. The policy of administrative decentralization described in the second half of the chapter may serve as an example of the type of bold initiative which has brought Kenya to the (*relatively* speaking) favorable economic situation it enjoys today in Africa.

The Rescheduling of Commodity Prices

The early 1980s witnessed considerable changes in the government-controlled prices of key agricultural commodities in Kenya. Under pressure from the World Bank and the IMF, Kenya initiated numerous increases in prices to agricultural producers with consequently higher prices to consumers. While on the surface these policies may appear to be favorable to producers, it has been suggested that, in the case of farmers, the poor may actually be net purchasers of agricultural produce and therefore suffer a loss as a result of the price increases (Due, this volume). Herein lies a major difference between agriculturalists and pastoralists. Historically, even cattle pastoralists such as the Orma have consumed very little beef. In fact, cattle were typically slaughtered only prior to imminent death or for ceremonial occasions (weddings, Islamic holidays, and funerals). Even goats and sheep were slaughtered relatively rarely, usually in the dry season to supplement depleted milk yields. Only recently have some wealthy Orma households been consuming larger quantities of meat (usually sheep or goat), which they purchase by the kilogram from makeshift "butcheries." In other words, while poor pastoralists benefit from any increase in the price of meat to the producer, they are virtually unaffected by increases in the price of meat to consumers.

Those households which do purchase meat are most definitely net beneficiaries of higher prices, as they consume only a fraction of the increases they realize as producers. However, to the extent that the government's policy is consistent across grain and meat prices, pastoralists are affected by increases in the price of grains and other regulated commodities. Table 12-1 provides data on changes in the terms of trade as they were experienced by the Galole Orma over the period from 1980 to 1987. While the government does not control the price paid to producers for cattle, it does control the price which may be charged to consumers, thus effectively accomplishing the same result for those sales which go through formal market channels. Table 12-1 demonstrates that overall the Orma have been net beneficiaries of a favorable turn in terms of trade between 1980 and 1987. While their main cash-earning commodity for sale (cattle) yielded 116 percent more in 1987 than 1980, their total consumer price index increased by 93 percent, and their food costs increased only 89 percent. Not coincidentally, the Kenyan shilling was devalued by exactly 100 percent over this same period. The result is a net gain in purchasing power of about 23 percent for the Orma.

Even a 23 percent increase in the terms of trade does not prepare us for the findings on household and per capita consumption in Table 12-2.

Table 12-1. Terms of Trade for the Galole Orma at Waya: 1980 to 1987 (in Kenyan Shillings).

	1980 (41 households)	1987 (104 households)	1980–87 % increase
Price to Orma Producers			
Cattle: 1–2 years	366 (n = 49)	787 (n = 150)	115%
Cattle: 3–4 years	753 (n = 64)	1741 (n = 27)	131%
Cattle: Over 5 years	988 (n = 74)	2072 (n = 47)	110%
Price to Orma Consumer			
Sugar (1 kg)	5	9	80%
Maize Flour (2 kg packet)	5	11	120%
Tea Leaves (50 g)	$1/50$	$1/90$	27%
Simsin Oil (700 ml)	12	16	33%
Rice (1 kg)	4	11	175%
Kanga Cloth	65	130	100%
Paraffin (700 ml)	3	6	100%
Exchange Rate			
One U.S. Dollar in Kenyan Shillings	8	16	100%
Increase in Cattle Prices Received by Orma Producers[a]			116%
Increase in All Commodity Costs to Orma Consumers[a]			93%
Increase in All Food Costs to Orma Consumers[a]			89%

a. Price indices are calculated on the basis of increase in prices weighted by the percentage of the household budget spent or received per commodity in 1987 (n = 127).

Here we see in the last entry at the bottom of the table that even poor households (the poorest one-third of the population based on wealth per capita of the household) have increased their total household consumption by 87 percent in real terms (1987 prices), while the figure is 125 percent for the middle third of the population and 39 percent for the richest third.[1]

It is important to note that I take increased consumption in real terms to be a sign of greater economic well-being. Expenditure increases in Table 12-2 are *after* inflation; thus they represent *real* increases in the level of consumption.[2] It is also my belief, having collected a great deal of household economic data, that expenditure reports are a more accurate reflection of household income than are income reports. Another way of interpreting these data, therefore, is to say that in 1987 households had significantly higher real incomes.

Having said this, however, it is equally important to stress that an increase in the percentage of the household budget spent upon food and even a real increase in food expenditures are not necessarily indicators of improvement in economic well-being. It is more likely in this case that they reflect a substitution of purchased foods for losses in subsistence production. For example, one might suspect that the large increase in purchased food in 1987 was due to the fact that 1987, although not a drought year, was a dry year and thus necessitated considerably higher food expenditures than would ordinarily be the case. However, 1980, the year of baseline comparison, was also a dry year. Much of the higher food expenditures by households in 1987 can be attributed to the fact that herd size (and thus milk yield) were substantially lower than in 1980, due to the relatively recent heavy losses of the 1985 drought. Increased sedentarization and resultant overgrazing also had a similar effect.

Several other peculiarities of the years 1980 and 1987 served to inflate the relative food expenditures for 1987. Especially since 1985, Galole households have periodically enjoyed substantial yields of maize from floodplain agriculture along the seasonal Galole River. Due to the dryness in 1987, no homegrown maize was being consumed throughout the duration of the survey period, thus resulting in higher than normal food expenditures. Finally, 1980 was a year of exceptional food shortages of all major food commodities—maize flour, rice, and sugar. In fact, from July to October 1980, food was frequently rationed and almost never were all three staples available at the same time.[3] This most certainly depressed food expenditures during that survey period and to some degree the increased expenditures in 1987 probably do actually reflect higher caloric intake.

Table 12-2. Mean Consumption Expenditures Per Capita for Three-Village Sunset: 1980 and 1987 (in 1987 Kenyan Shillings).

	Poor		Middle		Rich	
	1980	1987	1980	1987	1980	1987
Number of Households[a]	17	46	11	35	28	26
Mean Size of Household	8.4	8.1	10.0	10.3	12.4	16.4
Total Food Consumption[b]	472	1,047	463	1,156	585	963
Food as % of Total	56.7%	67.3%	57.1%	63.3%	43.3%	59.5%
Sugar	169	219	169	234	198	218
Flour	106	450	99	479	88	370
Tea & Ginger	62	90	60	92	74	96
Oil	33	180	29	204	25	183
Rice	58	43	66	60	88	59
Other Food	44	65	40	87	32	37
Total Non-Food						
Consumption[c]	360	509	348	670	660	656
Household	98	142	96	165	142	150
Clothing	144	158	172	239	290	241
Other Non-Food	118	209	80	266	228	265
Total Consumption	832	1556	811	1826	1165	1619
Real % Change 1980–87						
Food		+122%		+150%		+91%
Non-Food		+41%		+93%		−1%
Total Consumption		+87%		+125%		+39%

a. The samples sizes within wealth categories do not appear to agree (given household size) with the definitional breakdown of these groups into thirds of the population. The reason for this is that the wealth groups are defined on the basis of the full Galole sample in 1979 (n = 174 of 230) and the same population again in 1987 (n = 203 of 230), while the data in these tables come from only three villages (1979 n = 56; 1987 n = 107). A disproportionately large number of wealthy households lived in these villages in 1979, thus accounting for the large sample size of rich households, while the wealth of households in these villages in 1987 was far more representative of the population at large as measured by wealth. See Table 12-3 for a comparison of means of wealth per capita between the two samples.

b. In order to maximize comparability between survey periods, a few relatively insignificant food items were omitted from these data. Thus they do not fully represent total food consumption. They are, however, complete for the commodities listed.

c. These data exclude contributions to the mosque, *harambee* projects, gifts, and some insignificant miscellaneous items not surveyed identically in 1979 and 1987. In general, such expenditures were far higher in 1987 than in 1980, and were they included here they would strengthen the trend reported.

However one wishes to interpret the data on food consumption, it is clear from the data on non-food consumption that all but the rich in 1987 were consuming a great deal more in real terms of less essential commodities than they were in 1980 (41 percent more for poor and 93 percent more for middle households). Given these data, I conclude that the average poor and middle households were better off economically in 1987 than they were in 1980, and further, that this was not due entirely to a favorable turn in terms of trade for livestock in relation to grain and other commodity prices.

It is worth noting that this finding is all the more unexpected, as 1987 was a brief two years after an extremely serious drought in which the Orma lost 70 percent of their cattle. Nineteen-eighty, on the other hand, had been a full five years after a similarly serious drought in which the Orma also lost nearly 70 percent of their stock. This is reflected in Table 12-3, which shows the mean 1979 and 1987 stock holdings per capita for both the entire Galole sample and the three-village subset reported in Table 12-2. Per capita holdings declined on average 35 percent for the original full Galole sample from 1979 to 1987.

Table 12-3 also provides data on a comparison of means between the Galole population at large and the three-village subset whose consumption is reported in Table 12-2. With one exception, the means of wealth per capita by wealth group are extremely close, indicating that the sample subset is not biased on the most crucial variable. The exception occurs among the poor in 1979 (1.41 TLU per capita for the subset versus 1.17 TLU for the full sample), indicating that they are considerably wealthier than the "poor" population at large. However, since consumption is positively correlated with wealth, the bias goes against the direction of the findings reported here. In other words, had the poor sample in 1979 been more representative of the poor at large, we would have expected to find an even larger increase in their consumption between 1980 and 1987.

Another possible explanation for the trend of increased consumption seen in these data would be selective migration out of the area by poor households between the two survey periods. Indeed, there was a substantial migration in and out of the 15 by 20 mile survey area around Wayu. For the most part, these moves were precipitated by the 1985 drought and follow the pattern noted years ago by Barth (1961), whereby poor pastoralists settle in urban areas in times of stress. To control for this phenomenon, the "full Galole sample" data in Table 12-3 are based upon actual and, where necessary, estimated wealth per capita of the original 1979 sample population again in 1987, including those who migrated

Table 12-3. Mean Wealth Per Capita in Tropical Livestock Units[a] by Wealth of Household for Full Galole Sample and Three-Village Subset: 1979 and 1987.

	Poor		Middle		Rich	
	TLU	n	TLU	n	TLU	n
1979 Full Galole Sample	1.17	58	4.01	57	11.51	59
1979 Three-Village Subset	1.41	17	3.96	11	11.75	28
1987 Full Galole Sample[b]	0.64	80	2.05	72	8.15	51
1987 Three-Village Subset	0.64	46	2.02	35	8.25	26

a. A tropical livestock unit is equivalent to one head of cattle. Sheep and goats in 1979 were converted at 6 to 1, while in 1987 they were converted at 5 to 1, consistent with local exchange values.

b. The 1987 data for the full Galole sample are for the original population resident in the area in 1979, rather than the population within the survey area in 1987, in order to control for selective in-and-out migration. The three-village subset, however, is based upon actual residents in those villages over time. For many households which migrated out of the survey area, the chief's estimates of household size and wealth were used. In six cases where surveys of such households were later carried out, his estimates agreed quite closely with the actual surveys.

out of the survey area. In-migrants are not included in the 1987 data for the full Galole sample. The fact that the three-village subset (including in-migrants) still closely resembles the original sample reflects the fact that the small market towns represented in that sample are like mid-way stations in the process of in-and-out migration, and the wealth of those migrating in and out of these villages is relatively close. I am satisfied that the data are not confounded by either sampling bias or selective migration.

As further documentation that the well-being of the population may actually have improved between 1979 and 1987, I include 1987 data on weight per height by gender, age group, and type of residence (Table 12-4). Weight per height is regarded as a relatively good proxy for nutritional status. As there has been a significant transition to residence in market towns over time (from 39 to 63 percent of the population), roughly corresponding to the shift from nomadism to sedentarism, these data may be indicative of the longitudinal trend. We find a statistically significant improvement for both male adults and male children, comparing the mean weight per height of the bush and market-town samples. For females (both children and adults) there is no statistically significant difference. Thus, while we may conclude from these data that there is some

Table 12-4. Mean Weight Per Height[a] for 1987 Resident Galole Survey by Type of Residence, Gender, Age Category, and Wealth of Household.

| | Males | | Females | |
	Age 2–18	Age 19+	Age 2–18	Age 19+
Market Town	0.182[b]	0.333[c]	0.188[d]	0.308[e]
	(n = 266)	(n = 158)	(n = 261)	(n = 191)
Bush	0.170	0.319	0.185	0.307)
	(n = 105)	(n = 57)	(n = 98)	(n = 84)

a. Within age/gender categories a higher ratio of weight to height is generally indicative of better nutritional well-being; women's ratios are typically lower than men's. Comparative ratios from Turkana pastoral nomads are 0.331 for adult men and 0.302 for adult women and 3.31 for adult women (Galvin 1985: 232).

b. A difference of means T-Test for market town versus bush male children is significant at the 0.0001 level.

c. A difference of means T-Test for market town versus bush male adults is significant at the 0.0001 level.

d. There is no statistically significant difference between market town and bush female children.

e. There is no statistically significant difference between market town and bush female adults.

support for improved nutritional well-being of males in all age groups as a result of town residence, there is no change, for better or worse, for females.

In summary, I would argue that several economic and anthropometric indices bear out my impressionistic observations of economic change among the Galole Orma between 1980 and 1987, namely, that on average even the poor were at least slightly better off in 1987 than they had been in 1980. I do not conclude, however, that these tendencies can be attributed entirely to the effect of structural adjustment policies affecting agricultural prices, though a 23 percent favorable turn in terms of trade may account for about half of the improvement for the poor.

To a certain extent, the improved economic circumstances are attributable to increased government expenditures which have created some employment for the Galole. For example, the few Orma with secondary education are employed as clerks and schoolteachers. The government has also employed Galole on construction and road building projects. However, much of the increase in construction employment can be traced to increased trade and commerce rather than government building. For example, there is a local stone quarry in Wayu which supplies building stones for construction to the district headquarters. Many poor and some rich households have members who earn considerable incomes there. While some stones are used for government buildings, most are used in the construction of new shops and private residences in the district headquarters.

Perhaps more significant to the Orma economy than any other single change is the opening of new livestock markets (at Kitui and Bengal) paying approximately 30 percent more in 1987 than the Orma's traditional coastal market. The Orma sell stock to middlemen and do not always know the final destination of their stock. However, it was reported to me that the higher prices offered by the two new markets resulted from the fact that these stock were destined for export to the Middle East via Nairobi. If this is the case, the higher prices offered there since 1984 could be the direct result of Kenyan currency devaluations, which have the effect of making exports more competitive.

The increased competition of two new cattle markets has also had enormous secondary consequences. By breaking the virtual monopsony (i.e., presence of one buyer) of one coastal Arab trader, more local Galole have been able to get involved in livestock trading. Consequently, more of the money from such trade is staying in the district and helping to fuel the development of many service industries. For example, when I left Galole in 1981 there were no tea kiosks in Wayu Boro. I returned in 1987 to find not one, but six! One of these is owned and operated by a woman, while women operate all of the others and manage them together with their husbands.

Another small example of the increased specialization and division of labor is that one finds wealthy households now more typically buying handicrafts that they previously produced for themselves. Similarly, specialized traders in tobacco, miraa, and skins have developed.

All of the new sources of cash income (from casual labor, civil service jobs, livestock trading, commerce, and service industries) pay a special dividend for the poor, who are now no longer dependent upon shopkeepers for all of their cash needs and have to a great extent managed to free themselves from much of the debt bondage to shopkeepers which existed in 1980. Previously, those who took credit at a shop had to trade their livestock there or risk losing their credit in the future. Effective interest rates were 60 percent per season if one compared the prices the shops paid for livestock to those received by households who sold directly to outside traders (Ensminger 1984: 120).

Obviously not all of these changes can be attributed merely to increased government expenditure and currency devaluation. They also stem in part from an institutional structure which is facilitating the development of trade, increasing specialization, and the division of labor, which are essential to economic take-off (North 1981, 1990; Ensminger 1990). The government's recent effort toward administrative decentralization is but one example of such institutional change, and I turn now to an examination of this policy.

District Development Focus: Decentralization 1983–1987

On July 1, 1983, the Kenyan government launched a major governmental decentralization initiative described in what has come to be known as the "Blue Book" (Government of Kenya 1987). The 1970s had seen much lip-service paid to attempts to decentralize the government bureaucracy (Rondinelli et al. 1984:30; Oyugi 1983), but unlike these earlier attempts, what happened in 1983 had an impact in the rural area. The difference may be due to President Moi's political motivations and consequent commitment to the initiatives, which resulted in far greater attention to the undertaking than had previously been the case. The stated objective of district development focus was to move the center for much development decision-making closer to the respective recipients. It also meant that initiatives for rural development were expected to come more from below than had previously been the case.

A further, though often unstated, goal of the policy was to return to the districts more responsibility for the maintenance of development projects once begun. This meant a reversal of the long-standing national policy of taking over successful locally initiated projects (*harambee* schools, for instance) and in future leaving the maintenance of such development efforts more in the hands of the district. This was necessitated because districts had learned from past experience that the best strategy for getting more funds from the government was to initiate as many projects as possible to the required level of functioning and then petition for government takeover. The government eventually found that the recurrent costs of this policy were far too great. It also took too long for projects to become fully functional, and thus resources were being tied up inefficiently in projects dangling for years in various stages of half-completion (Alan Johnston, Ministry of Finance and Planning, personal communication).

An obvious danger of decentralization to poorer districts such as Tana

River is that it will lead to less redistribution from central government funds. This of course presupposes that such redistribution existed in the past. On the positive side, decentralization has been argued to increase responsiveness to local needs and to lead to greater political equality and leadership training (see Smith 1985:Chapter 2 for a review of these and other arguments). Decentralization also alters who wields power (Smith 1985:206), and thus its effect upon women has a great deal to do with women's position vis à vis the previous political structure. In the next two sections of the chapter I review how the Orma experience with decentralization has affected women in these critical areas.

A New District Focus: Effects upon Redistribution and Responsiveness to Local Needs

One of the most striking changes I noted upon return to the Orma in 1987 was the degree of commitment the population expressed for local fund-raising initiatives. While numerous fund-raising efforts were imposed upon the Orma between 1978 and 1981, they were almost invariably in support of projects in different districts. Typically, the provincial commissioner or the district commissioner (always from outside the district), would organize *harambee* (self-help) fund-raising drives in support of projects in their home districts. The pressure put upon local chiefs (the local governmental representative in remote rural areas) to raise funds for such foreign projects was enormous. Chiefs were typically assigned a quota for collection. By 1987, this practice had altered dramatically. Since the beginning of "district focus" in 1983, not one collection for outside the district was undertaken in the Wayu area, although the chief acknowledged that receipt books for external collections were still piling up in his office. The difference was that the Orma could now argue that collections for other districts were incompatible with the ideology of "district focus." Over and over again one heard the words "district focus" spoken with a nationalistic-like fervor. For the first time the local community had a pride in building for its own development. Needless to say, contributions increased substantially.

Local fund-raising drives in rural areas such as Tana River are a major means of taxation in Kenya. The Orma pay no official income taxes to the central government, although there are taxes on commercial transactions. Many of the funds for basic social services such as school buildings, therefore, must come from the initiative of the local community, although the government picks up the costs of paying the teachers and staff. Such funds are collected in a highly formalized manner, however, representing a system quite close to an income tax, albeit a relatively regressive one. For example, the elders, together with the chief, agree upon appropriate levels of payments for each household based upon their wealth in livestock. For a major school fund-raising drive in 1987, for example, the tax rate schedule was as shown in Table 12-5. Should a household resist paying, the chief exercised such sanctions as were at his disposal; the compliance rate was very high.

Table 12-6 provides data on one of the outcomes of the fund-raising efforts. When I left the Galole Orma in 1981 there was only one primary school then serving the population of approximately 2,400. During my absence a neighboring village had just completed a substantial fund-raising and was in the process of constructing a high-quality permanent school building. Enrollment of school-age boys increased between 1979 and 1987 from 26 percent to 50 percent. Even more impressive, while only 4 percent of school-age girls were enrolled in 1979, that figure rose to 30 percent in 1987. The chief notes that the addition of new classrooms, facilitated by *harambee* contributions, was essential to his being able to put pressure upon households to send their female children to school.

In addition to the positive effect that district focus had upon local development initiatives, there were many signs that central government expenditures had also increased. For example, Table 12-6 also provides data on adult education participation, which is a program begun in Wayu town in 1983 and funded entirely by the central government. The striking finding here is that it is the women, not the men, who are the most keen participants. While 26 men in the survey reported some participation in the program, 47 women had participated. Far more striking was the fact that only 1 male from Wayu town was continuing his adult education, while 31 adult Wayu women (41 percent of those in the town where it is offered) continued in the program. One of the reasons women are so anxious to study is because they have learned that lack of fluency in

Table 12-5. Structure of 1987 *Harambee* Tax Contributions in Galole by Wealth of Household.

Wealth of Household in Cattle	Type of Contribution	Value of Contribution (in Kenyan Shillings)
200+	Large Sanga Male	2500/=
80–200	Hawicha Female	1500/= to 2000/=
50–80	Cash	1000/=
30–50	Gabicha Male	500/=
1–20	Cash	100/= to 150/=
No Stock	Cash	10/= to 20/=

Table 12-6. Education by Gender for Resident Galole Sample 1979 and 1987.

	Males		Females	
	1979	1987	1979	1987
Some Schooling	119	253	13	132
As Percent of Pop. over Age 6	17%	30%	2%	18%
In School	82	158	9	84
As Percent of Pop. Age 7–16	26%	50%	4%	30%
Some Adult Education	0	26	0	47
As Percent of Pop. Over Age 18[a]		12%		19%
In Adult Education	0	1	0	31
As Percent of Pop. Over Age 18[b]		2%		41%

a. Adult education was originally offered in two villages. This figure represents the percentage of the population age 18 and above with some adult education for those two villages.

b. The adult literacy program was offered in only one village in 1987. These figures represent the proportion of the population age 18 and above continuing in adult education in that village.

Swahili and illiteracy have disadvantaged them in the courts and in promoting their interests through government channels.

Table 12-7 provides data on vaccination histories for children in the Galole area. At the time of my departure in 1981, only sporadic mobile vaccination campaigns had taken place. In the early 1980s, however, a major vaccination program through the permanent dispensary in Wayu town was initiated. Several findings surface from the inoculation data. First, there appears to be considerable diligence on the part of the population to see series of vaccinations through to their completion, as evidenced in DPT and polio vaccinations, which require two and three return visits respectively at specified intervals. Second, it is worth noting that no discrimination against female children exists such that males are more likely to be vaccinated than females.

Other government efforts of note during this time period include the upgrading of several significant roads in the area. This has considerable import for the quality of life of the population, as food shortages are common during the rainy season when roads are typically washed out in this flood-prone district.

Another of the most beneficial outcomes of the bureaucratic decentralization has been the effort to upgrade the level of civil servants in all ministries in the rural areas. This did not mean an expansion of the civil service but rather the posting of civil servants out of urban areas and into the

Table 12-7. Frequency of Vaccinations for Galole Survey by Gender: All Children Age 0–16 in 1987.

		n	No Vacc	1 Vacc	2 Vacc	3 Vacc	4 Vacc
DPT	Male	351	135 (38.5%)	17 (4.8%)	14 (4.0%)	185 (52.7%)	—
	Female	333	124 (37.2%)	20 (6.0%)	14 (4.2%)	175 (52.6%)	—
Polio	Male	351	133 (37.9%)	9 (2.6%)	13 (3.7%)	26 (7.4%)	170 (48.4%)
	Female	334	127 (38.0%)	15 (4.5%)	18 (5.4%)	31 (9.3%)	143 (42.8%)

rural areas where they could be most effective—no small accomplishment in any African bureaucracy. From the schools, to the dispensary, to the district development office, both the numbers and the qualifications of civil servants were increased in the mid-1980s.

The mid-1980s brought many new civil servants to Wayu, the center of Galole. For instance, while in 1980 one almost never saw a veterinary officer even visit the remote Galole area, in 1987 one was actually permanently posted there. The government also built an impressive house for the local nurse who attends at the dispensary. The better accommodation allowed for the posting of a far more qualified health officer. An assistant nurse was also brought permanently, thus ensuring that the dispensary could remain open when the nurse left for leave or to collect medicine. The number of administrative police in the area was also increased fourfold, thus contributing to greater security in an area continuously plagued by bandit attacks.

Finally, perhaps the single most significant activity of the government during this period was the provision of famine relief during the 1985 drought. Famine relief has been functioning intermittently in the Galole area since colonial times, but households noted with considerable appreciation that the effort in 1985 was one of the best organized and most responsive. While the initial shipments could certainly have been used two months earlier, once begun, they were both sufficient and timely, and continued for over a year at a significant level. The local chief's correspondence files clearly document the government's responsiveness. Maize sometimes arrived as quickly as five days after the request was communicated. There is no question but that the effort was more responsive than that during the 1974 drought.

In summary, it does not appear that the policy of decentralization has imposed costs on the Orma population generally or women specifically. On the contrary, given that in the past the Galole probably made a net contribution to other districts, usually substantially wealthier ones, the policy has actually improved the situation from the point of view of redistribution. Meanwhile, the ideology of "building for local development" has thus far helped raise an unprecedented amount of funds for local schools.

A word of caution is in order, however, regarding the future allocation of central government funds. It remains to be seen whether the government will continue to distribute its own funds in ever more generous amounts to districts such as Tana River. It has been suggested, for example (personal communication from sources in the Ministry of Finance and Planning), that the decentralization initiative, by placing the burden for initiation and maintenance of development projects upon the local areas, could be setting the way for a more focused use of national development resources in those areas where the economic return is likely to be highest—in other words, the high-potential agricultural areas. Should this be the case, and should resources be taken out of social services such as veterinary services, rural dispensaries, and schools, the Orma could yet see a decline in their area—both relatively and absolutely.

Political Equality and Leadership Training for Orma Women

I will close the section on the effects of decentralization with a brief discussion of what it has meant to women to bring the locus of decision-making closer to the rural areas. In theory, it is fair to assume that those most excluded from the upper echelons of power would be benefited by efforts that succeed in moving the level of real decision-making down the power hierarchy. It remains to be seen whether or not district focus will succeed in this, one of its stated objectives. In theory, however, it is hard to imagine that women would not be positively affected by such a change. The closer the political process gets to the rural village, which Galole women rarely leave, the more potential one would predict women have to make a real contribution.

There are very small signs that this is beginning to happen. It is mandated by the government, for instance, that women be included on local development committees. This committee meets in the chief's office in the small village of Wayu in the heart of Galole.

To my surprise, upon checking the minutes of meetings held in the mid-1980s, I did find women in attendance as members of the committee. Of 25 present at one meeting, 9 were women. At that meeting, when the members were asked to propose projects, the women spoke up in favor of a local nursery school and more resources for the dispensary. Both motions were acted upon by the committee.

Between 1980 and 1987 there was also a noticeable increase in the presence of women at village meetings (local *barazas*) organized by the chief. While most women even in 1987 still played only a limited role in these public forums, they were at least getting access to information, which is certainly a necessary step in the direction of exercising power.

In conclusion, I would say that decentralization in theory promises tremendous benefits for women, who have historically been excluded from the centers of power in virtually all societies. By the same token, one may wonder how long such a system will last once those to whom authority has been delegated begin to use it for purposes not to the liking of those who still retain the power to again change the institutional structure.

Conclusion

We should all be cheered by the fact that the Orma bring some good news to the subject of development and structural transformation in Africa. However, it is important to carry away the correct interpretations from these findings. While there are certainly lessons for Africa in the specific Orma and Kenyan experiences, it is also important to note the ways in which this case study may not be generalizable.

First of all, not all of Kenya has benefited from economic improvement in the 1980s. One need only look to the Orma's neighbors, the agricultural Pokomo, to find a people whose economic fortunes appear to have declined considerably over this period. In the case of the Pokomo, a major contributing factor has been the damming of the Tana River, which has substantially reduced the seasonal floods upon which the Pokomo depend for their livelihood. It would be premature to make the case that either the Orma or the Pokomo or some other experience is the more typical one for Kenya. Only more case studies with longitudinal data will resolve this. Second, the Kenyan experience itself is not typical for Africa. Due to a history of *relatively* good economic management, Kenya never fell to the depths that most other African nations experienced by the late 1970s. Consequently, the structural adjustment policies which Kenya has implemented are not nearly as harsh as those of other nations such as Nigeria and Tanzania. We must be most cautious, therefore, in generalizing from a positive experience in Kenya, to the very dissimilar conditions which brought very different policy prescriptions to places like Nigeria and Tanzania.

While the Orma case study may not be typical of the rest of Africa at the present time, one might hope that there are lessons in it which may be *transferable*. Both the Orma and the Kenyan experience generally have much to teach us about the factors which facilitate structural transformation. First of all, increasing prices to producers has made a difference, but it is not the whole story. Obviously this policy also needs to be weighed by planners against the hardship imposed at the other end, that is, to the consumers. Second, in the Orma case governmental institutional development appears to be crucial to the proliferation of trade and commerce, which finally took off in the mid-1980s to the point that it generated significant economic diversification. While many Orma are still terribly poor, their condition is somewhat improved by the new employment prospects afforded by this increasing diversification and division of labor. As the Orma experience with the tea kiosks indicates, such diversification need not exclude women, even in a Muslim society. The current decentralization initiative which the Kenyan government has embarked upon is but the most recent example of institutional change which appears to be paying off in the rural sector. Other African nations might do well to study this experiment.

NOTES

1. Due to the large difference in household size between poor (8.1 persons) and rich (16.4 persons) households, it takes many more poor households to make up the bottom third of the population. The divisions represented here, however, are based upon percent of the population, not percent of households, as was the case in Ensminger 1984. This makes a significant difference in the analysis, as the richest third of households actually represents 50 percent of the population.

2. The case I am making here, that increased *real* expenditures are a reflection of economic well-being rather than deterioration, does not contradict the argument made by others in this volume, that *inflated* prices have brought economic hardship to women in many areas as a result of structural adjustment. In those cases, income has not kept up with inflation, which consequently has lead to a *real* decline in consumption.

3. A general note regarding the policy of "getting prices right" is in order. To the extent that government-controlled prices of grains are so low that they depress production (as argued by many, including Bates 1981), one must consider *upon whom* the resultant shortages are most likely to fall. In 1980 Kenya suffered severe shortages of maize flour, the nation's primary subsistence crop. While the proximate cause for this shortfall was drought that year, one could argue that had production been higher in good years, reserves might also have been higher. Equally, had prices been higher, black-market exports to neighboring countries might have been reduced. Whatever the real cause, it was clear in Tana River that year that pastoral areas, some of the nation's poorest, were some of the last to get grain shipments during times of scarcity. Within the district, it was the poor who

were the last to get access to supplies during rationing. With little question, even the poor would have preferred to pay higher prices for maize flour to ensure supply rather than go without, as they often had to do that year. I would stress that the economically and politically weak, among which groups we often find women, are likely to be the first to suffer during times of scarcity.

REFERENCES

Barth, Fredric
    1961   *Nomads of South Persia: The Basseri Tribe of the Khamseh Confederacy.* Boston: Little, Brown and Company.

Bates, Robert H.
    1981   *Markets and States in Tropical Africa: The Political Basis of Agricultural Policies.* Berkeley: University of California Press.
    1989   *Beyond the Miracle of the Market: The Political Economy of Agrarian Development in Kenya.* Cambridge: Cambridge University Press.

Ensminger, Jean
    1984   Political Economy among the Pastoral Galole Orma: The Effects of Market Integration. Ph.D. dissertation, Department of Anthropology, Northwestern University.
    1990   Co-Opting the Elders: The Political Economy of State Incorporation in Africa. *American Anthropologist* 92(3). In press.

Galvin, Kathleen
    1985   Food Procurement, Diet, Activities and Nutrition of Ngisonyoka, Turkana Pastoralists in an Ecological and Social Context. Ph.D. dissertation, Department of Anthropology, State University of New York at Binghamton.

Government of Kenya
    1987   [1983] District Focus for Rural Development. Nairobi, Kenya: Government Printing Office.

Jaycox, Edward
    1988   What can Be Done in Africa? The World Bank's Response. *Africa's Development Challenges and the World Bank*, Stephen K. Commins, ed., pp. 19–52. Boulder: Lynne Rienner Publishers.

North, Douglass
    1981   *Structure and Change in Economic History.* New York: W. W. Norton & Company, Inc.
    1990   *Institutions, Institutional Change, and Economic Performance.* Cambridge: Cambridge University Press. In press.

Oyugi, Walter Ouma
    1983   Local Government in Kenya: A Case of Institutional Decline. *Local Government in the Third World: The Experience of Tropical Africa*, P. Mawhood, ed., pp. 107–40. New York: John Wiley & Sons.

Rondinelli, Dennis A., John R. Nellis, and G. Shabbir Cheema
    1984   Decentralization in Developing Countries: A Review of Recent
            Experience. World Bank Staff Working Papers No. 581. Washing-
            ton, D.C.: The World Bank.
Smith, B. C.
    1985   *Decentralization: The Territorial Dimension of the State.* London:
            George Allen & Unwin.

IV

Debate on the Economy of Affection: Is It a Useful Tool for Gender Analysis?

Goran Hyden and Pauline E. Peters

Introduction

The following is a transcription of a debate on the gender implications of "the economy of affection," a term coined by Goran Hyden, University of Florida, and questioned by Pauline Peters, Harvard Institute for International Development. The two-hour debate took place on the first day of the conference and addressed this question: Is the economy of affection a useful model for addressing gender differences in Africa and for tracking structural adjustment and its impact on women farmers? The reader should note that what follows are not, strictly speaking, papers but are based on the debaters' notes and on the edited transcriptions of the taped debate, which proved lively, cordial, and informative. It may also be helpful to know that Hyden initiated the debate with 10 minutes of description of the economy of affection. Peters then followed with 30 minutes of insightful argument, which in turn was followed by 20 minutes of rebuttal and counterrebuttal.

Hyden's Opening Statement

Hyden: Other conference participants (e.g., Lele, O'Brien, Johnston) have reported that, during the 1960s and 1970s, what was being done in the name of development was based on the idea that somehow a state and market could penetrate Africa, if it didn't already penetrate Africa. The debate then was very much about the extent to which one

Goran Hyden spent about 20 years in East Africa, before coming to the political science department at the University of Florida in 1986. He taught at Makerere University in Uganda, the University of Nairobi, Kenya, and the University of Dar es Salaam, Tanzania. Subsequently, he joined the Ford Foundation and worked there for 8 years, first as a social science research advisor and finally as its representative in East and Southern Africa.

Pauline E. Peters is an anthropologist and institute associate at Harvard Institute for International Development, and teaches in the department of anthropology, Harvard University. She has a Ph.D. from Boston University and has extensive fieldwork experience in Malawi.

could provide the right support for what was to be either a state or market-based approach. As early as the late 1970s, a number of people—including people at the World Bank—were becoming increasingly concerned about the fact that these prevailing approaches were essentially *top-down* approaches. Structural transformation was the catchword for what was being done. But whether it was structural transformation or not, the notion was that it had to be done from above. And what we were talking about was essentially the Africans as objects rather than as subjects or actors in their own rights.

I think it was in the light of the emerging failures of these approaches that people like myself and others in the late seventies began to question the conventional wisdom of the day. I was writing the first of two books—*Beyond Ujamaa in Tanzania*—which was published in 1980 but really written in 1978. It paid attention to the fact that if we were to understand where Africa was going, if we were to understand what was happening with development efforts in Africa, we really needed to think *beyond the market* and *beyond the state*. It was in that context that I suggested that the African economies have a logic—rationality—of their own that cannot just be subsumed under either market or bureaucratic rationality. I suggested in my own writing at that time that what we were really witnessing in Africa was the growing penetration of this social logic. The market and the state were becoming *less*, not more, prominent in African society.

What I suggested was that it might be useful to think of there being a peasant mode of production in African countries that is separate from what was essentially a capitalist mode of production which had been considered by everybody at that time as predominant. The peasant mode of production was characterized by the following: First, no real exploitation of peasants by another class was occurring, although there was obviously surplus extraction going on, but that was confined within essentially lineage or clan or kinship units. Second, land tenure and the control of the means of production remained in the hands of those units—the peasants themselves—rather than in the hands of a landlord class that had alienated the land from the peasants. Third, the technology used by the peasants was very rudimentary and therefore there were no real functional or structural linkages—backward or forward linkages—between agricultural and nonagricultural sectors as is found in other parts of the world, where peasants have become much more integrated into either market- or state-controlled production systems, e.g., in the East or West or Asia or Latin America. We're talking, therefore, about a situation where the units of production are by and large rather *autonomous.* On the basis of that, I suggested that the peasants themselves were, if not fully uncaptured, then *relatively autonomous and uncaptured,* compared to peasants in other parts of the world.

Then the question is, if these units of production and these economies are so weakly linked together, structurally and functionally, what is it that holds them together? I suggested that what really holds them together is *affection.* Affection here is a word that describes what is essentially the networks of support, communication, and interaction that exists among not only kinship units but also communities and other groups that might be described as held together on the bases of mutual sharing of positive sentiments for each other. Now some of you might say that affection is a universal value: we all seek affection. We seek it in love on a person-to-person basis and we seek it in many other contexts: we want to be feeling good in our relations with other people. The point is not the existence or nonexistence of affection. Rather, it is the historical difference between Africa and most other societies. Affection, particularly in Western societies, has been relegated essentially to the private realm. Being or showing affection in the public realm, here in the U.S. or Europe, or wherever market or bureaucratic rationality has taken over, suggests that you are actually doing something wrong, i.e., you are seeking favors or you are doing something contrary to the rules of those systems, the market system or the state system. In Africa, I'm suggesting that because markets and state are so weak and have not really penetrated societies, affection is not just a marginal or peripheral phenomenon, but sits there in the middle and is actually the core that holds societies together. Vis-à-vis both market and state, affection in Africa plays both a proactive and a reactive role.

Affection is not the same as kinship. It goes beyond kinship, although kinship is obviously one unit in the economy of affection. The economy of affection is not the same as the "moral economy" that so many have written about, especially with reference to Southeast Asia. The moral economy talks about the subsistence ethic of farmers who experience, what Marxists or neo-Marxists might call a "reproduction squeeze." I am not talking about the moral economy when I speak about the economy of affection. It's more than a defense mechanism; it's actually the way people are trying to get ahead, as well as protect themselves. It thus has a more universal applicability. It's not the same as the "informal economy," although such an economy often depends on affection when it operates in a parallel fashion to official institutions. The important thing to remember is that the economy of affection permeates bureaucracies and official markets, and therefore segments markets and creates systems of operations, networks of operations in government institutions and in public enterprises that very often go counter to what is the expected logic or rationale of such institutions.

I should also add that I see the economy of affection incorporating the concept of "ethnicity," thereby suggesting that people are sticking together on a lateral or horizontal basis. It also incorporates the notion of "clientelism" that my colleague Rene Lemarchand has been such a fervent advocate of over the years. Thus, the economy of affection also operates vertically, that is to say, people actually seek patrons or patrons seek clients in order to get things done. Affection does not exclude conflict. Affection is the kind of currency that exists out there. It is both a means and an end in itself. But because it becomes increasingly difficult to manage in a more complex society, affection is bound to lead to conflict and disaffection in many situations where the management of affection does not actually succeed. Therefore, conflict and disaffection are as much a part of the economy of affection as is solidarity or reciprocity.

Finally, let me conclude with two observations. First, these largely invisible institutions—these affective networks—exist out there and really make things work, whether we like it or not, or whether it goes against what we think is right. Whatever they achieve, right or wrong, good or bad, these invisible institutions are clearly in much more need of understanding when it comes to such things as we're talking about now, i.e., structural adjustment and impacts on women's production and consumption. Second, I also want to suggest that these institutions are not really based in a material condition that dictates its logic, but are really held together by affection. What we are talking about here is something that is very tenuous but also flexible. In that sense, "institution-building" or "capacity-building"—the current catchwords of not only the World Bank but also a lot of other institutions—is obviously not going to be a very easy task. It certainly has to be seen in the light of the particular concerns that I have discussed here and in my writings. Thank you.

Peters's Response

Peters: I wish to argue that the answer to the question of this debate, of whether the concept of the "economy of affection" (Hyden 1980, 1983) is useful for tracking structural adjustment programs, is no. As an analytical framework, the economy of affection fails to elucidate the dynamics of African rural transformation and of African political economy. It is useful neither for the scholar/researcher nor for the policymaker. Its major shortcomings are its failure to disaggregate rural producers and to provide ways of identifying the key social groups and categories, as well as the interconnections among them. In particular, the removal of "petty-capitalist farmers" from the peasant mode of Production obscures more than it clarifies. Finally, the complete absence of gender from Hyden's chosen "paradigm"—the economy of affection—is a particular, and particularly unfortunate, outcome of his reliance on a framework which is blind to social difference.

Although I want to contest Hyden's promoting "the economy of affection" as a new paradigm for understanding African political economies, I do so because I consider the questions he poses to be important. Hyden raises issues central both to scholarship on Africa and to analysis of policies, including those concerned with structural adjustment. They are, first, analysis of the purported "crisis" in Africa, the state of African political economies, the process of capitalist transformation, and, second, the analytical means to comprehend these. I think Hyden has headed off into a wrong direction with the economy of affection and the peasant mode of production (as defined by him), but I have sympathy with his insistence that conventional analytical approaches have not served the task of understanding Africa's experience well. Even less do they help policy analysis and formation. His goals are important and, in my opinion, correctly formulated but I do not think that the economy of affection is the solution. I think I am not alone in finding Hyden's written works stimulating; they contain insightful commentaries but I also think that the insights come from his years of experience in East Africa as a researcher and resident and do not depend on the theoretical framework he wishes to promote. Obviously, this is contrary to what Hyden himself says. My contention is that his experience in Africa, which he rightfully emphasizes, explains why much of his analysis "rings true" empirically. It is for this reason that his work is found useful for inquiries into the current political economies of Africa. But there is a large and uncomfortable gap between this experientially informed analysis and his favored "new paradigm." And now, to explore this gap....

My primary task here is to argue that the economy of affection is not a useful way to approach these concerns and questions. The economy of affection has been a key concept in Hyden's thought since his influential book *Beyond Ujamaa in Tanzania* (1980). Introduced in that work, it received more emphasis in *No Shortcuts to Progress* (1983), and in his most recent writing is given the status of an alternative theory in comparative politics to those based on models of the state, market, property rights, and "associative social action" (Hyden n.d.:16). In this later work, the economy of affection is also glossed as a "community" model, since "[t]he economy of affection ... functions as a model of social order through its central institution, the community" (ibid.).

Arising out of the "peasant mode of production," the economy of affection is one "in which the affective ties based on common descent, common residence, etc., prevail" (Hyden 1980:18). It "denotes a network of support, communications and interaction among structurally defined groups connected by blood, kin, community, or other affinities, for example, religion" (Hyden 1983:8). In a footnote to the 1980 citation, Hyden pointed out that his "economy of affection" conveys "the same meaning as implied in the reciprocal mode of economic organization identified by Polanyi as typical of simple agrarian societies." This idea has continued up to his most recent writing where reference is made to the economy of affection as a "community model of simultaneous reciprocities" (Hyden n.d.:4). Critically, the peasant mode of production and economy of affection are understood by Hyden to be "pre-capitalist."

The economy of affection is grounded in the peasant mode of production: these seem to be conceived by Hyden as mutually determinant. I shall argue that the characteristic features of the economy of affection and peasant mode of production are empirically untenable in Africa; and that, as concepts, they are curiously ahistorical, despite Hyden's call for more historically sensitive analysis. On these grounds, I consider that Hyden's "new paradigm" based on the economy of affection does not provide an adequate basis for understanding the questions listed above. Still less does it lend itself to being a useful tracking model for policy effects.

Hyden's characterization of the peasant mode of production as typifying African rural economies is quite unconvincing. In particular, the propositions that African rural producers or "peasants" are divided into isolated, autonomous units and are so independent of market and state that they can withdraw into subsistence, hence avoiding "capture," do not stand up to the empirical evidence from most parts of Africa. Hyden has stated the following:

> Without any real product specialization there is very little exchange between the various units of production. There is no functional interdependence bringing them into reciprocal relations with each other ... Each unit is independent of the other and the economic structure is cellular. To the extent that there is co-operation among producers ... it is not structurally enforced but purely a superstructural articulation.... (Hyden 1980:13).

An almost identical description appears in his most recent work in progress (Hyden n.d.:11).

Most studies indicate, contra Hyden, that there are extensive links among units of both reciprocal exchange and unequal dependence. Moreover, the evidence is that such links are rooted in the conditions for livelihood, and that, far from being some "superstructural" attitude floating above the realities of production and consumption, these relations underwrite the patterns of production described. The literature documents the importance of a wide range of exchanges: transfers among kin, friends, and neighbors in the form of work-groups (work parties) based on reciprocal exchange of labor; a wide range of share contracts (involving labor, other services, draft animals, and land); and work done for remuneration (cash or in-kind). Such transfers enable production and consumption to be carried out and act as "insurance" over the longer and shorter term (Mahoney 1977, Lewis 1981, Swindell 1985, Robertson 1987).

Hyden does refer, at several points in his work, to examples of transfers, but he insists that these are peripheral, temporary, or ad hoc activities. His position is contradicted by large numbers of research studies which show that such relations are not aspects of "co-operation [which] is temporary, for example, at the time of an emergency, rather than regular and formalized" (Hyden 1980:13), but, on the contrary, provide the specific conditions and terms of production and exchange which *differ* for *different* categories of rural dwellers.

A further consequence of Hyden's dismissing interdependence as unimportant among peasants is that he thereby dismisses a key dynamic in the very processes of agricultural transition and class formation that engage him. Very similar forms of exchange to those involved in the collective reproduction of rural groups can also facilitate unequal mobilization of scarce resources and, thereby, feed into a process of differentiation within and across generations (Spiegel 1980, Swindell 1985, Peters 1983, Behnke and Kerven 1983, Donham 1985, Robertson 1987). I suggest that Hyden's failure to "see" this is a function of the blinders of the economy of affection and is located in the very definitions of his key concepts. Following the critique by Kasfir (1986), I am referring to the way in which Hyden defines peasants separately from, and in some opposition to, "petty-capitalist" farmers, who adopt modern, capitalist methods of production. By excluding the very category of rural producers who have undergone a transition from the precapitalist economy of affection to capitalist production, (1) he is able to maintain that this transition is not happening among the "peasants"; (2) he fails to understand the ways in which the production strategies of the "petty-capitalist" producers are interconnected with those of the other producers ("peasants"); and hence (3) fails to recognize that the dynamics of rural economies lie in the interconnections between differences or solidarities based on "affinities" *and* those based on class. For these reasons, I contend that Hyden's proposing African rural producers to be understood in terms of a *precapitalist* mode of production is totally misconceived. While I accept Hyden's point that they are not "capitalist" either, I think the analytical and empirical tasks are precisely to understand the mix of behaviors, practices, and ideas that are influenced by a precolonial, precapitalist past and by a capitalist, colonial, and postcolonial past and present.

Hyden's misrepresentation of the conditions under which producers produce and consume leads him to a further conclusion that is untenable. This is that the peasants can withdraw from "the national economy" because they can "secure their own subsistence and reproduction without the assistance of other social classes" (Hyden 1980:29). Their ability to withdraw depends on their self-sufficiency. Although Hyden, at several points, vacillates on the issue of self-sufficiency—for example: "While peasant household units of production are not completely self-sufficient, management decisions are made in the light of domestic needs and capabilities" (Hyden n.d.:11)—his argument about the uncaptured peasantry *depends* on their being self-sufficient. Yet, on my reading, it is precisely this condition that is challenged by available empirical evidence from Africa.

First, on the basis of the kind of literature mentioned above on relations of reciprocity and dependence linking peasant units, it is clear that the conditions for production and consumption for large numbers of rural producers in various countries *are* determined, in part, by transfers of labor and other services by the poorer to the richer. Second, Hyden greatly overestimates the extent to which rural dwellers are independent of the market and the state. He states that peasants "simply must be made dependent on the other social classes if there is going to be social progress that benefits the society at large" (Hyden 1980:31). To explain this lack of dependence, Hyden reasons as follows: "the things that the peasants value ... are not absolutely necessary, only desired" (ibid.), and thus, they are able to withdraw into their own self-sufficient productive activities, to the frustration of the "petty-bourgeoisie [which] has been in strong need of the surplus product of the peasants" (ibid.). Available studies, however, suggest a much greater level of dependence on markets and other classes and a much greater influence of state action on the conditions of rural production. Large proportions of family and individual budgets are expended on purchased foods, clothes, personal and household items, cultivation tools, bicycles, radios, school fees, medical treatment, transportation, etc. Even when there had been indigenous methods of acquiring salt or iron goods, or of weaving cloth, making pots, leather goods, etc., in much of Africa these skills and activities have long been displaced by imported or locally manufactured goods. Dependence on these goods and services is hardly a matter of apparently easily dismissed "desires."

Moreover, many rural dwellers are dependent for their basic necessities, including food, on markets, and their ability to produce or purchase food is fundamentally affected by state action. The evidence completely belies the ability of peasants, posited by Hyden, to "withdraw" into autarchy. Studies in Tanzania show that almost half of full-time farmers' cash income (acquired from participation in markets through sales of agricultural products and wage work) is spent on purchasing food, and that the cost of "the minimum annual market purchases" required about one-third of the total year's available days in the fields (cited by Kasfir 1986: 345). A study carried out in western Kenya found that 40 percent of rural households depended on purchased food. When other necessities for "reproduction" (fertilizer, wages for farm laborers, machine contracts) are included, the proportion dependent on market purchases increases to 60 percent (Kongstad and Monsted 1980). In a recent study of smallholders (including those who would be petty-capitalist in Hyden's definition) in Malawi, virtually all household units purchased some of their staple maize, and under 15 percent were fully self-sufficient in maize (Peters and Herrera 1989). Even in Zimbabwe, which has been an exporter of maize, "only 45 percent of households in low-rainfall areas were net sellers of grain in 1984/5 while 25 percent were net buyers" (Weber et al. 1988). In a year of poor rainfall the proportion dependent on the market for staple grains doubled.

I noted above that Hyden excludes petty-capitalist producers from the peasantry, and, in positing lesser dependence on outside markets by the latter, implies a greater dependence and lesser self-sufficiency among the former. This too can be challenged as a general proposition. Existing studies show that the more commercialized farmers, who usually have larger landholdings, more access to cash and other resources, and larger incomes, tend to produce their staple foods in larger quantities than the mean *at the same time* that they also produce larger quantities (and values) of non-food cash crops (Peters and Herrera 1989).

I suggest that underlying Hyden's distinction between peasants and petty-capitalist producers and his assumption that the former are far less dependent on the market and state than the latter is an older distinction, but one which is equally flawed. This is the opposition between "subsistence" and "commercialization." In the past, theorists of agricultural transformation assumed that, as producers became "more commercialized" by adopting modern methods of production and by selling a larger proportion of their product, they also became less "subsistence-oriented." The opposition between subsistence and commercialization in fact *assumed* this transition. Numerous studies in various countries in Africa, however, have shown that, far from the more commercial producers reducing food production, they usually have the land and the ability to acquire labor and other inputs to be able to increase their production (and sale) of non-food cash crops as well as the staple food crops.

In contrast, the poorer producers are more often forced *out* of "subsistence." That is, they are often caught in the classic bind of the agrarian poor: they are not able to produce enough for their own subsistence and cash needs yet have to work for wages (cash or in-kind) in the agricultural peak season; and although their staple food harvests are too small for their consumption needs, they have to sell part immediately after the harvest because of their immediate cash needs (often to repay debts incurred during the preharvest food-deficit period). As Kasfir (1986) suggested, it is, at best, only a middle category of rural producers who are able to begin to approach the self-sufficiency posited by Hyden, and, given the seasonal and longer-term fluctuations in production, it is likely that even then this is variable.

Of course, there are some producers in some places and at some times who are able to rely on their own ability to provide for themselves. Hyden (1986:691), in a response to Kasfir, cites two recent studies (one in Guinea-Bissau and the other in Tanzania) in which rural households put a low emphasis on selling their food crops, in the face of a rapid "shrinking" in the resource base. But rather than offering these two examples as proof of peasants' "autonomy," one would be better off trying to understand the specific circumstances of these different outcomes—that is, inquiring into the relationships between food production, food consumption, food crop sales, and the production and sale of non-food cash crops, and between these and levels of resources, political environment, etc. In other words, the degree of dependence on the market, or of self-sufficiency in food or other basic necessities, is *not a given* for rural dwellers in Africa but *a critical question*.

Furthermore, the strategies of richer and poorer (or "petty-capitalist" and "peasant") are joined in respect to the production and sale of food versus non-food crops. The bigger producers not only are often able to produce their own food supply but can use their surplus food crops to hire farm laborers (either directly with food or by selling food at a point in the season where prices are highest—contrary to what poorer producers are able to do). Hence, food production is as much a factor in the processes of commercialization and socioeconomic differentiation as in levels of self-sufficiency. By excluding, *by definition*, the more commercial or capitalist smallholder from his economy of affection, Hyden excludes a key component of the rural dynamics he is trying to capture.

In his discussions of the ability of peasants to remain uncaptured by the state and/or "other classes," Hyden places a great deal of weight on his claim that African producers retain control of the land. Throughout his writing, Hyden points to a fundamental difference between sub-Saharan Africa and the regions of Asia, Europe, and Latin America, namely, that "there was no indigenous tradition of land alienation and concentration in Africa" (Hyden 1986:680) and hence, limited stratification. I agree that this particular part of the history of Africa is a critical part of our understanding of both past and current formations. However, its significance is read differently by writers on Africa. For example, Hyden cites Guy Hunter's assessment in 1969 that "without an established landlord and merchant domination of the rural community, there is no obstructive power which needs to be broken" in the process of "modernizing peasant societies" (Hyden 1980: 210). Hyden feels that two main outcomes of this situation have been more negative than Hunter's optimistic forecast supposed. These are, first, that donor agencies and governments tended to see the African social landscape as a *tabula rasa*, a place for experiments in social and economic engineering. The second, his main thesis, is that the absence of "an obstructive power" masked the fact that the peasant mode of production itself, with its companion, the economy of affection, was to prove the main obstacle to economic growth. In his 1980 book, the necessary economic revolution (though this word was not used by Hyden) was to take place through socialism, directed, if necessary, by force. In the 1983 and subsequent works, it is to take place through the promotion (by means of less clearly specified methods) of capitalism.

In Hyden's view, then, the ability of peasants to retain access to land on which they can provide themselves with subsistence and livelihood has proven to be the "obstructive power" which Guy Hunter had assumed lay only in appropriative and jealous landed elites. Indeed, Hyden has frequently pointed out that the freedom and independence of African peasants resides precisely in the fact that in Africa no "lords" rose to power over the peasants (Hyden 1986:680). I would agree that the *relative* lack of widespread land alienation and, hence, of landless groups in Africa has to be incorporated into an understanding of sociocultural organization in which "the accumulation of people" rather than land has been a key element. On the other hand, as Hyden emphasizes, one has to recognize that these are historical phenomena. Thus, I would argue that the current situation with regard to access to land is less simple and less rosy than Hyden says. While relative ease of access continues to be a dominant influence in the patterns of production for many smallholders, in some places and for some categories of producers, there is increasing pressure on available land, evidence of concentration of land, new forms of legal and practical constraints on gaining access to land, as well as new wealth to be gained from its use, and the existence of landless groups. (On appropriation and concentration of land see Reyna 1987, Mbagwu 1978, Okoth-Ogendo 1975, Little 1985, Hitchcock 1982, Koehn 1983, Mhone 1987, Schoepf and Schoepf 1988; on landlessness, also Shipton 1987, Brokensha 1987; on constrictions, Benneh 1974, Haswell 1975, Hecht 1983.)

The literature indicates the inappropriateness of Hyden's assumption that African smallholders, by definition, as it were, continue to have access to the land they need. In conditions of land shortage, the Chayanovian model of household production expanding and contracting as the consumer/worker ratio shifts over the developmental cycle does not hold. At the same time, other studies across Africa showing a "proliferation" of land rights or a nonexclusionary trend in land use also indicate that there is no single trend throughout the continent; indeed, in even one part of one country, trends may appear contradictory. But that is why an a priori definition of peasants as having a sufficient and protected access to land is unacceptable, and why more carefully specified research has to be carried out. Even if Hyden's description of Africa being egalitarian in respect of land allocation held in the past, it does not hold everywhere now.

A final set of problems with Hyden's insisting on the independence of the peasantry has to do with the fact that rural dwellers in much of Africa are not only farmers but are also heavily engaged in "off-farm" employment and in wage labor. Both are seriously misunderstood and underestimated by Hyden. Hyden's treatment of off-farm work by peasants is rather idiosyncratic. He suggests that such activities represent a way for peasants to acquire more income without the "drudgery" of increased farm production. This interpretation of peasants choosing to avoid farm drudgery by taking up work that is often hard, underpaid, and necessitating long absences from home and family contrasts starkly with studies which interpret off-farm employment, including labor migration, as either required by declining returns to farm production (due to land shortage, land deterioration, or unfavorable economic conditions such as pricing and marketing policies), or as a complementary strategy for acquiring necessary income. For the poorer and/or land-short producers, off-farm employment is a way of supplementing the income they can derive from their farm production. As noted above, this strategy can have cyclically negative repercussions for individual families and for whole categories ("classes"). For the better-off and/or land-rich producers, off-farm employment often provides cash income which is used (a) to increase the level of investment in, and returns from, their farm production and (b) to provide the means of educating children. It is clear that these different routes for poorer and richer have implications for intergenerational differentiation.

The extent of waged work, whether casual or temporary work among smallholders or in multiple nonagricultural employments, including self-employment and "informal sector" activities, are similarly underestimated by Hyden. Once more, the issue is not to suggest that all forms of remuneration in African rural areas are equivalent to the stereotypical proletarian wage. I'd have thought that with the empirically rich and theoretically subtle work done on this issue (e.g., Swindell 1985, Robertson 1987, Cooper 1980, Freund 1984), we should not have to be stuck in a yes/no position on wage work. The point is the same: the task facing Hyden and the rest of us is to document and analyze the range of exchanges of work, services, and land, which *vary* for different categories of producers.

In recent publications, Hyden considers "diversification" (which includes off-farm activities) as part of the risk-minimization strategies inherent in the peasant mode of production and also suggests that diversification represents for the economy of affection "the seed of its own destruction" (Hyden 1987b:122). One might suppose that this intriguing idea indicates that Hyden perceives the kind of dynamics of uneasy dependence and differentiation I have suggested above. But instead of pursuing this thought, which I believe would end in his rethinking the economy of affection, Hyden appears to shift theoretical ground. He refers briefly to patterns of investing in "networks of trust ... to spread risk or create resources", and suggests that, as these expand beyond the local area, "the costs exceed the benefits, and actors look for new ways of organizing society that permit higher levels of both expansion and productivity" (Hyden 1987b: 123). This sounds to me like the new institutional analysis in political science and economics in which rational actors create new institutions as responses to economic bottlenecks (e.g., Bates 1988). What is unclear is how this theoretical approach can be incorporated into the economy of affection framework.

The Economy of Affection and Gender

Up to now, I have been arguing that the economy of affection misrepresents the conditions under which most African rural dwellers live and work. It does not provide the analytical framework with which to explore the variations in the mix of unequal exchange as well as reciprocities across rural populations, or the variations in the degree of dependence on markets or state. Within this general problem of Hyden's chosen framework, a particularly acute problem is the exclusion of any attention paid to *gender relations.* My interpretation is that Hyden is unable to attend to this crucial aspect of African rural systems because the economy of affection excludes social differences of all kinds, including those based on gender.

Even if this argument for the neglect of the concept of gender is accepted, one might still want to ask "where are the women"? They too are virtually absent from the texts and totally absent from the analysis. The very few references (literally two or three, according to my count) include one to women in the context of high levels of drudgery in "domestic" work, and to "females and children ... as dependents" in African households (Hyden 1980:86). In one elliptical reference, Hyden notes that the economy of affection provides "collective security" but then, as a shadow of a doubt about the equal benefits of such security arises, he refers to "females and children as dependents" in African households. He nevertheless concludes that "there is little doubt that to its members, particularly those who control it, there are many intangible and invisible benefits offered [by the economy of affection]" (Hyden 1980:86). He does not inquire into these differences between controllers and controlled.

Why is this exclusion so damaging to Hyden's important attempts to explain African rural economies? African production and consumption patterns have been shown overwhelmingly to be differentiated by gender, as well as by the differences of resource levels, income, etc., which I have been discussing so far. Although the notion of "female farming systems" can be misleading if interpreted too literally, sub-Saharan Africa has the highest average proportion of female labor in agriculture in the world. The clearest implication of this in the now large literature on these matters is that labor is *not* mobilized simply by "the household" or "family." While labor is mobilized on behalf of the larger units of production/consumption (I shall come back to the household in a moment), these larger units are made up of mini-units or individuals who also have rights to their own labor. Thus, the allocation of labor is based in most groups on differences of gender and age (juniority). The negative consequences for development activities of not understanding this have been well documented (e.g., Dey 1981, Guyer 1981).

The literature also documents that while women's contribution to agricultural work (not to mention many off-farm activities and the necessary reproductive or "domestic" work) is extensive and critical, in many cases the returns to them of that work are not proportionate to the effort. The "dependent" status of women (mentioned but unanalyzed by Hyden) results in their receiving lower levels of benefit than their husbands or male relatives. Women in Tanzania complained about their increasing work burden: "We go to the village shamba [farm], then to women's shamba, then to individual family shamba"; "We have no time to weed the women's farm; we're stuck at the village farm; we are oppressed there and at home" (Mbilinyi 1988:573). Such reports of women's sense of being "oppressed" by both government demands and the division of effort and rewards with their husbands contrast with Hyden's reference to complaints about work burdens by unspecified "villagers" in Tanzania (Hyden 1980:73). Yet surely both comprehension of the organization of these rural systems and the need for tracking policy/program action require the more precise specification that, without attention to gender differences, escapes Hyden's paradigm.

While some studies have explored the indigenous methods used by women to negotiate with their husbands the "returns" to their work (Jones 1983, Guyer 1988), it is clear that their position vis à vis the male authority holders in their lives has been fundamentally affected by actions of the state. It is commonplace now to say that women have suffered discrimination in their access to agricultural extension services, credit, information, markets, and well-paid jobs (see Staudt 1987 for a recent summary). To that extent, Hyden's (1980:73) comment that peasants do not have access to extension services because they do not wish to (for fear of getting too close to government) is particularly egregious applied to women.

Where Hyden's fondness for the economy of affection really gets in the way of addressing the particular gendered relations of production and consumption in Africa is his insisting on the Chayanovian peasant household. His frequent references to household or family labor are glaringly inadequate in the face of the large literature documenting gender-differentiated patterns and criticizing the use of a "household" or "family" model for African producers (Boserup 1980, Bukh 1979, Guyer 1981, Jones 1983, Moock 1986, Staudt 1987; on the household, see Jones 1983, Moock 1986, Guyer and Peters 1987).

The "lessons" for tracking policies or other influences on agricultural production in Africa that emerge from this literature on the role of gender difference in rural economies would seem to include the following. If one wants to increase output and productivity, then one must attend to the gendered division of labor and to gendered patterns of income allocation and expenditure patterns; one must attend to the discrepancy in services and support received by women farmers (whether as heads of their own households or as wives of farmers). Where there are pressures to cut back on state services, women's position at the *end* of the queue needs to be recognized in understanding the likely effects on production and consumption. Administrative or legal specifications in programs intended to boost production that negatively affect women's claims to land, or newly introduced technology that disproportionately benefits male farmers at the cost of women, will change the expected outcomes. Why should services be extended to "households" registered in the name of the household head, who in most instances is male? Why not register in the names of the adults responsible for the work being done?

Such questions cannot even be posed with the economy of affection framework, let alone receive answers. Hyden's analysis leads him to the prescription that the only route for progress towards capitalist accumulation and economic growth is to appropriate the "peasant's" surplus product. Since the process of production and accumulation in Africa is so clearly gendered, and the relative disadvantage to women found to be greater, the appropriation is ultimately at the cost of women.

Why has Hyden not even posed the question of gendered forms of organization and accumulation? I have already suggested that his failure to do so can be persuasively attributed to the incapacity of the economy of affection to carry out socially disaggregated analysis. But might there be another reason?

In trying to figure out why Hyden has been so faithful to the economy of affection over all these years and in face of the attempts by many critics, of whom I'm only the most recent, to disabuse him of its charms, I was struck by the following comment in one of his recent papers. After noting studies that have shown no improvement in the skewed distribution of wealth in African countries, Hyden comments: "Liberals and socialists alike, particularly expatriates with little or no sensitivity to African social and political processes, apply a set of criteria and expectations with regard to equality that are both ahistorical and downright unfair to Africans" (Hyden 1987b:131). I suddenly realized that Hyden's clinging to the economy of affection might be seen as a type of apologia for Africa, an explanation for the failure of the continent to move smoothly into capitalism. If this is so, then Hyden's failure to attend to gender differences may be interpreted as his not wishing to recognize one of the most strongly argued positions for widespread and deeply embedded inequality. Hyden, in the same paper, goes on to say, that "expecting Africa to adopt the same criteria of equality and redistribution as are current in mainstream development thinking in Europe and America, [critics] are imposing a double standard, because what ought to apply in their analysis of Africa are the criteria that were valid when European or other societies went through the equivalent historical process" (ibid.). It seems to me that there are many African voices, male and female, who would reject this position and who do invoke contemporary "criteria" when pointing out the bases of discrimination in Africa.

A further support to this interpretation is another recent statement. Addressing the constraints in the way of African peasant response to price change incentives, Hyden notes the dependence on "family labour" and adds that a further constraint is "the fact that there is a legacy of division of labour that militates against flexible allocation among household members" (Hyden 1986:692). This opaque judgment is not explained and it is not clear whether this "inflexible ... legacy" refers to the gender division of labor. But if the future of Africa depends on the further development of capitalist production, with its increasing "economic ... and emotional ... nucleation," it may be that the subordination of women to the household or nucleated form of production is assumed by Hyden to be a necessary cost of that development. Hence, his silence on gender difference.

Whatever the outcome—and I should think we should leave room for specifically African forms of accumulation that will diverge from the classic patriarchal and class mode of Europe and elsewhere—I suggest that in the shorter term of policies like structural adjustment as well as broader policies and programs affecting rural production in Africa, we are ill-advised to continue to ignore gender differences, and we should *not* look to the economy of affection paradigm for help in understanding African rural economies.

The Rebuttals

Hyden: I'd like to reply to two things which I think Dr. Peters has

stressed in her excellent presentation. First, she suggests that the economy of affection does not pay attention to stratification; and second,
that it does not pay attention to gender differences. These are partly
related and I'd like to address them together. In all fairness, what we're
talking about here is to some extent a moving target. I have obviously
developed my position on some issues since I first used the concept of
economy of affection. I'd like to believe I've developed my own position more fully; in that sense what I said in 1980 may not necessarily
be what I'm saying in 1990. I don't think Dr. Peters did an unfair representation of some of these things, although I felt on the specific
issues of stratification and on gender differences perhaps she came
across, in my perspective, as being a little unfair. Let me try to
explain....

Peters suggests that the economy of affection paradigm cannot
accommodate stratification. The point I'm trying to make is, what are
the grounds of stratification? Are they rooted in the market? Are they
rooted in state control? Or are they rooted in some other phenomena
that are out there which explains why, for instance, people are accept-
ing to be unequal or living in such different standards. The point I'm
trying to make here is that the criteria for differentiation or social stratification is not solely—and not even primarily—the market or the
state, but there are other criteria which are what you might call the
legacy of the precapitalist mode of production or the economy of
affection which I see as the economic network that operates in this
context. The question here is, how do people actually accept stratification? How do people actually operate, you might say, in this situation?
Let me also clarify that I'm not suggesting that Africans operate completely out of the market or out of the state and that all these things
that are the economy of affection are outside of the market or outside
of the state. The state and the market in this perspective become the
arena in which these processes take place.

Criteria that we would normally not assume in our own models
about the state or market become important in determining why certain things do take place. For instance, we talk about such things as
weak or poorer households engaging in wage labor for the richer farmers. In many countries that would be a clear-cut example of capitalist
exploitation. What I'm suggesting is that those relations which lead to
stratification should not be solely interpreted as if they were capitalist
penetration. What I'm suggesting to you is that these are still being
justified with reference to what is essentially the precapitalist logic or

system. People accept these relations because they have not been alienated by either state or market. They are embedded in an economy of affection which serves to conceal this emerging stratification. It provides nonmarket criteria for justifying stratification and exploitation. In this respect, the economy of affection is controversial to everybody concerned with progress and equality.

Now with reference to gender, I agree that I have not addressed that sufficiently in my earlier work, but I don't see why the economy of affection could not be used to study gender differences. In Africa the economy of affection provides African males with a very wide range of both material and symbolic weapons to perpetuate gender exploitation. Men dominate the economy of affection and the latter gives them more tools to do so than what is typically available to men in market economies. What I am saying here is that gender exploitation takes on special or extra dimensions because of the continued existence of precapitalist social formations.

This raises the question, which I know is very controversial, if it is a step in the right direction or not, as I have argued in *No Shortcuts to Progress*, that further market penetration may *open up* new opportunities for women that were not there before. I suggest that market penetration is an asset to women at least as much as it is a constraint. I'm not suggesting that it should be looked at in terms of either/or categories, because I believe it's obvious that women can be exploited more nakedly under certain circumstances in the market situation. But given the legacy of the precapitalist formations that exist and therefore given the reasons that can be mobilized by men to justify their exploitation, then you do gradually take away some of the reasons for exploitation when you bring in the market, assuming that it begins to have an effect on the way people think. Second, it does provide an opportunity for women to get alternative sources of income. And it's not a coincidence that women do engage in a lot of work in groups on their own. Women are so strongly inclined to work in groups, because it gives them a chance to come out under the prevailing male domination and gain control of economic resources of their own. I would suggest, therefore, that the current policies pursued under the name of structural adjustment are potentially *beneficial* to women. At least, they are not *a priori* harmful to women under the prevailing circumstances.

I would suggest, therefore, that the problem we have here is that the economy of affection does provide the rationale for stabilizing relations among different people. It is being used as well as being abused.

Sometimes it is used for what we might call "good" things; other times it is used for what we consider "bad" things. The economy of affection is a controversial phenomenon that has to be dealt with. How we do that is clearly a challenge both for policymakers as well as for academics. I agree with Pauline about the need for disaggregating the units of social action, but I disagree with her point that it can't be done within the conceptual framework proposed by myself. That would be tantamount to throwing the baby out with the bath water, or perhaps better put, not seeing the forest for the trees. Gender issues cannot be fully understood in isolation from the peculiar social structures Africans have put in place, the ones I subsume in my conceptualization of the economy of affection.

Finally, let me stress that the economy of affection obviously does not exist in a social vacuum. It is versatile and flexible but also shaped by its interaction with market or state. In my perspective, it flourishes particularly well where state rather than market prevails. The structural adjustment or more market-oriented policies now being proposed or pursued constitute a threat to the basic precapitalist foundation of social and political action in Africa in a way that state-centered policies do not.

There are two threats that I see as particularly serious if structural adjustment policies succeed. The first is that social tensions—the propensity to engage in "disaffective" action—will increase and the task of holding African societies together will become much more difficult. The second threat is partly related to the first. It relates to the ability of African leaders to rule their countries. Because they do not have effective access to self-reproducing mechanisms derived from the prevalence of a "market" or "bureaucratic" rationality, they invest a lot of their time in personal maintenance of their political systems. Affection is the cement that holds these systems together and makes them move. As we know from all African countries, the mode by which things get done is highly personalistic. The physical presence of a leader is almost always necessary.

Now, this is not a very efficient system and the impatience of the global finance institutions threatens its very foundation. That is why African leaders have difficulties with structural adjustment, not because they are wedded to socialism. The dilemma that African leaders face, therefore, is whether in the interest of long-term development to give up the economy of affection or in the short-term interest of political stability to stick with it and undermine structural adjustment. This dilemma is no smaller than that facing leaders in Eastern Europe and the Soviet Union. In fact, structural adjustment in truly socialist economies may prove to be easier than in those where the economy of affection still exists. Certainly, the latter deserves as much attention as structural adjustment policies when it comes to understanding African development, whether in macro terms or in micro terms such as gender differentiation.

Peters: I think that Goran's beginning comments about the economy of affection being "a moving target" is precisely the problem. It has been expanded to cover too huge an array of things: e.g., he talks about the way that people organize their production, the rationales that they use to talk about the way they employ someone, the relationships between husbands and wives, and the kinds of bureaucratic corruption that we see. I think it was Gavin Williams in the journal *Development and Change* who said that he thought that the kinds of things that we see at the bureaucratic level should be referred to as "rampant kleptocracy" rather than an economy of affection! My problem is that much of what Goran says in terms of what he sees happening in Africa I can sympathize with; I can resonate with; I can understand what he's saying. When someone is hired by another farmer, the way that they are hired makes a difference. If, for example, that person's an uncle, he might get more or less remuneration than someone who is a stranger from outside. We all see that. My argument is that the economy of affection does not provide us with the analytical means to interpret these observations. That is my basic position.

Now let me try to flesh this out a bit in the next few minutes. First of all I do not think that we're talking about either the economy of affection or capitalism. I think one of the problems, precisely, is that dichotomy. Goran suggests that those who have become petty-capitalist producers are somehow *outside* the economy of affection and the economy of affection will itself *disappear* when capitalism finally penetrates. Although it does seem that there is a slight tension between that and your (to Hyden) position that the economy of affection is somehow penetrating the state and the market, like a kind of virus—a rampant virus through the system. I think that what we have to do is to be able to conceptually disaggregate more than you allow. When Goran talks about the economy of affection, anthropologists would talk about cultural rationales, ideologies of relationships, ideologies of residence, the way that conjugal relationships are thought about, and so on. Some of what Goran talks about are what we would call social organization. How is production carried out? How is labor mobilized? Is it mobilized through a kin form of organization or through a conjugal unit or through a women's association? In other words, there are far more discriminating analytical categories that we can use that would get us much further to a new understanding than with the economy of affection.

The economy of affection is a kind of *blanket* that doesn't allow us to discriminate amongst the various forms of organization that one is interested in. For example, it isn't that the remuneration that a worker gets from another farmer is either a *wage*—a capitalist exploitative wage—or that it is something rooted in the precapitalist economy of affection. It is precisely the question of how determinate is that relationship in the whole pattern of production of that wage worker— himself or herself. In other words, how important is it for certain categories of farmers that during the cropping cycle they have to take three months out to work for another category of farmers who have more land, more access to the market, and more access to state supplies? In other words, what we are talking about here is a structure of dependence. We are not talking about "superstructural" ideas that somehow inflect the way people organize themselves. It's rather a question of the degree of determination of people's ability to produce and consume for themselves.

I think that the notion of the economy of affection and its opposition to capitalism is rooted in yet another type of analysis which I think ill serves Hyden's attempts to understand what is going on in Africa, and why I'm suggesting that we should not follow him. When he refers, for example, to "symbolic capital" in relation to the economy of affection in his writings, he claims that the precapitalist economy of affection does not have what are called self-perpetuating mechanisms of domination—drawing here on the work of Pierre Bourdieu. There's a contrast set up between, on the one hand, the precapitalist economy of affection, the absence of self-perpetuating mechanisms—i.e., institutional mechanisms of domination, the presence of symbolic domination and symbolic violence, as Bourdieu calls it, and on the other hand, a capitalist system where affection has been relegated to the margins of the private realm, where relationships are impersonal, rationally instrumental, rationally based, and where one has no need for symbolic violence and symbolic domination—precisely because there are self-perpetuating mechanisms of domination. This is absolutely wrong. Capitalist systems themselves require and use symbolic violence. They use symbolic capital. Similarly, many of the precapitalist institutions and political systems that we try to analyze also have self-perpetuating mechanisms of domination.

An example used by Bourdieu from his ethnography of the Bedouin is of the *khamme*—a kind of client or sharecropping tenant who is tied to his patron not only by the obligation to give a large share of the crop but also by personal services, debts, etc. Although we can see here the personal investments of "symbolic capital" by the patron in this relationship, we also see (I suggest contra Bourdieu and hence Hyden) that the relation *also* constituted a self-perpetuating mechanism of domination. In addition to the relationship of production there is a relationship of dependence: they are *both* patron-client and father-child. The two, in other words, go together.

What I think Hyden has done with the contrast is to remain with the nineteenth-century dichotomy of two different sorts of society. As we move from the precapitalist into the capitalist society, from the pre-modern into the modern, the affective relationships are left behind. Instrumental and impersonal relations become more dominant. But that is not so. You've only got to look at politics in the United States to see the incredible importance of symbolic capital, the incredible importance of symbolic domination as well as of self-perpetuating mechanisms of domination. Similarly, if we look at the precapitalist system there were self-perpetuating mechanisms there too. I absolutely agree with Hyden that we have to take very seriously—this is where I feel I'm on the same side with Goran Hyden—*absolutely* seriously the rationales, the understandings, the ideologies, the beliefs, the attitudes of people that we try to study. All I'm saying is that we cannot do that by using the economy of affection. We can do it by drawing on other traditions of analysis in anthropology, some in sociology.

There's a last thing on the theoretical side. At one point in the discussion about self-perpetuating mechanisms of domination, Hyden refers to power. He uses the classic Weberian definition of power as the imposition of will on someone else. There's a whole new form of theory located in feminist theory but also in other fields where power is being rethought. Maybe power can be thought of not as the imposition of will upon another person, but power as the ability or the capacity to act in concert. If power is redefined in that way, our whole structure of analysis derived from the sociology and anthropology of the nineteenth century is completely undermined.

What I would suggest, therefore, is that Hyden should ditch the economy of affection. He should say he is experientially rich. He is analytically rich, feeling for the differences wherever they are in Africa. He will not capture them with the economy of affection. That also goes for gender.

Let me give another example of the problems of the simple opposition of precapitalist and capitalist/modern. Hyden (1980:221) said that "polygamy, gerontocracy, funeral feasts and other institutions supported by the economy of affection, are not reconcilable with the socialist mode of production." In 1983, he said, "Ceremonial functions like weddings and burials ... are clearly depriving the national economy of resources that could be productively employed" (Hyden 1983: 13). This is a fundamental misunderstanding that goes against everything else that Hyden is saying. In other words, what he is saying here is that these have nothing to do with production, consumption, and domination. They have *everything* to do with production, consumption, and domination. In these weddings, in these funerals not only do people talk about affective relations amongst themselves, they talk about cattle prices. They talk about who knows which gate to cross over the border with their coffee, cocoa, or diamonds, or whatever it is. Ceremonial functions are therefore intrinsically involved in the structure of production and consumption. They are not capitalist systems; but neither are they precapitalist systems.

I'll end with this final example. In Zambia and Zimbabwe, some of the biggest commercialized farmers are petty-capitalist producers in Hyden's terms, using modern techniques of production and integrated with the state and the market. Many of these have increased their use of polygyny, because wives are their major labor force. One of them in Cheater's work refers to his chief wife as his "boss boy." In other words, she was his foreman. He recognized the importance of her labor. For that reason, too, some men are refusing to allow their wives to have their own separate fields: they are afraid of losing the wives' labor. In other words, what we see is commercialization being managed and being promoted through a form of conjugal relationship that is not precapitalist. It may be rooted in the precapitalist past, but the implications are capitalist for that woman who's being excluded from having her own fields, precisely because her labor is important to her husband. Other wives, on the other hand, are glad to be members of such households, because they are able to get more money to send back to parents or educate children. Those are absolutely and firmly embedded in situations where the state and capitalist production are absolutely determinate. We still have to understand the rationales. We still have to understand the culturally specific ways of doing them. But to understand them as precapitalist is quite unilluminating.

Concluding Statements

Hyden: As I think has become clear from this debate, Pauline and I come at the same set of issues from different perspectives. She stresses the micro, I the macro perspective. This may reflect, at least in part, our respective disciplinary backgrounds, she being an anthropologist, I being a political scientist. Having said that I have a lingering feeling that on many issues we aren't that far apart. Yet, there are differences, both small and large, remaining. I wish to return to at least a few of these before time is up.

Let me start by picking up a few points that she made in her second intervention. First, I agree with her that we cannot isolate the "petty-capitalist" farmers from the peasants. I don't do that. All I am suggesting is that although the former may have adopted a capitalistic logic, they are unable to ignore the economy of affection altogether. They need the support of the peasants and there is little, if any, evidence that this type of "petty-capitalist" farmers have cut their ties with other groups in society. It is in this respect that the economy of affection rather than capitalism has a hold on society.

The second point is that I am surprised that Pauline is ready to attach so much importance to the potential benefit of the agricultural extension service to women in Africa. Her statement on this issue overlooks the overwhelming evidence from across the continent that these extension services have failed to serve the farmers. The heavy-handed methods used by the extension officers, both in colonial and postcolonial days, have alienated peasant farmers. It is unlikely that these services are going to be crucial to reversing gender imbalances, even if they were to employ more women. We need to think of alternatives that go beyond the existing institutional arrangements.

My third point may be a matter of clarification. I refer to the subsistence orientation in my own work, but I do not imply thereby only self-sufficiency. I realize that self-sufficiency is hardly a realistic objective in today's world, even in the peripheral parts of Africa, though we should not underestimate the extent to which people in countries where the market economy has not been allowed to develop have actually withdrawn from market transactions. The main point, however, is that "subsistence orientation," in my mind, refers to the preoccupation of household members with their own immediate needs. These are not necessarily identified in an identical fashion. For instance, Goheen's paper on Cameroon demonstrates the differential perspectives that men and women have on what is an "immediate" need. Yet, the point is that in an economy where affection, as opposed to impersonal mechanisms like the market or the bureaucracy, dictates social relations, the concerns of the micro units of social action tend to take on primary significance, so much so that the national economy reflects this "parochial" orientation. The market or the state simply do not constitute strong enough "countervailing" forces.

The fourth point concerns the concept of power. I don't agree that I am using it in a classical Weberian fashion. What I am pointing to is the underlying relations of dependence as prerequisites for the exercise of power. In more advanced economies these relations are many; nobody tends to be exclusively dependent on another. As a result, pluralism is possible. In Africa, the situation is different. Structurally determined dependencies are still few and weak. As I have suggested before, production units are both structurally and functionally quite autonomous. Their involvement in the market exchanges puts them under some pressure, but these are not basic or inevitable. People can, as has been proven, withdraw from them. Power, then, rests on more feeble ground in Africa. It is essentially "superstructural," determined by the claims and counterclaims that the economy of affection generates. These tend to be ephemeral, thus making the power structures both fluctuating and unstable. It is for this reason that in the context of national politics power often is being exercised in a blatant fashion, the reason being that the leaders have no strings to pull, i.e., their power is not determined by preexisting structures on which they can rely. They have to recreate relations of power all the time, using patronage and "symbolic capital" to ensure compliance. This does not exclude, of course, the possibility that power is the ability to act in concert, as Pauline suggested. This new, feminist perspective is in fact very much present in the economy of affection. Women, in particular, have proved that by working together they can exercise power in a new way. I agree with Pauline that we need to incorporate such a definition in our study of social relations in Africa.

My final point deals with the basic question of the usefulness of the concept of economy of affection. If I hear Pauline right, she says that she agrees with me that we must take the rationales, the beliefs, etc., of the people we study seriously. At the same time, she recognizes that there are peculiar African forms of accumulation. If the latter is the case, we need to have a conceptual formula for dealing with such a peculiarity. I have offered the concept of economy of affection as one way of looking at it. I haven't heard what Pauline's alternative concept is. She has only decided to throw my concept out. I think that is unfortunate. We need to be conceptually innovative and explore the limits of these ventures. I am the first to admit that the economy of affection may still appear as a "half-baked" concept but that doesn't mean that it cannot be further refined. If anything, developments in Africa in the 1980s have convinced me that the assumption that there is a precapitalist social formation still competing successfully with the forces of capitalism is basically correct. Thus, whether we apply the concept of the economy of affection to "structural adjustment" or "gender analysis," it provides a guide to understanding the social logic within which both macroeconomic interventions and microeconomic action have to be conceived and analyzed.

Peters: I disagree with Goran's suggestion that the economy of affection as a framework for analyzing African societies and that my critique of it can best be glossed over as a macro and micro perspective. On the contrary, Goran's use of the economy of affection to analyze *both* peasant household behavior *and* the state (soft or otherwise) indicates that in practice the economy of affection framework purports to be both micro and macro. My critique, in turn, is concerned not with *levels* of analysis but with the sets of concepts used in all analysis.

Goran ended by suggesting that those who, like myself, doubt the analytical utility of the economy of affection fail to offer an alternative "conceptual formula" for dealing with the African specificities. First, I should point out that while I agreed that there were specific aspects of African societies (please note that I'm using the plural) that have often escaped, or been obscured by, interpretive frameworks drawn from other situations (in which I included "peasant" models of Chayanov and Sahlins), I also would argue that there are clear similarities between African cases and other regions. For example, certain types of labor sharing or other forms of share contracting are remarkably similar to types documented in Asian and Latin American countries. Or take, for example, some gender-related patterns of authority or control over income. What this leads me to suggest is that, like Goran, I feel too simple a transfer of the Western understanding of capitalist evolution fails to capture what is going on in Africa. But I also, *contra*

Goran, feel there is much in Africa that is not unique. What this means, I think, is that we don't need to construct an analytical framework peculiar to Africa, whether the economy of affection or another, as much as we need to pay more attention to the particular forms of production and consumption, cooperation and conflict, reciprocity and dependence, equality and inequality in African countries. This is so for analysis of individuals, families, villages, regions, nations; for the workings of the farm or of the office of the president. (I must say that I am more and more dissatisfied with the opposition of micro and macro, introduced, I suppose, from economics, which tyrannizes much of our thinking about social process. If political alliances or conflicts within a cabinet or political party affect agricultural policy-making, why is that "macro" when political alliances or conflicts within a village or lineage are "micro"? But that would be another debate!)

On a second point, Goran moves from typifying African peasants as having a subsistence orientation or preoccupation with their own immediate needs to argue that the national economy reflects this "parochial" orientation and that the state and market are less powerful than that orientation. Again, I don't think this is a useful way to describe what we know about Africa. I'd rather say that we find in the studied groups (farmers, traders, etc.) different *mixes* of behaviors described as commercial/capitalist/market-oriented and subsistence, rather than see them as opposed states. Existing studies show, in fact, that the two more often go together: farmers who produce for the market have been found (e.g., in Malawi, Kenya, Rwanda, Gambia) to also produce much of their own food. And, in contrast, many of the poorest cannot manage to be subsistenceoriented. I fear that Goran's approach tends to *underplay* the influence of the state and of the market on "peasants." In addition, in trying to understand the determinants and effects of strategies of commercial and subsistence production, use of the economy of affection framework leads one to conflate very different phenomena—for example, both the production/consumption patterns of farm families and the bureaucratic inefficacy of ministries. Developing a more precise understanding of these rather different sets of phenomena (which, of course, are interrelated), is not to assert a more "micro" perspective.

I have already said that I reject the notion that power is superstructural or the state is ineffectual. Recognizing the degrees of power and the different sources of power is not helped by the notion of superstructure or of the economy of affection. That some people sometimes can rely on their own resources to achieve livelihood is important to document and analyze, but the economy of affection framework *overestimates* this capacity and underestimates the "structural" pressures of power.

Finally, I suppose that if we are to take seriously the notion of differential power, we have to be prepared to talk not only of states and individuals, of class, gender, markets, and communities, but we also have to recognize that Africa has its own history but that that history is connected to our own Western history. The current programs of structural adjustment, like other political, economic, and social processes, must be seen within the differential power relations in specific national and subnational situations but also within the differential power relations of the global economy.

REFERENCES

Bates, Robert H.
  1988   Macro-Political Economy in the Field of Development, Working Paper 40, Duke University Program in International Political Economy.

Behnke, R., and C. Kerven
  1983   FSR and the Attempt to Understand the Goals and Motivations of Farmers. *Culture and Agriculture* 19: 9–16.

Benneh, George
  1974   Land Tenure and Sabala Farming System in the Anlo Area of Ghana. Land Tenure Center, University of Wisconsin at Madison.

Bledsoe, Caroline
  1980   *Women and Marriage in Kpelle Society.* Palo Alto: Stanford University Press.

Boserup, Ester
  1980   *Women's Role in Economic Development.* London: George Allen and Unwin.

Brokensha, David
  1987   Inequality in Rural Africa: Fallers Reconsidered. *Manchester Papers on Development*, III(2):1–21, Institute for Development Policy and Management, Manchester.

Bukh, Jette
  1979   *The Village Woman in Ghana.* Copenhagen: Centre for Development Research.

Cooper, Frederick
  1980   *From Slaves to Squatters.* New Haven: Yale University Press.

Dey, Jennie
  1981   Gambian Women: Unequal Partners in Rice Development Projects? *African Women in the Development Process*, N. Nelson, ed. pp.

109–122. London: Frank Cass.

Donham, Donald
  1985   History at One Point in Time: "Working Together" in Maale, 1975. *American Ethnologist* 12(2):262–84.

Freund, Bill
  1984   Labor and Labor History in Africa: A Review of the Literature. *African Studies Review* 27(2):1–58.

Guyer, Jane I.
  1981   Household and Community in African Studies. *The African Studies Review* XXIV, 2/3:87–137.
  1988   The Multiplication of Labor: Historical Methods in the Study of Gender and Agricultural Change in Modern Africa. *Current Anthropology* 29(2):247–72.

Guyer, Jane I.
  1987   Introduction. Special Issue on Conceptualizing the Household. *Development and Change* 18(2):197–213.

Haswell, Margaret
  1973   *The Nature of Poverty.* London: Macmillan Press.

Hecht, Robert
  1983   The Ivory Coast Economic "Miracle": What Benefits for Peasant Farmers? *Journal of Modern African Studies* 21(1): 25–53.

Hitchcock, R. K.
  1982   Tradition, Social Justice and Land Reform in Central Botswana. *Land Reform in the Making*, R. P. Werbner, ed., pp. 1–34. London: Rex Collings.

Hyden, Goran
  1980   *Beyond Ujamaa in Tanzania: Underdevelopment and an Uncaptured Peasantry.* Berkeley: Univ. California Press.
  1983   *No Shortcuts to Progress: African Development Management in Perspective.* Berkeley: Univ. California Press.
  1986   The Anomaly of the African Peasantry. *Development and Change* 17(4): 677–705.
  1987a   Final Rejoinder. *Development and Change* 18(4):661–67.
  1987b   Capital Accumulation, Resource Distribution, and Governance in Kenya: The Role of the Economy of Affection. *The Politcal Economy of Kenya.* New York: Praeger.
  n.d.   Beyond State and Market: African Politics in Comparative Perspective. (With D.C. Williams.)

Jones, Christine
  1983   The Mobilization of Women's Labor for Cash Crop Production: A Game Theoretic Approach. *American Journal of Agricultural Economics* 65(5):1049–54.

Kasfir, Nelson
  1986   Are African Peasants Self-Sufficient? Review Article. *Development and Change* 17(2):335–57.

Koehn, Peter
    1983   State Land Allocation and Class Formation in Nigeria. *Journal of Modern African Studies* 21(3):461–81.
Kongstad, Per, and Mette Monsted
    1980   *Family, Labour and Trade in Western Kenya.* Copenhagen: Centre for Development Research.
Lewis, John van D.
    1981   Domestic Labour Intensity and the Incorporation of Malian Peasant Farmers into Localized Descent Groups. *American Ethnologist* 8(1):53–73.
Little, Peter D.
    1985   Absentee Herd Owners and Part-Timer Pastoralists: The Political Economy of Resource Use in Northern Kenya. *Human Ecology* 13: 131–51.
Mahoney, Nicholas
    1977   Contract and Neighbourly Exchange Among the Birwa of Bostwana. *Journal of African Law* 21(1):40–65.
Mbagwu, T.
    1978   Land Concentration Around a Few Individuals in Igbo-land of Eastern Nigeria: Its Processes, Scope and Future. *Africa* 48(2): 101–15.
Mbilinyi, Marjorie
    1988   Agribusiness and Women Peasants in Tanzania. *Development and Change* 19(4):549–83.
Meillassoux, Claude
    1981   *Maidens, Meal and Money.* Cambridge: Cambridge University Press.
Mhone, Guy
    1987   Agriculture and Food Policy in Malawi: A Review. *The State and Agriculture in Africa,* Thandika Mkandawire and Naceur Bourenane, eds., pp. 59–87. CODESRIA Book Series.
Moock, Joyce (ed.)
    1986   *Understanding Africa's Rural Households and Farming Systems.* Boulder: Westview Press.
Murray, Colin
    1981   *Families Divided: The Impact of Migrant Labour in Lesotho.* Cambridge: Cambridge University Press.
Okoth-Ogendo, H.W.O.
    1975   The Adjudication Process and the Special Rural Development Programme. *IDS Working Paper,* Nairobi, Kenya.
Parkin, David J.
    1972   *Palms, Wine and Witnesses.* London: Chandler.
Peters, Pauline E.
    1983   Gender, Development Cycles, and Historical Process: A Critique of Recent Research on Women in Botswana. *Journal of Southern*

    African Studies 10(1):100–122.

Peters, Pauline E. and M. G. Herrera
    1989   Cash Cropping, Food Security and Nutrition: The Effects of Agricultural Commercialization Among Smallholders in Malawi. Mimeo, Harvard Institute of International Development.

Reyna, Steven P.
    1987   The Emergence of Land Concentration in the West African Savanna. *American Ethnologist* 14(3):523–42.

Robertson, A. F.
    1987   *The Dynamics of Productive Relationships: African Share Contracts in Comparative Perspective.* Cambridge: Cambridge University Press.

Schoepf, Brooke, and Claude Schoepf
    1988   Land, Gender and Food Security in Eastern Kivu. *Agriculture, Women and Land*, Jean Davison, ed., pp. 106–30. Boulder: Westview Press.

Shipton, Parker
    1987   The Kenyan Land Tenure Reform: Misunderstandings in the Public Creation of Private Property. HIID Development Discussion Papers, Cambridge, MA.

Spiegel, Andrew D.
    1980   Rural Differentiation and the Diffusion of Migrant Labour Remittances in Lesotho. *Villagers in an Industrial Society*, Philip Mayer, ed. Cape Town: Oxford University Press.

Staudt, Kathleen
    1987   Uncaptured or Unmotivated? Women and the Food Crisis in Africa. *Rural Sociology* 52(1):37–55.

Swindell, Ken
    1985   *Farm Labour.* Cambridge: Cambridge University Press.

Weber, Michael, John Staatz, J. Holtzman, Eric Crawford, and Richard Bernsten
    1988   Informing Food Security Decisions in Africa: Empirical Analysis and Policy Dialogue. Paper presented at American Agricultural Economics Association Meetings, Knoxville, TN, July 31–August 3.

V

Where Do We Go from Here?

1

New Women's Organizations in Nigeria: One Response to Structural Adjustment

Lillian Trager and Clara Osinulu

The severity of economic conditions in sub-Saharan Africa during the 1980s is well known. Many African governments have adopted stabilization and structural adjustment programs in an effort to remove distorted "macro prices" and invigorate their stagnating economies. In the short term, however, some of the policies adopted have worsened conditions for some of the most vulnerable groups in the populations of these countries, particularly women, children, and the poor. While effects on specific groups are still in the process of being determined, there is increasing concern among governments and international agencies to find ways to address the continuing crisis and to both alleviate some of the negative short-term impacts and ensure that long-term benefits reach the poor and vulnerable as well as other groups in the population (Serageldin 1989). For example, the World Bank has recently begun the Social Dimensions of Adjustment (SDA) projects "to ensure that the needs of the poor and most vulnerable will be given primary consideration from the very outset of the adjustment process" (Jaycox 1989:39). To date, however, it is uncertain whether SDA projects can fill the gap in social services left by government cutbacks.

Lillian Trager is associate professor of anthropology at the University of Wisconsin-Parkside. She specializes in the study of marketing systems, the informal economy, and rural-urban linkages in West Africa and the Philippines. From 1985 to 1987 she was assistant representative and program officer for the Ford Foundation, Lagos, Nigeria. Her publications include *The City Connection: Migration and Family Interdependence in the Philippines*.

Clara Osinulu is director of the African American Institute in Nigeria. She was trained as an anthropologist at University College, London, and University of Birmingham Centre for West African Studies, where she focused on the changing status of African women. She is currently a member of the Central Committee on Better Life for Rural Women in Lagos State. Among her publications are "The Changing Status of African Women," "Voter Education for Nigerian Rural Women," and "Religion and Status of Nigerian Women" in *Women and Development*.

In this context, one set of institutions which have drawn increasing interest and attention have been nongovernmental organizations (NGOs) and other organizations concerned with local-level development activities. As it is increasingly recognized that governments do not have the capacity to undertake all development activities, especially in local areas and remote regions, a variety of types of local and nongovernmental organizations have come to be seen as increasingly important. According to *The Urban Edge* (1989:1), "NGOs ... of all types are becoming the rage." Women's organizations, in particular, have been seen as appropriate and viable institutions to undertake a variety of development activities, such as health and family planning programs, income-generating projects, and literacy and education activities that governments have been forced to cut as part of structural adjustment.

Nigeria is no exception to this general trend. Despite, or more likely because of, its oil wealth, Nigeria has undergone a severe economic crisis in recent years, leading to the implementation of a structural adjustment program under the present government. Whereas in the past—and especially during the oil boom era—it was largely assumed that government had the funds for a very wide range of development activities and that it was the appropriate role of government to undertake those activities, now it is increasingly recognized that this is not the case. At the same time, nongovernmental organizations have been increasingly suggested as appropriate vehicles for carrying out development, especially in local communities.

In the past several years, a number of women's organizations have formed in Nigeria, and others that previously existed have taken on explicitly development-oriented activities. Some of these are formally organized nongovernmental organizations, while others are local-level associations that do not have formal recognition as NGOs, and still others are tied to government institutions. In this paper, we examine the current role and activities of women's organizations in Nigeria, arguing that the economic crisis in general and structural adjustment in particular have affected the formation and activities of these organizations. The first section of the paper reviews the effects of structural adjustment and argues that in the present economic context NGOs and local development organizations have become increasingly important. The second section examines the types of women's organizations and the range of their activities. In the third section, a number of questions are raised about the impact and importance of these organizations. What effect do their activities have on the development process? What is their impact on women who are members and participants? What are the problems and difficulties that are encountered by these organizations in carrying out their activities? And, in the overall context of economic crisis and structural adjustment, to what extent can women's organizations be effective, or is too much now expected of them?

Structural Adjustment Programs and Women

To what extent are women detrimentally affected by the adoption of structural adjustment programs (SAPs) or, conversely, are they benefiting from these policies? Any definitive answer is impossible, as studies are only now being conducted. In many countries, data on impact are simply unavailable (Hugon 1988:2). However, in a series of well-known studies, UNICEF has argued that there has been widespread deterioration in the conditions for children during the 1980s (Cornia, Jolly, and Stewart 1988). Other studies, such as those presented in this volume, have begun to consider specific effects of adjustment on women and to advocate disaggregation of data by gender (Collier 1989, Spring and Wilde, this volume). Joekes has examined implications of adjustment policies on women's income, on women's consumption patterns, and on women's participation in various sectors. For women in the informal sector, for example, she suggests that while there may be some expansion and increased opportunities, overall evidence shows decline in informal sector incomes as "the reduction in formal sector employment throws the newly unemployed, and new entrants to the labor market, into the informal sector to compete for available business" (Joekes 198:39). With respect to women in agriculture, she argues that structural adjustment may exacerbate existing biases in the access that women have to productive resources "by overlooking, if not denying, women's access to and consumption of the type of productive resources and services such as extension, credit, and input subsidies that are targeted to export production" (Joekes 1988: 36).

There is little direct evidence on the effects of adjustment policies on rural nonfarm enterprises. However, since much of the rural nonfarm activity for women involves the processing and distribution of locally produced and consumed food, there may not be much immediate effect. Over the longer term, if agricultural production increases, there should be increased opportunities in such activities (Guyer, this volume). However, without improved access to technology, credit, and markets, both local and international, women may not be in a position to exploit such opportunities.

As other papers in this volume document, women—both rural and urban—are key producers as well as central to the sustenance of households throughout sub-Saharan Africa. As incomes decline, and as men employed in the formal sector lose their jobs, the economic activities of women are likely to become even more central to household and family sustenance and maintenance. As dependence on women's income-earning activities increases, the variety of demands on their time also increases. Already responsible for childbearing and rearing and for productive work, women are increasingly taking on what Moser (forthcoming:4-5) terms a "community managing role," to try to ensure provision of basic services such as water and health care.

There is a tendency to consider the effects of recent policies on urban and rural households separately. Throughout African societies, however, there are extensive linkages maintained among rural-based and urban-based kin. These may be increasingly relied on for assistance in times of great economic need. For example, one of the authors sends money and food every two weeks to an aunt in the village. But with SAP-induced wage freezes or firings, such remittances may well diminish or disappear. When an urban worker loses his job, or a school leaver is unable to find urban employment, he may well depend on rural-based kin for sustenance. Again, the burden is likely to fall on women more than on men, and particularly on rural women who find themselves with more dependent kin to support.

Nigeria began implementing its own structural adjustment program about four years ago. Although Nigeria has had greater wealth than most other countries in the region, its economy had become almost entirely dependent on revenue from oil exports. As a leading Nigerian business expert has reflected:

> Our economy became dominated by a single commodity—oil and ... it provided 25% of our Gross Domestic Product, 95% of our foreign exchange earnings and 60% of Federal Government revenues in 1985. At the same time the world economy reflected a fall in oil prices and Nigeria's earnings from oil exports became less than half of what they used to be. Nigeria had a crushing debt service burden which was consuming 40–50% of the foreign exchange and part of the remainder was swallowed by imports of the agricultural products which were necessary to feed the population but which we should be capable of producing in the country (Shonekan 1985:1-2).

When Nigeria undertook its structural adjustment program, much of the emphasis was placed on renewing agricultural production. In the long term, this should benefit women, both those engaged in farming and those in processing and distributive activities. Much will depend on how the policy is carried out and on what types of agriculture (large vs. small scale, export vs. food crops) are in fact supported and encouraged (Guyer, this volume). In the short term, however, the standard of living for many women and their families has worsened, as a result of withdrawal of subsidies, wage freezes, and government fiscal restraint (Elabor-Idemudia, this volume). For those dependent on purchasing food, prices have increased substantially while incomes have declined. Many are having difficulty paying for the education of their children; access to various public services such as health care is less. In addition, the continuation of restrictions on importing manufactured goods and certain staple foods such as wheat and rice, as well as the devaluation of the Naira, has had severe repercussions on those women engaged in trade in imported commodities, especially in urban areas.

In recent months, the Nigerian government has responded to public pressure to seek ways to alleviate some of the negative effects of its SAP on vulnerable groups in the population. Most of its efforts are directed towards those in rural areas, through four major government programs— the Directorate of Food, Roads, and Rural Infrastructure (DFRRI), the National Directorate of Employment (NDE), Better Life for Rural Women, and the People's Bank. Many of these programs, as well as others, call for or rely on the participation of women's groups. At the same time, nongovernmental organizations have also begun to respond to perceived needs and problems of local populations and to try to solve some of them. It is in this context—of economic crisis, structural adjustment, and recent efforts to alleviate negative effects—that the current emphasis on women's organizations must be considered.

Women's Organizations

Structural adjustment has not caused the formation of women's organizations in Africa. Rather, organizations and associations of women have a long history in the continent and have been important in a variety of contexts. However, existing groups have taken on new functions, and new types of organizations have come into existence in recent years. Their increasing prominence is, in part, a result of the current economic crisis and structural adjustment policies. In this section of the paper, we consider the types of women's organizations that are oriented towards development and socioeconomic issues, and then describe the range of their activities. Following a brief overview of organizations throughout sub-Saharan Africa, we concentrate on those in Nigeria. We suggest that three types of organization are particularly important: local, usually village- or community-level groups; nongovernmental intermediary organizations; and government-linked intermediary organizations. In many cases, the activities of the latter two types of organization rely on the existence and participation of the first type.

Historically, women's organizations in Africa are organized primarily at the local level, around a variety of concerns and for a variety of purposes. Some are basically social groups or clubs, such as the many *egbe* found among the Yoruba of Nigeria (Fadipe 1970). Others are organized for the purpose of generating savings and providing access to credit; the *esusu* among the Yoruba and other Nigerian groups and *njangis* or *tontins* in Cameroon are rotating savings organizations which provide the major source of credit for many West African small businesswomen; such associations also exist among women in Kenya (Thomas 1988:406). In some societies, local associations involving both men and women are organized explicitly for community development purposes; for example, among the Igbo of Nigeria, whose self-help organizations are wellknown (Uchendu 1965), women may belong to associations focused on improvement activities for their own hometowns as well as the hometowns of their husbands.

However, with the exception of the community improvement organizations, most of these groups have not been concerned with "development" issues as such. The organizations are typically small and focus on parochial concerns of interest to their own membership. Few are incorporated in any formal sense; even in those areas where the cooperative movement has played a role, women's organizations have rarely been registered as cooperatives.

In recent years, efforts have been made to base development activities on local-level groups. For example, in Kenya, Tototo Home Industries has worked with existing women's groups to develop village-level income-generating projects (McCormack, Walsh, and Nelson 1986). Similar projects have been designed elsewhere, usually aimed at small and micro-enterprise development and skills training for rural women, but also based on savings and credit programs. Several analysts have also considered the problems and feasibility of transforming indigenous, local organizations into development organizations (Esman and Uphoff 1984; March and

Figure 13-1. The economic crisis in general and structural adjustment in particular has encouraged the formation of local women's organizations aimed at micro-enterprise development, skills training, and savings and credit programs for rural women.

Taqqu 1982), but for the most part local organizations continue to carry out their functions for members (such as providing a way to save small amounts of money) without undergoing any fundamental transformation.

At the same time, new types of organization have come into existence which have modeled some of their activities on those of local women's groups and have sought to draw on the existence of those groups to carry out their activities. The newer organizations include formally organized nongovernmental organizations as well as organizations linked to and/or stimulated by government.

While there are many different types of nongovernmental organization, including the well-known international relief and development organizations, our focus here is on indigenous NGOs, and especially on those which operate as intermediary organizations (Bratton 1989:571). Intermediary organizations typically operate at a national level, or in a region of a country, and seek to attract resources and develop programs which can be implemented at local levels, usually by local groups linked to the intermediary. For example, in Senegal, Service International D'Appui a la Formation (AFOTEC) has focused its attention on women's income-generating activities, and especially on the improvement of technology used in those activities. Led by several professional women with considerable experience in rural development, it works with local women's groups in specific regions of the country, such as the Casamance. Because organizations such as AFOTEC are formally registered, they are able to attract external funds (e.g., from international donor agencies) that local women's groups cannot attract.

African governments have frequently sought to co-opt the activities of indigenous NGOs through the establishment of what Bratton calls quangos (quasi-NGOs), that is, "publicly-sponsored NGO's which [are] organizational affiliates of a government ministry" (Bratton 1989:579). In some cases, the government establishes an organization, often in the ministry of social welfare, to which NGOs must be attached. In other cases, the government seeks ways to link NGOs to government officials and agencies. In Kenya, "the governing party gradually exerted control over [the] umbrella organization of women's groups known as *Maendeleo ya Wanawake* by incorporating it into the patronage networks of party leaders" (Bratton 1989:579). In Nigeria, government has itself established organizations, some of which are explicitly governmental bodies that act as intermediaries, while others of which are "semi-governmental" (Trager 1989) in that they are mandated by government but have leaders who have sought to transform them into membership-based NGOs.

Nigeria is a particularly interesting arena in which to examine recent developments regarding women's organizations as there has been relatively little activity on the part of international NGOs. Throughout the oil boom period it was largely assumed that government could assume responsibility for *all* aspects of development, and it is only quite recently that there has been a shift both in government rhetoric and in the orientation of much of the population. As a result, although local women's groups have long been influential in Nigerian society, the formation of NGOs and of government-sponsored women's organizations is largely a phenomenon of the 1980s. Certainly, there were NGOs previously, including a wide variety of professional and service organizations, many with international links, such as Girl Guides, Zonta, Soroptomists, Nigerian Association of University Women, etc. The National Council of Women's Societies is an umbrella organization to which all women's groups are supposed to belong. While some of these organizations have undertaken service projects directed towards improving conditions in some way or for some group, that is not their fundamental raison d'être.

In contrast, several new NGOs have been formed with explicit goals addressed to development issues. For example, in Lagos State, the Lagos State Women's Association for Home Gardening and Farming is concerned with increasing food production and encouraging women to grow food for their own consumption. The All Nigerian Women Association, led by Lady Oyinkan Abayomi, a prominent and longtime women's leader in Lagos, has been acting as a pressure group that brings together groups such as market women and those who are educated, to improve conditions of women. Women in Nigeria (WIN) has played an important role in examining government and societal issues as they affect women and has published research results on the status of Nigerian women (Women in Nigeria 1985a, 1985b).

The best known of the development-oriented NGOs in Nigeria is the Country Women Association of Nigeria (COWAN), founded originally in Ondo State but now seeking to establish branches throughout the country and operate as a national intermediary organization. The overall objectives of the organization are as follows:

1. to increase the productivity and consequently the earning capacity of the rural folks for better living standard;
2. to promote programs that have an inbuilt self-sustaining growth that could be replicated in the various ecological zones of the states;
3. to diversify economic opportunities available in the rural areas by promoting rural crafts, processing of agricultural products, and by creating jobs for artisans in various fields;
4. to develop rural-based technologies for increased cottage industries and home products;
5. to train rural women in relevant improved skills and management of small enterprises and to enhance self-reliant rural development; and

6. to associate itself with the government's aspiration to develop the rural areas, feed its teeming population, and become self-reliant.

Formed in 1982, COWAN has registered as a multipurpose cooperative in Ondo State, giving it institutional legitimacy and access to certain types of resources. It works with local women's groups in communities throughout the state, mainly in rural areas but also in towns and cities. The groups are organized around economic activities in which the women are engaged—farming, food processing, fishing and fish marketing, pottery, weaving, and so on.

COWAN's main activity has been to work with these groups to improve access to productive inputs such as improved seed varieties for farming groups and processing equipment for food processors. In 1987, it established a revolving loan fund to provide small loans to the groups for their productive activities; by January 1989 forty groups had received loans ranging from 1,000 to 6,000 naira.

COWAN is a membership organization; individual members pay 2.50 naira to register and can buy shares in the society at 50 naira per share. Each member society is also supposed to pay 250 naira to the organization. Of the local groups belonging to COWAN, there is considerable variation in the extent of their organization and their success to date in carrying out activities. One of the best established and best organized groups consists of women engaged in fishing, fish smoking, and fish marketing in a town in the riverine area of the state. This group used an earlier COWAN loan to build a warehouse for storage and had established a marketing system under their own control; their goal was to obtain their own boat. Other groups are much less well organized.

In roughly the same time period in which COWAN and other NGOs have formed, the Nigerian government has taken steps towards the formation of women's intermediary organizations and has also called for the development of local-level organizations. The first effort in this direction was made in 1982 with the establishment of the Committee on Women and Development, with the goals of examining women's contribution to development, strengthening women's participation, and working with government and NGOs. Both state and national-level committees were established (Johnson 1989). In the mid-eighties, however, the committee's role changed and it began to be directly involved in development programs, such as income-generating projects, leadership training for women, and development of loan schemes. In some states, such as Oyo State, the committee sought to transform itself into a membership organization working with local women's groups, and its leaders began to argue that they were really a nongovernmental organization, even though they had originally been appointed by the government. At present, the organization may best be considered a "semi-governmental organization" (Trager 1989).

The change in the orientation of the Committee on Women and Development can be seen as a response to the economic crisis and structural adjustment, as the necessity for direct involvement of women's organizations in the development process became more evident. An even more direct response has been the establishment of several other government programs and agencies, including the Directorate of Food, Roads, and Rural Infrastructure (DFRRI), the National Directorate of Employment, and the People's Bank. These are not specifically directed towards women, but they do draw in several ways on local groups. For example, DFRRI has called for the formation of Community Development Associations in all communities in the country (Trager 1989), and the very recently established People's Bank will give small loans only to individuals through cooperative or trade groups of which they are members.

In addition to these broad development programs, the Nigerian government has established a program directed specifically to concerns of women, the Better Life for Rural Women program (although the name was later changed to Better Life for Rural Dwellers) established in September 1987 by the president's wife. Better Life programs have been established in all states and are directed by the governor's wife in each state. The stated objectives of Better Life are:

1. to improve the living standard of rural women, their life-styles, families, and environment;
2. to generate a new awareness in the field of education, creative pursuits, and recreation;
3. to evolve appropriate technologies to lessen hard and cruel rural life and resultant drudgery in such areas as farming, cooking, weaving, and water collection;
4. to curb the ignorance of their basic and legal rights; and
5. to provide solutions to the poor health care provisions, scarce and unsuitable methods of evacuating farm produce to the market, as well as the inadequacy of essential commodities (Ekaette 1989).

The Better Life program has attracted considerable attention, and at least in some states, a variety of activities has been undertaken. For the most part, these seem to be local-level income-generating projects. For example, Lagos State has compiled a list of about thirty projects ranging from fish smoking to *gari* processing to farming and trade activities. Most have been—or are in the process of being—undertaken by local women's groups, some of which have been formally changed to cooperative societies, which can then receive loans of 5,000–1,0000 naira for their projects. (See Table 13-1 for a list of groups and projects.) In Anambra State, according to the governor's wife, 300 cooperatives had been registered by September 1989, compared to only 16 two years earlier; again, these cooperatives are formed around various economic activities in which the women are involved (*Newswatch*, Jan. 15, 1990).

In some areas, attempts have begun to improve access to land. For example, in Borno State, Better Life acquired 50 hectares of land in order for women to be able to go into wheat production. Elsewhere, attention has focused on access to equipment, markets, and transport, as well as on health and education issues.

In effect, Better Life seems to be operating as a government umbrella organization, presumably seeking to find ways to link local women's groups to resources that are difficult for them to gain access to. Since it has only been in existence since 1987 it is very difficult to evaluate any results of this program.

Impact of Women's Organizations in Nigeria

Given the length of time the organizations under discussion have been in existence, consideration of their impact must be speculative. The most significant of the NGOs involved in development—COWAN—was formed only in 1982 and much of its activity has occurred only since 1985. The major government program—Better Life for Rural Women—has only been in existence for two or three years, and while government publicity suggests a great deal of activity in that brief time, there is no way to evaluate what has actually occurred. In this discussion, therefore, we seek to examine both the potential for these programs and organizations and the problems and difficulties they are encountering. Furthermore, since both NGOs and government organizations are relying on local-level women's groups to carry out their activities, we need to look at the impact on those groups.

What problems and difficulties are being encountered by NGOs such as COWAN and government programs such as Better Life? As embryonic institutions, still really in the process of formation, they have a variety of organizational weaknesses which affect their impact (Bratton 1989:572).

Table 13-1. Women's Groups Associated with Better Life, in Selected Areas of Lagos State.

Name	Activity
I. Epe Local Government	
Orimedu Women Society	fish smoking
Oriba Women Cooperative	gari processing, fish smoking
Tiwadipe Noforija Cooperative	gari processing
II. Ikeja Local Government	
Ijegun Women Cooperative	gari processing and fufu
Isheri Olofin Cooperative	farming, gari processing
Sasa Women's Club	cloth weaving
III. Ikorodu Local Government	
Irewole Farmers Club	farming, fishing, fish smoking
Ifelodun-Araromi Village	farming, gari processing
Ifelodun Thrift and Credit	farming, gari processing
Agbelonionje Cooperative	farming, gari processing
Ibese	fish smoking
Igbogbo	gari and fufu processing
Oreta	fishing, farming, fish smoking
IV. Mushin Local Government	
Ayenuga Cooperative Society	tie and dye
Olorunsogo Brick Making	roofing sheet and brick moulding
Akinwumi Soap Making	soap and pomade making
Ireakari	soap and pomade making
Ejigbo	gari processing
Mafoluku Cooperative	baby clothes, poultry farm
V. Badagry Local Government	
Ilado Oro	coconut oil extraction
Apa	gari processing
Oredunni Multipurpose Group	multipurpose
Whedako Fishermen and Women Cooperative	fishing, fish smoking
Home Gardening and Farming Association	farming, processing
VI. Shomolu Local Government	
Ilaje Ifelodun Fishing Association	fishing, fish smoking
Ago-Egun	fishing
Igbehinadun	fishing, fish smoking
Ajegunle	fishing, fish smoking, mat weaving
Orile Maidan	farming

One major problem is that of leadership: there tends to be dependence on a single strong, dominant leader, usually the founder or one of the founders. While these leaders have a clear vision of what they hope to accomplish and a great deal of energy and dynamism, in these early stages it may be difficult for other leaders to emerge. This can become a problem particularly as the organizations become better known and involved in a wider range of activities. In the government organizations such as the Committee on Women and Development and Better Life, there are also problems of leadership. Here, the leadership is assigned—e.g., to the governor's wife in the case of Better Life. Yet this in itself can be problematic. The assigned leader may be able to exercise leadership and authority because of her status, but there is no basis for it in terms of a clear commitment to the goals of the organization. Therefore other second-level leaders who have that commitment must become involved; in those situations where the government organizations have begun to play a significant role, such as the committee in Oyo State and Better Life in Lagos State, this seems to be what has happened.

A second set of problems derives not from the structure of one specific organization but from conflict between organizations. Bratton (1989) has recently considered at some length relationships between NGOs and government in development activities and the potential for conflict between them. In Nigerian women's organizations, with both NGOs and governmental bodies with similar goals and working with similar types of local-level women's groups, the potential for conflict is very real and has in fact already occurred in at least one situation. Conflict has arisen over whether a particular NGO or government organization working in the same area is responsible, and hence should get the credit, for the establishment and success of specific women's groups projects in the state. The issue here is not simply one of government control (Bratton 1989), although that is certainly part of it. Given the scarce resources which both NGOs and government organizations are trying to draw on and mobilize, it is also a question of who gets access to and controls those resources, and who gets the credit and recognition for having done so, which of course may lead to access to additional resources.

Beyond the problems and conflicts, what is the potential impact of these organizations on women and on the development process? We will address three questions here. First, how does the current emphasis on women's organizations affect women's participation in the development process? Second, what is the effect on local women's groups? And third, what impact is there on the overall development process and specifically in response to the conditions generated by structural adjustment?

In the current literature on development in general and on women in development in particular, there is considerable emphasis on "empowerment;" nongovernmental organizations have been viewed as an especially important instrument for empowerment. We should therefore ask whether involvement of NGOs in development activities leads to increased empowerment for women. This leads to a further set of questions: Who has organized the program? Who provides the leadership? Who makes the decisions? What is the role of local women?

In considering these questions, a fundamental distinction can be made between governmental and nongovernmental programs and organizations. Essentially the government programs are inherently top-down. No matter how concerned they are with local development, the authority and leadership come from government. Where local women's groups are involved, as in the Better Life program, the local activities may help empower women. But the authority for such groups and the decision to fund specific projects still rests with state government or more specifically, the wife of the state governor. It is one of the contradictory aspects of Nigerian government programs—not only programs focused on women—that they advocate local community organization and leadership but the mandate for that organization comes from a central authority!

On the other hand, efforts of nongovernmental organizations—especially indigenous NGOs—seem to have greater potential for empowerment of women. In terms of both its organizational structure and the types of activities undertaken, an organization like COWAN has the potential to foster the empowerment of women through local women's organizations that make up the larger organization. However, without specific research on these groups, it is difficult to judge to what extent this has actually occurred. Some of the local groups affiliated with COWAN, such as the fish processors described above, are well organized and have strong local leadership. They have undertaken actions, such as building a storage shed and establishment of a new system for marketing fish, that suggest considerable decision-making and leadership power. These decisions certainly affect others in their communities, and it is likely that the fish processor organization has become a significant local force and has been aided in doing so by its membership in COWAN. Other groups, on the other hand, are much less well organized and not likely to have much economic or political muscle. In other words, women's intermediary NGOs have the potential to lead to increased empowerment for women; the extent to which they have done so, however, remains in question.

Second, what is the impact of intermediary NGOs and governmental organizations on local women's groups? It is striking that both the rhetoric and the organizational structure of an NGO like COWAN and government organizations like Better Life call for the participation and formation of local women's groups. This focus has meant increased recognition and attention to the importance of such local groups, groups which are often categorized as "informal" and therefore somehow not worthy of attention. In addition, there is recognition that local associations are likely to have good ideas about what is needed at the local level and hence an increased attention to local knowledge and local awareness of problems. However, this is not always the case; intermediary and national-level organizations can also simply use local groups to implement programs formulated at national levels without taking local conditions or problems into account. In other words, there is an important issue of *whose agenda is being followed*.

In addition to recognition, local groups may benefit in more concrete ways by their association with an intermediary or umbrella organization. They can gain access to information and resources that would otherwise be difficult to obtain. For example, through its revolving loan fund, COWAN has made it possible for small, local groups that are not formally recognized to get access to credit. It has also helped some to register as cooperatives, which gives them access to specific goods and services through government programs. Better Life seems to be operating in a similar manner, by helping village-level groups to obtain equipment for food processing and other income-generating activities.

Questions must also be raised about negative aspects of this reliance on local women's groups. The basic issue is *whether too much is now expected of them.* These are, after all, primarily organizations that formed for other reasons, and even when they are concerned with community improvement or generating savings, they have specific forms of organization that may not be amenable to transformation into development organizations. Most are small and bring together a set of women with a specific set of interests or attributes in common. If left that way, they may function well and benefit their members. But if they are asked to become community-wide or larger organizations, encompassing more people with more varied interests, such a transformation may be problematic. As March and Taqqu (1982:119) have pointed out in their discussion of informal associations as the basis for development, what is being called for is the transformation of informal associations into formal ones; and "the formalization of informal associations as groups ... alters their internal dynamics and can undermine mutual trust and flexibility among members." Like March and Taqqu, we suggest that in Nigeria, as elsewhere, results are likely to differ based on the preexisting structure and raison d'être of the groups involved, as well as on the type of new structures and functions adopted. As noted in our discussion of COWAN for example, preexisting groups organized around common economic interests, such as the fish processors, appear to be having greater success than some of the other groups.

Conclusion

Finally, what is the overall impact of women's groups on the development process and as one response to structural adjustment? We suggest it is great, that local women's increased access to information and resources through links with intermediary organizations are key ingredients to local development. To what extent development is now occurring in Nigeria, in the era of structural adjustment, is more open to question. Certainly, some local development projects of importance have been undertaken. But it is too soon to evaluate their success or failure and certainly far too soon to know if they will fundamentally counter, in some cumulative way, the negative impacts of structural adjustment "reforms."

There is also the danger of too much being expected of these organizations. Just as government before structural adjustment was expected to do everything, women's organizations may now be expected to solve all development problems. Particularly in light of a macroeconomic situation where structural adjustment continues to be the key word, and where the economy has not yet revived, it is difficult to know the extent to which women's organizations can mitigate the situation. What seems most likely is that, in some contexts and for some groups, women's groups will result in better access to resources and opportunities. To the extent that food crop production and agro-processing activities are encouraged and stimulated, some of the local-level projects concerned with these activities should help those involved. But much will depend on the specific activities as well as on the macroeconomic environment.

An additional danger is that too much may be expected of the individual women involved in the groups. As NGOs and government organizations develop programs for women's groups, the time and energy demanded of individual women may simply overburden them. New sorts of income-generating activities, carried out in addition to women's daily tasks (enumerated by Elabor-Idemudia, this volume), may result in more (self-) exploitation of women. If, on the other hand, income-generating projects are based on activities already part of women's daily work plans, then they may benefit them by providing greater inputs or resources. As with other issues considered here, the actual results are likely to vary considerably from case to case.

In sum, the current situation of women's organizations in Nigeria, and elsewhere in Africa as well, is both exciting and problematic. It is exciting that women's organizations are being recognized as viable institutions that can make an important contribution to development. It is at the same time problematic, because there are still many questions about whether the existing organizational structures can in fact do all the things that are now expected of them.

REFERENCES

Bratton, Michael
    1989   The Politics of Government-NGO Relations in Africa. *World Development* 17(4):569–87.

Collier, Paul
    1989   Women and Structural Adjustment. Washington, D.C.: World Bank.

Cornia, Giovanni Andrea, Richard Jolly, and Frances Stewart
    1988   *Adjustment with a Human Face.* Volumes I and II. Oxford: Clarendon Press.

Ekaette, U.J.
    1989   Overview of the Achievements of Women in National Development. Paper presented at the Workshop on the Role of Women's Voluntary Organizations and Support Groups in Development, Lagos State, Nigeria, Oct. 5–6.

Esman, Milton J., and Norman T. Uphoff
    1984   *Local Organizations: Intermediaries in Rural Development.* Ithaca: Cornell University Press.

Fadipe, N.A.
    1970   *The Sociology of the Yoruba.* Ibadan: Ibadan University Press.

Hugon, Philippe
    1988   The Impact of Adjustment Policies on Microenterprises. Paper presented at World Conference on Support for Microenterprises, Washington, D.C.

Jaycox, Edward V.K.
    1989   Structural Adjustment in Sub-Saharan Africa: The World Bank's Perspective. *Issue* 18:36–40.

Joekes, Susan
  1988   Gender and Macro-economic Policy. Paper prepared for AWID
          Colloquium on Gender and Development Cooperation,
          Washington, D.C.
Johnson, Simi
  1989   New Strategies for Integrating Women in National/State
          Development and the Role of Women's Organizations and Support
          Groups. Paper presented at the Workshop on the Role of Women's
          Voluntary Organizations and Support Groups in Development,
          Lagos State, Nigeria, Oct. 5–6.
McCormack, Jeanne, Martin Walsh, and Candace Nelson
  1986   *Women's Group Enterprises: A Study of the Structure of Opportunity
          on the Kenya Coast.* Boston: World Education Inc.
March, Kathryn S., and Rachelle Taqqu
  1982   *Women's Informal Associations and the Organizational Capacity for
          Development.* Cornell University Rural Development Committee
          Monograph Series. Ithaca: Cornell University Press.
Moser, Caroline O. N.
  forthcoming   Gender Planning in the Third World: Meeting Practical and
          Strategic Gender Needs. *World Development.*
Newswatch
  1990   Supplement on Anambra State, January 15:29.
Robinson, Pearl T.
  1989   Transnational NGO's: A New Direction for U.S. Policy. *Issue*
          18(1):41–46.
Serageldin, Ismail
  1989   *Poverty, Adjustment and Growth in Africa.* Washington, D.C.:
          World Bank.
Shonekan, Ernest A. O.
  1985   Economic Outlook—1985 vs. 1983. *Nigeria's Economic Recovery.*
          New York: African American Institute.
Thomas, Barbara P.
  1988   Household Strategies for Adaptation and Change: Participation in
          Kenyan Rural Women's Associations. *Africa* 58:401–22.
Trager, Lillian
  1989   Local-Level Development in Nigeria: Institutions and Impact.
          Paper presented at the African Studies Association meetings,
          Atlanta, Georgia, October.
Uchendu, Victor C.
  1965   *The Igbo of Southeast Nigeria.* New York: Holt, Rinehart and
          Winston.
The Urban Edge
  1989   NGOs Gain Clout, Recognition. *The Urban Edge* 13(8):1.

Women in Nigeria

    1985a   *Women in Nigeria Today.* London: Zed Books.

    1985b   The WIN Document: Conditions of Women in Nigeria and Policy Recommendations to 2000 A.D. Zaria: Women in Nigeria.

14

The Role of Home Economics Agents in Rural Development Programs in Northern Nigeria: Impacts of Structural Adjustment

Comfort B. Olayiwole

Women's participation in rural development programs has increasingly become an important focus for governments of Third World countries and international agencies. Ensuring that women are active participants in rural development not only fulfills the equality issue but also makes economic sense since women make up over 50 percent of the rural labor force. Equity and social justice are said to be some of the reasons for justifying priority on rural development. In Nigeria, the population is predominantly rural and depends on agriculture and its related actives for livelihood. Therefore any effort to develop the rural areas requires the mobilization of rural resources, human and material.

It is also generally agreed that rural development is an essential and primary part of overall economic development. Thus rural development must include not only improved agriculture and increased production, but also improvement of the standards of living of the rural households. In discussing rural people's participation in development, FAO (1979) observed that "the key steps towards effective participation include: encouraging organization of the rural population, decentralizing decision-making and, if necessary, reforming local government institutions and involving the beneficiaries of the development programmes."

Participation thus implies that rural women are actively involved in the decision making, planning, and execution of rural development programs beneficial to them, their households, and communities. In the northern states of Nigeria, as in the rest of Nigeria and Africa in general, women play vital roles in the survival of their households. Their contribution in raising children—the future labor force—as well as their agricultural and

Comfort Olayiwole is principal, Samaru College of Agriculture, Ahmadu Bello University. She has a Ph.D. in Home Economics from Kansas State University, where she studied on a Ford Foundation fellowship. She is the author of numerous articles on Nigerian women's roles in food production and marketing and the role of home economics in rural development.

livestock production and other economic activities are central to rural development. In fact, in most rural communities, women are responsible for the provision of basic needs of their households. For example, the availability of food, clothing, household goods, water, and fuel all depend on the women in the household.

Therefore, considering the economic, social, and political importance of women in rural development, their contributions can no longer be ignored. Yet women in general and rural women in particular have suffered serious neglect in past development plans of Nigeria. Studies have shown that even in well-structured rural development programs, *women as farmers* have been ignored by rural development agents, who happen to be predominantly male. Data in Table 14-1, collected in Muslim and non-Muslim communities in northern Nigeria, agree. They show that men in 93 percent of households in Zango have contacts with extension agents, whereas only 50 percent of men in Kenye households have extension contacts; but almost no women in all four communities have extension contacts.

Yet women have tremendous potential impact on the future social and economic development of Nigeria. Rural women hold the key to raising the rural levels of living in relation to their family responsibilities as well as their agricultural and nonagricultural activities. The old proverb is true: "If you educate a man you educate an individual. If you educate a woman you educate a family."

Figure 14-1. Women as farmers have been ignored by rural development agents who happen to be predominantly male.

Table 14-1. Households with Extension Contacts (%).

Male/Female Contacts	Zango (N = 30)	Kajuru (N = 30)	Unguwar Jaba (N = 30)	Kenye (N = 30)
Males only	93	13	87	50
Females	0	0	3	3
Males/Females	0	0	3	10

Source: Olayiwole (1984:122).

Home economics is the discipline in agricultural schools which has traditionally been responsible for training women. In general, it is a family-oriented discipline that plays an important role in the readjustment of the family to new socioeconomic situations and new functions, to fit into the developing yet ever-changing economic, social, and political nature of Nigerian society. Yet the discipline of home economics itself is undergoing enormous changes, from a discipline focusing almost exclusively on the "domestic arts" of food processing, cooking, and sewing to a discipline which focuses on women as agricultural producers and income generators. It is the purpose of this paper to describe the changing roles of northern Nigerian women, the changing roles of home economists in Nigeria, and their new duties in the era of economic crisis and structural adjustment in Nigeria.

Northern Nigerian Women's Participation in Rural Development

Farming is the primary industry of people in the rural areas of northern Nigeria. Women are actively engaged in on-farm operations, either on their own income-generating operations or in an operation complementary to the farming activities of their husbands or employers. Recent research findings have shown that women provide between 60 percent and 80 percent of the agricultural labor in Nigeria, depending on cultural and religious factors. Women are engaged in the production process of crops and livestock, in most cases including farm work such as planting, weeding, applying manures/fertilizer, harvesting, transporting crops to home and market, distribution, storage, poultry and small-livestock keeping, food processing, and marketing of the produce (Table 14-2).

Most women who consider farming as their major occupation cultivate crops not only for household consumption but also for income (Table 14-3). These data show that in Zango, for example, 7 percent of women

Table 14-2. Women's Participation in Farm Tasks (%).

| Task | Muslim | | | | | | Non-Muslim | | | | | |
| | Zango (N = 30) | | | Kajuru (N = 30) | | | Unguwar Jaba (N = 30) | | | Kenye (N = 30) | | |
	F	M	C/WF	F	M	C/WF	F	M	C/WF	F	M	C/WF
Land Clearing	4	96	0	0	100	0	17	33	50	87	0	13
Hand and Plow												
Tilling	0	100	0	0	100	0	0	90	10	7	77	16
Planting	0	100	0	–	100	0	93	0	7	100	0	0
Fert./Manure	0	100	0	0	100	0	23	0	77	7	77	16
Weeding and												
Thinning	0	86	14	0	97	3	0	53	47	60	17	23
Harvesting	0	72	28	0	93	7	0	27	73	7	0	93
Threshing and												
Husking	24	0	76	62	0	38	87	0	13	83	7	10
Transportation	9	53	38	0	55	45	90	0	10	60	0	40
Storage (Home)	86	9	5	7	90	3	3	47	50	3	37	60
Marketing	0	89	11	0	100	0	93	0	7	67	10	23

Key: F–Females (Adults).   M–Males.   C–Community Labor.   WF–Whole Family.
Source: Olayiwole (1984:93).

report farming to be their primary occupation, while 17 percent report farming to be a secondary occupation. (Clearly, the remaining 76 percent of Zango women do not farm.) Data also show that women in non-Muslim communities farm more than women in Muslim communities. Their involvement in farming is said to be dependent on their access to land for personal cultivation. Barkaw (1972) and Olayiwole (1984) report that non-Muslim women farmers in Kaduna State who have personal plots cultivate crops and control the proceeds as they wish. Similarly, Ngur (1988) reports that Jarawa women in Bauchi State cultivate both cash and food crops on their own personal plots. She noted that rice is cultivated mainly for a cash crop by the women.

Livestock

Among major activities of women in the northern states of Nigeria is the keeping of livestock. Olayiwole's (1984) study reveals that both Muslim and non-Muslim women are known to rear small animals such as poultry, sheep, and goats. In addition, non-Muslim women rear pigs (Table 14-4), while the rearing of large animals such as cattle is mainly done by the

Table 14-3. Distribution of Women's Primary and Secondary Occupations (%).[a]

	Muslim				Non-Muslim			
	Zango (N = 30)		Kajuru (N = 30)		Unguwar Jaba (N = 30)		Kenye (N = 30)	
Occupation	Primary	Secondary	Primary	Secondary	Primary	Secondary	Primary	Secondary
Farming	7	17	3	7	37	63	63	37
Food Processing	12	17	70	3	13	0	13	17
Handcrafts[b]	43	23	10	0	0	0	0	0
Beer Brewing	0	0	0	0	43	0	0	20
Others[c]	3	17	17	10	4	3	4	17
None	43	27	0	80	3	34	0	39

a. Percentages in rows of this table do not necessarily add to 100 percent, as some women do not have this occupation.

b. Handcrafts included embroidery work, weaving, and spinning.

c. Occupations reported in this category included firewood fetching and selling, mat making, pottery, and petty trading in commercial products such as salt, sugar, soap, and paraffin.

Source: Olayiwole (1984: 81).

Fulani, nomadic cattle rearers. Simmons (1976) and Olayiwole (1984) both observed that rural women in the villages of Kaduna State considered livestock keeping as a banking system rather than an occupation.

Processing

Activities women engage in as their income-generating occupations include crop and milk processing such as dehusking, threshing, winnowing and milling of grains and legumes, and milk processing into butter, *nono* (yogurt), and *wara* (cheese). Other food processing such as the extraction of groundnut oil, the pounding of grains, preparation of food and snacks for sale (e.g., the making of *kosai, kunun, zaki, danwake*, etc.) are done mostly by secluded women (Table 14-3). Their predominance in off-farm occupations is to be expected because, according to Simmons (1976), accepted occupations for Muslim-Hausa women include food processing. Studies have also found that non-Muslim women are also engaged in food processing, particularly local beer brewing from grains. These activities are carried out mainly on market days and/or during the nonfarming seasons (Olayiwole 1984, Ngur 1988).

Table 14-4. Female/Male Participation in Small Livestock Production (%).[a]

| | Muslim | | | | | | Non-Muslim | | | | | |
| | Zango (N=30) | | | Kajuru (N=30) | | | Unguwar Jaba (N=30) | | | Kenye (N=30) | | |
Livestock	F	M	F/M	F	M	F/M	F	M	F/M	F	M	F/M
Poultry	93	4	3	70	13	0	37	17	37	30	23	37
Sheep	10	54	0	7	17	17	3	7	0	0	7	93
Goats	10	47	0	10	7	13	40	13	37	3	63	17
Pigs	0	0	0	0	0	0	67	3	23	53	17	17
Others[b]	3	7	8	0	3	4	0	0	0	4	0	3

a. Percentages in rows of this table do not necessarily add to 100 percent, as some households do not raise this type of livestock.

b. Other livestock, including rabbits and turkeys.

Key: F–Females.   F/M–Females and Males.   M–Males.

Source: Olayiwole (1984:107).

Marketing and Trading

It is established that a large proportion—up to 80 percent—of traders in West Africa are women. This fact is also true in the northern states of Nigeria. In a study of Katsina area, Hill (1969) found that Muslim-Hausa secluded women trade in agricultural produce and snacks from the confines of their compounds. The important roles played by secluded Hausa women were comparable in significance and scale to those played by the open-market women in southern Nigeria. Other studies by Olayiwole (1984) and Ngur (1988) also found that women market agricultural produce. Olayiwole (1984) observed that rural open markets are dominated by non-Muslim women. Muslim secluded women, on the other hand, operate from the confines of their compounds, using young children as their intermediaries (Simmons 1976, Olayiwole 1984, Ajala 1988).

Providing Labor

Several studies among rural women in the north show that elderly Hausa-Muslim women hire their labor for tasks such as weeding, harvesting. and processing of crops (Simmons 1976, Jackson 1978, Longhurst 1980, Norman et al. 1982, Olayiwole 1984).

In view of the foregoing, it becomes obvious that unless and until rural

Table 14-5. Distribution of Subjects (Programs) Desired Most by Respondents (%).

Subject/Program	Muslim		Non-Muslim		Total
	Zango (N = 30)	Kajuru (N = 30)	Unguwar Jaba (N = 30)	Kenye (N = 30)	
Reading and Writing	93	97	87	93	92.5[a]
Sewing and Handcrafts	60	83	70	77	72.5
Food Preparation	33	60	30	77	42.5
New Farming Techniques	7	37	47	63	38.3
Health and Sanitation	20	43	23	57	35.8
Home Management	30	50	33	30	35.8
Raising Animals	20	47	27	43	34.2
Home Improvements	30	40	23	43	34.2
Nutrition Education	17	37	23	50	31.7
Maternal and Child Care	17	37	13	23	22.5

a. An average of 92.5 percent of women in the four villages desire reading and writing programs.

Source: Olayiwole 1984: 128.

families, especially women, are organized and made aware of their ability to identify their own problems, actively participate in the design of suitable intervention measures, and successfully implement such measures themselves using their resources, Nigerians' aspirations for a better life will continue to be a mirage. True and meaningful development can be attained only when the rural populace in Nigeria's over 90,000 communities are able to acquire the necessary capabilities to do things for themselves.

Average Nigerian rural homemakers are illiterate and have very little education. But their roles, like those of women everywhere in the world, are significant both within the family and society, as the data in Tables 14-1 through 14-4 clearly show.

Women in the northern Nigerian villages studied desire education and other development programs. Data in Table 14-5 show what kinds of extension programs are desired by women in the four communities studied. Clearly, programs that teach reading and writing skills, handcrafts, food preparation, and new farming techniques are the more popular programs, although there is much intercommunity variation.

The Role of Home Economics Extension Agents in Rural Development

Home economics extension agents are trained to reach women and their families/households using the extension approach. The discipline of home economics in Nigeria, as in other African countries, is very susceptible to criticism at this time. To the casual observer it is very "Western" with not much relevance to the socioeconomic conditions of developing nations. Other critics simply see the profession as strictly and only for women; it is therefore considered to be a "cheap" academic program to undertake at college level. Home economics is an applied science, however, concerned with the development and effective use of human and material resources to meet the needs of the individual, family/household, and community for a better quality of life. It synthesizes knowledge drawn from its own research and other fields in the physical, biological, and social sciences, as well as the arts. It applies this knowledge to improving the standard of living of rural peoples.

A review of the history of education in Nigeria indicates that home economics education was introduced in the country as far back as the early 1850s. The first known teacher was Mrs. Anna Hinderer, a missionary's wife, whose daily notes showed that girls were taught sewing while boys were taught farming in addition to religious education. From 1874 up to the early 1960s, home economics was offered as a "domestic science" or "housewifery" in various educational programs. Trends over the last two decades, however, show remarkable developments and changes that reflect both new ways of thinking about women's roles in production and reproduction as well as new ways of viewing the roles of home economists themselves.

That these changes should occur in Nigeria as well as in the United States and Europe is not surprising. By its very nature, home economics is susceptible to disciplinary change because of its emphasis on the family and society, both of which are changing. Both of these components are influenced by changing cultures and material conditions of life, themselves affected by changing government policies. Therefore the discipline has now assumed an important role in the total educational system because of its relevance in meeting the needs of the ever-changing Nigerian society.

A survey of the home economics profession in Nigeria in 1985 revealed that there are over 4,000 educational institutions from primary to university level offering home economics or related programs (Olayiwole 1985). For example, the government has mandated that home economics be offered to both boys and girls in the junior secondary schools (Federal Ministry of Education 1989). Also, the two newly established universities of agriculture have home economics departments that place emphasis on meeting technical manpower needs in home economics extension and rural technology.

In most of the northern states, traditional cultural norms and practices, especially in areas of land tenure, rights to inheritance, access to extension information, and agricultural inputs, tend to favor men so much that rural women are placed in a state of perpetual childlike economic dependence vis à-vis men. This situation prevents rural women from developing their productive capabilities as potential producers. In order to address some of these serious constraints, home economics training for extension agents was established in the mid-1960s to help reach and provide rural women with development programs to improve and raise the quality of life in the rural areas. They work directly with rural women and their households to help women and girls acquire knowledge and skills necessary in improving their living standard.

The Federal Government's Agricultural Policy document (1987: 197–198) states the role of home economics as follows: there is a felt need to formulate a sound program to cater to the special requirements of rural women since they play a dual role in rural development, involving farm production and home management. The home economics program is designed to take account of this dual role. The program calls for the establishment of a Home Economics Department at the federal level and a home economics division at the state level, both in conjunction with local governments. All will be responsible for the execution of home economics projects which include:

1. agricultural extension to rural women in food production, rural health, and human nutrition.
2. home management and technological development to reduce women's drudgery in food processing and the utilization of feed products and agricultural by-products as well as provide advisory services in home and household related activities.

Several federal and state government programs such as DFRRI, Better Life for Rural Dwellers and Women, and the Agricultural Development Projects have also been developed to assist with a conscious involvement of women in the production of goods and services, decision making, and efficient management of their farms and households—all necessary for an improvement of rural life.

The Better Life Programme (BLP) which was initiated in 1987 by the first lady, Mrs. Maryam Babangida, has set in motion a chain of events that has created a high degree of awareness among women and drawn the attention of government to problems and needs of women. This led to the establishment of the Centre for Women in Development in the federal capital for the following purposes:

1. to collate and disseminate information on the activities and achievements of women;
2. to process information/data into consumable/usable form for women to improve their life;
3. to hold conferences, seminars, workshops, public lectures, and debates on policy issues which would enhance the dignity of womanhood and provide improved opportunities;
4. to provide a forum for guidance and counseling on problems peculiar to women;
5. to provide a forum for mobilizing and training women not only for leadership but also for effective utilization of opportunities offered by the system; and
6. to serve as a center for skill development for women in general and specific vocations, basic industrial skills, basic home craft skills, catering and domestic food processing, beauty science and interior decoration, etc.

Home economics extension agents represent the largest cadre of trained female extension workers within Nigeria's rural development programs. Their training is in line with requirements for development work among women. Agencies employing home economics extension agents are:

1. State Ministries of Agriculture and Natural Resources
2. State and Federal Ministries for Rural and Community Development
3. Local governments
4. State Agricultural and Rural Development Authorities
5. State Agricultural Development Projects (ADPs)
6. River Basin Development Authorities

Within the framework of agricultural development, home economics extension agents assist the agriculture extension services by teaching and helping women through improvement of living conditions for the rural family/household, the efficient use of the resources which are available to the family, and the production, storage, preservation, and utilization of foods and fiber. Projects fall under the following categories:

- Income generation through the sale of crops, breeding of animals, poultry, petty trading, production and sale of handicrafts, running small businesses, operating group savings and loans schemes.
- Skill training, making articles for home use or for sale. They make dresses, adapt, and improve traditional technology and handicrafts; they also learn agricultural techniques and vocational skills for self-employment.
- Learning new ideas in maternal/child health, nutrition, home improvement and management, leadership, responsible parenthood, and functional literacy (the latter is in conjunction with the Agency for Mass Education, Women's Units).

They also assist in explaining policies and objectives of government and other "outside" agencies to the rural women and their families so that rural households can see their role in relation to these agencies and therefore actively participate in the effort to develop a new society within their communities.

Impact of the Structural Adjustment Program (SAP)

The introduction of SAP by the Babangida administration in 1986 brought with it policies such as devaluation of the naira, withdrawal of subsidies, elimination of low interest rates, and the elimination of all food imports. The effects of these measures are runaway inflation and high prices of essential goods and services, including food. The escalating food prices would seem to suggest that food is increasingly becoming inaccessible to most Nigerians, particularly the poor, the most vulnerable members of the society. *Analyst Magazine* (May 1988) reported that people in northern parts of the country have resorted to famine foods, notably *dusa*, hitherto fed to animals. The *Nigerian Economist* found out that only workers who earn from 8,600 naira upwards could survive, while others are vulnerable to hunger. These reports tend to validate the report that a high proportion of Nigerians are undernourished because of food shortages (*World Bank Report 1988*). This is evident from the radical shift in feeding habits resulting in kwashiorkor and marasmus, diseases of malnutrition in children.

In the light of these observations, home economics extension agents were asked about the impact of SAP in their local regions. A total of 20 home economics extension officers and supervisors volunteered their opinions, presented in Table 14-6. Results show that, surprisingly, rural women are now more actively seeking the help of home economics exten-

Table 14-6. Impacts of Structural Adjustment Program on Women's Participation.

Opinion	Response	
	Number	Percentage
Women now deliberately seek assistance of the trained professionals to teach them income-generating skills, unlike in past years when agents were begging women to participate in programs.	5	25
Women are now willing to form cooperative groups for group farming and also to seek loans and other inputs only available to groups rather than to individuals.	5	25
Women are willing to try any new skill that is said to be useful for improving their farming or commercial ventures.	3	15
Women are forced to look inward for alternative sources/resources of getting their basic needs met.	1	5
Women that were formerly wholly dependent on their husbands have been forced to begin thinking and finding means of meeting personal needs.	2	10
Women cannot afford the imported goods and therefore try to make substitutes (e.g., soap, pomade) for use and income.	1	5
Very high costs of essential commodities necessary for family survival have forced women to seek new ways to meet family needs.	1	5
No opinion given.	2	10
Total	20	100

sion agents, unlike in past years when agents were begging women to participate in programs. The severity of life due to structural adjustment reforms and the cutting off of all food imports has thus forced women to begin thinking on their own and finding means of meeting personal needs, independent of their husbands. They are now willing to form cooperative groups for group farming and to seek loans to do so. They are actively looking for ways to produce substitutes for imported goods. In short, they are trying anything to survive during this economic crisis.

Conclusion

Women in Nigeria, including the northern states, have major roles in all aspects of crop and livestock production, as well as in food processing and marketing. However, the level of participation in each of these tasks varies from state to state and even from village to village. The differences are said to be due to ethnic, cultural, and religious norms.

Home economics extension agents offer nonformal development programs to rural women of all ethnic groups. Home economics extension agents are of the opinion that structural adjustment has helped *increase* women's participation in rural development. Rural women are now more actively seeking the help of home economics extension agents, unlike in past years when agents were begging women to participate in programs. The severity of life due to structural adjustment reforms and the cutting off of all food imports has thus forced women to begin thinking on their own and finding means of meeting personal needs, independent of their husbands. They are now willing to form cooperative groups for group farming and to seek loans to do so.

In consonance with the realities of Nigeria's changing society, home economics extension agents have been in the forefront promoting women's development programs. They have been involved in organizing women for income-generating activities through skills improvement programs. They have disseminated skills and appropriate technologies directed at solving some of the problems brought about by structural adjustment.

Women's groups and projects are no longer isolated ventures easily ignored by government or community members. As women increase the level of their contribution to family income, women are organizing themselves into a formidable political and social movement which is quite often outspoken on current issues and the current crisis. The main objectives of their activities are to improve the economic welfare of their families and to bring women together to share in projects that will make them strong and help them achieve self-reliance.

REFERENCES

Ajala, Margaret K.
   1988   *The Impact of Kano River Irrigation Project on the Socio-Economic Role of Women.* Master's thesis. Ahmadu Bello University, Zaria.
Barkolo, Jerome H.
   1972   *Hausa Women in Islam.* Paper presented at the Annual Meeting of the Canadian Sociology and Anthropology Association, Montreal, Canada.
Hill, Polly
   1969   Hidden Trade in Hausa Land. *Man* 4(3):392–409.
Jackson, Cecile
   1978   A Study of Rural Hausa Women: An Outline of the Methods Used and the Problems Encountered. Seminar paper, Department of Agricultural Economics and Rural Sociology, IAR/ABU, Zaria.

Longhurst, Richard W.
1980   Rural Development Planning and the Sexual Division of Labor: A Case Study of a Muslim Hausa Village in Northern Nigeria. WEPI INP/10. Geneva ILO.

Ngur, Nema
1987   Women and Development in Crop and Livestock Production in Northern Nigeria: What Changes? Paper presented at the Seminar on Women's Studies: The State of the Art Now. Women's Research Documentation, Institute of African Studies, University of Ibadan, Ibadan.

1988   Notions of Work and Independent Income Among Rural Women: A Case Study in Northern Nigeria, Association of African Women for Research and Development (AAWORD). Research project on Women and Employment in Africa: Monograph.

Norman, David W., Emmy B. Simmons, and Henry Hays
1982   *Farming Systems in Nigerian Savanna: Research and Strategies for Development.* Westview Press.

Olayiwole, Comfort B.
1980   Motivation and Mobilization of Nigerian Women for Integrated Rural Development. Proceedings of the Agricultural Extension Conference, AERLS, A.B.U. Zaria, pp. 222–238.

1984   Rural Women's Participation in Agricultural Activities: Implications for Training Extension Home Economics. Ph.D. dissertatoion, Kansas State University, Manhattan, Kansas.

1985   Home Economics Resources and Agricultural Development in Nigeria. A research report submitted to the Home Economics Association of Africa, Nairobi, Kenya.

Simmons, Emmy B.
1976   Economics Research of Women in Rural Development in Northern Nigeria. OLC Paper 12. Washington, D.C.: Overseas Liaison Committee, American Council on Education.

15 Curriculum Planning for Women and Agricultural Households: The Case of Cameroon

Suzanna Smith and Barbara Taylor

In Cameroon, as in other African countries, women are the major agricultural producers (Goheen, this volume). Cameroonian women produce an estimated 90 percent of subsistence production and comprise about 53 percent of agricultural workers (Pentang 1989). Women's agricultural production is frequently hampered, however, by lack of access to both formal and extension education and to other resources, such as improved technologies and inputs such as fertilizer and credit (Kilo 1989, Gladwin, this volume).

Recent Cameroonian government policies have recognized the fundamental roles women play in increasing food crop production and self-sufficiency and have urged that agricultural training, outreach, and development be aimed at women farmers (International Agricultural Development 1987). In response, the University Center of Dschang (UCD), Cameroon's agricultural training institution, has begun to determine how to bring into the curriculum the subject matter that will prepare graduates to work with rural women. UCD is revising its curriculum as part of the Agricultural Education Project funded by USAID and, in the process, has initiated planning for a women and agricultural households program.

Establishing a new curriculum is difficult under any circumstances,

Suzanna Smith is assistant professor of human development, Department of Home Economics, University of Florida. Her degrees are in child and family development (Ph.D.), social work (M.S.W.) and sociology (B.A.). Her research interest is gender and employment in rural areas of the southeastern U.S. and West Africa.

Barbara Taylor is a professor, program development, Home Economics Department, University of Florida. Her degrees are in home economics with a minor in sociology (Ph.D. and M.S.) and home economics education (B.S.). Her interest is in curriculum and program development in rural areas of West Africa and the U.S.
The authors are grateful to Camilla Harshberger for assistance and funds from the Program Support Grant and the Cameroon Agriculture Education Project, funded by USAID.

and in this case there were few, if any, guidelines or models. From the outset, UCD administration considered establishing a home economics program, because this has traditionally been the area in which women's household work has been addressed. Training in food-related sciences, which was of particular interest to UCD, is frequently provided under the home economics rubric. In 1986 UCD invited the University of Florida to conduct a needs analysis with UCD faculty and government representatives to determine interest in establishing a program, and priority areas of training that would prepare graduates to work with rural women. In this way UCD administration began to assess whether specified needs could be addressed within the agricultural curriculum. In brief, findings from the needs analysis indicated support for a program and the need for training in the following areas: food production, preservation and storage, nutrition and food preparation, family health and hygiene, child development, marketing and resource management, and women's roles in agricultural production. In addition, the findings indicated that a program at UCD that combined an empirical base with practical and field experiences was considered highly desirable.

The scope of training needs identified by the needs analysis spanned home economics and agriculture, incorporating aspects of both household and agricultural production. Consequently, when UCD requested assistance from the University of Florida (UF) in developing a curriculum, we recommended a general term for a program be used, a "working title" that could span disciplines—"Women and Agricultural Households." We also suggested that the shape of the program be determined as an outcome of training in curriculum planning. In 1989, we offered a shortcourse on curriculum planning with an emphasis on Women and Agricultural Households at UCD. Our primary goal was to provide participants with the knowledge and skills that would enable *them* to design and implement a women and agricultural households program. As a result of the course, participants developed and delivered to UCD administration a set of recommendations regarding the type of program needed and preliminary steps in program planning. We discuss the shortcourse in detail in the following sections, including conceptual foundations, format, content, and outcomes.

Overview of Shortcourse

Effective curriculum considerations begin with establishing communication channels within and outside the institution (Doll 1986), including potential employers who need competent graduates. A crucial aspect of the Cameroonian shortcourse was the participation of representatives of ministries and other organizations, who provided current information about the needs of women farmers and the skills of field staff and program administrators. The shortcourse bridged two areas of study, women and agricultural households and curriculum planning. Our goals regarding women and agricultural households were to introduce fundamental concepts, provide current information and a common knowledge base, and demonstrate the importance of women to agricultural production. We based much of this material on the work of Overholt, Anderson, Cloud, and Austin (1985) and Cloud (1985). Their frameworks for household activity analysis and resource allocation helped us to more effectively synthesize and organize our concepts on gender division of labor in Cameroon.

We designed the course to take participants through the steps of a curriculum planning model to apply concepts and skills to the development of a women and agricultural households program. We were particularly interested in presenting a learner-centered rather than a knowledge-centered curriculum development model because this seemed most appropriate to UCD's interests. First, UCD graduates needed technical skills, and programs built on learner-centered models are usually defined on the basis of competencies rather than subject matter area. In addition, the research literature indicates that women's activities and needs include animal production, horticulture, and agriculture, and take place in social contexts in which rural economics, sociology, community development, and extension education impact on efforts to improve productivity. Learner-centered models are also suited to the development of multidisciplinary educational programs, which we anticipated would be the case for a women and agricultural households program. The shortcourse was structured around Hunkins' (1980) five-step curriculum planning model, which focuses on the needs and interests of learners and has been found to be useful in creating new programs and improving curricula of existing programs at educational institutions. The model was modified for our purposes and is presented in Figure 15-1.

The shortcourse took participants through the steps of the curriculum planning model. The first two modules provided participants with conceptual and practical tools for analyzing women's roles in agricultural production; five other modules were based on the components of curriculum development (Hunkins 1980, Doll 1986). Through this process, participants developed the essential components of a curriculum proposal, including needs analysis, mission and goals statements, objectives statements, analysis of curriculum content, and implementation. Written information was provided in a participant training manual or sourcebook

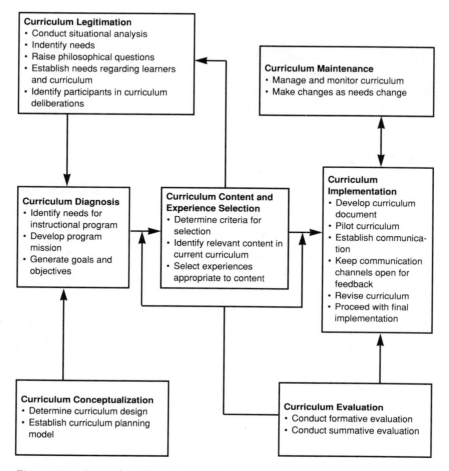

Figure 15-1. Curriculum Planning Model.

that presented background information, handouts, and exercises for each segment of the course.

The workshop required a high level of group participation so participants could practice skills and emerge with a final set of program recommendations for UCD administration. Work groups of five to seven faculty and ministry and organization representatives completed exercises for each step of the curriculum planning process and each small group presented their results to the large group for further discussion and clarification. Throughout the workshop each "product" was based on the outcomes of the previous group exercise. The following is a detailed description of each segment of training.

Figure 15-2. African faculty themselves developed the curriculum proposal, including needs analysis, mission and goals statements, objectives statements, analysis of curriculum content, and implementation.

Shortcourse Format

Needs Analysis of Women and Agricultural Households

The first three days of the course were devoted to an analysis of women's needs in Cameroon. Speakers from government made formal presentations that discussed their unit's activities and progress in addressing the needs of women and agricultural households. In small work groups, participants continued to identify needs. A nominal group technique was used to maximize the opportunity for participants from the various ministries and organizations to contribute valuable observations from their field. Groups considered needs at two levels: (a) women's needs and (b) ministry or organizational needs for personnel to work in programs for women. Participants identified seven broad areas of women's needs, as presented in Table 15-1.

After the large group agreed on these needs, facilitators began to provide conceptual information and analytic tools to organize thinking about women and agricultural households and curriculum planning. We used a modified activity analysis framework (Table 15-2) to expand participants' notion of production to include farm and household tasks and informal

Table 15-1. Needs of Women and Personnel Needs

Women's Needs	Personnel Needs
1. Health and welfare: nutrition, primary health care sanitation, child care, family planning.	Educators in family health, nutrition, hygiene, and sanitation; child care advisors and supervisors.
2. Income-generating resources: land, credit.	Coordinators and managers of women's cooperatives.
3. Agricultural technologies: inputs to improve production, methods for food processing, conservation and storage, livestock production.	Subject matter specialists in agriculture and food technology; trained technicians.
4. Household technologies: labor-saving technologies that improve access to water and electricity	Technicians trained in labor-saving technologies.*
5. Marketing skills: marketing for food crop products, household productions and services, business management.	Subject matter specialists and trained technicians in post-harvest practices, marketing, and business management.*
6. Adult education.	Teachers for secondary schools and specialized training centers; literacy instructors and supervisors.
7. Control and influence in household decision-making.	

*Added by authors.

and wage-labor employment, and to provide a strong visual representation of women's responsibilities relative to other household members. The framework visually represented differences between men and women in production priorities and access to resources, and the impact of resources on individual and household decision-making. Using case studies, participants applied the concepts to actual situations in developing countries. With this conceptual and experiential foundation in place, we began the actual curriculum planning process.

Program Mission and Goals

Participants developed mission statements for a women and agricultural households program, emphasizing a long-term vision of what the program is or is striving to become. At the core of the mission statements was an emphasis on providing, through research, extension, and resident instruction, the information and personnel that would enable women to participate in rural development.

Participants then developed more specific goal statements that pro-

Table 15-2: Example of a Completed Household Activity Analysis.

Type of Production	Gender/Age					
	Female Adult	Male Adult	Female Child	Male Child	Female Elder	Male Elder
Agricultural						
Food Crops	X					
Cash Crops	X	X				
Livestock	X	X				
Household						
Food Preparation	X		X		X	
Housekeeping	X		X		X	
Water	X		X			
Fuel	X		X	X		
Forage	X		X	X		
Ceremonies	X	X			X	X
Construction		X				
Human Capital						
Childbearing	X					
Childcare	X					
Informal Marketing	X					
Wage Labor		X		X		

Source: Cloud (1985:48).

vided an overall direction for a program and expected outcomes or measures of intended program accomplishments. In keeping with the mission statements, goal statements emphasized UCD's role in instruction, research, extension, and continuing education. Mission and goals statements are presented in Table 15-3, with statements somewhat condensed for brevity and clarity.

Objectives and Curriculum Content

How can these very general goals be realized in the program? We hoped to specify objectives of the program and even the course content or curriculum. To do this, facilitators synthesized five major program areas from small group work and large group discussions: agricultural and livestock production; "problems" of women and agricultural households; health, education, and environment; women's income; and community and gov-

Table 15-3. Mission and Goals Statements.

Mission Statements	Goal Statements
Address women's needs by generating knowledge, disseminating information, and training personnel to help women contribute to the developmental process, and to improve the general well-being of the population.	Provide teaching programs to ensure a supply of competent trainers, teachers, field workers, and advisors. Provide continuing education programs to improve understanding and integrate knowledge about women and agricultural households into existing programs.
Study and access the rural environment, and transmit knowledge to ensure a better standard of living in the rural areas and to more fully integrate women into rural development.	Through research, broaden the knowledge base for addressing current problems of women and agricultural households. Improve rural agricultural productivity and family welfare through adapted extension services.

ernment organizations. Participants proceeded to pinpoint program objectives for desired student outcomes. They determined what students would need to know to address the needs of women and agricultural households on the job in their future employment. Participants then identified the course content UCD should offer in order for students to meet these program objectives (Table 15-4). Participants also emphasized the importance of providing training in practical skills such as communication techniques and field research.

Implementation and Evaluation

Actual implementation of a curriculum takes place within the context of available resources. Participants evaluated available resources, including personnel, space, and specialized needs such as laboratories and equipment, as well as existing limitations. In the final plan, they recommended a sequential planning process that would enable UCD to build on existing resources while developing a more expansive program.

Respondents strongly supported providing some type of educational program in the area of women and agricultural households. The group

Table 15-4. Recommended Program Areas, Objectives, and Course Content.

Program Area and Objectives	Course Content
Agriculture and Livestock Production	
Improve agricultural production including food crop production and livestock production	Soil chemistry Climatology Fertilization Plant protection Seeds Forestry Animal production techniques Farm management Conservation, processing, and storage of food crops
Through extension programs, introduce to households new research-based ideas and appropriate technologies while strictly respecting societal norms and values	Appropriate technology for food crop production
Problems of Women and Agricultural Households	
Identify needs and problems of women and agricultural households	Land tenure Education Agricultural credit
Propose research topics that have application to household sociocultural and economic problems	Responsibilities of women in agricultural households Integrated approach to solving women's problems
Generate interest in women's issues among potential students, the public, and other rural organizations	Instructional techniques for adults
Health, Education, and Environment	
Raise family living standards through health education, functional literacy, and home management skills	Family health and hygiene Sanitation Primary health care Maternal and child care
Improve nutritional health status of women and their families	Basic nutrition Understanding and solving nutritional problems
Improve the woman's environment	Environmental studies
Increase household management skills	Household management and economics
Develop courses and teaching aids that reflect women's needs	Family structure, economics, and cultural influences
Improve access to adult education	

(continued)

Table 15-4 (*continued*).

Income	
Promote socioeconomic changes enhancing rural productivity and family welfare	Marketing, exposition, and sales
Identify nonagricultural problems and seek assistance	Small business management
Raise rural women's income by helping them diversify their activities and organize marketing of their products	Income-generating potential for women (i.e., indigenous handicrafts and art, apparel production in home, child care, processed foods)
With government support, assist rural families in identifying their problems and resources for improving progress in development	Women's cooperatives

Leadership and Policy	
Develop women's management capcities and leadership potential (increase capcity in decision-making)	Study and analysis of women's status in rural communities Leadership and decision-making skills
Identify the structural imbalances which compound and perpetuate women's disadvantages at the family, community, and national level	Rural environment and societies Demography Survey techniques in rural areas Data collection and analysis Group dynamics Communication patterns
Evaluate the impact of agricultural policies	Study of institutions working in rural areas Legislation and agricultural households Community development Project analysis

recommended that UCD strengthen existing courses and add new courses aimed at meeting the specific needs discussed in the workshop. The group also recommended that this approach be carefully evaluated to determine its effectiveness and the subsequent need for a more concentrated program, such as a full-blown department.

Participants also felt they had developed the skills to launch a pilot program. Virtually all (100 percent) respondents to the overall evaluation (n = 22) said the curriculum planning model had been useful in planning how to address women and agricultural households at UCD. Over three-fourths (77 percent) felt that they personally could develop a curriculum development plan. Those who expressed uncertainty indicated a need for

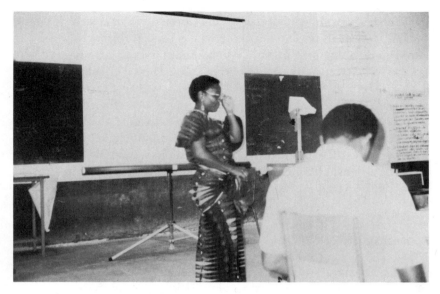

Figure 15-3. Participants used a household activity analysis framework (Table 15-2) to understand farm and household tasks of men, women, and children.

Figure 15-4. Participants then identified the course content UCD should offer in order for students to meet the women and agricultural households program's objectives.

greater collaboration with others already working in this area, or for more indepth information about social sciences or more knowledge of the women in development literature. In addition, the vast majority (92 percent to 100 percent) found that training on specific curriculum planning skills was helpful. All respondents (100 percent) believed women's work is important to Cameroon's food production and self-sufficiency. Over 80 percent felt their knowledge had increased regarding the "household" concept, men's and women's work in farm and household activities, and resources that affect productivity. Unfortunately, we did not collect baseline data so we do not know if there was a change in attitudes as a consequence of being exposed to the training.

Conclusion

When we began to work with faculty at UCD, we were struck by the lack of available models for institutions in developing countries that seek to establish programs to prepare graduates to work with rural women. Our previous needs analysis, knowledge of the literature, and personal experience suggested that one model, either a traditional home economics program or a traditional agriculture program, was not the most appropriate. We chose curriculum planning with an emphasis on women and agricultural households so that UCD faculty themselves could analyze and select the most effective approach for their needs and resources. We also wanted to provide information about the importance of women to agricultural production as well as household functioning and the planning skills to guide the direction and development of such a program.

Several themes emerged from discussions and observations that have implications not only for the University Center of Dschang but also for other institutions developing a women in agriculture program.

Although participants recommended that eventually a concentration or even a department be considered, they concluded that a full-blown program was impractical until specific needs were determined. In their official recommendations, participants urged UCD to strengthen existing courses that already include content on rural women and to add material to other courses. In part this direction was chosen because of resource limitations, such as heavy faculty course load, in part because the process of getting new courses approved at the national level is a lengthy one. Results of evaluations suggest that faculty fully support both integration of material and addition of new courses: 95 percent of respondents favored including content in existing courses and 88 percent favored developing new courses.

Participants emphasized the need for a research-based teaching program to provide graduates with a solid academic background in subject matter areas. In addition, participants urged UCD to provide opportunities for field experiences and activities that train graduates in practical skills and effective outreach. These approaches require designing courses that provide conceptual frameworks and analytic tools for use in the field, and supervised field experiences to help students apply theoretical and research-based knowledge, as well as practical skills. While generic technical skills are needed, there also appears to be a need to expose students to the literature on women in development, which is lengthy even if confined to Cameroon.

Participants identified program content in many disciplines (agricultural and livestock production; health, education and nutrition; community and government organizations; women's socioeconomic and political problems), which suggests that a future program should be multidisciplinary. Such a program would require a conceptual perspective to bridge both social and technical aspects of agriculture. It would also require social and agricultural scientists to loosen their disciplinary ties to provide multidisciplinary education and field experiences.

At an even more fundamental level, however, these issues raise questions about women's roles and training in agricultural institutions. At present outreach efforts have difficulty reaching rural women in Cameroon, not only because graduates have not been trained specifically to target women's needs, but because *women* have not been trained. The university is currently exploring ways to attract qualified female applicants and provide the necessary academic and field experiences.

Unfortunately, home economics programs have tended to concentrate women in a subject matter that limits their knowledge of agriculture. This division between agriculture and home economics also limits agricultural students' knowledge of the integration of household and agricultural production. The integrated and multidisciplinary approaches discussed above may enable UCD to avoid some of these problems.

In summary, although institutionalization of a new program takes time, we found the shortcourse format an effective vehicle for initiating the first steps in curriculum planning for the women and agricultural households program at UCD. We think this approach would be effective at other agricultural institutions that are developing women in agricultural development programs.

REFERENCES

Cloud, Kathleen
 1985   Women's Productivity in Agricultural Systems: Considerations for
         Project Design. *Gender Roles in Development Projects,* C. Overholt,
         M. B. Anderson, K. Cloud, and J. E. Austin, eds., pp. 17–56. West
         Hartford: Kumarian Press.

Doll, Ronald C.
 1986   *Curriculum Improvement: Decision Making and Process* (3d ed.).
         Newton, MA: Allyn and Bacon.

Hunkins, Francis P.
 1980   *Curriculum Development: Program Improvement.* Columbus: Charles
         E. Merrill Publishing Company.

International Agricultural Development
 1987   The Successful Face of African Agriculture. *International Agricul-
         tural Development* 7(2): 7–8.

Kilo, Regina
 1989   Problems and Potentials for Rural Women in Cameroon. Paper pre-
         sented at the shortcourse on Curriculum Planning with an Empha-
         sis on Women and Agricultural Households, University Center of
         Dschang, Dschang, Cameroon, July 10–15.

Overholt, Catherine, Mary Anderson, Kathleen Cloud, and James Austin
 1985   *Gender Roles in Development Projects.* Boulder: Westview Press.

Pentang, Rosalie
 1989   Problemes et Potentials de la Femme Rurale au Cameroon. Paper
         presented at the shortcourse on Curriculum Planning with an Em-
         phasis on Women and Agricultural Households, University Center
         of Dschang, Dschang, Cameroon, July 10–15.

16

Women Farmers, Structural Adjustment, and FAO's Plan of Action for Integration of Women in Development

Anita Spring and Vicki Wilde

Many of the same problems, barriers, and needs of rural women that have been documented over the past twenty years are receiving new attention with the focus on structural adjustment and the larger macroeconomic influences. These include women's lack of land rights, inadequate access to credit, productive inputs and extension training, as well as the heavy burdens placed on them to meet the productive and reproductive needs of their households.

What is new is the recognition of a slowdown or even reversal in women's economic and social progress that was made during the 1950s to the 1970s, in which the economies of many developing countries grew at an annual rate of almost 2 percent per capita. Social progress was even greater than economic progress—life expectancy increased, infant mortality rates fell, and school enrollment rates increased at every level. Women participated in this progress, despite inequality in employment, income, education, and basic services. However, economic growth began to slow down in the late 1970s and early 1980s. A number of developing countries experienced a rapid accumulation of debts and slid into recession. With the economic crisis that followed, women's incremental steps for-

Anita Spring is chief of the Women in Agricultural Production and Rural Development Service of the Food and Agriculture Organization (FAO), where she oversees programmatic efforts on women. She formerly directed the Women in Agricultural Development Program at the University of Florida and has a Ph.D. from Cornell University. She is the coeditor of *Women Creating Wealth: Transforming Economic Development.*

Vicki Wilde is a consultant for the Women in Agricultural Production and Rural Development Service at FAO, where she coordinates the WID training program for FAO staff. She is completing a Ph.D. at City University of New York.

Valuable comments on this chapter were provided by the heads of various technical units of FAO, including E. Morris-Hughes, H. Hjort, T. Aldington, and C. Morojele. The views expressed by the authors are theirs alone and do not reflect those of the Food and Agriculture Organization of the United Nations.

ward have been severely hindered. Cuts and deteriorations in the public and social sectors have been felt by all but the wealthy, but most particularly by women (Commonwealth Secretariat 1989).

These issues are particularly apparent in Africa where women farmers are estimated to contribute up to 80 percent of agricultural labor, mainly as unpaid family labor, to produce approximately 60 percent of the food that is consumed by rural households, and to generate a third or more of all household income, predominantly through small scale agro-industry, trading, craft work, and casual labor (FAO 1984).

In this chapter, conclusions with respect to the impacts of structural adjustment policies on women's agricultural work and their access to resources and inputs based on the research studies and the lessons learned from field projects are briefly reviewed. Second, an outline of some of the structural adjustment-related activities of FAO is presented. While FAO has a diversified portfolio with respect to adjustment, this paper focuses on those activities that are related to women in agriculture. Finally, a review of FAO's Plan of Action for Integration of Women in Development and the plan's relevance to structural adjustment impacts on rural women are discussed.

Shifts in Agricultural Production

A major implication of structural adjustment for agriculture is the provision of incentives for the increased production of certain crops. Shifts in agricultural production to export crops or tradeables are encouraged through currency devaluation, input subsidies aimed at creating price incentives, the easing of credit restrictions, the application of differential tax rates for the agriculture sector, and the reduction or dismantling of agricultural marketing boards (Griggs 1989). These incentive policies create changes in the demand for labor, resource allocations, land values, and farm management strategies, all of which strongly impact on income distribution and food production (Joekes 1988). For at least two reasons, policies that encourage export crop production can have enormous impact on women farmers. First, women encounter discrimination outside the household at many levels including differential access to wage employment and, perhaps more importantly, differential access to credit. Second, within the household, women live with asymmetric obligations. They work considerably longer hours than men and are obliged to grow, process, and prepare food; gather fuel and water; and rear and educate children. Consequently, women's labor tends to be concentrated in activities that are internationally "nontradeable" and that provide relatively low incomes. If women are less able to transfer their resources to the tradeable activites that expand during adjustment, they become economically handicapped.

Because women's agricultural work is focused on "self-provisioning" for the household, policies that encourage cash crop production subsequently raise the issue of competition for household level resources between tradeables and domestic crops, often called nontradeables (Palmer 1988). Cash crops can further catalyze gender differentiation since those who can adopt export crops are often already better endowed with productive resources.

Land Issues

The fact that adjustment policies put emphasis on the production of tradeable crops has important implications in terms of women's access to land. The greater emphasis on export crops, and the subsequent increase in competition for land and increase in land values, may result in marginalizing women farmers. Since the allocation of land held under usufruct rights is controlled by senior males in the lineage, it is likely that adjustment-induced shifts into more profitable crops will result in men taking over land previously cultivated by women or with women having access to less productive, more distant plots (Goheen, this volume). This phenomenon was observed following the introduction of irrigation in Gambia that made land more valuable (Dey 1984). Palmer notes that when women's access to land worsens and labor becomes too asymmetrical in the household, women are more likely to seek wage employment rather than to keep on working for their husbands full time (Palmer 1988). She notes:

> Any shift towards greater asymmetry in women's and men's access to land can only contribute to greater asymmetry of obligations and reciprocities because of the inherent decline in women's bargaining position. The terms of labor trade will move further against women and, with that, there will be further misallocation of women's labor time. The terminal situation of total subordination of the family

labor force to one spouse's production management means that there is no way of valuing labor against opportunity costs within the household ... If the land situation vis-a-vis women worsens, more and more women are likely to seek wage employment. There is evidence from the WID literature that women are already doing this rather than work for their husbands full time (Palmer 1988:9).

Access to Agricultural Inputs

By far the largest part of women's economic activities is financed by informal savings and credit services. However, such services are hardly present in some areas and others have limited development potential (Jiggins 1989; Gladwin, this volume). Clark and Manah (this volume) note that in the informal sector women must compete with men who, because of structural adjustment reductions to credit programs, can no longer get formal sector loans. Women's lack of firm land title restricts their access to formal credit and banking services, thus restricting opportunities for increasing assets. Social biases constrain them from attending extension and training courses, operating mechanized farm equipment, and dealing with input supply and marketing personnel. Female-headed households are particularly disadvantaged in this respect. However, the complete or partial withdrawal of the public sector from these services as part of many structural adjustment packages, will increase privatization and may afford greater access of women to these services, unless constrained by a social tradition of male dominance in commercial activities (Development Assistance Committee 1988).

Agricultural Modernization

Given women's initial inferior position with respect to access to agricultural inputs and equipment, agricultural innovations will have different effects on men and women (Agarwal 1984). The underlying sexual division of labor conditions whether mechanization increases or decreases the workload of men or women, or both, or results in the displacement of either from their economic activities. For example, the introduction of draft animals and tractors lessen male, but increases female, labor because larger areas can be cultivated. Mechanization of post-harvest processes, on the other hand, may lead to substantial displacements of women (Scott and Carr 1985) or will enable men to take over occupations previously dominated by women. In Nigeria, men took over mechanized cassava processing and thus gained in terms of income, while women were constrained from adopting the new technology by their lack of credit, extension services, transportation, and storage facilities (Adekanye 1984).

Innovations in African smallholder agriculture are mostly in the form of high-yielding varieties (HYVs) and irrigation, while the labor changes are met predominantly by the family (Griggs 1989). The use of HYVs, for example, requires more agricultural labor and therefore can increase the workload of women. Where the new varieties generate increases in income, particularly on large farms, men may withdraw female labor and thus undermine women's relative economic status (Griggs 1989). Women need fair access to the innovations designed to increase agricultural production for export as well as access to innovations/appropriate technologies designed to reduce the time- and energy-consuming daily tasks, particularly with respect to food, water, and energy. Clearly, women can benefit from innovations, but only if given equitable access to the appropriate resources.

Employment

Structural adjustment may create increased employment opportunities for women by stimulating the production of certain types of agriculture and food processing industries and by expanding the service sector, the latter two usually in urban or peri-urban areas. By favoring exports and efficient import substitution, structural adjustment policies could provide the opportunity for rural women to engage in small-scale nonfarm production, processing, and marketing in the informal and rural industrial sectors. The extent to which women can take advantage of such opportunities will depend on their access to household capital resources and to credit markets.

Similarly, adjustment policies may play a role in expanding the service sectors with a consequent increase in employment opportunities for women. However, the severe contraction of the domestic economy in many cases means that job insecurity is high; layoffs of workers are common; wages, fringe benefits, and promotion may be cut back severely; and, in general, the legal obligations of employers towards their workers are not enforced (FAO 1985).

Heightened unemployment and downward pressure on wages for men may mean that the burden of supporting the household falls increasingly on women, and that women have to increase their work in the informal sector, where wages and work conditions are far below those of the formal, government-regulated sector. Consequently, women's cash incomes may become more essential, especially in cases of male unemployment, but they may also become inadequate to meet the basic needs of the household (Mies, Lalita, and Krishina 1986). Elson (1989:69) notes:

> The market appears to treat women as individuals in their own right. If women can sell their labor or their products and get a cash income of their own, this lessens their economic dependence upon men, increases their economic value, and may increase their bargaining power within the household. Access to an income of their own tends to be highly valued by women, not only for what it buys, but also for the greater dignity it brings. However, so long as women carry the double burden of unpaid work in the reproduction and maintenance of human resources, as well as paid work producing goods and services, they will be unable to compete with men in the market on equal terms.

Health, Nutrition, and Education

Many argue that, with the increased production of export crops, women continue to grow food for their families, often from increasingly marginal land, while their labor also is drafted to work on the tradeable crops. Consequently, they have less time for self-provisioning activities and compensate by working longer hours, enlisting their children's assistance, and changing to less nutritious foods that are easier to cultivate and prepare. Further, any structural adjustment-related reductions in public expenditure on health, education, and rural infrastructure will affect women's reproductive activities, including their time and energy available for food production. Women's workload and family nutrition are also affected by the loss of male labor caused by out-migration, and the introduction of intensified technologies that often give women more tasks to perform (Holmboe-Ottesen, Mascarenhas, and Wandel 1989). Another factor is that emphasizing export crop production as a policy may raise the price of purchased food on the market. Consequently, food that is purchased may become less affordable and less nutritious foods may be substituted. A related phenomenon is that as the incomes of the households that are export crop producers rise the demand for purchased food may also increase at the same time that resources are being drawn away from food production. Such trends may create a gap between the demand and the availability of affordable, nutritious foods. The balance will depend on the individual setting.

Women are most affected by reductions in education, social services, and infrastructure such as water supply. In some places, girls have been withdrawn from school to help or even to replace their working mothers in the home. A recent United Nations study of 17 countries, including 5 in Africa, found that since 1980 there has been a slowdown in the improvement of the enrollment of girls in schools compared to boys, the deterioration being more evident in primary and middle-level schools (UNCsDHA 1989; Due, this volume). Female students in secondary schools have been largely unaffected, reflecting the fact that girls who reach that level of education generally come from better-off households. Current advice on structural adjustment programs is that funds for education be reallocated in favor of primary and secondary education.

Impacts of Structural Adjustment on Women

Empirically, the impact of structural adjustment policies on women are difficult to separate from the effects of both economic crises in general and of the sociocultural constraints traditionally faced by them. Indeed, any direct causal links between structural adjustment programs and a modification in the situation of women requires care. Gender disaggregated data are particularly scarce with respect to the impacts of structural adjustment on women. Nevertheless, two recommendations can be drawn from the points above.

First, any structural adjustment-stimulated impacts or changes that further hinder women's already difficult/inequitable position in agricultural production should be delineated to inform the design and implementation of proper mitigation or intervention packages. Second, understanding any changes in gender relationships concerning labor and remuneration as a result of shifts in agriculture is necessary to strengthen women's capacities to participate in the new productive opportunities brought about by structural adjustment. There is no automatic link between economic growth and improvement in women's situation. Targeted legislation, programs, and actions are necessary to induce a change in their social and economic position.

These recommendations prompt an examination in terms of what FAO is doing about structural adjustment programs in general and about their impact on women in particular. In order to address this issue, it is first necessary to review some of FAO's structural adjustment activities and then to focus specifically on women farmers and related programs. Finally, FAO's Plan of Action for Integration of Women in Development and its potential to mitigate the adverse effects of structural adjustment on women are described.

Some Structural Adjustment Activities of FAO

The Food and Agriculture Organization (FAO) has a long history of assisting member governments to improve agricultural and food production, nutrition, and the living conditions of rural people. Its mandate and the consequent scope of its activities are supported by policy advice, field projects, statistical analysis, and research studies. Many of FAO's country-level activities in agriculture, forestry, and fishery sectors can be seen, in one way or another, as related to or influenced by adjustment policies. FAO's direct approaches to the issue of structural adjustment include collaborations with other international agencies, advice and assistance to member governments, and research studies; increasingly field projects are being designed to mitigate or enhance the effects of structural adjustment. FAO's work on structural adjustment began with a number of studies in 1984, and in 1987 it joined the multi agency Social Dimensions of Adjustment Project (SDA) for studying the social impacts of adjustment in Africa.

Collaboration with Multilateral and Bilateral Agencies

The complexity of structural adjustment programs and their implications across sectors in the economy raise issues of consultation and coordination among multilateral and bilateral agencies involved in the process of adjustment either as funding or as technical assistance partners. Correspondingly, FAO has stressed the need for greater collaboration between the World Bank, the International Monetary Fund, and other UN agencies in the context of structural adjustment. This issue is of high priority, not only because of the responsibilities of each agency according to its mandates, but also because no single institution is the sole repository of knowledge and experience in matters of policy reforms.

As noted above, FAO is a member of the Steering Committee for the World Bank-led Social Dimensions of Adjustment (SDA) Project in Africa that aims to assess the social impacts of structural adjustment, particularly on the poor and vulnerable sections of the population, and to formulate measures to offset or mitigate the adverse effects. Thirty-two countries in Africa have currently ongoing adjustment programs; 27 of them are included in the SDA Project that pursues country-level support (1) to assist with long-term documentation and monitoring of the dynamics of structural adjustment; (2) to assist with the development of short-term social action programs designed to compensate for the short-term negative effects of adjustment; and (3) to secure core funding for social sector and public sector programs within the macroeconomic loan processes.

To strengthen the capacity of participating countries to conduct empirical and policy-oriented investigations into the social dimensions of adjustment, the SDA Project has formulated "analysis plans" on poverty, labor and employment, smallholders, health, education, food security and nutrition, and the role of women. The analysis plans are designed as operational tools to help governments identify and address these issues. Further, the analysis plans are written to guide participating countries in the development of prototype household surveys. FAO provided comments to the project on the analysis plans on food security and nutrition, and on women.

A second collaboration is FAO's participation in the Informal Group of Multilateral Agency Representatives on the Impact of Economic Adjustment on Food Security and Nutrition in Developing Countries, established at the initiative of the World Food Council in collaboration with UNICEF and ILO in May 1987. The initial and continuing value of the group is the forum it provides the agencies for informational exchange with respect to structural adjustment, primarily through technical and country studies. A useful output of the group is its development of a list of qualified consultants who can provide expertise on economic adjustment, including food security and nutrition-related issues. Another purpose is to provide technical advice to countries applying for structural adjustment loans. Support for Togo, for example, is planned for 1990.

Third, the UN Administrative Committee on Co-ordination (ACC) Task Force on Rural Development, chaired by FAO, has prepared methodological guidelines for countries to use in monitoring the impacts of macro-level economic policies on the rural poor. The first phase concluded with the UNDP publication, "The Impact of Macroeconomic Policies on the Rural Poor: Analytical Framework and Indicators" (Azam et al. 1989). The second phase, now underway, is designed to test and refine the methodologies developed with case studies in Niger, Jamaica, and two other African countries.

Advice and Assistance to Member Governments

FAO works with other multilateral and bilateral organizations to support governments requesting assistance in their structural adjustment efforts, especially in reforming their food and agricultural sectors. Early in 1990, FAO had 66 ongoing country policy projects that were directly or indirectly linked to the structural adjustment process. Of particular importance were projects in eight countries: Mali, Guinea, Comoros, Ghana, Nicaragua, Senegal, Nigeria, and Jordan. A regional planning program in policy analysis and planning also has been proposed by FAO for sub-Saharan Africa.

Subject to requests from member governments, FAO provides advice and technical assistance on food security, nutrition, environment, rural development, women in development, agriculture, forestry, and fishery. With respect to each of these topics, FAO is developing its capacity to offer assistance with appropriate policies and programs to accompany structural adjustment programs; with designing compensatory measures where necessary; with training national policy analysts; and with executing and backstopping field projects to monitor and assess the impacts of adjustment. Specific FAO field projects that focus on fertilizers, irrigation, or fish drying techniques, for example, could serve as vehicles to help mitigate the negative impacts of macro-level adjustment policies at the local or household levels.

Research Studies

Since 1984, FAO has prepared or initiated about 30 studies on the impact of structural adjustment on food production, food security, household welfare, smallholders, land tenure, women, and other agricultural issues (FAO 1985;1987a; 1987b; 1989a; 1989b). Upcoming is a special chapter on agriculture and structural adjustment currently being prepared for FAO's annual publication, "The State of Food and Agriculture 1990." The question of gender is seen as one of the key policy issues, and is discussed thematically throughout the chapter. One underlying premise is that structural adjustment programs are not gender-neutral in their operation and effects. The imposition of additional burdens or costs on women in terms of jeopardizing their nutritional status, health, and education must be avoided. Therefore, incentives and investment specifically for women farmers must be provided to enhance agricultural performance, particularly in the food sector, vital for structural adjustment efforts.

Focusing specifically on women farmers and structural adjustment,

FAO has prepared three reviews which support the argument that structural adjustment programs have different impacts depending on economic class and gender. The first considers the impact of structural adjustment on rural women with reference to four solutions for raising primary incomes through the adjustment process (FAO 1989). These can be summarized as: (1) increasing access to productive assets such as land, irrigation, and production inputs; (2) increasing the rates of return on assets held by the poor by dismantling inefficient marketing boards and eliminating market distortions, raising output prices, or lowering input prices; (3) increasing access of the poor to employment through improvements in the operation of the labor market; and (4) protecting the human capital of the poor by guaranteeing their access to health and education services through a restructuring of public sector resource allocation (Addison and Demery 1987).

An FAO study on food security notes a number of structural adjustment-related social impacts and concludes that the majority of impacts documented to date are *negative* for women. As the main providers of household food security, especially among lower socioeconomic classes, women have been more seriously affected than men by such policies as elimination of government subsidies, cuts in social services, rises in consumer prices, higher priced imports, the reduction of public sector employment opportunities, and the freezing of wages and salaries. A major policy concern is that reduced food subsidies, reduced income opportunities, and cutbacks in health and environmental services may be related to lowering the food intake and thus the nutritional status of the poor (FAO 1990b).

Finally, a third study investigates the interconnection between structural adjustment policy at the macro level and women's ability to manage family resources for the achievement of food security and nutrition at the household level (Elson 1990a). The paper concludes there is enough evidence now to be reasonably confident that adjustment policies increase the demands on the time for *all* women except those in high-income households. Among the most crucial factors are rises in the price of food and nonfood crops as well as agricultural inputs such as fertilizer and credit; reductions in infrastructure expenditure and public sector employment opportunities; increases in employment opportunities in export-oriented activities; and falling wages in the informal sector. The key policy issues are targeting more resources to women so as to increase their entitlements and improve their abilities to acquire food while reducing the degree of risk that they face in provisioning their families (Elson 1990a).

Field Projects

FAO executes about 2,500 projects in all agricultural sectors around the world at any one time. The Women in Agricultural Production and Rural Development Service is the organization's principal unit addressing women's issues and acts as the coordinating unit for the promotion of the integration of women in the activities of all FAO technical units. FAO takes a two-pronged approach to projects on women in development (WID); there are those that are exclusively for women (about 40 of FAO's 2,500 projects) and those that promote the integration of WID issues into the mainstream (about 28 percent of FAO projects). The integration of WID issues into mainstream activities is to be given primacy under the new Plan of Action for the Integration of Women.

In 1989, FAO was directly involved in about 50 field projects (both women-specific and mainstream) and a number of project task force meetings concerned with rural women in Africa. The projects address various aspects of women's needs and roles such as training, appropriate technology, promotion of women's groups and associations, vegetable production, agricultural extension, credit, and mechanization. They either strengthen the capacities of women farmers and their families to participate in the new economic opportunities stimulated by structural adjustment, or they mitigate some of the negative effects brought about by structural adjustment-induced deteriorations in social and public services. Examples include:

1. *Ghana:* "Promoting Population Education Communication and Income Generating Capacity in the 31st December Women's Movement." The project provides support to the national women's machinery to provide inputs, training in food production, and population education to rural women.

2. *Kenya:* "Support to Small, Low-Income Women Producers in Arid and Semi-Arid Lands" aims to increase the country's food self-sufficiency and improve employment levels in rural areas by securing the access of vulnerable groups to food and jobs through the establishment of economically sustainable food production and small rural industrial and service units.

3. *Lesotho:* "Women's Integrated Agricultural Project Through Community Action" aims to increase women's food production and income from agriculture through various supporting services such as increasing the number of female extension workers and enhancing their work with rural women.

4. *Mali:* "Assistance to the Women's Groups in Kayes-Nord Region to Increase Their Food Production" provides training to members of women's groups in vegetable production techniques and management of income-producing activities. A revolving fund was established for the collective purchase of basic equipment such as agricultural tools, pumps, and grinding mills.

5. *Malawi:* "Income Generation for Women Farmers" aims at assisting the ministry of agriculture to provide training programs to women farmers; to promote income-producing activities for women to increase household income; and to strengthen the outreach capacity of rural development services reaching rural women.

6. *Nigeria:* "Strengthening Agricultural Extension" aims at developing Nigeria's capacity to evolve extension policies, strategies, and systems for the development support communication component and extending and strengthening agricultural outreach and services to rural women. A recent workshop at Aboekuta University was focused on the revision of home economics curriculum.

7. *Senegal:* "Rural Promotion in the Senegal River Valley" is testing a methodology and developing a program for the training and socioeconomic promotion of women and youth groups. The activities are supported by a functional literacy program that enhances the capacities of group members towards self-management of economic activities.

8. *Sudan:* "Training in Income-Earning Activities for Rural Women" promotes leadership abilities among rural disadvantaged women by increasing their capacity to meet their own needs and those of their dependents.

9. *Tanzania:* "Women in Irrigated Agriculture." The project aims to increase food security at the household level through nutrition education, agro-forestry, and small-scale irrigation.

10. *Zimbabwe:* "Strengthening Women's Role and Work in Rural-Development" investigates ways to remove the constraints that prevent women from participating effectively in agriculture. As part of a credit and savings scheme, farmers' groups, consisting of 80 percent women, receive training in crop selection, methods of planting and cultivation, fertilizer application, harvesting, record keeping, and evaluation of production activities.

11. *Regional:* In the pipeline is a UNDP/FAO regional project, "Improving African Women Farmers' Access to Appropriate Technologies" covering Ghana, Sierra Leone, Tanzania, Zambia, and Zimbabwe. The major objective of this project will be to increase women

farmers' agricultural productivity through identification, dissemination, and institutionalization of improved agricultural technologies.

Almost all of the above projects are in countries undergoing structural adjustment, and in most cases the countries also participate in the SDA project. FAO's project in Senegal, for example, is designed to increase rural women's literacy skills and training opportunities. Senegal has had structural adjustment loans since 1979 and participates in the SDA project. The questions important to this project may now include: What kind of training is most important to the women? Do they need training to participate in the new opportunities brought about by structural adjustment policies, e.g., to switch to different crops, to acquire credit and land, or to improve their management skills? Or, do they need programs to help women protect their families from the negative impacts in nutrition and food security? Clearly, it is important for FAO to strengthen its field projects with respect to structural adjustment.

Plan of Action for the Integration of Women in Development

The integration of WID issues into mainstream activities is to be given primacy under the Plan of Action for the Integration of Women, a medium-term plan covering the period 1989 to 1995. It was unanimously approved by the FAO's governing bodies in 1988, reaffirmed in 1989, and is currently one of FAO's nine overall priorities (FAO 1988). The plan's objective is to bring about change in order to ensure that, in FAO's sphere of responsibility, women are accorded equal rights and opportunities and that their contributions to rural development be supported and rewarded. The strategy proposed is to work for this change at three levels: (1) to increase the information base on women in agricultural development; (2) to formulate and promote policies based on this knowledge; and (3) to develop programs and projects.

Substantively, the focus of activities is to support women in their roles as producers and workers in agriculture, including fisheries and forestry. The emphasis is on women's special needs for income-producing activities and control of income; for obtaining extension services and training opportunities; and for the introduction and development of technologies and other means to ease their burden and to increase their productivity and their access to markets.

The plan is a comprehensive document and identifies measures in four spheres of action—the civil status, economic, social, and decision-making spheres. In the civil status sphere, the plan calls for efforts to improve legislation on women's access to land, credit, and membership in development organizations and cooperatives. It foresees FAO providing advisory and training services to countries that desire to bring national legislation into conformity with standards being suggested by various UN bodies. In the economic sphere, the measures foreseen aim at enhancing women's role in the agriculture and rural economy and at maximizing benefits from economic activities to women. FAO is to contribute to raising overall economic efficiency by increasing the capacity and productivity of women and by expanding their economic opportunities. In the social sphere, activities are geared to improving rural women's access to education at all levels and to modernizing agricultural and home economics training and degree programs. The integration of population and nutritional considerations and of social components in sectoral policies and programs is also given systematic emphasis. In the decision-making sphere, efforts are concentrated on improving women's participation in institutions and in people's organizations through promotion of specific policies and programs including leadership and management training to women.

Program Priorities

To implement the plan, seven priorities have been selected by FAO for the period 1989–1991.

1. *Staff Training on WID.* FAO's staff capacity to understand and account for the concerns of WID in the various technical fields and to integrate gender issues into project and program planning will be increased under this priority. Twelve hundred FAO staff members in headquarters, regional offices, and FAO program offices will attend workshops and orientation sessions.

2. *Policy Advice to Member Governments.* On request from member governments, FAO will provide assistance in terms of legislation and programmatic efforts. Some examples of FAO's planned activities that directly relate to the impacts of structural adjustment programs include assisting member governments interested in revising their agrarian legislation to concur with the guidelines provided by the UN Convention on the Elimination of All Forms of Discrimination Against Women; offering a program of policy advice to national ministries of planning, agriculture, and rural development for the purpose of building and strengthening Women in Agricultural Development units and understanding the effects

of structural adjustment on women farmers; and giving special attention to including women when providing assistance to governments on people's organizations, cooperatives, and other rural groups.

3. *Project Development and Monitoring.* FAO is increasing gender considerations in the planning, implementation, monitoring, and evaluation of projects at all project stages. Special attention is being given to the identification of women as project participants, in presenting disaggregated agricultural data by gender, and in the inclusion of women in project formulation and implementation. Activities include: designing projects that mitigate the effects of structural adjustment through credit and training programs, dissemination of new technologies, and the creation of diversified income-producing enterprises and management strategies; conducting farm management surveys and including the study of gender roles in agriculture and domestic labor for the purpose of designing and implementing projects; offering training seminars focused on improving the level of agricultural extension support for women and on teaching women retailers marketing techniques; working with rural bankers to extend credit to women, and, where traditional financial institutions do not exist, identifying alternative credit channels for women farmers; setting up small-animal production pilot projects, channeled through local NGOs; and implementing integrated dairy development activities for small-scale milk producers, especially for women's groups; assisting women in resource and environmental conservation projects; promoting energy-related technologies (in food processing and the provision of water and fuel); and promoting the expansion of women's income-producing activities in nonwood forest products.

4. *Reorientation of Home Economics and Agricultural Curricula for Extension Workers.* By including training in agriculture in home economics curricula, and by including WID issues and women participants in agricultural courses, extension workers of both sexes will be better equipped to give appropriate advice and training to rural farmers, especially women. FAO staff will assist member governments with staff training and redesign curricula to reflect WID concerns in home economics and agriculture degree programs in educational institutions. They will offer nutrition training that is sensitive to gender issues to government and agricultural college staff.

5. *Preparation of WID Guidelines and Manuals.* In order to assist decision-makers and technical assistance staff to include WID concerns in all stages of project development and implementation, various guidelines are planned. Some will focus on the project cycle, on women's participation

in horticulture, irrigation, forestry, seed selection, integrated pest management, animal husbandry, and fertilizer programs, on WID and population, and on statistical indicators on women in agriculture.

6. *Data Collection, Research Studies, Communication, and Public Information.* To improve the knowledge base on WID, FAO will strengthen the database on women in agriculture to provide and analyze standard agricultural data by gender, and will carry out studies on women's participation in agriculture and their access to rural services and technology. Activities include: reviewing case studies to identify legal problems hindering women's participation in rural development and studying legal standards and women's accessibility to resources; collecting data and analyzing case studies on women in irrigated agriculture and on women's importance in the environment, on fuelwood, biomass fuels, and other forms of rural energy; analyzing technological changes in agro-processing and its impact on women's employment; studying the effects of structural adjustment programs on women's roles in agricultural production, marketing, and family nutrition; setting up a database on women in agriculture and preparing a manual for the collection of statistics on women in agriculture.

7. *Including Population Education and WID.* Projects that improve the status and quality of life of rural women and their families and that collect more grassroots-level information on the relationship between women, demography, and population factors in agricultural development are being developed. Population components will be integrated into agricultural, fisheries, and forestry development projects in which women participate.

As a result of the Plan of Action, requests from 25 governments, 12 of which are in Africa, have been received. The requests fall into two main categories. The first is a request for setting up or strengthening WID units in government ministries, as in the countries of Congo, Cape Verde, Madagascar, Mozambique, and Mauritania. The second consists of requests for WID projects in extension and technology development.

The Plan of Action and Structural Adjustment

The issues of concern to rural women outlined within each of the four spheres and seven priorities of the Plan of Action can be evaluated with respect to structural adjustment. Many of the plan's strategies reflect those mentioned in the literature to mitigate the negative impacts of structural adjustment on rural women. Improving women's access to credit and productive inputs, promoting their participation in marketing organizations, advising national governments on ensuring their rights to land, water, and new technologies, assisting with policy making and programs on food and nutrition, and encouraging appropriate and time-saving technologies are only a few examples. Further, the Plan of Action explicitly includes the study of the effects of structural adjustment on women and the assessment of the participation of women in cash crop production. Two strategies are currently in process: the collection of gender-disaggregated data that will document the productive roles of rural women during structural adjustment and the explicit consideration of structural adjustment processes in the design of women-specific and mainstream field projects.

The gender-disaggregated database will cover such areas as access to productive resources, productivity, income, consumption and wage rates, educational attainment and extension, health and nutritional status, housing and household conditions, and women's roles and participation in decision-making. FAO aims to improve data collection and compilation programs in the countries to provide reliable gender-specific data from population and agricultural censuses and from household surveys such as those conducted under the United Nations National Household Survey Capability Program and the SDA Project. These results will also be used to improve the collection of data on women in various FAO programs and projects.

Conclusion

The advantages and disadvantages of structural adjustment programs are being discussed and evaluated by the World Bank, the United Nations Economic Commission of Africa, FAO, various multinational and bilateral agencies, and by the affected governments themselves. The purpose of adjustment policies is to improve the economic vitality of developing countries, as a continuation of economic crisis in developing countries is not a promising option. However, research on the effects of structural adjustment in general and on selected groups, such as women, has shown that there have been severe consequences for the poor in both rural and urban areas, with poor women being particularly disadvantaged and general female social and economic progress being slowed. The negative impacts are particularly apparent in the early stages of adjustment when drastic cuts are made in services in a number of social and public sectors and the predicted economic growth is yet to materialize. Structural adjustment programs need to be formulated so that the negative aspects are minimized and the positive maximized. Such programs must include policies based on an explicit acknowledgement of the constraints on and potentials of rural women. Fortunately, the knowledge base on the effects of structural adjustment programs is increasing and remedies for addressing the problems are being formulated. The database on women in agriculture and the large number of studies and surveys carried out by FAO will assist in enhancing this knowledge.

The long-term prospects for rural women are highly dependent on whether or not they are included as participants in the process of economic change and growth. The picture thus far is one where women bear the brunt of the negative impacts of structural adjustment, while being severely constrained from participating in the positive impacts. National governments and international agencies must broaden their approaches to structural adjustment programs so as to incorporate explicitly women's roles and contributions to economic production and household management and reproduction. The current record indicates that women farmers have been generally neglected by the programs designed to promote appropriate technologies, modern inputs, and economic rewards. The latest FAO data on women's access to agricultural extension training show that worldwide women represent only 6 percent of all extension clientele. In Africa, only 7 percent of the agricultural extension clients are female (FAO 1990c). Women's access to land, credit, inputs and key services, including employment, must be enhanced in order to increase their economic opportunities. Indeed, given women's substantial role in agriculture, particularly in Africa, the argument to be made is that economic growth cannot be realized without their participation.

Several units of FAO are studying the effect of structural adjustment and either have or are in the process of developing the capacity to discuss these issues with national governments as they formulate and implement their policies. Documentation on women's roles in the agricultural sector is proceeding, to enrich the planning process. Many of the projects specifically targeted to women include credit programs and training. The provision of assistance to member governments which request the strengthening or creation of units on WID, food security, and/or nutrition surveillance units is a strong part of FAO's mandate, and WID units are a priority under the Plan of Action. Finally, as more of the mainstream projects of FAO include women as participants, a greater percentage of project and field program resources will reach them, either through general rural development or through specific projects designed to mitigate the effects of structural adjustment.

REFERENCES

Adekanye, Tomilayo
  1984   Innovations and Rural Women in Nigeria: Cassava Processing and Food Production. *Technology and Rural Women,* Iftikhar Ahmed, ed., pp. 252–83. London: George Allen and Unwin.

Agarwal, Bina
  1984   Women and Technological Change in Agriculture: The Asian and African Experience. *Technology and Rural Women,* Iftikhar Ahmed, ed., pp. 67–114. London: George Allen and Unwin.

Azam, Jean-Paul, Gerard Chambas, Patrick Guillaumont, and Sylviane Guillaumont
  1989   The Impact of Macro-economic Policies on the Rural Poor: Analytical Framework and Indicators. New York: United Nations Development Program.

Commonwealth Secretariat
  1989   *Engendering Adjustment for the 1990s.* Report of a Commonwealth Expert Group on Women and Structural Adjustment. London: Commonwealth Secretariat.

Development Assistance Committee (DAC)
  1988   The Socio-Effects of Structural Adjustment on Women. Background document for the discussion on structural adjustment at the DAC meeting on 5 October.

Dey, Jennie
  1984   Women in Rice-Farming Systems: Focus on Sub-Saharan Africa. Women in Agriculture and Rural Development Service 2. Rome: FAO.

Elson, Diane
  1989   How Is Structural Adjustment Affecting Women? *Development* 1989(1): 67–74. Rome: Society for International Development
  1990   Economic Adjustment and Women's Role in the Management of Family Resources for Achievement of Household Food Security and Nutrition. *The State of Food and Agriculture 1990.* Rome: FAO.

Food and Agriculture Organization of the United Nations (FAO)
  1984   Women in Agricultural Production. Rome: FAO, Women in Agriculture 1, Women in Agricultural Production and Rural Development Service.
  1985a   Impact of International Monetary Fund/World Bank Recommended Structural Adjustment Policies on Food Production and Consumption in Africa. ARRD:AF/85/5. Rome: FAO. Paper presented to the Government Consultation on Follow-up to WCARRD in the Africa Region, Harare, Zimbabwe, 3–6 September.
  1985b   Women in Agriculture. Women in Agricultural Production and Rural Development Service 4. Rome: FAO.

1988 FAO Plan of Action for Integration of Women in Development. CL 94/13. Rome: FAO.

1989a Effects of Stabilization and Structural Adjustment Programmes on Food Security. CFS:89/3. Rome: FAO, Committee on World Food Security, Fourteenth Session, Rome, 3–7 April.

1989b Structural Adjustment Programmes in Sub-Saharan Africa: A Review in the Context of Training Proposals for Agricultural Policy Analysis. Rome: FAO, Training Material for Agricultural Planning, No. 15. ESP/TMAP/15. Development Policy Studies and Training Service.

1989c Women, Food Systems and Agriculture. *1990 World Survey on the Role of Women in Development,* Chapter III, pp. 75–128. New York: United Nations.

1990 Gender Issues in Food Security in Developing Countries. CFS: 90/4. Rome: FAO.

Griggs, J. M.

1989 Women and Structural Adjustment: A Review of the Literature. University of Warwick, Development Economics Research Centre.

Holmboe-Ottesen, Gerd, Ophelia Mascarenhas, and Margareta Wandel

1989 Women's Role in Food Chain Activities and the Implications for Nutrition: New York: United Nations, Nutrition Policy Discussion Paper No. 4, State-of-the-Art Series, Administrative Committee on Coordination/Subcommittee on Nutrition.

Jiggins, Janice

1989 How Poor Women Earn Income in Sub-Saharan Africa and What Works Against Them. *World Development* 17(7): 953–963. Oxford: Pergamon Press.

Joekes, Susan

1988 Gender and Macro-Economic Policy. Paper prepared for AWID Colloquium on Gender and Development Co-operation, Washington, D.C., 11–12 April.

Mies, Marie, assisted by K. Lalita and K. Krishina

1986 Indian Women in Subsistence and in Agricultural Labor. Women, Work and Development Series, 12. Geneva: International Labor Organization.

Norton, Roger D.

1987 Agricultural Issues on Structural Adjustment Programs. Economic and Social Development Paper 66. Rome: FAO.

Palmer, Ingrid

1988 Gender Issues in Structural Adjustment of Sub-Saharan African Agriculture and Some Demographic Implications. WEP 2-21/WP.166. Geneva: ILO, Working Paper No. 166, Population and Labor Policies Programmes, World Employment Programme Research.

Sarris, Alexander H.
  1987   Agricultural Stabilization and Structural Adjustment Policies in Developing Countries. Rome: FAO, Economic and Social Development Paper 65.
Scott, Gloria L., and Marilyn Carr
  1985   The Impact of Technology Choice on Rural Women in Bangladesh: Problems and Opportunities. World Bank Staff Working Paper 731. Washington, D.C.: World Bank.
United Nations Center for Social Development and Humanitarian Affairs
  1989   *1989 World Survey on the Role of Women in Development.* New York: United Nations.

Index

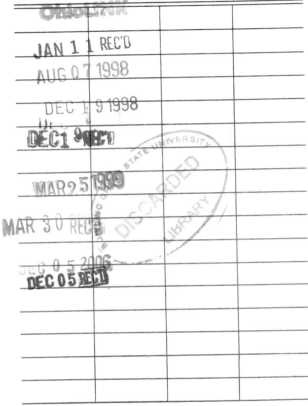

Structural adjustment and
African women farmers